Created and Directed by Hans Höfer

INSIGHT
GUIDES

The Rockies

Project Editors: Diana Ackland and Janie Freeburg
Field Editor: Sriyani Tidball
Updated by Lisa Cavanaugh

HOUGHTON MIFFLIN COMPANY

APA PUBLICATIONS

THE ROCKIES

Third Edition (2nd Reprint)
© 1994 APA PUBLICATIONS (HK) LTD
All Rights Reserved
Printed in Singapore by Höfer Press Pte. Ltd

Distributed in the United States by:
Houghton Mifflin Company
222 Berkeley Street
Boston, Massachusetts 02116-3764
ISBN: 0-395-66248-6

Distributed in Canada by:
Thomas Allen & Son
390 Steelcase Road East
Markham, Ontario L3R 1G2
ISBN: 0-395-66248-6

Distributed in the UK & Ireland by:
GeoCenter International UK Ltd
The Viables Center, Harrow Way
Basingstoke, Hampshire RG22 4BJ
ISBN: 9-62421-032-2

Worldwide distribution enquiries:
Höfer Communications Pte Ltd
38 Joo Koon Road
Singapore 2262
ISBN: 9-62421-032-2

ABOUT THIS BOOK

Joining the growing number of American titles in Apa Publications' *Insight Guide* series is this guide to the Middle Rockies, stretching through the five states of Colorado, Utah, Wyoming, Idaho and Montana. Apa Publications is a Singapore-based publishing house founded by designer **Hans Höfer** whose innovative approach to creative travel chronicles has won awards throughout the world.

Heading the *Insight Guide: The Rockies* project were two California-based editors, **Diana Ackland** and **Janie Freeburg**, who coordinated each stage of the massive project from concept to finished product. They organized field editors, writers, photographers and shaped the book carefully during its nine months of production.

Diana Ackland's editorial background started in New York where she was an editor in the Features and Articles Department of *Good Housekeeping* magazine. From there she moved on to Los Angeles where she became Promotion Manager for the *Los Angeles Times* Syndicate. Now she serves as Vice-President of Sequoia Communications, the Santa Barbara company Ackland and her husband Donald run. She fell in love with the Rockies during her first visit there in the summer of 1984. The Wapiti Valley between Cody (Wyoming) and Yellowstone Park is particularly close to her heart.

Janie Freeburg, managing editor of Sequoia Communications, brings a variety of experience to her editorial work. She has planned, edited and designed a number of publications in several years as a public relations specialist. Freeburg graduated from the University of California, Irvine, with a degree in Comparative Cultures, followed by studies in commercial art and graphic design – a combination that she says makes her a good conversationalist who loves to produce books.

In addition to the California project editors, Field Editor **Sriyani Tidball** was indispensable to the project. Tidball gathered a strong group of writers from the Rockies area, helped develop the editorial format, met multiple deadlines, worked on the preselection of her husband's photos and wrote several pieces herself – including the massive *Travel Tips* section in the back of this book. Tidball's previous experience with Apa Publications included work on the *Insight Guide: Sri Lanka*. A Sri Lankan herself, Tidball was educated at the University of Sri Lanka, the Royal Institute of British Architecture and the University of Nebraska and holds a degree in Architecture. Her work has been published in several Asian inflight airline magazines.

Tom Tidball, who wrote the National Parks section and contributed the majority of the photographs for this book, runs the Tidball Photographic Company in Sri Lanka. Tidball came back to America specifically to work on *Insight Guide: The Rockies*. He and his wife and children traveled throughout the five Middle Rockies states one summer shooting approximately 4,000 slides of Rockies landscape, festivals, people and their lifestyles. His photographic archive was invaluable to this book.

The Tidballs wish to extend special thanks to Richard Grant, Dr Maryanne Parthum, the Denver and Colorado Conventions and Visitors Bureau, the Aspen Chamber of Commerce, the Salt Lake City Visitors Bureau, the Wyoming Travel Commission, Montana Travel Promotion, the Idaho Travel Committee and the Shoshone Bannock Tribal

Ackland

Freeburg

S. Tidball

T. Tidball

Viesti

Council – all of whom assisted with their Rockies trip and research.

Photographer **Joe Viesti**, based in New York City, went to the Rockies on special assignment to shoot winter scenes, activities and ski resorts in a vast winter wonderland. Viesti has combined his profession, photography, with his love of travel and his desire to focus on positive and colorful images. His work has previously been represented in the *Insight Guides* to *Florida, Southern California, American Southwest, New England, Continental Europe* and *Texas*. He has shot for American Express, the National Geographic Society, and various airlines.

Barbara Fifer who wrote "Rocky Mountain Highs and Lows" and "Bozeman, Montana" is the assistant editor of *Montana Magazine* in Helena, MT. **Linda Zuick**, author of the Rockies history section and the "Jackson Hole, Wyoming" piece, is from Lincoln, Nebraska. She knows the Rockies like the back of her hand since spending summer vacations and winter ski trips there.

Virginia Hopkins did an outstanding job writing four major pieces for this book: "Rocky Mountain People", "Colorado Mountain Towns" and "The Aspen Mystique". Hopkins knows North America well having lived in Aspen, Colorado and in New York City after her graduation from Yale University, Connecticut. Her vast knowledge of the Southwest United States formerly won her the role of project editor for Apa's *Insight Guide: American Southwest*.

Professional rodeo barrel racer, **Patty Jones**, was the perfect choice for the "Blazing Saddle" feature. Jones' writing has appeared in the *Texas Longhorn Journal*, *Western Horsemen*, *Pro Rodeo Sports News*, and the *High Plains Journal*.

Betty Stevens, author of "Native Americans Then and Now" and "Colorado's Canyon Country", is a reporter for the *Lincoln, Nebraska Journal* and the *Durango (Colorado) Herald*. She has reported on Indian interests since 1971.

Pamela Stenmark, as a ski expert and author of the book *Skiing for Women*, was the ideal writer to tackle "The Outdoor Experience" and "Ski Resorts" pieces. Stenmark lives in one of the most glamorous Rockies ski resorts – Vail, Colorado – earning a living as public relations manager for Vail Associates, Inc.

Sheila Andren's western roots go way back to her grandfather, Jim Corder, who came to Wyoming from Kentucky in a covered wagon. Andren was raised in Cody, Wyoming, and is now director of public relations at the Buffalo Bill Historical Center.

Historical consultant, **Anthony Godfrey**, author of the "Salt Lake City, Utah" piece has written for *Arizona and the West* magazine. The author of "North Utah" and "Mormons" is **John R. Alley, Jr.**, editor of Howe Brothers Book Publishers in Salt Lake City.

Photographer **Hara** wrote the special sidebar on "Taking Good Photographs". Her work has appeared in *National Geographic's Traveler*, *Better Homes and Gardens*, *Smithsonian Magazine*, *Mademoiselle*, *Glamour*, *Seventeen* and *Esquire* among others, plus many books.

Others who assisted in putting the book to bed are **Bruce Bernstein**, a graduate student at Princeton University, who photographed many of the historical reproductions in this book, and the **Princeton University Library** which was generous to open its fine collection of photographs, prints and illustrations to Apa's cause.

Fifer

Zuick

Hopkins

Jones

Stevens

History

People

Places

Maps

TRAVEL TIPS

**For detailed information
see page 291**

WELCOME TO THE ROCKIES

Your first encounter with the Rockies is one of life's magical moments. You will be treated to a breathtaking panorama of some of America's most awe-inspiring natural beauty: sweeping colorful vistas, towering mountains, sprawling ranches with farmlands that stretch as far as the eye can see, and the occasional, unexpected metropolitan cities that surprise the visitor with their very existence after endless natural splendor.

The Rockies present a wealth of unsurpassed virgin beauty – what former United States President Theodore Roosevelt called "scenery that bankrupts the English language". Shimmering blue lakes, scenic roadways, parks, forests, recreation areas and wondrous rock formations are free for all to enjoy. And, as if this were not enough, there is also the added thrill of the rodeo, skiing on choice mountain slopes, ballooning over snowpeaked mountains, and whitewater rafting down a rushing river…not to mention the abundant fishing, sailing, camping and backpacking on hand at every turn.

The air here is really fresher, the water clearer, the sky bigger than any place you will ever see. The clean, crisp atmosphere penetrates the senses. A combination of adventure, natural beauty, wildlife, sports, history and art is to be found in all five Middle Rocky states: Colorado, Idaho, Montana, Utah and Wyoming.

The Rockies today are as unchanged as when the first pathfinders, Lewis and Clark, unlocked the American West. They were followed by mountain men, fur traders, gold and silver prospectors, land and cattle barons, cowboys and ranchers, copper kings, countless visionaries, and today, those in search of the robust life.

Welcome, then, to the Rockies. Enjoy everything they have to offer: the varied recreational activities, the scenery, the wildlife and the history. Memorable adventures await you here…

Preceding pages: aspens in Rocky Mountain National Park; a future bronco buster straddles his horse trailer; Blackfeet Pow-wow; springtime snow-melt near Medicine Bow; yellowing aspens signal an end to summer; a sea of mountain wildflowers near the West Teton foothills; a charming Queen Anne style Colorado home. **Left**, participants in the Avon Balloon Race rise to the occasion.

ROCKY MOUNTAIN HIGHS AND LOWS

Because of their many snow-capped peaks, the Rocky Mountains were called the "Shining Mountains" by the Native Americans who lived or traveled within sight of them. That poetic name was recorded by the Verendrye brothers, French explorers who were the first whites to see the Rockies, in what are now known as Montana and Wyoming, in 1742–43.

Plains Indians, such as the Cheyenne, who lived east of the Rockies in the flat country of the High Plains, considered the mountains a place where only spirits could safely go and humans dared not venture – a place to hold in awe, but not one to explore.

When Europeans began to come into this area, they pragmatically called the range filled with bare-rock crests the "Stony", and then the Rocky Mountains. These ranges were, to them, not a forbidden place, but a barrier to be challenged. The mountains slowed, but could not stop, the westward push of the United States population. The first whites to appear in this area were fur trappers who lived in isolation; then, wagon trains heading for the lush Pacific Northwest forests and the California gold fields found advantageous passes that let them through the barrier.

The land of the Rockies to this day still hasn't been conquered, however. Populations in the five Rocky Mountain states are among the lowest in density in the United States today. For example, the western half of Colorado is in the mountainous portion of the state. Of the 34 counties there, 11 have from 5 to 20 residents per square mile (2 sq. km), 12 have two to five, and the remaining 11 have fewer than two people per square mile of land.

Much of the land in these five states is owned by governments, state or federal. In order of amount, the federal shares are: Montana, 30 percent; Colorado, 36 percent; Wyoming, 48 percent; Idaho, 64 percent; and Utah, 66 percent. Mineral extraction and forestry, as well as recreational uses of such

Left, bull moose are common sights in the Grand Teton National Park. **Right**, dramatic Yellowstone Falls sets a rainbow in motion.

land, is carefully controlled by the government. Among these publicly owned lands are "wilderness areas", portions protected even more completely where, by law, humans may only visit.

The concept of a "wilderness area" continues to be hotly debated in the United States. At one extreme are those who believe that the mineral and timber resources "locked away" there should be fully utilized. At the other extreme are those who believe that not only current wilderness areas cannot be

opened to development, but that still more land should be added to the system. Most US citizens, naturally, fall between these two viewpoints, and seek a compromise solution. While acknowledging the nation's and the world's need for resources located in the Rocky Mountains, they believe that preserving these remaining true wilderness areas is a worthy goal. They are aware that, besides providing a home for wildlife, these pristine mountain forests also benefit human ecology and supply one of the West's most precious resources: water.

And so, today's Rocky Mountains are no longer the abode of mysterious spirits, or a great wall separating one part of the nation from the other. They are settled lands – if lightly populated – clustered around intact wildernesses. Their future is a point of national concern, but for now people who come to live or vacation in this area seek spiritual and physical refreshment among the beauties of the Shining Mountains.

Grand mountains and great rivers: Traveling through the Rockies gives a sense of seeing earth's geology at work, as a wide range of conditions vividly illustrates this planet's shaping forces. In Wyoming, Grand Teton Mountain abruptly rises to 13,737 ft (4,100 meters), towering 7,000 ft (2,100 meters) above the fertile valley named Jackson Hole.

stantly boiling mud, spew their sulphurous smells into the otherwise sweet air. A plume of steam at the edge of a cold stream alerts the visitor to a hot spring emptying into the icy, melted-snow water.

Mighty rivers rising in these mountains leave their mark, too. North America's deepest gorge is Hell's Canyon in Idaho – it's 1 mile (1.6 km) deep, cut through rock by the coiling, well-named Snake River. In Colorado, the Arkansas River has cut more than 1,100 ft (335 meters) through granite to form Royal Gorge; from its headwaters, the Arkansas drops 6,600 ft (2,000 meters) in elevation within only 150 miles (240 km) before reaching flat land.

Around the valley that holds Salt Lake City, Utah, and the Great Salt Lake, the Wasatch Range rises 6,000 ft (1,800 meters) above the valley floor. These mountains without foothills show how the tremendous forces of colliding continental plates uplifted the Rocky Mountains.

While mountains may seem to show the thickness of the earth's surface crust, Yellowstone National Park in Wyoming demonstrates how comparatively thin this crust is and what forces are constantly at work beneath it. Here, geysers periodically spout boiling water from the depths. "Mudpots", or rock basins filled with con-

The entire Rocky Mountain chain of mountain ranges extends for 3,000 miles (4,800 km) from Alberta and British Columbia, Canada, into Mexico, and at most points is several hundred miles wide. The highest peak in this entire cordillera is Mount Elbert in Colorado, which stands at 14,431 ft (4,400 meters). Because of different climate and geographical conditions, the Rockies' ranges are conveniently divided into the Northern, Middle and Southern Rockies. The states covered within this book are within the Middle Rockies, which includes the Wyoming Basin – the desert-like "hole in the mountains" used as a wagon-train passage by the

Mormon, Overland, and Oregon Trails of the 19th century.

The Rocky Mountains are young ones on the North American continent, formed as what was once the western coastal edge of the great Canadian Shield tectonic plate pushed westward – butting against the eastern edge of the eastward-moving Pacific plate. The result of this powerfully grinding but gradual "collision" was the upward thrust of the Rockies. Land that had been at sea level rose so that today the base of the Rockies is about 1 mile (1.6 km) above sea level.

Slow and steady sculpture: Glaciers of the later Ice Ages sculpted these uplifted mountains, and inland seas of their melting waters

Park, one August night, the lake bottom tipped 20 feet towards the northeast, and a massive landslide tragically buried 50 campers before they could flee. Earthquakes are common throughout the Rockies, but most are small tremors causing little or no damage – usually unsensed by people. A half-century ago, though, throughout the year of 1935, a series of earthquakes damaged buildings in Wyoming and Montana.

High and dry: The landscape of the Rockies further demonstrates the youth of these ranges. Its soil is thin and stony because fewer eons of erosion have gone into its creation. In this shorter time period (60 million years), fewer species of trees have

filled mountain valleys as the last Ice Age closed. Major volcanic action further shaped some mountains, building upon the upthrust rock masses, as in the San Juan Mountains of Colorado.

Although most geological changes occur too slowly for humans to witness, an event in 1959 demonstrated that the block faulting which built the Rockies does indeed continue. At Hebgen Lake in Yellowstone National

Left, an aerial view of the Rocky Mountain peaks and valleys in Wyoming. **Above**, elements of time take their toll on rock formations at Capitol Reef (Utah).

evolved to survive here than in the Appalachian chain (225 million years old) that parallels the eastern US coast.

Vegetation in this high country is as much a product of altitude as of longitude and latitude. In fact, the higher peaks rise well above the "timberline", the point after which trees can no longer grow. The western side of the mountains receives more moisture than the eastern, as clouds cool when rising over the land mass and their moisture condenses to fall as rain – or, in greater quantity, as snow. Tall and dense fir woods characterize the lower elevations on the wetter westward side, with pine forests on the drier east, and spruces braving the higher slopes towards the timberline.

Climate throughout the Rockies is generally dry, making for clear skies that enhance the ability to see for long distances. Nights are much cooler than days in summer (and much *colder* in winter). Because snow forms a greater proportion of annual precipitation than rain, "snowpack" throughout the area is carefully monitored. This is each winter's snow accumulation, whose melt feeds rivers supplying the region's comparatively scarce water. Where the coolness of altitude is too great for snowpack to melt in the summer sun, glaciers form.

From April into June each year, spring-

Hearty lifestyles: In the Middle Rockies, the rugged land and climate dictate what major industries can flourish. After the native people, who lived off the land's wildlife and its natural crops, those who came and stayed participated in what are called extractive industries. They harvested the pelts of fur-bearing animals; mined precious and then basic metals (and more recently, radioactive ores); cut the forests (originally "clear-cutting", or removing all trees without re-planting, a practice no longer followed).

Agriculture began as mining camps sprang into being, but in these dry lands before irrigation was introduced, cattle and sheep ranching predominated. In "open range" days,

time in the Rockies means the flooding "run-off" season as snow melt runs into streams, whose mergers form the headwaters of several major rivers. The Arkansas, North and South Platte, Rio Grande, Missouri, and Colorado rivers all rise in the Rockies. The Continental Divide, which generally follows the crest of the mountains, is the great watershed of North America. Precipitation falling or melting down the east side of the Continental Divide flows ultimately into the Atlantic Ocean; that falling to the west of the Divide flows to the Pacific. Of the major rivers mentioned, only the Colorado flows to the Pacific.

this meant letting the herds of cattle or flocks of sheep graze where they chose, taking the natural grasses. It is only in the 20th century that tourism became a major "industry" for the Rockies, affecting delicate ecosystems in some locations, but not permanently removing resources.

Because this land is rough to travel and ungenerous in agricultural soils and water supplies, major cities have not developed in the Rockies. The two metropolitan centers of the Middle Rockies, Denver and Salt Lake City, are much like cities of their size elsewhere in the US – but not representative of the smaller settlements in the region.

Friends in the wild: A "small town" friendliness and casualness pervades life throughout these five states (even in Denver and Salt Lake City). Manners are less formal and dress answers as much to practicality and comfort adapted to weather conditions as it does to fashion. The lack of pretension may be a legacy of the frontier heritage, when all were equal in scrabbling for a living in a tough land.

People who live here are proud if they can trace their families back as residents over three or four generations. They are proud, also, of the beauties of the land, and are pleased to share them with visitors. If their hearty openness with strangers offends, it

buffalo (American bison). They are the rarest, largest, and most dangerous animals found in today's Rockies.

Although a few buffalo are privately owned (and experiments continue in cross-breeding them with cattle to produce "beefalo" meat), the only two herds remaining in the United States are in Yellowstone National Park and at the National Wildlife Refuge at Moiese, Montana.

Visitors to Yellowstone in summer and winter will see buffalo grazing stolidly. The adult male stands up to 7 ft (2 meters) tall and weighs up to 2,000 lbs (900 kg). When stampeded, these massive animals can outrun humans; when frightened, they will de-

should be remembered that the friendliness is intended as a compliment.

Wild animals abound in the Middle Rockies, both in the "wilderness areas" where no humans may live, and in the national parks with their thousands of visitors each year. Some species delicately coexist with human settlements – deer, antelope, and even elk.

By far the two most spectacular animals to be seen here are the grizzly bear and the

Left, bison have been at home on the range in Wyoming since the days of the Native Americans. **Above**, fascinating formations in Arches National Park in Monument Valley.

fend themselves by goring with their short curved horns. They are not to be approached on foot – or surrounded by a group.

Grizzly bears do their best to avoid humans, but backpackers in wilderness areas may encounter these huge omnivores. Grizzlies have poor sight and hearing, and may move towards the unknown in order to understand it. They will try to flee from humans unless in pain, or feeling trapped, or unless someone comes between a sow and her cubs. The best advice, of course, is to keep your distance.

Adult females weigh from 350 to 450 lbs (150 to 200 kg) and males range from 800 to

1,000 lbs (360 to 450 kg). Their coloring ranges from dark brown to straw-colored blond with silvery tips to the hairs, giving the grizzled look for which they are named. A noticeable hump at the shoulders and an indented face above the snout distinguish them from their bear cousins. Fewer than 800 grizzlies are thought to exist in the United States outside of Alaska, with half of those in Glacier and Yellowstone National Parks and their adjacent wilderness areas.

Black bears present more danger to people, because more of them exist and because they have become less afraid of the human presence. In the national parks of the Rockies, some even adapted quite happily to foraging

in garbage dumps and "begging" for food at campsites or by the roadsides. Modern management policies helped alleviate this harmful adaptation, but human encounters with black bears are a constant concern of park rangers.

This bear may be brown or reddish ("cinnamon") in color, as well as black, but usually has a brown face and a white blaze on the chest. Adults are 5 to 6 ft tall (about 2 meters) and weigh from 200 to 500 lbs (90 to 230 kg).

Four members of the deer family are common to the Rockies, including the moose. Today's bull moose weighs from 1,000 to 1,400 lbs (450 to 630 kg); he stands about 6 ft (1.8 meters) high at the shoulder. Their antlers are the largest grown by any mammal, with five to seven prongs spreading out from solid "shovels" nearer the head. Record antler widths from prong to prong begin at 5 ft (1½ meters). Moose are fond of marshy areas and the grasses that grow along river banks. They are strong swimmers and will even take to open waters.

The slightly smaller elk also carries large antlers, in this case, open prongs sweeping upward and back from the head, nearly as large as the moose's. The elk's "rack", or set of antlers, may weigh 50 lbs (23 kg). When fattened by summer forage, a bull elk weighs from 500 to 700 lbs (225 to 300 kg), with a shoulder height of about 5 ft (1½ meters). Elk range through the lower-elevation forests and on to the plains.

Where the deer and antelope play: Mule deer and white-tail deer, smaller relatives of the moose and elk, live wherever human populations are thin enough in the Middle Rockies. The mule deer is recognizable because of its long ears and stiff-kneed, springing manner of running. The white-tail is named for its "warning flag" tail, white on the underside, which snaps upright when the animal is frightened.

Residents of the Rockies call the slight pronghorn an "antelope" even though it is unrelated to Old World antelopes. The animal's delicate appearance – it weighs only about 100 lbs (45 kg) – belies a strong constitution designed for survival by flight. Antelope eyesight has been compared to humans using seven-power binoculars, and the animals also have enlarged lungs and windpipes. Thus, they range freely in open country, sensing danger and running from it. Herds of antelope can be seen in open grasslands, even along busy roads.

Visiting the Middle Rockies means enjoying a great variety of spectacular scenery, having opportunities to view many types of wild animals, small as well as large, and being warmly welcomed by the people. It is a land of extremes in climate and geography, but the hardness of the land has bred a robust people who are happy to share the rugged beauties around them.

<u>Left</u>, wildlife thrives in the clear mountain air of the Rockies. <u>Right</u>, a rare close-up of a Rockies Bighorn Ram – now an endangered species.

Billions of years of heat and movement formed the rock base upon which the Rocky Mountains were built. There is geological evidence that at one time they lay at the bottom of a sea; then this rock base slowly but steadily broke apart and pushed upward. It was eroded by rivers, blown by winds, heated by volcanoes, shaken by earthquakes and frozen by glaciers.

These centuries of incredible fluctuation and the constant pressure from beneath the earth's surface, with the semi-liquid land bubbling up like porridge, were essential to the formation of the Rocky Mountains as we know them today. The rock rose, fractured and cracked, pushing ever upward to form cliffs thousands of feet high.

In Colorado, these mountains take up an area more than six times the size of the Swiss Alps – with 53 snowy peaks towering more than 14,000 feet (4,260 meters) above sea level and a total of 1,143 mountains rising to altitudes of 10,000 ft (3,040 meters) or more.

In Idaho, the landscape gaps between the mountains were depressed and filled by lava flows and carved by the violent Snake River itself. The lava plains here are second in size only to the Columbia River Plateau of Oregon and Washington. Craters of the Moon National Monument at the north edge of these lava fields preserves their breathtaking volcanic features.

Evidence of the ancient rock layers bending and turning upward can be found everywhere in the Rocky Mountains. Lifted, folded, mangled, crushed and broken rock formations created today's magnificent scenic features. The vast mineral wealth there, concentrated deep in the earth's cracks and crevices, has challenged man for hundreds of years to make a living from the important natural resources before him.

The concept of the movement of the earth is difficult to grasp as the infinitely slow uplift of great landmasses brings forth the mountain peaks and valleys. The uplift goes on too slowly for the human eye to perceive. But today, landslips occur occasionally as if to remind us that the eternal hills are still changing. In 1925 near Jackson Hole, Wyoming, a cowboy outran a mile-and-a-half long rain-soaked avalanche of hillside while six of his cattle died.

Cave dwellers' secrets: One of the natural wonders of the world, the Rocky Mountain range today still shares its ancient secrets.

CLIFF-DWELLINGS SOUTHERN COLORADO.

The sides of these mountains reveal ancient marine life fossils, fascinating dinosaur remains and rocks which were formed in the hot interior of the earth – invaluable links to our planet's history.

Near the southwest corner of Colorado is a green tableland 15 miles (24 km) long and 8 miles (13 km) wide rising 1,500 ft (455 meters) from the surrounding valleys. Tribes of peace-loving Native Americans lived in homes on these tablelands or mesas until about 700 AD. They were followed by another group, the Anasazi (or ancient ones), who inhabited pueblos on the mesa and later built sheltered caves in the walls of the canyons

Preceding pages: ancient Native American petroglyphs on a rock slab in Arches National Park. **Left,** Bryce Canyon National Park (Utah). **Right,** remnants of an ancient tribal civilization in cliff dwellings in southern Colorado.

that supported it. The Navajo and Ute Indians lived for many years on the lands surrounding the mesa but stayed away from the cliff dwellings that were abandoned by their ancestors until the 14th century, believing that they were inhabited by spirits of the departed.

"Far View House" is a well-preserved pueblo dwelling which gives some clues about the lives of the Native Americans. Fireplaces, pottery, utensils and grinding stones were found in the rectangular living rooms; larger circular rooms, called "kivas", were thought to be ceremonial halls.

Mesa Verde National Park: More of these Anasazi structures were found in 1888, when

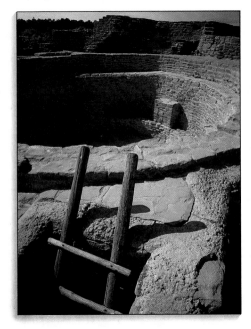

two cowboys hunting cattle stopped to rest their ponies and discovered a group of ancient dwellings in a huge cave about 50 ft (15 meters) below the rim of the mesa. They found what is now called "Cliff Palace". This structure with its 200 living rooms is thought to be the largest group of dwellings of its kind. The four-story rooms have walls decorated with red and white primitive art designs. There is a 30-ft (9-meter) tower in the Palace, most impressive because each of the stones which contributes to the curvature of the tower has been shaped with the crudest tools. Grinding bowls and storage bins for corn were found in the Palace, and there may

have been a spring to furnish water for the ancient Indian population, estimated to have been about 400.

In 1906 by an act of Congress, the archaeological ruins were set aside as a national park. That portion of the mesa which contains the cliff dwellings is now known as Mesa Verde National Park and can easily be visited today.

Little else is known about the Rockies' history until the 16th century when white men ventured into the southern part of the mountain area. Francisco Coronado set out from Mexico City in New Spain in 1540 searching for the Seven Cities of Cibola to the north. Rumors were rampant that the seven cities were stocked with gold and gems. The Spaniards were so angry when they discovered that Cibola consisted of nothing more than a collection of pueblos and caves that they ransacked the place from kiva to kiva, killing the men and raping the women. Thus they provided the Native Americans with a sample of what was to come for the next 300 years.

Coronado nevertheless continued north and no one is sure where he concluded his fruitless search. He returned to Mexico City with the members of his unfortunate expedition having accomplished two things. He had destroyed the myth of great golden cities to the north, and he had given the Indians a deep and bitter hatred of the Spanish.

Expeditions north, however, continued for various reasons: some of the explorers were devout men who wanted to convert the Native Americans to Christianity and others were interested in elevating their family's social status and gaining land.

But the Spanish, continually harassed by the hostile Native Americans in their attempts to conquer the frontier to the north, were ultimately defeated by the French when Napoleon took the Louisiana Territory from Charles IV of Spain. Thus the Louisiana Territory, which had passed from French to British to Spanish hands, reverted to France in 1802. It did not remain so for long, however, for the following year Napoleon sold the entire territory, also known as the Louisiana Purchase, to the American government.

Left, ladders connected the multi-levels of the Anasazi Indian cliff dwellings. Right, the famous Cliff House in the Canon de Chelly.

EXPLORERS, TRAPPERS AND TRADERS

The Louisiana Purchase occupies some 827,987 sq. miles (2,1500,000 sq. km) of land between the Mississippi River and the Rocky Mountains, stretching from the Gulf of Mexico to the Canadian border. The purchase took place in 1803 during President Thomas Jefferson's first administration. The price was $15,000,000, which made it the greatest land bargain in the history of the United States.

Within weeks of the purchase, President Jefferson sent his private secretary, Captain Meriwether Lewis, and Lewis' friend William Clark, off on a mission to gather information about this newly acquired territory. They were to investigate the plants and animals, the Native American culture and trade, and the possibility of discovering a route over the mighty mountains to the Pacific.

The Lewis and Clark expedition: Lewis and Clark set out from a spot near St Louis on May 14, 1804, with a party of 45 men, most of them rugged frontier men whom they recruited and trained themselves. The records of Lewis and Clark tell of an 8,000-mile (13,000-km) round trip to the Pacific Ocean.

A French-Canadian trapper named Toussaint Charbonneau and his family joined the group in North Dakota. He and his wife, Sacagawea, were to serve as interpreters and horse traders for the party as they traveled through the Shoshoni Indian country.

The Lewis and Clark expedition set out from Fort Mandan for the west in the spring of 1805. They fought the Missouri's currents, struggled through deep canyons, and learned from the Native Americans as they went. Across the Continental Divide, and down the Columbia River, they traveled until they finally saw the Pacific Ocean on November 17, 1805. They spent the winter and started back the way they had come. The party divided there with Lewis going north and Clark following the Yellowstone River east. In August of 1806, they were reunited and the expedition was complete, having brought to the nation a real sense of pride and the first glimpse of understanding about the northern reaches of its territory.

Before Lewis and Clark had returned, President Jefferson sent Thomas Freeman with a second party to the southern portion of the Louisiana Territory. Although Freeman's expedition didn't cause quite the stir that the Lewis and Clark one did, it nevertheless provided valuable information about the extent of Spanish military operations in the area and the appropriate waterway to the Rocky Mountain country.

That waterway was the Arkansas River and Captain Zebulon Pike was selected to explore it. In 1806, while making a map of the Arkansas and Red rivers east of the

Rockies, he followed the Arkansas into Colorado and discovered the peak which carries his name. He noted it on his map as "Highest Peak" and it was officially named "James Peak" after the first man who scaled it. But trappers and hunters persisted in calling it "Pike's Peak" and, in 1835, "Pike's Peak" it became. Zebulon Pike's notes on his exploration were of a military intelligence nature as he was an army officer at heart and not so concerned with the possibilities of the development of the territory.

In 1818, Congress ordered an expedition to continue Pike's work and to investigate animal, vegetable and mineral life and trade with the Indians, as well. Major Stephen H. Long was to be in charge of the expedition.

Like Pike, Long named the first mountain he observed in the Front Range of the Rockies "Highest Peak". That peak is the highest summit in Rocky Mountain National Park and is now known as "Long's Peak". Otherwise the group contributed little toward the knowledge of the region.

By 1841, proof of the riches of the West were filtering back and exploration began anew. Always the travelers were at the mercy of the Indians and the weather. John C. Frémont made five expeditions across the mountains mainly for the purpose of publicizing the West. Until this time, an artist was

But Frémont's attempts to find the central route proved futile and the man who did find it was John Gunnison. He died when he was struck by an arrow while trying to explain to a Native American that he was an explorer not a settler. The Gunnison expedition brought the United States government to the realization that any further explorations would have to be by military men.

The history of the real pathfinders can be traced in the story of the Rocky Mountain fur traders. From Lewis and Clark's expedition until the middle 1840s, commerce in the West was controlled by the fur trade. The employees of the fur trading companies and the free trappers (who sold furs they trapped

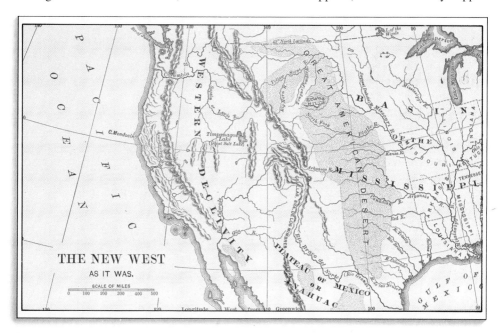

THE NEW WEST

AS IT WAS.

SCALE OF MILES
0   100   200   300   400   500

sent along with each expedition to sketch significant scenery, but Frémont was the first explorer to make use of the new invention, the camera. In addition, he was distinguished by his determination to find a central route to California as there was increasing talk of a railroad being built through to the Pacific Ocean.

Preceding pages: *The Fireboat* by western artist Charles Russell depicts the uneasy coexistence between early settlers and Native Americans. **Left**, early explorers became great leaders of the West. **Above**, map of the "New West" in the 19th century.

themselves) were the first real explorers of the West. Unfortunately, they left few records of their discoveries behind. These mountain men didn't write, but they read trails and tracks and weather signs. Trusting their instincts and sense of direction, they carried a more complete map of the Rocky Mountain country in their heads than any expedition hired by the government was able to put together.

Beaver was the fur that lured men to the West. The skins were used for hats and muffs, coats and linings and collars. Two hundred thousand pelts a year were sent to China alone during this period for the Emperor's garments. The demand for the pelts nearly killed off the beaver, but a change in fashion saved them from extinction in the nick of time.

The trappers in their buckskin suits and coonskin caps lived entirely in the open with their Native American wives and families. They met other trappers at the annual "rendezvous" where white men and Native Americans gathered to drink, trade and gamble. The heads of fur companies met their employees, paid them for their furs and gave them supplies for the year. The free trappers brought their furs and the Native Americans came to gamble and trade. The business transactions at a rendezvous usually took

one of two brothers who trapped; Thomas Fitzpatrick, "Broken Hand" as he was called by the Native Americans who both feared and admired him; and Old Jim Bridger whose prowess as a storyteller was almost as great as his skill with a rifle. All of the mountain men in one way or another had a profound influence on the history of the Rockies.

Besides these mountain men, pioneers seeking a way West on wagon trains were the next settlers. William Sublette proved that wagon wheels could negotiate the mountain passes and this opened the trails for them in the 1830s. In addition to supplies, the wagon trains brought tourists and journalists who talked and wrote about the Rocky Mountain

JAMES BRIDGER—See following page.

about a week. The furs were graded and bargained for and this was followed by two to three weeks of carousing. Gunpowder and whiskey were the medium of exchange and more than one trapper went back to the wilds with nothing to show for a year's work but a bad headache, while the owners of the fur-trading companies were the ones to profit.

William H. Ashley was the owner of the Rocky Mountain Fur Company. He employed some of the West's most famous mountain men: Jedediah Smith, the tough Methodist who went West with a gun in one hand and a Bible in the other; David Jackson, who gave his name to Jackson Hole; William Sublette,

country and its wonders, one of which was the warm and versatile buffalo robe. This, in turn, produced increased demands on the fur business and necessitated the cooperation of the Native Americans who could slaughter great herds of buffalo.

Forts and trading posts started to replace the annual rendezvous. Fort Laramie, the midway point between the Missouri and Salt Lake on the Overland Trail, was built on the site of a rendezvous in 1834. It operated as a private trading establishment until 1849 when the government bought it to use as a holding place for the troops that protected the gold rush caravans. There were 12 buildings surrounded by a 4-ft-thick (120-cm) adobe wall that was 20 ft (6 meters) high. It could corral 200 animals if need be and 40 men were employed there as traders, tailors and buffalo hunters. Fort Laramie was the capital of the Rocky Mountain country until the discovery of gold.

Jedediah Smith, Sublette and Jackson bought the Rocky Mountain Fur Company from Ashley and trapped up and down the Rocky Mountain territory. Smith enjoyed the dangerous life of the trapper. He met a grizzly bear in the Black Hills and was so badly chewed that he nearly died, but was sewn up with a needle and trapped on.

It wasn't the danger of his work that led

Indians before he ever reached Sante Fe.

Kit Carson was another hunter and trapper with a vast knowledge of the Rocky Mountain country that he shared with exploring parties and military expeditions. Soon his name was famous throughout the Rocky Mountain range. He was known and feared by the Native Americans and envied and respected by the other trappers and mountain men during his eight years as a buffalo hunter. His second wife was Josepha Jamarillo, the sister of Charles Bent's wife and one of the members of the family who witnessed Bent's murder by the Indians when he was the governor of New Mexico. With the Indians and whites no longer trusting each other and

Smith to give up the trade but the fact that the beavers were over-trapped and fashions had changed. The pack of furs he delivered to St Louis in 1830 was his last and he sold his holdings in the company and set his sights on the Sante Fe trade. From the start he encountered trouble with the weather and the Indians. Finally, he was killed by a band of

Far left, Jim Bridger – early explorer and mountain man; and left, holding on for dear life on the Colorado River. Above, turn-of-the-century Sioux Indian moccasins fashioned from porcupine quills. Above right, covered wagons hauled freight through the Ute Pass.

the chaos created by Bent's death and the start of the gold rush, the day of the mountain man was drawing to a close. Kit Carson died in 1868 having outlived the last act of the mountain man drama.

Thomas Fitzpatrick, called "Broken Hand" (after his new rifle exploded, maiming several of his fingers), was a trapper and hunter who became the first federal Indian Agent in the Rocky Mountain country.

The practical experience he gained dealing with the Native Americans while he was trapping was to come in handy 20 years later when the government was formulating the official Indian policy in the Rockies. With the buffalo disappearing and the hunting grounds of the Indians being devastated, Fitzpatrick urged the Indians to turn to agriculture and tried to persuade the government to start a program to equip them for that agricultural life. Under his leadership, the first great treaty between the whites and the Indians was drawn up with 10,000 Indians present at the meetings at Fort Laramie in 1851. It could truly be said that Thomas Fitzpatrick set a firm foundation for trust and understanding between the two peoples.

James Bridger, a hunter, trapper, fur trader and guide was one of the mountain men who bought into the Rocky Mountain Fur Company in 1830. He was one of the first white men, exemplified the real attributes of courage and freedom from fear. During the summer of 1863 the daring and violent Espinoza brothers terrorized the southern region of the Rockies, killing, raping and thieving. The commander of one of the military units in the area hired Tom Tobin to solve the problem. Tobin knew the mountains in the area as well as any man alive and set out in search of the brothers. He found the culprits when he spotted crows circling over them in a canyon and there he killed them both single-handedly. Not wanting to waste gunpowder, Tobin merely wounded the two, then cut off their heads with his knife. Tobin needed proof of his kill to collect his pay. The

men to see the area that was to become Yellowstone National Park and he may have also discovered the Great Salt Lake. In 1843, when the fur trade declined, he built Fort Bridger in southwest Wyoming, a way station to supply immigrants on the Oregon Trail. By 1850, the fort had been taken over by the Mormons and Jim Bridger was among many old trappers and mountain men who went to live at Fort Laramie. Many of the tales he told there are still repeated in the West; that he'd come West so long ago that "Pike's Peak" was nothing but a hole in the ground at the time is one among them.

Tom Tobin, one of the last of the mountain bodies were too cumbersome to haul across the mountains, so he threw the heads in a sack and returned to Fort Garland and deposited his bloody trophies at Colonel Tappan's feet. When he died in 1904, he had outlived by nearly 50 years the other legendary mountain men he'd known.

Squabbles with Mexico: Explorations to the Rockies were interrupted by the Mexican War of 1846. The squabbles between Mexico and the United States were 20 years old. Idle mountain men were harassing Mexican wagon trains and the United States was worried about the Mexicans exciting the Utes and Apaches. At Taos, Mexicans and Pueblo

Indians raged into the home of Charles Bent, the military governor of New Mexico, scalped him in front of his family and rode off with his scalp tacked to a board. To achieve peace and extend its frontiers, the United States became involved in what many historians felt was an unnecessary attack on a weaker nation. By the treaty of Guadalupe Hidalgo, the United States acquired California, Nevada and Utah and parts of Arizona and New Mexico, Colorado and Wyoming.

William Gilpin was appointed as the first governor of the new Colorado Territory in 1861. Having visited the Rocky Mountain country in the days of the Mexican War, he must have been astonished as he rode into

side of the Union, didn't waste any time squashing the secessionist idea before it had a chance to take hold.

The Confederates swept north up the Rio Grande intending to seize the Colorado gold fields in 1862 but were forced to retreat. Even as the Civil War was won in the Rockies for the Union, another war was started with the Native Americans.

War crimes: The War Department had withdrawn most of the weapons and regulars from the Rocky Mountains and sent them east to fight the Southerners. The Native American tribes all through the western mountains, realizing that the white man was at a disadvantage, were tired of being con-

Denver on a stagecoach. What had once been a favorite camping ground had turned into a bustling city of several thousand people with hotels and restaurants.

There was a method to President Lincoln's madness when he offered Gilpin the post of Governor of the territory. Colorado with its gold rush was important to the economy of the Union. But Colorado and New Mexico had an inordinate number of secessionists in their midst. So Gilpin, a Southerner on the

Left, Buffalo Bill Cody triumphs. **Above**, Mormon pioneers make peace with the Native Americans, on the way to the New Jerusalem.

fined to various uninhabitable reservations. For 10 years they had suffered in silence and now they were intent on moving to more bountiful hunting grounds as had been their custom before. Their revenge was swift as they overtook anything from stage routes to isolated settlers.

War parties on the rampage in 1863 and 1864 continued their destruction despite vigorous United States military operations. Colonel Chivington, who had won the Civil War for the Union in the Rockies, took over the handling of the Native Americans. Governor Evans, who had replaced Gilpin, felt things were headed for a truce until Colonel

Chivington and his 600 men marched into a camp at Sandy Creek and methodically shot every man, woman and child there.

News of his treachery reached the other tribes around Fort Laramie and they began a full-scale war led by Chief Sitting Bull. Communication between Denver and the east became non-existent and settlements were pillaged and burned. The economy was in ruins and the whole territory was on the verge of starvation. Chivington was reprimanded and the Massacre at Sandy Creek was denounced as the most unjustifiable crime in American history, but the war with the whites didn't end until the Battle of the Little Big Horn in 1876.

Heeding the "call": Religion was one of the reasons that settlers first undertook the trip west across the Rocky Mountain country. Once William Sublette proved to them that wagon trains could cross the mountains, missionaries felt sure that they possessed the time, energy and courage to move their households west. Marcus Whitman was such a missionary; commissioned in 1835 by the Presbyterian and Congregational churches, Whitman was to go west and report back to them on the feasibility of setting up a mission. He reported that not only could women and wagons cross the Rockies but that milk cows could be herded, guaranteeing a solid agricultural foundation. In 1836, a missionary party of six set out to make the overland journey through the Rocky Mountain country and on to the Pacific, two of the six being the first women to make such a trip.

While Whitman and his group were settling in Oregon, other men were looking to another part of the West as their Promised Land. The Mormons were being persecuted for their beliefs, which at first were much like the beliefs of any other religion (later Mormonism came to include the doctrine of polygamy). The Mormon Church was founded by Joseph Smith who left his home in New York State about 1830 seeking the New Jerusalem he'd been told of in a "revelation". He teamed up with Brigham Young in Independence, Missouri, and the Mormon Church grew by leaps and bounds, alienating people as it went. Smith's "revelation" on plural wives caused an explosion that resulted in his death and Brigham Young took his place as head of the church.

Young organized the Mormons for a journey west in 1846 to a remote New Jerusalem where they would be safe. There was nothing haphazard about the Mormon migration – they knew exactly where they were going. Wagons, horses, seeds for crops, cows, oxen, men, women and children traveled west in military formation and rarely had trouble with the Native Americans. They ran across mountain men in the Rockies who scoffed at the idea that they could grow corn in the dry Great Basin, but they didn't know Brigham Young had studied irrigation.

In July 1847, they reached the valley of the Great Salt Lake and went to work planting crops, building irrigation ditches and planning their city. Some of the original 150 settlers went back east for their families and soon there was a long line of Mormons winding through the Platte Valley, over the sand hills, past Fort Laramie, across South Pass down to the valley. By October, they were 4,000 strong, and they had indeed found their New Jerusalem.

The Oregon Trail: Except for Captain B.E. Bonneville's dress rehearsal with a train of 20 covered wagons headed west in 1832 and the Mormons' pilgrimage, it wasn't until the discovery of gold in 1848 that the covered wagon mass migration started. One observer in the spring of 1849 estimated that there were 12,000 wagons in the Rocky Mountain country headed for California. Fifty-five thousand travelers were said to have stopped at Fort Laramie in the summer of 1850 alone.

The Oregon Trail was the longest of the overland routes used in westward expansion. Ruts left by wagon wheels can still be seen today along the trail. Families traveled up the Platte River to Fort Laramie, Wyoming and along the North Platte to its Sweetwater branch; across the South Pass in the Rocky Mountains to the Green River Valley at Fort Bridger, Wyoming; through the Snake River area and on to Idaho; across the Blue Mountains to Marcus Whitman's mission and down the Columbia River to Fort Vancouver, Oregon. Settlers dealt with flooded rivers, Indian attacks on their wagons, outbreaks of cholera and scarcity of food, wood and drinking water. The journey took six months and was a severe test of endurance and strength.

Right, courageous pioneers settled the West in *The Homesteaders*, by John Clymer.

SACAGAWEA

Of the many characters in American history, few are as idealized as Sacagawea, the Shoshone Indian girl who was the guide and interpreter for the Lewis and Clark expedition to the Pacific Northwest in 1804–06.

Sacagawea, whose name means "bird woman", was kidnapped when she was a young girl by the Hidatsas Minatarees tribe in Atsina country, and taken to North Dakota. She was sold as a slave to a French-Canadian trapper Toussaint Charbonneau who subsequently married her. It was at about this time that Lewis and Clark and their party were spending a winter in Mandan, North Dakota, waiting for the spring to start their expedition. Two French-Canadian interpreters were employed by Lewis and Clark so they could intercede with the Indians for the expedition. One was Toussaint Charbonneau who came with his 16-year-old pregnant wife, Sacagawea. Both captains were delighted when she joined the group, for they thought she could help them bargain with the Native Americans for the horses they needed for the mountain crossing. That February, Sacagawea gave birth to a son who was named Jean Baptiste and called "Little Pomp" meaning "First Born" in Shoshoni. The little boy at two months was carried by Sacagawea on her cradle board on this 3000-mile (4,800-km) adventure. He was loved by all and especially by Captain Clark. Throughout the journey Sacagawea proved to be very resourceful as she guided the group through the wilderness, showing them what berries and roots could be eaten. Great courage and good temperament were her attributes and Meriwether Lewis wrote of her "…if she had enough to eat and a few trinkets to wear I believe she would be perfectly content anywhere."

Once, when one of the boats almost turned over, she calmly recovered all the valuable articles from the water. Her amiable disposition made her one of the most popular people on the expedition next to "Little Pomp", the favorite.

Sacagawea helped tremendously when the expedition reached her native tribe, the Shoshonis, at Beaver Head Valley, Montana. Their young Chief Cameahwait turned out to be Sacagawea's brother whom she had not seen since she was kidnapped. When she realized this she threw her blanket over him "…weeping profusely. The chief himself was moved not in the same degree. After some conversation between them, she resumed her seat, and attempted to interpret for us, but her new situation seemed to overpower her, and she was frequently interrupted to tears," Clark wrote.

That first winter: In two weeks' time the explorers were ready to proceed. Sacagawea helped bargain with the Shoshonis for 21 horses and two guides. This next part of the journey took almost a month as the party traveled through the rugged Bitterroot Mountains. The winter set in and they struggled with freezing rain, sleet, heavy snowfall and some frost-bitten feet. On top of this there was a terrible food shortage. They ate unfamiliar boiled yams, bear grease and candles which resulted in many digestive problems.

During the entire adventure the warm-hearted Captain Clark was devoted to "Little Pomp". He tried to persuade his parents to let him bring up the boy as his own son with a proper education. On the return journey, he named a 190-ft (60-meter) rock column pillar "Pompy's Pillar" along the Yellowstone River, which is still located about 25 miles (40 km) from Billings, Montana. In August 1806, the party returned to Fort Mandan where Charbonneau, Sacagawea and Jean Baptiste left the expedition.

When Jean Baptiste was six years old, Charbonneau took another wife – a total of three wives for "the polygamous old interpreter". Charbonneau was a constant pursuer of young Native American girls and even at the age of 80 he married an Assiniboine girl of 14. Sacagawea later left him and moved to St Louis. There William Clark educated and cared for "Little Pomp".

There are two versions to Sacagawea's

life at this point. Some records say she died in her twenties in South Dakota. Native American tradition and other records say she had a long life.

The lost woman: These other accounts say that later on she lived with the Comanche Indians in Oklahoma, marrying a man named Jerk Meat. She lived harmoniously here giving birth to two (some records say five) children. Jerk Meat was killed in battle and Sacagawea began wandering again. The Comanches, not knowing her whereabouts, called her "Wadze-wipe" (Lost Woman). She did spend time in Fort Bridger where she lived with Jim Bridger's wife. Bridger was one of the most respected and well known mountain men of the Rockies, who married three times, each time to a Native American woman from a different tribe – first to a Flathead, then to a Ute and his third wife was a Shoshone, like Sacagawea. In 1871, Sacagawea moved to the Wind River Reservation where she decided to live with her own tribe.

Sacagawea was the first woman to speak in tribal councils. She introduced "sundance" to her tribe. "Sundance" is an event that takes place for four days and nights in which the dedicated participants fast and seek a vision or fulfill a vow. Due to her good relationship with the whites, she was instrumental in keeping her tribe from getting involved in the terrible Indian wars as the Shoshone and their Chief Washakie served as scouts for the US army.

The burial site: Sacagawea died when she was nearly 100 years old, and was buried in the Wind River Reservation. Her grave can be visited today. It is located west of Fort Washakie across from the Wind River Valley, where "she sleeps with her face towards the sunnyside of the Rocky Mountains". Beside her grave is the grave of Brazil, her adopted son according to Shoshone customs, who was the orphan of her dead sister. He lived and died with her on the reservation.

It is remarkable that Sacagawea's son, Jean Baptiste, who was educated in the court of a European prince, returned to the Rockies to try for a career as a mountain man. At the end of his life he went home to his mother's people, the Northern Shoshonis, and died in the Wyoming country of the Wind River Mountains.

Today Sacagawea is considered one of the six most important women in American history. She traveled from Missouri to the Pacific Coast, and it was her contribution that made the Lewis and Clark expedition a success. Her services as an interpreter, horse trader and a native to the wilderness cannot be overestimated. The Shoshone girl from the Rocky Mountains left an enduring image in a very literal sense. There are said to be more statues erected in her honor than to any other woman in the history of the United States.

Sacagawea sculpted by Larry Jackson, 1980.

PONY EXPRESS

CHANGE OF **TIME!**
REDUCED **RATES!**
EFFECTIVE JULY 1st, 1861

10 Days to San Francisco!

LETTERS

WILL BE RECEIVED AT THE

OFFICE, 84 BROADWAY,

NEW YORK,

Up to 4 P. M. every TUESDAY,

AND

Up to 2½ P. M. every SATURDAY,

Which will be forwarded to connect with the PONY EXPRESS leaving ST. JOSEPH, Missouri, the following SATURDAY and WEDNESDAY, respectively, at 11:00 P.M.

TELEGRAMS

Sent to Fort Kearney on the mornings of MONDAY and FRIDAY, will connect with PONY leaving St. Joseph, WEDNESDAYS and SATURDAYS.

EXPRESS CHARGES.

LETTERS weighing half ounce or under *(reduced from $5.00)* $1.00
For every additional half ounce or fraction of an ounce $1.00

In all cases Express CHARGES are to be Pre-paid.

RIDERS WANTED

Young, skinny, wiry fellows. Anxious for adventure and chance to see our great WEST. Must be expert riders, willing to risk death daily. Orphans preferred. $60 PER MONTH and keep. Apply at above address.

Transportation to the West improved with the emergence of the stagecoach in the mid-1850s, 10 years before the Pacific railway was finished. Stagecoaches were to travel in the 1800s what the airplane is to travel today. The stage drivers solved the problem of the need for speedy mail and passenger service. Ben Holladay, a well-known character in the saga of the lusty stagecoach days, was a driver-turned-boss of his own firm. He knew first-hand that the success of the coach company lay in the hands of the drivers, and he is credited with immortalizing their role. Ben Holladay sold out to Wells, Fargo and Company in 1865 after a series of disasters, not the least of which were attacks by Native Americans. The stagecoach disappeared almost completely with the coming of the railroad. It was soon relegated to the fundamental business of freighting over the back roads of the Rocky Mountain country that the railroads couldn't reach.

An even faster method of transportation was the Pony Express. Galloping through the central Rockies, its primary purpose was speed. The riders changed ponies frequently, and in the 18 months that it was in operation, the riders raced the clock and the Native Americans. Some of the greatest stories of the old West come out of the courage and endurance of the Pony Express riders.

Making tracks: The opening of the Rocky Mountain country for rails began in 1853. Grenville Dodge, nominated by President Lincoln, was to decide what route it should take, from Julesburg over the Continental Divide. Trappers and traders had told Dodge of a way through the Continental Divide below South Pass but it wasn't until he was accidentally led by a group of Native Americans through an outlet to the West that the Granite Canyon route was finally complete.

Dodge went to work recruiting thousands of young men recently discharged from the Union and Confederate armies, and the operation for the completion of the lines ran with military precision. By 1867, a total of

250 miles (310 km) were already laid and the Continental Divide had been crossed. On May 10, 1869, the Union Pacific tracklayers met the Central Pacific tracklayers and drove a golden spike to mark the railroad's completion at Promontory Point in Utah. The Pacific trails chapter was complete and the Rocky Mountain country was a real part of the United States at last.

Cattle and sheep feuds: When the railroads extended their tracks West, ranchmen looked West likewise for new pastures. Hesitant

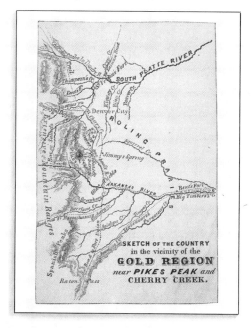

SKETCH OF THE COUNTRY in the vicinity of the GOLD REGION near PIKES PEAK and CHERRY CREEK.

about taking their cattle into the mountains, the ranchers were worried about the weather and the altitude. After years of reluctance, they started moving into the mountain valleys and found them more than agreeable for their livestock. The water was abundant and the grass nutritious. The cattlemen came to believe that their pastures produced the best grades of beef.

The sheep and cattle men were in real competition for the best pastures on the government-owned lands of the West. Each group felt that the other was making life impossible for them and their families. Many a gun battle was fought between rivals until

Left, the bottom lines of a Pony Express ad point out the dangers of the job. **Right**, the Gold Boom region near Pike's Peak, Colorado.

the government established national forests and assigned pastures to various ranchmen.

Most ranchmen held two roundups each year. In the fall, the cowboys gathered the cattle together and separated them according to their brands and selected the marketable beef to be driven to the nearest shipping center. In spring, another roundup was held to brand the calves. Early roundups were great social occasions with bronco busting, horse racing and all kinds of contests, much like a modern-day rodeo.

Many settlers took advantage of the Homestead Acts to start farming the mountain country and selected places near the streams in the Rocky Mountain country where water

reservation in northwestern Colorado. He won neither their respect nor their confidence and he and 11 of his employees were killed in a massacre. Colorado's outrage over the hideous atrocity drove the Utes forever out of their beloved Rocky Mountains.

When gold was discovered in California, adventurers started scurrying through the Rocky Mountains on their way to the Pacific Coast. Some camped by promising-looking streams on their way West and never left the Rocky Mountain country. Others remembered it and returned when they failed to make their fortune in California. However, when they got there by 1860, there were hundreds of men looking for "pay dirt" in the

was readily available and the valley lowlands were more fertile for farming. Nathan Meeker was the patron saint of these Rocky Mountain agriculturalists.

Building Utopia: With the success of irrigation and the beginnings of the cattle industry, Meeker was consumed with the idea of establishing a model farming community in the late 1860s. Many Easterners went along with his scheme and during the spring of 1870, 400 families went West by train to set up their Utopian-like colonies. When the colonists turned toward capitalism, Meeker reapplied his puritan agrarian ideas to the Ute Indians on the

mountain streams. They were followed by thousands more prospectors looking for mineral wealth.

There are endless stories carried around in the heads of the old-timers in the mountains. One of them is the "lost-cabin-mine" theory. The versions vary, but basically the story is that a Spanish explorer found gold in the Rockies, built a cabin and carried away all that he could along with a map to show where his claim was. After he died, one of his descendants searched for the cabin and the mine and when he couldn't find it, he sold the map to an American prospector. The possibilities of the map changing hands were as numerous as the gullible prospectors who believed the story.

A party of men in 1858 heard that some Cherokee Indians had found gold in the streams near "Pike's Peak". These nine men did indeed find a decent little deposit, but it was nothing compared to the rumor that spread like wildfire of the quantity of gold around "Pike's Peak". Thousands of people loaded up their wagons and headed West with "Pike's Peak or Bust" painted garishly on the side. Some were lucky, but most were disappointed and went limping back a few months later with "Busted" labeling their wagons this time.

Mining is big business: Cripple Creek ap-

refining business and they established the Guggenheim Foundation to support research and the arts.

Virginia City, Nevada, grew up on the site of the Comstock Lode, made up of several rich veins of silver and gold. One part alone was rumored to produce 200 million dollars' worth of ore. Ethan and Hosea Grosh discovered silver at the site in 1856 and died before they could develop their claim. It was rediscovered in 1859, and the stampede that was to be called the Comstock Lode began.

Probably the mining city with the most sensational career is Leadville. In 1877, there were 200 people in the whole Leadville region and three years later there were over

MAMMOTH HOT SPRINGS — MAIN TERRACE

peared on the mining maps upon its discovery by W.S. Stratton. He found an ore called telluride not known to miners in the 1890s, which was to make the Cripple Creek region one of the most famous mining centers in the world, and proved the need for large-scale lode mining. Mills needed to be built so the ores could be treated and the concentrates taken to the smelters in Denver or Pueblo.

Meyer Guggenheim and his seven sons had phenomenal success in the smelting and

Left, *Post Office in Cow Country* – a painting by Remington. **Above**, early tourists at Mammoth Hot Springs, Yellowstone Park.

14,000 in the city itself. The story was a familiar one. Two relatively inexperienced fellows struck it rich and the roaring mining camp took off. Saloons, dance and gambling halls grew like mushrooms and fortunes in gold and silver were made and lost.

Of all the fantastic things that happened in Leadville at this time, one of the most spectacular was the opening of the Crystal Castle. It was a ballroom, skating rink, dining hall and riding gallery and was composed almost entirely of blocks of ice. The rooms were heated and lit by electricity with massive pillars and towers throughout the building.

Horace Tabor's personal story is at least as

fantastic as that of the Crystal Castle. He backed the two men responsible for the claim that set Leadville awhirl. The mines he bought and sold brought him great fortunes and he was free with his money. He built a bank and an opera house and gave freely to philanthropic institutions.

He kept his mistress, Elizabeth McCourt Doe, well-situated in a suite in the Clarendon Hotel in Leadville. Once he set his sights on becoming the US Senator from Colorado, he divorced his wife. He wanted to marry Elizabeth "Baby Doe" in Washington, so he bought himself a Senate position which did little to popularize him with either his colleagues in Washington or his constituency at home.

ROCK CUT, NEAR ASPEN.

Tabor and his new wife were never really accepted in society, and when the silver market collapsed, their happy days came abruptly to an end. Tabor's debts mounted faster than he could add them up and he gave up everything. Tabor died a pauper and when he was buried a great part of Colorado's past went with him. "Baby Doe" lived another 35 years and never gave up hope that the price of silver would revive itself, and in the process rehabilitate her own fortunes.

Ups and downs in the mining business were common. Ghost towns exist in all the old mining districts. When the streams were emptied of gold, one by one the miners and their families moved away. The last to leave was usually an old prospector whose hopes were not so easily crushed.

Vacation time: With the 20th century and the advent of the family vacation, the Rocky Mountains portion of the United States became known to millions of people. Every grade of accommodation was available: from campgrounds in the national parks where only water was provided; to chateaux in the mountains with every modern convenience. Dude camps with pack animals and old-fashioned ranches took in boarders who wanted a peek at life a hundred years ago. Providing recreation and inspiration, the tourist business probably brought more money into the Rocky Mountain country than all the mineral wealth taken out of it.

During Teddy Roosevelt's presidency, preservation of the national parks, monuments and primitive areas that attract tourism was nourished. That meant alienating the ranchers in the Rocky Mountain country who had been grazing their livestock on public lands. The fight was bitter and long but the fireworks were confined to Congress – not a shootout as might have occurred in the old days.

The time between the World Wars was, for the Rockies, one of uncertain change. The depression that was death to stock investors and the railroads brought a flicker of life back to the mining industry. The clean-up operations in the mines were boosted in 1934 when President Franklin Roosevelt devalued the dollar. Gold prices leaped from $20.67 an ounce to $36 an ounce. It wasn't a true resurgence, though. Actually mining just shifted its course to copper, lead, zinc and other minerals. Improvements attributed to the war turned surviving mines into giants.

The influx of tourists slowed down during World War II but soon revived when hostilities ended. Towns overwhelmed by crowds of visitors rebuilt themselves to look as they once had in the past. Today the great Rockies range with its rich history still exerts a strong pull. Its spectacular beauty, part of the nation's heritage, sits in wait for the contemporary explorer.

Left, trains cut paths through the Rockies; and **right**, palatial living on the Pacific Railroad in the 19th century.

PALACE-CAR LIFE ON THE PACIFIC RAILROAD.

PEOPLE

The history of the Rockies tells the tale of many outdoors-lovers who came to unlock the beauty of the mountains. Fur trappers like John Colter and Jim Bridger; mountain men like Jedediah Smith and Kit Carson; explorers like Lewis and Clark; all were enthralled by the opportunity for adventure in this land. And even long before they arrived, Native American tribes including the Arapahoe, Bannock, Shoshone, Crow, Nez Perce, Paiute and Ute inhabited this mountainous country.

The rich resources of the Rockies have rewarded many fortune seekers with gold, silver, copper, timber, furs, cattle, oil and coal. All have had their heyday and some are still prospering. The Rockies was the land of the Spanish explorer, the cliff dweller, the Oregon Trail, the Mormon Trail and the gold rush. Today, the gold that lures people to the Rockies is the clean, crisp, invigorating and sparkling air. The "rush" is still on! Backpackers, campers, mountain climbers, whitewater rafters, river-runners, fishermen, balloonists, skiers, hunters, windsurfers and hang gliders all flock to this year-round playground to enjoy unlimited outdoor adventures.

There is more to the Rockies than its breathtaking vista points, national parks and famous museums. The Rockies today means diverse people – cowboys, cattle barons, shepherds, ranchers, miners, fruit farmers, park rangers, naturalists... Most of the people who live here reflect the environment. Names like Big Horn, Wind River, Medicine Bow, conjure pictures of more than mountain ranges – they bring to mind images of real people: the Mexican vaqueros, whose families inherited generations of ranching expertise; Native American families on vacation in a resort on a Colorado reservation; the first settlers who originally came to the American West from Europe in search of a place to call "home", where they could work and worship freely. All these people and even the thousands of outdoors-lovers who now live in the Rockies are tied by birth or choice to the Rocky Mountains – a part of the country in which might lie the very soul of America.

Preceding pages: a western landscape adorns a street wall in Silverton (Colorado); Miss Coors, Shelly Burmeister, and her trusty steed. <u>Left</u>, a cigar-chomping farmer on his Rockies ranch.

There's no doubt in the minds of those who live in the Rockies that they are a breed apart, whether their families have been here for three generations, or whether they came for a year off from college and never left.

The mountain men who ventured into the unexplored and nearly impenetrable wilderness of these mountains were the first whites to come under the spell of the Rockies. When the demand for beaver pelts died out, the mountain men became guides and scouts for the wagon trains heading West. A relatively small handful of people heading West in wagon trains stopped at the eastern plains and foothills of the Rockies and became farmers and cattle ranchers.

The next group to invade the Rockies were the miners, and though most of them followed the siren call of big strikes and easy riches from valley to valley or mountain range to mountain range, many stayed even after the silver had played out. The first white men to settle in the lush and spectacularly beautiful Estes Park area in northern Colorado were Joel Estes and his son Milton, who built a cabin in the grassy meadows at the bottom of the valley in 1859. They later sold their property to the Earl of Dunraven, who wanted to turn it into a game preserve.

Joe Shipler was among the first to stake out claims in the Never Summer Mountains at the headwaters of the Colorado River in 1879. Though he never got much silver out of Shipler Mountain, he and his family lived in the Kawuneeche Valley until 1914.

Though the 100,000 people who headed West for Colorado in 1859 were ostensibly on their way to make a fortune panning gold in the mountains, they were spurred by a depression, and by the promise of new beginnings. Only half of them made it, and very few stayed on. The 5,000 or so that were left a year later were a determined, hardy bunch.

There was "Uncle Dick" Wooton, who opened the first tent saloon in Denver. He arrived on Christmas Eve with a wagonload full of groceries and 10 kegs of whiskey, one

of which he cracked open with an axe, and handed out free drinks. Wooton was a Virginian who later made his fortune by hacking out a 27-mile (43-km) road over Raton Pass, on the New Mexico border, then charging a hefty toll to those who wanted to cross it. He wisely let the Native Americans pass without charging them, probably to save his own skin, but also perhaps out of a sense of justice, considering that they had been using the route long before the white man appeared on the scene. When the Santa Fe railroad

wanted to use his pass, Wooton sold his rights to the company, and helped build the graded track.

The freewheeling atmosphere of new mining towns spawned or attracted many a character, male and female. One of them was Poker Alice, a widow in her early twenties, who ended up in Denver after the Civil War. When she was unable to find a "respectable" way to make a living, she took a job dealing cards in a saloon, and found she had a talent for gambling. Like most gamblers, Poker Alice made the circuit of mining towns, earning a reputation along the way for toughness. She packed a gun, smoked long, fat

Left, "old friends" enjoy a stroll through the aspens. **Right**, a park ranger shows the valley's natural beauty.

cigars and is said to have shot a few men who tried to cross her. When she tired of the itinerant life of the gambler, she opened a bordello.

Women in the Old West are divided into two categories, good and bad. However, the "hurdy gurdy" girls, as saloon waitresses and prostitutes were called, often ended up marrying, and with the scarcity of women in the West, they were usually in a position to be choosy. The "good" girls were almost by definition married or had parents who were wealthy enough to support them until they found a husband.

While most mining towns established law and order within a matter of months, there

into their own hands. Eventually Sheriff Plummer was given away by one of his men, exposed as the leader of the notorious band and hung.

There was a great fascination with the early West not only back East, but in Europe as well. Oscar Wilde toured the mining camps of the Rockies, and said the miners were the best audience he'd ever had. Silver bricks were laid in Leadville for the visit of President Grant. Dukes, lords, barons and other dignitaries from Europe came to invest in the mines and hunt grizzlies. Susan B. Anthony and Elizabeth Cady Stanton spent months among the women of the Rockies, lobbying furiously for women's rights. In the late

were also those that remained lawless, spawning legends of gunfighters and outlaws. Henry Plummer was one of the "baddest" of the Montana outlaws but, handsome and charismatic as he was, he literally "got away with murder" for years. At the height of his checkered career, Plummer led a band of more than 100 men, calling themselves "The Innocents". They robbed stagecoaches and mines in Montana – and at the same time he managed to get himself elected sheriff of Bannack and Virginia City. After years of being terrorized by "The Innocents", a group of citizens calling themselves the "Vigilantes", led by John X. Beidler, took the matter

1800s and early 1900s, celebrities flocked to the health spas and hot springs of the Rockies in much the same way as they flock to the ski slopes today.

Town origins: Throughout the Rockies, the pattern of settlement was similar. Mining towns sprang up overnight and disappeared just as quickly when the silver or gold failed to live up to its promise. Those towns that survived and grew, such as Helena, Montana, and Boise, Idaho, were favorably located along roads or railways. Nearly every town in the Rockies has its origins in mining – the ranchers, farmers and merchants followed the miners. Some towns continued to flourish because ores such as copper, coal and uranium were found. Others such as Glenwood Springs, Colorado Springs and Idaho Springs became health spas. Jackson, Wyoming, grew because it borders on Yellowstone. Today there are towns that exist solely because of their ski mountains – Vail and Beaver Creek are two prime examples. Aspen was almost a ghost town when the skiing craze hit and revived it, as were Steamboat Springs and Breckenridge.

Mining is still a major industry in the Rockies, from the massive open-pit copper mines of Montana and the Climax molybdenum mine near Leadville, Colorado, to small gold and silver mines that are privately owned. Mining is very much a way of life. The hours are long, the pay is low, the work is hard and dirty, but for some it's the only life they know, and the life they choose.

The promise of wide open spaces, freedom and opportunity inspired a variety of religious and Utopian groups to settle in the Rockies, of which the Mormons were the largest and most successful. Greeley, Colorado, was founded as a cooperative agricultural colony that sold its goods to the mining towns. The original members were religious and conservative, banning drinking and gambling, encouraging church socials, setting up libraries and schools. Other towns along the Front Range of Colorado, such as Longmont, Fort Collins and Colorado Springs, became thriving towns in the same manner. Though they soon ceased to be communally owned the settlements were very successful, and established a tradition of conservatism that survives to this day.

Tourists began flocking to the Rockies within a few decades after the miners arrived, to gaze at the splendor of the snow-capped peaks; to hunt for elk, bear and mountain lions; to fish for trout in the streams; to cure illness in the hot springs; or to play cowboy at the dude ranches. One narrow-gauge railway that followed a creek bed survived by catering to trout fishermen, who were dropped off at likely-looking spots along the way. Colorado Springs became a famous health resort for the wealthy, beginning a tradition of sumptuous *grande dame*

hotels in the middle of nowhere, many of which still stand.

The skiing boom: Throughout the early and mid-20th century, the Rockies remained somewhat obscure. Denver, Cheyenne and Helena were little more than sprawling cow towns, hanging on for their economic life to mining, agriculture and ranching through booms and busts, droughts and depressions. Tourists continued to trek West in the summers, but the winters found most towns semi-deserted and economically impoverished. It was skiing that finally made the Rockies a year-round tourist attraction. What began after World War II as a somewhat eccentric industry catering to a select group of wealthy

clients, has done nothing but mushroom ever since. The birth of the ski industry created a mini-boom of immigrants to the mountain towns; people who were willing to forego the convenience and money of the cities for the easy-going lifestyle and beauty of the ski resorts – not to mention the opportunity to spend a good part of each winter's day on downhill skis.

The growth of the ski industry in the 1960s coincided with the era of the hippies, the flower children who, at least for a while, rejected the values of their parents in favor of a simpler, less ambitious lifestyle. Of the thousands who moved to the mountains,

<u>Left</u>, western artist Micky McGuire at his easel. <u>Right</u>, a young rodeo contestant says his prayers before entering the ring.

most were eventually absorbed into the mainstream of the mining, ranching and resort towns, but there are still plenty of holdouts who live in log cabins with no electricity or running water and lead a largely self-sufficient lifestyle. Bearded and long-haired mountain men and their female counterparts are still a relatively common sight in the mountain towns of the Rockies. For these people, the Rockies represent the same things as they did to the first immigrants – the space, freedom and opportunity to live their lives as they choose.

The ski bums who came and never left are a similar group in ski towns. They came on vacations, or during a year off from college.

tain towns. Typical of them would be the successful New York City advertising executive who made a lot of money, got fed-up with the frenetic lifestyle, took his life savings out of the bank, moved to a resort town and opened up a shop, a real estate office, or a lodge. Many of these immigrants also brought with them a firm commitment to preserving the beauty of the mountains. Thousands of young people have moved to the Front Range of Colorado where, they believe, they have the best of both worlds – the sophistication and excitement of a metropolis, with the recreational playground and pristine wilderness of the mountains only a few miles away. The Front Range has at-

They fell in love with the thrill and adrenalin of downhill skiing and with the mountains. When the idyllic summers came, they couldn't bear to leave, and they put down roots. Their first few years in town are usually spent washing the dishes, cleaning the hotel rooms, running the ski lifts, waiting on tables, and performing all the other services so vital to a resort town. An equal number stay only for a season. Most ski resorts have an ample supply of young transients who are willing to do menial labor in exchange for the chance to ski.

The 1970s saw an even larger wave of young immigrants to the cities and the moun-

tracted many hi-tech industries in the past decade, creating its own Silicon Valley and lucrative jobs for young professionals.

Outdoor attractions: If there is one easy generalization to make about those who live in the Rockies, it's that they love the outdoors. Health and physical fitness is virtually a regional obsession. It often seems that everyone under the age of 40 is involved in jogging, bicycling, aerobics, athletic clubs or exercise classes of some sort. The goal is not only staying thin and fit, but excelling in one or more of the many mountain sports, from riding clunker bikes over mountain passes to skiing, hiking, rock climbing, kayaking and backpacking. If those sports are too taxing, there are always trout fishing, ice fishing, bird watching, gardening, horseback riding, jeeping, snow-mobiling, ballooning, and golf – the point is getting outdoors, enjoying the wilderness, the scenery, the crisp air and the blue skies.

For every sport in the Rockies, there are races, contests, celebrations and festivals, from marathons to rodeos, that are well and enthusiastically attended. Summers are all too fleeting in the Rockies, so they are approached with gusto, with a sense of now-or-never, take-it-while-you-can. When the hunting season arrives in the fall, hunters flock to the mountains by the thousands –

from the dancers of Ballet Aspen to the top-notch musicians of the Telluride Jazz Festival. Acting troupes, film-makers, classical musicians, craftspeople, painters and sculptors flock to the mountains where, it seems, their creative juices flow like nowhere else. To celebrate these artists, every resort town has its concerts, festivals, fairs and shows.

Every resort town also has its part-time resident celebrities – some of them come for the skiing, some for the cultural events, some simply for some peace, quiet and mountain air. Former President Ford prefers Vail. Jack Nicholson, John Denver and a host of others like Aspen. Billy Kidd swears by Steamboat Springs, and others prefer Jackson Hole, or

many say it's as much an excuse to get out into the wilderness before winter sets in as it is a desire to shoot a deer or an elk. And even with the long winters, there never seems to be time to get in enough skiing – there's always one more run to make, or one more turn to carve out of the powder.

Higher arts: Though the Rockies are something of a cultural wasteland in the winter – with the exception of the big cities – the idyllic summers attract artists of every kind,

Left, Boulder (Colorado) cheerleaders in motion. **Above**, all eyes are on this bronco bustin' cowboy at the rodeo.

Park City, Utah. Writers seek the solitude and big horizons of Montana and Wyoming, while painters look for Victorian towns, weatherbeaten cowboys and vistas of snow-capped peaks.

The Rockies melting-pot: The Rockies have always been an Anglo melting-pot, with heavy German and Slavic populations in the mountains. Other ethnic groups, such as blacks, Chinese and Hispanics, tend to be concentrated along the Front Range, in urban settings. Blacks played a large part in the settling of the West – the Museum of the Black Cowboy in Denver covers this history in fascinating detail. The Chinese came to build the railroads in the late 1800s, and many settled in Denver. Southern Colorado is a part of the Southwest that has been settled by Hispanics for centuries, and there has been a natural migration to the cities. In some of the small isolated Hispanic villages in the San Juan mountains of southern Colorado, English is a second language, and the cultural milieu is much the same as it has been since the 1500s. Adobe houses, strings of red chilis hanging in the sun, and the cadence of Spanish mark these villages. In Denver, Hispanics are by far the dominant ethnic group, accounting for over half of the population of Denver's public schools, and the Hispanic community is playing an in-

creasingly important role in local politics.

In contrast to the large reservations in the Southwest, there are relatively small Ute, Cheyenne, Crow, Shoshone, Bannock and Arapahoe reservations scattered about the Rockies. Each tribe has its own celebrations and ceremonials, but they aren't widely publicized off the reservation, so the best way to find them is to stop and ask. The Plains and Mountain Indians tended to be more warlike than their Pueblo neighbors to the south, and their land was more valuable to white settlers. As a result, they were nearly wiped out by the late 1900s, and have slowly made a comeback both in terms of population and in preserving their cultural heritage.

Another unusual and disappearing group of people in the Rockies are the Basque sheepherders. It was only a little more than a decade ago that large herds of sheep created traffic jams on the streets of Aspen and other Rocky Mountain towns in the spring and fall. Overgrazing and the competition of large ranches spelled the demise of the independent Basque sheepherder, but many can be found working for large ranches, living a simple life in primitive trailers.

Rangers at work: Travelers who venture into the national parks, forests and wilderness areas of the Rockies are more than likely to meet a ranger working for one of the numerous government agencies that maintain, regulate and watch over them. Most have degrees that make them experts in the conservation, management, identification and preservation of the plants and animals of the Rockies. Their job description may include giving nature talks and walks, keeping the peace at crowded campgrounds, picking up litter and looking for lost backpackers. It can also include spending weeks at a time alone in the wilderness on foot or horseback, maintaining trails and signs and cataloging flora and fauna.

Winter visitors to the Rockies are more than likely to meet another group whose jobs entail more than meets the eye – ski instructors and the ski patrol. Competition is stiff for these jobs and those who make it are highly qualified and certified. On any given day, a member of the ski patrol may have set off an avalanche with dynamite, marked a dangerous spot on the ski slope, put a broken leg in a temporary splint and hauled the injured party off the mountain in a sled, and gone on an out-of-bounds search looking for a missing skier.

The people of the Rockies are much like people anywhere else in the United States but there is a certain exuberance, a *joie de vivre,* a keen appreciation among those who have fallen under the spell of the blue skies and snowcapped peaks. It's right there in the eyes and the hearts of the people, and it can be contagious!

Left, representatives of Denver's ethnic mix. **Right**, the ultimate Fourth of July costume on a modern Uncle Sam.

Cowboys, a vanishing breed? Only time will tell, and it will be a long time before the Rocky Mountain cowboys vanish. Working cowboys (cowpunchers), rodeo cowboys, cattle and sheep ranchers, even farmers, in this western region are collectively referred to as cowboys.

Cowboys still wear their well-known traditional outfits: broad-brimmed cowboy hats, pointed, high-heeled boots, rawhide belts with fancy buckles, denim jeans, shirts that snap all the way down, and sometimes neckerchiefs that protect them from dust and wind when pulled up "bank-robber style". You'll be sure to hear a cowboy at a distance because his spurs "jingle-jangle" as he walks.

Some have skin that's as weathered and wrinkled as the clothes they wear, some sport shirts of flashing, bright colors and wear smiles that are just as "shiny". You won't see all of them whirling a rope, or with a "chaw" of tobacco tucked inside a cheek. Rarely will you see a cowboy shed tears or be unkind to the opposite sex.

There are cowboys working daily with machinery over acres and acres of crops. Some are seen on horseback "moseying along" with their herd of cows or sheep flock, and some will be found caring for fruit orchards.

A cowboy's life is a lonely one, his best friend is sometimes his horse or his own company, and it hasn't changed much over the past hundred years.

Endangered species: The "old cowboy lifestyle" may be a dying way of life today. Modernization has moved in over the past century. From a time when fence lines didn't even exist to present-day barbed wire, electric fences, truck power, and modern equipment. The cowboy may soon be put on the endangered species list.

Some say, "As long as people are eating beef, we'll have cowboys." We all know that cowboys "won the West". Now, it seems,

they're just trying to keep from losing it.

A cattle rancher used to be called a cattle baron or a cattle king, depending upon the number of cattle he owned.

It wasn't unusual to own a ranch covering more than 1,000 sq. miles (2,500 sq. km) teeming with cattle and a few cowboys to tend the herds.

Cattle ranches today are few and far between compared to those operating in years past. But traveling across the golden plains of Colorado and Wyoming into the mountain

regions, you can see a little history come vividly to life.

From Herefords to Texas Longhorns, every breed with beef on its sides can be found grazing the endless grasslands. If you keep your eyes open, you might also notice antelope or deer, maybe even a hawk or an eagle. You won't have to look hard to find jack rabbits, but you may strain yourself in an attempt to avoid hitting one: they frequently insist on jumping out in front of unsuspecting drivers, especially at night when they are mesmerized by the on-coming headlights.

Woolly America: Heading north from colorful Colorado into the great Wyoming range

Preceding pages: an exotic belly dancer at the Colorado Renaissance Festival; a Crow Indian in clown costume; and calming a roped steer, Wyoming. **Left,** horse and rider hit the lonesome western trail. **Right,** a specially bred longhorn.

area, you'll notice that cattle decline and sheep begin to appear. Wyoming, originally known as "cow country", is now a heavily populated, wool-producing state.

Range wars between sheep and cattle ranchers during the 19th century became a major theme in Wyoming's history. It was the cattlemen in Wyoming who claimed first-come, first-serve rights to the land. However, as sheep vied for space, the conflict grew violent.

In one skirmish, more than 150 masked men attacked a sheep ranch killing at least 2,000 sheep and a number of sheepherders, who tried in vain to protect their important and valuable woolly charges.

punchers or gunmen. "Go West Young Man," stated Greeley, a Colorado farmer – and they did, literally by the thousands.

Farmers flocked into vastly populated areas to feed miners attracted by the gold rush, cattlemen drawn by Federal land grants, and other pioneers. Sheep ranchers followed, giving the farmers one more reason to cultivate crops.

When the miners and traders moved on, the farmers and ranchers stayed behind to settle the states of Idaho, Wyoming and Colorado. These hardworking men and women, standing firm against adverse weather conditions, possessed an undying love for their land that made possible the

" CUTTING OUT."

These range wars, otherwise known as sheep slaughters, continued until the Wyoming Wool Growers' Association was organized. The organization attracted many members who eventually put a stop to the bloodshed.

In reality, sheep were more profitable than cattle. Sensing this fact, many cattlemen became sheepherders and the feuding ceased to exist. As a result, wool became the state's leading industry in the early 20th century.

Cowboy farmers: Pioneers made their way West, blazing the trails for the crowds who followed them. Those same pioneers soon became farmers, miners, ranchers, cow-

Rocky Mountain cowboy farmer of the 20th century. You'll find those farmers today harvesting everything from potatoes to wheat to fruit orchards.

Rocky mountain crops: Ask any American where potatoes are grown and chances are he'll say Idaho. Although potatoes are grown right across the United States, the largest crop is cultivated in Idaho, mainly in the irrigated Snake River area.

Luther Burbank is known as the "father of the russet burbank potato", developed in 1872 and still the leading potato variety grown in the state. Burbank accidentally found a seed pod in his New England garden and transferred it to Idaho. Then, Joe Marshall, the legendary "Idaho Potato King", developed the potato to its present value.

Marshall had such a love for "his" potatoes that any employee he observed handling them carelessly or bruising them was instantly fired. Thanks to Marshall, Idaho is the number one potato producing state in the United States.

The tall, amber-colored wheat grain seen all over Colorado's Rocky Mountain plains is the state's chief field crop, producing a record high of 117 million bushels in 1983.

Successful wheat farming in Colorado began in 1876, the same year Colorado reached statehood. Cowboy pioneers learned

or drought ruins the crop and waiting until the next year for another chance to win.

Two-thirds of the Colorado wheat is shipped to other countries, a blessed excess that feeds hundreds of million abroad. In turn, income from the fields feeds the farmers' families and their state taxes pay for schools, roads, parks and other systems – a boon to the state's economy.

As the Rocky Mountain regions in the United States evolved, cowboys found futures in what their soil would produce. Riches were made in potatoes, in wheat and some in mouth-watering, taste-tempting fruit.

Pounds of peaches: Peaches, peaches and more peaches are produced each year in

to cultivate their land for this golden crop, opening the door for the wheat-raising families of today.

Long, hard hours are spent planting, tending and harvesting a wheat crop. Fields are alternately planted. A crop is raised in one field one year and another the next year, enabling the fallow fields to rest to enhance the quality of future crops.

Wheat farmers are always gambling on weather conditions, losing when a hail storm

Left, roping and herding steer in the old days was called "cutting out". **Above**, herds roam the plains of a Wyoming ranch.

Colorado, mostly in the Grand Valley near Mesa Country. In fact, the town of "Fruita" is named for the massive amount of peaches grown in its vicinity. More than 7 million pounds were produced in Mesa Country in 1983. In April the western slopes of the Rockies are covered with the beautiful colors and smells of peach blossoms. About 400,000 peach trees are scattered over 2,700 acres (1,090 hectares) bearing fruit from July through September.

The soil of the western mountain valleys is the most fertile in the nation, and the land west of the Continental Divide gets more than two-thirds of the state's surface water from rain and snow run-off. The dry, warm climate is ideal for growing fruit. In addition to peach trees, orchards full of cherries, pears and apricots dot the countryside.

Local roadside stands, farmers' markets and grocery stores make fruit easily available to tourists at very reasonable prices. Plan your Colorado vacation during the summer months, and drive through this fruit-full area for sights, scents and tastes that you'll never forget.

Texas Longhorns: The first cattle in the Americas, hunted as wild animals in larger herds than the buffalo and eventually becoming more endangered, were the Texas Longhorns. Without them, all the romantic

legends about cowboys and their adventures wouldn't exist.

In 1493, Christopher Columbus brought Spanish cattle to this continent, and 200 years later, descendants of those cattle were grazing the Mexican ranges. In 1690, about 200 head of cattle were driven north to a mission near the Sabine River, land that would soon be known as Texas.

By the Civil War, nearly 300 years after setting hoof in America, millions of Longhorns ranged the southwestern plains. In the next quarter century, 10 million head were herded north as far as Colorado, Wyoming and Montana.

Charles Goodnight and Oliver Loving in 1860 created the famous Goodnight-Loving trail, driving several hundred Longhorns into Denver City for the Colorado goldminers. Around the same time, Lovell and Reed, a well-known firm of Texas cattlemen, brought in another herd, thereby starting the range cattle industry in a country now called Colorado.

The Longhorns could travel nearly 100 miles (160 km) without water, surviving on prairie or mountain grasses no other animal would even look at. Their calves stood up right after birth and traveled side-by-side with the mother. Longhorns were feisty, rangy animals, adept at protecting their young from natural predators, such as the coyote.

At the turn of the century, in less than 40 years, an overwhelming demand from Europe for American beef imports brought the Longhorn closer to extinction than the buffalo. The federal government then intervened and established two wildlife refuges in 1927 for the preservation of the Texas cattle.

In 1964, when the Texas Longhorn Breeders' Association was formed, fewer than 1,500 head of Texas Longhorns existed. Three years later, Darol Dickinson bought a few Longhorns, the first step in developing a Texas Longhorn empire.

Dickinson Ranch today comprises 20,000 acres (8,094 hectares) on three ranches in Colorado, running 1,000 head of mostly Texas Longhorns. The ranch is one of the pioneers in the new Salorn cattle breed, producing naturally lean beef and the Salers breed, hardy cattle from France that are similar to Longhorns.

Darol Dickinson and his Dickinson Ranch have claimed a spot in the history of tomorrow's Texas Longhorn by ensuring their popularity and survival in today's industry. Visitors are encouraged to "stop in", as they have for the past 18 years. Here is a good place to surround oneself in western lore. Those traditions are still alive on this busy, working ranch, located in the heart of Colorado's plains, just a few minutes east of Colorado Springs on State Highway 94. At the crossroads of Ellicott, just look for the "long horns" – and the cowboys.

Left, the sun highlights a symbol of the Old West – the pistol. Right, a thoughtful Wyoming ranch hand contemplates the outdoor life.

He rises from his pallet inside the Sundance corral. It is just before sunup on the ritual's third day. The Sundance participants have been without food and water since Friday evening. It is now Monday and they have been "standing thirsty" in a spiritual quest that will hopefully include renewal and rededication through individual visions. Outsiders have gathered in the morning darkness to seek a blessing at this high-holy moment of sunrise.

Leonard Burch, immediate past chairman of the Southern Ute tribe, takes the flute made from the bone of a turkey leg and the haunting notes he creates seem to pipe the sun out from under its mauve coverlet, over the mountain top. Burch's only garb is a bright red breech clout.

Two days later, dressed in a three-piece business suit, Burch has jetted to Washington DC, where he is explaining to the United States Congress the importance, to Native American and Anglo alike, of damming up the river waters of the state of Colorado before they flow into New Mexico and Southern California.

In just 48 hours, Burch has passed from the old way to the new.

Sundance kids: The Utes are just one tribe (with several bands) of Native Americans who called the Rocky Mountains home. Their neighbors were the Crow, Flathead, Blackfeet, Bannock, Shoshone, Crees, Nez Perce, Arapahoe and Cheyenne. Some of those tribes, like the Arapahoe and Cheyenne, were Plains Indians who moved West to escape the encroaching white settlers. The Cheyenne came to the Big Horn Mountains after the defeat of General George Custer at the battle of the Little Big Horn in 1876.

They were unique as tribes, but had some things in common. The Utes were known for their horsemanship. The Comanches had a reputation for their skill in warring, the Blackfeet for their cunning in dealing with the white aggressors.

As they intermingled, they learned from

each other. It was from the Shoshonis that the Utes learned the Sundance. The Sundance is the most sacred religious observance of Plains Indians. It includes fasting and dancing in an enclosed area, always facing the sun or some other sacred object such as a buffalo head on a pole in the center of the corral. The object is spiritual growth through a vision quest. Some tribes pierced their flesh as a sign they would fulfill their vows. The US government banned the Sundance for that reason, but it has been making a comeback since the 1960s as tribes recapture their culture. The Shoshonis obviously learned the Sundance from either the Arapahoes or Cheyennes.

The Shoshonis called themselves "the people" and except for the latecomers, if they were asked where they came from, they said they had been there forever. Rock art substantiates a very old history of the people whose lives were shaped by their geography. They followed the game to high country in the summer and to the valleys in winter. Before they were introduced to the horse, they used buffalo products for everything – food, shelter, clothing, tools and ceremony.

Totems and taboos: The Shoshonis knew the ways of both animals and plants and respected them even as they used them. They had a universal belief that animals, like humans, had souls that survived death. Their respect for animals stemmed from that belief. They thought animal souls reported to living animals how they were killed, butchered and consumed. Living game refused to allow their bodies to be slain by an unkind hunter, who thereafter found hunting more and more difficult.

When Native Americans saw an eclipse, they believed an animal was trying to swallow the sun or the moon. Many of their original legends and stories give human properties to animals like the coyote, the lizard, the eagle and the mountain lion.

Most tribes had taboos concerning pregnancy, birth, menstruation and going to war. Some tribes isolated the expectant mother immediately before birth and for 30 days thereafter. Isolation from the tribe was common for women who were menstruating and such women were barred from tribal rites

Preceding pages: a dramatic Shoshone Indian chief in full traditional garb. **Left,** the well-worn face of a member of the Crow tribe.

such as the sweat lodge. In some tribes, preparation for war included dancing, fasting and isolation to ensure abstinence from sexual activity.

Their medicine was a mix of religion, magic and herbalism. In most nonliterate cultures, marriage was a contract between kin rather than between two individuals. It was widely celebrated and served as a way to regulate sexual activity.

The Native Americans made beautiful works of art, such as beadwork, tanned leather, bone and teeth breastplates, jewelry and other adornments. Furs were worn not only for warmth but as hair ornaments or as a decorative part of their clothing.

probably encountered their first white men when the Spanish colonization of the Pueblos began about 1600. Contact with those Spanish invaders and Mexican explorers into the Rocky Mountain region is reflected in the Ute language.

Peter and Paul Mallet are credited with being the first men to have reached the Rockies by crossing the plains in 1739. The Spanish priests Dominguez and Escalante, exploring for Spain, got into the Rocky Mountains as they searched for a trail from New Mexico to California. When Lewis and Clark came West in an attempt to find a commercially feasible land route across the continent, their contact with the Rocky Moun-

White invasion: The functions of Native American societies were clearly defined, and these groups were a far cry from the "savage nomad" myth which was promoted by the white aggressors.

What happened to these early tribal societies is that they were made to trade the lands they called home for the most uninhabitable acreage their white oppressors could force upon them. They were beaten by disease, such as smallpox, to which they had no immunity; superior and unethical military attacks; and a US government that did not honor its treaties.

Native Americans in the Southern Rockies

tain Native Americans was the Shoshonis who were riding Spanish horses through their trade with the Utes and Comanches.

It was the introduction of the horse into tribal society that brought drastic change. Mounted, the tribe members could pursue both game and enemies over far greater areas. In their exchanges with neighboring tribes, they picked up new ways of warring and celebrating.

Traders and treaties: From 1795 to 1822, the US government operated trading posts. Indians' contact with traders was mostly friendly. Traders wanted the beaver and buffalo pelts that the Native Americans could supply;

while they wanted the utensils, firearms, fabric and liquor that traders could offer them in exchange.

The first treaty the US signed was with the East Coast Delaware tribe in 1778. From then until 1849, when the Bureau of Indian Affairs was moved out of the US War Department to the Department of the Interior, all Native Americans agents were military officers charged with protecting the interests of the fur traders, missionaries, miners and finally the settlers. No one was charged with protecting the interests of the Native American.

It was the California gold rush in the middle of the 19th century which alerted the

buffalo and other game but wantonly killed without utilizing their kill. That practice was an affront to the Native Americans; it also made it harder and harder to supply meat to their hungry tribes.

On the heels of the miners came the transcontinental railroad. The venture not only appropriated vast amounts of land to the railroad and its right-of-way, but decimated forests and buffalo herds. Twenty-five hundred railroad ties per mile stripped timber lands. Feeding railroad workmen further reduced the buffalo herds and for the majority of whites who favored exterminating the Native Americans, killing buffalo became a means to that end as they realized the tribes'

Native Americans to the fact that the resources on which they depended were finite and that the white invaders had little respect for either the land or the animals.

They began to fight back with attacks on forts, wagon trains and settlements. This encouraged the white invader to annihilate "the savages".

The miners who poured into the area for the Pike's Peak gold rush not only drove out

Left, a modern Zuni jewel at the Museum of Mesa Verde National Park. **Above**, buffalo provided food and clothing for Native Americans seen here in *Buffalo Hunt*, by Frederic Remington.

dependence on the shaggy beasts.

As Native Americans killed and looted in a vain attempt to protect their resources, the US government shored up its resolve to conquer by force.

Every tribe faced its military "Waterloo".

Weakened by a plague of smallpox, the Shoshonis and Bannocks had gathered on the Bear River in 1863. A military attack took the lives of 400 people. By the next year, 20,000 whites had entered Idaho's richest mining area.

In 1854, the Utes were called to a peace conference held in Taos, New Mexico. Blankets were given to the Native Americans as gifts and every person who received a blanket contracted smallpox. Even now, many Utes believe that plague was deliberately introduced by the whites who came to talk peace. With more and more settlers coming into their territory, the Utes joined the Apaches to drive the whites from the country around Fort Carson, Colorado.

Gaining entrance to Fort Carson on Christmas Day, the Native Americans staged an uprising, killing all but one man and taking the one woman in the fort and her two children captives. Kit Carson led the defensive action against the Utes, defeating them.

The Sand Creek slaughter: Colorado Governor John Evans ordered the Cheyennes and Arapahoes to lay down their arms and report to Fort Lyons. Native American agent Colonel John Chivington believed only a harsh lesson would persuade those two bands of warriors to behave. With the Cheyennes and Arapahoes encamped at Sand Creek, Chivington followed them there with 900 "military" men, most of whom were miners who had enlisted in the cause of exterminating the "savages".

More than half the Native Americans killed at Sand Creek were women and children. Soldiers also disemboweled several pregnant women. The event was termed "The foulest and most unjustifiable crime in the annals of America." It plunged Colorado into a state of emergency, martial law and economic crisis because of the whites who protested such brutality.

The Blackfeet, too, were suffering from a plague of smallpox in 1870. When they saw soldiers approaching their encampment on the Marias River, Chief Heavy Runner went out to meet the soldiers alone, carrying a sign of peace. He was shot, only the first of many Blackfeet killed that day.

Weakened by disease, beaten in battle, stalked by hunger and with their tribal society non-functional, tribe after tribe signed a treaty with the US government.

The Native Americans not only were with-

out options, but it is doubtful that they understood what they were signing. In a US Supreme Court Case in 1945, US versus Shoshone, Chief Justice Black wrote: "Ownership meant no more to them than to roam the land as a great common and to possess and enjoy it the same way they possess and enjoyed the sunlight, the west wind and the feel of spring in the air."

Mediator or traitor?: The Treaty with the Utes is a typical example of the misunderstanding. That treaty was signed in 1868 by Chief Ouray. It designated the land on which the Utes could live without intrusion by whites. But almost immediately, both gold

78

and silver were discovered in the San Juan Mountains and the mountains were filled with miners.

Ouray was considered a great mediator by the US government. The Utes considered him a traitor. Ouray felt the Native American had to change his way to survive and he joined the white effort to assimilate the Utes into white society. In 1873, Ouray signed another agreement with the US government that gave 6,000 sq. miles (15,540 sq. km) of Ute land to miners – almost one-fourth of the reservation agreement of 1868.

In an attempt to demonstrate to Indians that they could succeed in an agrarian civilization, Ouray and his wife, Chippeta, lived

cans to adopt white people's ways.

First they were all assigned to agencies where food and goods were to be distributed and Indians were forced to learn farming.

The Dawes Act of 1887 gave Native American heads of families 160-acre (64-hectare) allotments, opening the rest of the reservation lands to white settlers.

Native Americans were a highly spiritual people. Because the "superior" whites had no concept of any religion except their brand of Christianity, the move to "Christianize" the tribes diluted their native faith with a demoralizing result. Many Indian spiritual leaders see a direct result of that spiritual destruction in the high suicide rates among

on a farm near Montrose, Colorado, cultivating their lands and raising sheep and cattle. But after repeated contact with the Great White Father in Washington, Ouray died knowing his life's work had failed. Chippeta remarried and lived in a traditional teepee until her death in 1924.

Great white ways: By 1871, the US had stopped treaty-making with the Indians. Through a series of government programs, attempts were made to force Native Ameri-

Left, a Native American concentrates on the rodeo. **Above**, a native dance at the Crow Indian Festival and Rodeo in Montana.

the population today.

Attempts to educate Native Americans were even less successful. Teachers spoke English in boarding schools where using any native tongue was discouraged to the point of punishment if children were found speaking anything but English. Not only did children not understand subject matter, but they were separated from their families and tribes and experienced severe trauma because of those separations.

Native American lawyer and writer Vine Deloria Jr., of Denver, has written: " Tribal society is of such a nature that one must experience it from the inside. Being inside a tribal universe is so comfortable and reasonable that it acts like a narcotic. When you are forced outside the tribal context, you become alienated, irritable and lonely. In desperation, you long to return to the tribe if only to preserve your sanity."

All the government's attempts to assimilate the Native Americans were marked by a paternalism that encouraged dependence.

In 1924, Native Americans received citizenship from the US government, but it was not until 1948 that they could vote in every state in the union.

Policies and programs: In 1934, the Indian Reorganization Act reversed the Dawes Act, saying that no tribal lands should be par-

uted to individuals who were not prepared to handle either. The tribe was destroyed as a powerful economic unit.

Concurrent with the termination policy was the Relocation Program. It was designed to take Native Americans off reservations and place them in the city. It proved to be just a new form of disaster.

Indian assistance: In 1946, a Claims Commission was established to settle all grievances with Native Americans by cash payments with the objective of cutting off financial aid. By 1951, 852 land claims had been filed – a legal brouhaha that defied resolution since many claims overlapped each other.

In 1961, most tribes were represented at a

celled out in individual allotments. Annual authorizations of $2 million for the purchase of tribal land were established. Credit funds for incorporated tribes were set up. Loans for vocational training and academic study were provided. The power of tribes as self-governing units was established. Although funds to enact many of these provisions were never fully appropriated by Congress, the policies of the Indian Reorganization Act were theoretically much better than the federal government's next idea.

In 1953, the United States adopted a policy of termination in its relations with Native Americans. Land and capital were distrib-

government-called conference where a declaration of Indian purpose was drafted. "Indians ask for assistance, technical and financial, for the time needed, however long that may be, to regain in the America of the space age, some measure of the life they enjoyed as original possessors of the land."

Native Americans were ripe for the civil rights movement of the 1960s.

They staged a fish-in in Washington State where they had been denied the right to fish. They took over Alcatraz Prison in San Francisco Bay. In 1968, the American Indian Movement (AIM) was founded. Leaders said they formed AIM because they were tired of having nothing to say about their own destiny. That organization took over the Bureau of Indian Affairs (BIA) office in 1972.

Recovering the "loot": When they left the BIA, they took an estimated $750,000 worth of art objects which they said missionaries stole from the Native Americans many years ago. They left behind a statement which read: "Gentlemen: I do not apologize for the ruin nor the so-called destruction of the mausoleum. For in building anew, one must first destroy the old. This is the beginning of a new era for the North American native people. When history recalls our efforts here, our descendants will stand with pride, knowing their people were the only ones responsi-

ble for the stand taken against tyranny, injustice, and the gross inefficiencies of this branch of a corrupt and decadent government."

It is poetic justice that the arid lands many tribes were forced on to are now discovered to be rich with mineral resources.

Tribal energy: Rocky Mountain tribes are among the 25 who in 1975 combined to form an organization to protect their energy resources. That organization calls itself The

Left, Native American and Congressman, Ben Nighthorse, in his shop 'Campbell Creations'. Above, a wide-eyed young resident of the Fort Hall reservation.

Council of Energy Resources Tribes (CERT).

From a CERT annual report come these words: "On a hot and dusty western summer day in 1875, two cowhands stopped their horses by a creek running deep through Indian territory. The animals refused to drink and the men, looking closely, found the water to be covered with a thick, sticky black substance neither had ever seen before. They were the discoverers of oil on Indian land.

"A hundred years later, more than 13,000 oil and gas leases involving tribal lands were on record, accounting for over 23,000 separate producing wells. The largest open-pit uranium mine in the world and the largest surface coal mine in the country were both operating on Indian lands."

CERT was formed on the premise that if they took control of this energy and managed it wisely, it could become the foundation for economic development on their reservations.

Its goals are: To ensure an equitable return for resources, to assist tribes in protecting those resources, to aid each tribe in the capability to manage its resources for itself.

Peter MacDonald, chairman of the Navajo Nation and former CERT Chairman, said, "Federal support for CERT and for other tribal energy programs is proving to be among the most cost-effective investments yet made in our country's energy future.

"Real progress, in the view of my people, must transcend profits. It must outlast generations. It must help us realize a vision articulated by Chief Joseph of the Nez Perce a century ago: "Let me be a free man – free to travel, free to stop, free to work, free to trade where I choose, free to choose my own teachers, free to follow the religion of my fathers, free to think and act and talk for myself…for this time, the Indian race is waiting and praying."

There is an effort by most tribes to recapture their spiritual values, native tongue, history and legends. Tribes are still affected by high unemployment rates, high suicide rates, alcoholism and infant mortality.

The freedom MacDonald speaks of will be found in leaders like himself – articulate, well-educated and sophisticated. In common with oppressed people throughout the history of the world, Native Americans are gradually developing a leadership which will enable them to hold their own against further tribal and personal violations.

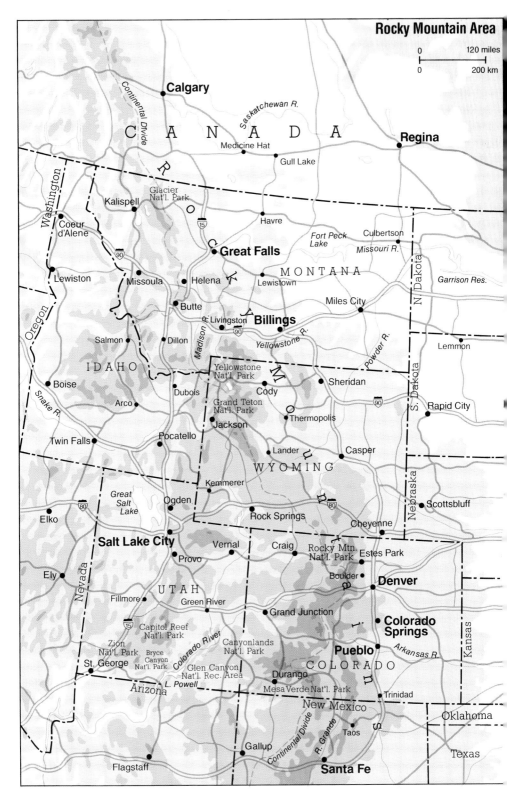

Rocky Mountain Area

0   120 miles
0   200 km

Calgary

Continental Divide

Saskatchewan R.

Regina

C A N A D A

Medicine Hat

Gull Lake

R O C K Y

Washington

Glacier Nat'l. Park

Kalispell

Havre

Culbertson

Fort Peck Lake

Missouri R.

Coeur d'Alene

Great Falls

M O N T A N A

Garrison Res.

Lewiston

Missoula

Helena

Lewistown

Oregon

Butte

Miles City

Lemmon

Livingston

Billings

Salmon

Dillon

Yellowstone R.

Madison

Powder R.

IDAHO

Yellowstone Nat'l. Park

Rapid City

Boise

Dubois

Cody

Sheridan

Snake R.

Arco

Grand Teton Nat'l. Park

Thermopolis

Jackson

Pocatello

Lander

Casper

Twin Falls

W Y O M I N G

Kemmerer

Great Salt Lake

Ogden

Elko

Rock Springs

Scottsbluff

Salt Lake City

Vernal

Craig

Cheyenne

Provo

Rocky Mtn. Nat'l. Park

Estes Park

Ely

Nevada

Boulder

Denver

U T A H

Fillmore

Green River

Grand Junction

Capitol Reef Nat'l. Park

Colorado Springs

Zion Nat'l. Park

Bryce Canyon Nat'l. Park

Canyonlands Nat'l. Park

Pueblo

Arkansas R.

St. George

Colorado River

Glen Canyon Nat'l. Rec. Area

C O L O R A D O

Durango

Arizona

L. Powell

Mesa Verde Nat'l. Park

Trinidad

New Mexico

Oklahoma

Continental Divide

Taos

Texas

Gallup

R. Grande

Flagstaff

Santa Fe

N. Dakota

S. Dakota

Nebraska

Kansas

The Rockies, once a vast, sprawling mountain land, now boasts mountain towns, sophisticated cities and exciting activities. Apa's *Insight Guide: The Rockies* helps you explore it all.

First we present you with themes basic to the hearty Rockies lifestyle. "The Outdoor Experience" describes the variety of outdoor pastimes available in these spectacular mountains.

The Rocky Mountains is ski country personified. Many claim here is the greatest snow on earth. Dude ranches, ski lodges and resorts have sprung up everywhere so you can ski the peaks in style. "Ski Resorts" tells you how to get the best out of it.

"Mountain Celebrations" helps you plan your trip to coincide with some of the greatest events and happenings.

Visitors also flock to the many National Parks and monuments scattered throughout the Rockies states. Some of the most dramatic landscape and wildlife in the world are here. The National Parks section gives you pointers on how to visit and what to look for in the Yellowstone, the Grand Tetons, the Rocky Mountain and in Utah's National Parks. Don't miss the helpful photographic tips following that section.

The Colorado Mountain Towns nestled in the Rockies are a treat to visit and are full of mining history. Aspen in particular, a Colorado mountain retreat rivalling Denver in popularity, has an aura all its own.

Then your drive to Durango, south of Denver, takes you through narrow passes and wide open meadows to authentic western streets almost frozen in time. And don't miss Canyon Country nearby. The Royal Gorge and the Black Canyon here reveal dramatic evidence of ancient geology at work.

Moving north to Wyoming, explore its wilderness and on the way visit Jackson Hole. Encounters with wildlife and the proximity of the Grand Tetons make this an awe-inspiring area. Then allow a few days at the Buffalo Bill Historical Center in Cody to view four superb museum collections. On the way out of town enjoy the Wapiti valley and some of the best dude ranches in the West on the outskirts of Yellowstone Park.

Also within reach is Bozeman in Montana "big sky" country. Farmers and modern cowboys here live with their rich lore of gold seekers and mountain men.

Traveling south through Idaho towards Utah you'll arrive at state capital Salt Lake City where 100 years of Mormon history come to life. This unique American subculture is a powerful social force today. From here the superlative ski areas in the Promontory Ranch north of the Great Salt Lake are close by.

The Rockies – a place well worth exploring. Come share in the adventure.

Preceding pages: Steamboat Springs (CO); the Zion overlook from Highway 14; van in Capitol Reef National Park.

THE OUTDOOR EXPERIENCE

From the first recorded history of Rockies settlement, adventurous travelers have been coming to the area for a variety of reasons. Not only to seek their fortunes in the rich gold and silver fields, but to settle the land and take advantage of the moderate climate and the vast resources of the varied terrain. The region's earliest history is not written down but is recorded in paintings on the canyon walls in protected locations along the Colorado River near Lake Powell and in the ruins of the cliff dwellings at Mesa Verde.

Those early Rocky Mountain residents were drawn to the area for the same reasons as the white explorers and adventurers who came later; and even more recently, as the vacationers who still make their way to the remote villages and mountain hideaways. The rich land and natural resources, spectacular scenery, and opportunity for adventure and personal fulfillment are what draw people, almost magically, to the Rockies, and have for more than 200 years.

The acquisition of the Rocky Mountain region with the Louisiana Purchase in 1803 made it accessible for settlers, trappers, hunters, and those seeking their fortunes in gold and silver. Brief forays or exploration parties made their way into the mountains. Included in their number was Zebulon Pike who, in 1806, discovered the mountain that bears his name, and Lord Gore whose reputation has been embellished as the years have gone by.

Lord Gore was an English nobleman who traveled in style during his hunting trips that included cooks and servants, and the luxury of frequent hot baths in his tent. His large brass bathtub was part of the equipment that normally accompanied Lord Gore. Today, an entire mountain range bears his name, and stirs curiosity and imagination in the campers and backpackers who take the time to trek the ancient trails.

More and more people ventured into the unknown territory from the 1830s to the 1850s. But not until the fall of 1858 was gold discovered in the hills west of Denver which sparked the rush that brought instant attention and tent cities to the relatively uncharted territory.

Just six years later, in 1864, the silver boom was on. Some of the rough-and-tumble mining towns turned quickly into rich and fabulous cities with opera houses and magnificent homes inhabited by men and women with broad and booming personalities to match them. Silver Baron H. A.W. Tabon, who established, lost and regained his fortune in Leadville, then made his mark on the society of Denver is among the most notable. He built the Tabor Opera House in Leadville and later the Tabor Grand Opera House in Denver. His first wife, Augusta, was a strong woman whose work ethic scorned Tabor's glamorous and flamboyant lifestyle. When Tabor moved to Denver, he married Baby Doe, a beautiful young woman who enjoyed the exciting society that Tabor's riches provided. Baby Doe died penniless trying to work the Matchless Mine near Leadville. Tabor admonished her before his death "never to sell the Matchless" because it would once again make her rich. Now, the Matchless Mine is open to visitors and takes history buffs into the rough world of the early miners. The Tabor Opera House has reopened as a visitor attraction, but the city of Leadville is far from the booming community that once boasted more than 12 theaters, many of which were "wine theaters" of questionable reputation.

On the trail to relaxation: Following the gold and silver boom, the region's cattle, agricultural and mineral resources boosted the economy and allowed cities to flourish along the rivers, at highway junctions, natural springs and hot springs. The hot springs, vacation spots for the earliest settlers and once believed by both Native Americans and whites to have exceptional healing powers, still attract thousands of visitors. Among the most noted are the mineral hot springs at Eldorado Springs, Idaho Springs, Hot Sulphur Springs, Ouray, Mount Princeton, Pagosa Springs,

Redstone and Glenwood Springs, home of the largest spring-fed hot pool in the world. While some of the hot springs are well-known and accessible vacation spots, many can be reached only by jeep road or hiking trail in summer or by cross-country skiers in winter.

Ironically, what draws people to Colorado most is also the state's biggest barrier: the Rocky Mountains. More than 50 peaks in the Colorado Rockies top 14,000 ft (4,250 meters), and more than half the state is covered by rugged mountain terrain or high plateaus laced with deep valleys and canyons. Etched by glaciers and erosion, layers of cliffs line canyon walls, creating the trails that early settlers faced and the adventure for today's hikers.

People still flock to the region to play or to seek their fortunes among the rocks and abundant resources. Most of the Rockies' industry relates to mineral resources or agriculture. The travel industry occupies an extremely important spot in the economy and it relies most heavily on the region's dramatic natural beauty of jagged peaks and wide open sky.

Recreation, relaxation, vitality, adventure, beauty, excitement – just a few of the varied reasons why people continue to visit the Rocky Mountains. An even greater variety of activities keeps them busy. From the sophisticated, modern and elegant resorts that entertain skiers, conventioneers, and summer guests in a planned and ultimately civilized manner, to the backcountry experiences where the hardy undertake almost the same risk and hardship as the early traveler, the Rockies have it all.

Because the Rocky Mountain states rely heavily on tourists, they have made it a point to develop a transportation and hospitality industry that encourages return visits. The interstate highway system allows easy access to major areas and links with well-maintained local roads which, in a few short miles, take visitors to regions that appear as untouched and pristine as they were 100 years ago. With a little extra effort, either by taking one of the numerous backcountry jeep trails or by going it

Balloons at the Avon Balloon Race in Colorado.

alone, on foot, horseback or trail bicycle – you can reach restricted wilderness areas where no motorized vehicles break the silence. The only sounds are of the wind in the trees, the rushing stream at the valley floor, and the wildlife that goes about its daily business with an occasional scolding at intruders. Only minutes from the door of many Rocky Mountain communities, you can get away from it all and feel alone in the solace that Mother Nature maintains to replenish the mind and soul.

Victorian elegance: As a Rocky Mountain vacation begins, in evidence are the quaint Victorian homes and buildings that sprang up at the peak of the gold and silver rush. Nothing was spared in many of the homes, with gingerbread woodworking surrounding the leaded glass windows that overlook mountain vistas. At the decline of the gold and silver boom, the rich communities suffered setbacks and homes fell into disarray. Beautiful and opulent landmarks, such as the Tabor Opera House in Leadville and Teller House in Central City, where the street in front was paved with 30 solid silver bricks and which was known for the large painting of a beautiful woman, commonly called "the face on the bar-room floor", closed their doors to the richly attired gentlemen and ladies of the late 1800s.

The recent rush of tourists has given new life to the Victorian towns. Homes have been restored either as private residences, bed-and-breakfast locations or even boutiques and museums. While visiting one of the mining towns, it is appropriate to dive completely into the romance of the Old West and stay in one of the rooming houses. Today, summer visitors enjoy opera, symphonies and plays at a number of the restored opera houses. The opulent chandeliers, woodwork and decor have been authentically restored so guests can feel they are living in the 19th-century affluent society.

Moving away from the atmosphere and relative formality of the villages and towns the pioneering spirit of the West remains. The hustle and bustle of modern cities begin to fall away as you enter the mountain communities. The transformation continues as you move into the spaces and activities that are now so accessible throughout the Rocky Mountains.

The rush to the Rockies is not impeded by lack of transportation. Those arriving by car and reluctant to venture beyond that mode of transportation can see a large part of the states. Roads to mining towns are generally good, and many of the historic locations or ghost towns are found on jeep roads. While not for the faint of heart in many cases, taking time to visit some of the ghost towns is greatly rewarding. Jeep trails are ranked from nearly passable by a normal passenger car to a white-knuckled ride in a four-wheel-drive vehicle. Narrow, winding roads that once provided access for residents traveling by wagon or on horseback are still the only ways to reach some of the ghost mining towns. But the vistas are spectacular, and, once at the destination, wandering among the fallen buildings and searching for artifacts left behind by departing citizens is rewarding. Tourists can let

Sailing through water and clouds at Grand Lake.

their minds wander and imagine what life was like in the encampments, from the bold and bawdy days when gold and silver finds were commonplace to the cold and desolate winters when the price of gold and silver dwindled and settlers suffered.

Jeeping to ghost towns is not the only choice, however. Taking restricted or jeep roads into the backcountry allows hikers to strike off on foot and push still deeper into the wilderness.

For those who wish to leave the driving and route selection to someone else, organized jeep tours are offered in almost every corner and valley of the Rockies. Local Chambers of Commerce or Information Centers can provide names of jeep outfitters and recommend routes that suit either the adventurous or the timid.

The great outdoors: The high mountain streams and lakes are a fisherman's dream, yielding brook trout, browns and firm-fleshed lake trout. Depending on the area, bait or fly fishing is recommended. For backpackers or hikers, find-ing a mountain stream is just as enjoyable as fishing itself. Most mountain communities boast a fishing guide operation that not only has checked out the finest and most productive fishing spots, but also constantly monitors the most effective bait choices for each season. Some guides all but guarantee that fishermen will leave with breakfast in their creels, but even if the fishing is unproductive, the Rocky Mountain scenery always makes the trip worthwhile. Guides can be hired to supply equipment as well as expertise in most areas, and, depending on season and location, will take their charges to the destination by boat or jeep.

For other sports enthusiasts, big game and bird hunting are abundant in the Rockies. Many guides and outfitters who handle jeep and fishing tours will also take care of details for hunters. A number of dude or working ranches accommodate hunters in the fall, and offer a range of services. Some ranches or outfitters handle only lodging, while others provide horses, guides, cooks

Grinning and pushing over Independence Pass (CO).

and every piece of equipment necessary for an extended stay in the woods. Materials supplied are almost certainly accompanied by many tall tales of years past and the big trophies that they didn't quite bring home.

Hiking and climbing into those unique and special wilderness spots is a pastime that can occupy a day, a weekend or entire summers in the Rockies. The area is networked with hiking trails maintained by the United States Forest Service. Maps are available through the Forest Service and at many information centers. Colorado has 11 National Forests that encourage everything from car-camping in the numerous campgrounds to a backcountry experience. Once again mountain guides and outfitters can help with equipment, guides and routes if visitors are novices to backpacking. No one should strike off into the wilderness without first becoming properly equipped and learning how to use the equipment. Mountain weather changes extremely frequently and rapidly, and what starts out as a sunny day can be punctuated by a snowstorm even at the height of summer. Many Rocky Mountain states boast – or caution – that somewhere in the high country, it snows every month of the year.

Come spelunking!: The unique outdoor activities that bring the hardy enthusiast to the Rockies include rock climbing and caving or spelunking. Neither of these demanding sports should be attempted by anyone who is unfamiliar with them. There are numerous rock-climbing schools throughout the area where, under the watchful eye of guides and well-trained instructors, students learn the art of rock climbing just as they learn to respect the technical knowledge needed to complete exercises and journeys successfully and smoothly.

Cavers and spelunkers should also be properly outfitted and guided to their destination. While caving can be exciting, it is surrounded by superstition and tales of wild adventure. The lure of the unknown is probably the basis for most of the spectacular stories about nature's underground, but those who venture

Rough and tumble rafting on the Colorado River.

into the deep should be well prepared, not only for where they are going, but also for what they are getting into. Climbers and cavers should check in with the regional Forest Service office both upon entering and leaving their destination.

For a more civilized approach to caving, Cave of the Winds, near the Broadmoor and Colorado Springs, is operated commercially for tourists. The stalactites, stalagmites, flowstones and other eleothems are typical of what cavers find.

Highways are not the only means of transportation throughout the Rockies. While the waterways are not noted for transport or big boats and sailing, river rafting has become a significant alternative for the adventure-seeking resident or guest. River rafting is generally done on inflated rafts carrying a dozen or more people but many prefer canoes, kayaks, or smaller inflated rafts. As a rule, because of the amount of whitewater throughout the region, only experienced canoe and kayak enthusiasts ply the wild rivers. Whitewater

rafting companies, on the other hand, are as abundant as other guide services provided in the Rockies.

Classifications identify the rivers' ruggedness – from Class 1, an easy river with small waves and generally sandy, accessible beaches; to Class 3 with medium-sized or high irregular waves and passages dotted with boulders and rocks; to Classes 5 and 6 where only the most experienced boatmen dare to travel. A thirst for whitewater adventure can be quenched in the Rockies. Rafting trips can be booked for part of a day or a full day or a week-long adventure that takes boaters through deep canyons otherwise inaccessible. Camping and river rafting go hand in hand; once on shore, a hike into the desert or woods along the river takes boaters even farther from the bustle and smog and pressure of everyday city life.

Networks of rivers throughout the mountains provide plenty of opportunity for a relaxed daytime float or a whitewater thrill in thundering torrents. **A quiet**
Water sports and campouts: Other wa- **resting place.**

ter sports are available in the Rocky Mountain states, but to a far different degree from coastal regions or states with vast waterways. Because of the rugged mountain terrain, lakes tend to be smaller and winds changeable and unpredictable. While the cold and often shallow water does not lend itself to swimming, sailboarding or water skiing in many locations, sailing can be exciting and a test of ability – the small size of the lakes and unpredictable winds require quick maneuvering.

Sailboarding with wetsuits is becoming increasingly popular at many lakes that allow body contact, largely because of the strong and active resident and visitor population and the relative ease of size of required equipment.

A number of mountain lakes allow motor boats and water skiing, but in some areas, skiers prefer wet suits. Some mountain lakes allowing water skiing are Bonny Reservoir, Grand Lake, Shadow Mountain and Green Mountain. Dillon Reservoir in Summit County allows motor boating and sailing, but

swimming, sailboarding and water skiing are not permitted. Lakes and reservoirs near metropolitan areas are abundant and full water-sport activities are usually permitted. Chatfield and Cherry Creek Recreation areas near Denver are particularly popular and accessible. Or a trip to Rifle Gap in the western part of Colorado, where artist Christo Jvaacheff hung the 400-ft-high (120-meter), 1,250-ft-long (380-meter) orange curtain, may be worth the time and effort, not only for the sailing but also for the scenery.

Back to the lure of the Old West, horseback trips into hidden canyons and valleys are among the finest and most relaxing ways to get acquainted with the wilderness. Guides and outfitters abound in nearly every mountain village and along major or secondary highways. For an hourly fee, guides take even the most inexperienced rider on a safe trail ride. Or, better yet, plan ahead for a breakfast ride at the crack of dawn in the crisp mountain air. The guide will have the horses ready and will take you to a camp where the cook has steaming hot

reshwater
sh are
bundant.

coffee and a hearty breakfast ready to appease the appetites of dudes and wranglers alike. For those less inclined to rise with the early birds, there is always the evening steak ride or wagon ride. Guests are led to a hidden spot where the fire crackles and the steaks sizzle. The evening almost always includes tales of the Old West or at least the wranglers' experiences when they "was just young-uns" pushing cattle or riding their horses to school in the blizzard of 1949.

Enthusiasts who want to go further into the mountains can take a packtrip lasting several days. Most outfitters will supply everything except personal articles. A packtrip by horse can be coupled with fishing or hunting for the real enthusiast; however, wandering off into the wilderness with a few good friends on horseback, and with no plans other than enjoying the scenery and each other, is fulfillment enough.

"Up, up and away": Getting high in the Rockies is easy, with the rarefied air, incredible scenery and changing vistas around each corner, and the variety of things to do. But for those who want to get even higher, hot-air ballooning has become a new and exciting pastime. Whether you want to soar over the meadows and villages just to snap a few photographs and for the thrill of it all or to learn something about ballooning as a sport, an increasing number of balloon ranches throughout the western states are ready to fulfill your desire. Some of the ranches are connected with dude ranches and offer a variety of activities; others specialize in ballooning and balloon rides.

You'll find balloon ranches or balloon rides in the plains areas, along the foothills, and in high mountain valleys that afford enough space for take-off and landing the large, colorful crafts. Don't forget to take your camera along, as the panoramas will excite you at every turn of the head.

The thoroughly active person will find bicycling in the Rockies a challenge. Steep climbs and exhilarating descents are the rule in all but a few mountain locations. In many communities and **Climbing Fremont's Peak in Wyoming.**

counties, a good system of bike trails links cities and towns 20 or more miles (32 km) apart. Some trails climb mountain passes or meander along mountain streams where the refreshing sights, sounds and smells of the outdoors take much of the effort out of the climb. Being in good physical shape before embarking on one of the mountain passes is imperative.

Renting a bicycle and pedaling around the villages and into the surrounding valleys is a pleasure that can be enjoyed by almost anyone. Many winter-time ski rental stores switch to bicycles and fishing tackle in summer. They can recommend trails that are a joy to those who want fresh air and light exercise or can point out the more challenging rides.

Bicycling in the Rockies has long been a local favorite. The richest bicycle race in the United States, the International Bicycle Classic, was born in the Rockies.

Tennis is one sport that requires equipment light enough to be taken along on almost any vacation or day trip, and tennis buffs will be delighted to find that nearly every resort town or mountain community has a number of courts available to guests. Many resort hotels have installed courts that are in use year-round. Equipment can be rented at most facilities, and lessons and full tennis shops abound. There are even high-altitude tennis camps that will literally take your breath away.

Try a hole-in-one: If you want more than a stroll in the woods, why not a stroll on the golf course? More and more 18-hole courses designed by luminaries such as Jack Nicklaus and Robert Trent Jones II are springing up in the Rockies. In Vail Valley alone, there are four public and one private course, and just an hour's drive away in Summit County is the beautiful Keystone course. The challenge to golfers extends beyond the usual as courses are frequently narrow and filled with many natural hazards. Designers have taken advantage of the natural lay of the land and complemented their courses with large stands of pine, mountain streams, rolls and hills, and turns that follow the valleys. Accurate ball placement is required on most mountain courses. In addition, because of the thin air, the ball travels farther. Major adjustments in club use are required. The pro shop will be able to advise you, or a lesson with one of the local pros giving tips on how the course plays will work wonders in keeping your scores low and spirits high.

But the Rockies aren't just for the active, the young and the brave. Spectator sports are numerous throughout the area. For one more taste of the old West, there is the rodeo – the sport that developed when cowboys turned skills required for their work into one of the nation's most popular events. Cheyenne Frontier Days is one of the most noted rodeos in the world, drawing crowds from across the country for a week of fun and competition. In January, cowboys flock to Denver for the National Western Stock Show and Rodeo. In summer, you'll find rodeos up and down the Rockies: at state and county fairs, local rodeos and wild rides. The essence and history of rodeo is captured at the

Between a rock and a hard place.

Pro Rodeo Hall of Champions in Colorado Springs.

While summer overflows with adventures and activities, fall becomes a wonderland as aspen trees turn to burnished gold contrasting strikingly with the deep green pine forests and bright blue skies. A weekend jaunt into the mountains is a regular fall activity for Front-Range residents and is a must for visitors in September and October. The aspen or "quakies" shimmer in the sunlight as they reach brilliant gold tones. Green and gold are primary fall colors here, and Indian summer days bring out the best in the aspen. Warm, sunny days beg you to take a hike in the woods to enjoy the fleeting days before snow falls, and coupled with the frosty nights encourage the leaves to turn gold. While it rains or more often snows a bit in October, Indian summer is generally the rule. Rocky Mountain locals will tell guests that fall is one of the best times in the mountains. Warm days that encourage outside play are precious, and the already spectacular scenery takes on new beauty.

Come ski the Rockies: Leaving warm weather behind is a natural for the Rockies. While winters were the bane of travelers, settlers and miners, they are the sustenance of the travel and tourist industries. Colorado and the Rockies have earned the name of Ski Country, USA, with hundreds of resorts and ski areas dotting the maps. From the luxury resorts such as Aspen, Vail, Deer Valley, Beaver Creek and Snowbird, to the smaller, intimate ski areas such as Loveland Basin, Telluride, Redlodge, or Jackson Hole, the Rockies offer an area for every taste and inclination. You can find accommodation fit for (and often used by) kings and heads of state or stay in bed-and-breakfasts, pensions or dormitories that are easier on the budget. But, once on the mountainside, the Rockies will make anyone feel like royalty. Downhill or alpine skiing is perhaps most popular throughout the mountain winter resorts, and it doesn't take an expert to enjoy the thrills. Complete programs are available for beginners who thought they would never venture into the cold mountain air; some become enthusiasts who readily join *après-ski* conversations with stories just as impressive as those of seasoned powder hounds.

In the steep and deep Rockies, expert skiers are constantly challenged, if not by taking lessons in the latest techniques, then by constantly changing conditions on expert slopes.

Cross-country skiing or touring is gaining in stature among Rocky Mountain skiers. It's easier on the pocketbook than downhill, both in equipment cost and because lift tickets aren't generally required. A skier no longer has to be a super-conditioned athlete to enjoy the sport. More sophisticated equipment, eliminating the need to be a waxing expert and adding instant ease and enjoyment to the sport, has made a tremendous impact over the past 5 to 10 years.

A number of resorts are grooming cross-country trails or setting tracks for guests, some without charge and some asking a track use fee. The US Forest Service marks and maintains trails throughout the National Park System which are usually free to the public. Maps can be obtained from the local Forest Service office or from information centers.

Winter pleasures: Cross-country centers or ranches are springing up around the Rockies. Here one finds comfortable rustic accommodation set in valleys that afford miles and miles of skiing during the day, often followed by dips in hot springs or hot tubs. Spend a week or a day and take the trails at your own pace. Cross-country skiing can be a lively workout or, like a stroll in the park, a leisurely enjoyment of the wonders that wintry nature has to offer.

The lure of the Rockies and the rush to enjoy its riches has not diminished over the past 100 years. Adventure is still abundant and remains the watchword for most visitors. For others, the sheer beauty, immensity and solitude create not only relaxation but also excitement. The private spots that many residents or visitors find may truly have exceptional healing powers. It's no wonder that the rush to the Rockies continues.

Right, Rockies hikers reflect on the natural beauty.

ROCKIES SKI RESORTS

Colorado is known as Ski Country, USA, a title obviously well deserved when one looks at a map of the state. Dotted with day ski areas and destination resorts, the map looks as if it has been sprinkled with snow, just like the abundant peaks. Colorado is home to more than 35 ski resorts and is known worldwide for its consistent "champagne powder", the light dry snow that makes skiing a pleasure and a thrill for these avid experts who seek out the face of Bell Mountain in Aspen or Vail's dramatic Back Bowls.

For most visitors, Denver is the first stop and the gateway to the Rockies. It is the largest city in the region and Colorado's capital. Busy Stapleton International Airport is the "fifth busiest" in the country, shuttling traffic from distant as well as nearby locations. While Colorado is still best known for its western flavor, it also has assumed, because of the great influx of winter visitors, an international flair that is evident both in the cities and resorts from the variety of languages and dialects that can be overheard in the streets.

Upon arrival in Denver, skiers can expect generally mild weather, frequently in the sixties, even in winter, and graced by regular snowfalls that often disappear in days without a trace. But the ski enthusiast should not despair. The weather in Denver and the surrounding plains is often surprisingly unrelated to the mountain areas where, when city folk are relaxing in the parks with a good book, skiers may be enjoying that peak experience of a run down a slope covered with 8 inches of newly fallen snow. Average snowfall throughout the region is nearly 350 inches (890 cm), with many resorts getting double that before the season ends.

From Denver travelers can reach their destinations quickly and easily with the assistance of coach and limousine services, a regular bus service and even taxis. Because the Colorado economy depends upon tourists for its health,

transportation in the state is efficient and well-organized.

While mountain travel is generally pleasurable, travelers are advised to check on current road conditions prior to leaving Denver for their destinations. Colorado Ski Country, USA, maintains an information booth in the Denver airport that carries current road conditons as well as skiing and weather conditions at 35 resorts. In addition, Colorado Ski Country, USA, can assist visitors with lodging, travel routes and a variety of other details.

Once on the road, take time to enjoy the mountain views and allow adequate time to reach your destination. Winter travel can be slow due to road and weather conditions or to drivers who are inexperienced on snow-packed roads. Exercise patience and the journey from the plains to the mountains will be more pleasurable.

The destination resorts: Towering snow-covered peaks, secluded valleys, Victorian mansions turned into quaint shops and restaurants, Alpine villages hiding boutiques and pizza parlors, luxurious hotels, festivals, competition, celebrations – all are part of the experience in Rocky Mountain ski resorts. From the rustic and once rich mining-towns-turned-resorts such as Aspen and Breckenridge or Telluride, to the new developments at Copper Mountain, Beaver Creek, Snowbird (in Utah) or Vail, skiers can find a full array of activities, day and night. The personalities of the old towns shine through in many locations and are assisted by traditional celebrations of the snow such as Ullr Fest, with new excitement added by the influx of today's adventure-seekers to the areas. The newly developed resorts springing up in sheep and cattle pastures have learned from the old, European styles that have been popular with skiers for so long. At times, visitors might feel that they are strolling down a street in St Moritz, rather than close to home, because of the Bavarian architecture and the number of international visitors. At the same time, visitors can expect the latest conveniences and luxuries, including gourmet meals, fast-food, shopping at its finest, and recreational activities to fill the days and nights of both skiers and non-skiers.

Ski the Summit, one of the first destinations for skiers traveling west from Denver, offers four ski areas and villages that suit many preferences. The **Keystone Complex** includes Keystone Mountain, North Peak and Arapahoe Basin ski areas, and the modern Keystone Village. **Arapahoe Basin** is Colorado's highest skiing point. At an elevation of 12,450 ft (3,800 meters), the views are as breathtaking as the rarefied air. Peaking well above the timberline, the jagged mountains are similar to the Swiss Alps. The season at Arapahoe Basin extends well into June. The Colorado sunshine combines with cool high-altitude temperatures to keep the snow light and moods high through-out spring skiing. Skiers of all levels find satisfaction on these slopes and the most advanced challenge themselves on the Pallavicini or East Wall in narrow chutes that cascade from rocky heights. During the week, the locals' favorite time to ski, there are smaller crowds and relaxed ski experiences remembered from seasons past.

Keystone Mountain has become known as "the cruiser" on slopes like "Jackwhacker", "Last Hoot" or "Go Devil" for those who want just enough of a challenge but with the security of well-groomed intermediate and beginner trails that boost any ego and style. Keystone takes most of its trail and lodging names from the logging and mining operations that first brought settlers to the area. The remains of disused mines are dotted throughout the valleys

Skiing in the olden days.

and contribute to the ambience of the Old West.

North Peak, opened in 1984, is a $15 million expansion that adds a six-passenger gondola, 14 new trails and exciting advanced terrains to neighboring Keystone Mountain. The new terrain is accessible from the Summit House at Keystone as well as from River Run Plaza, situated one-half mile east of Keystone Mountain Village on the Snake River. North Peak is for those who become bored with the consistent and reliable trails on Keystone Mountain; 58 percent of its terrain is for expert and advanced skiers. The gondola whisks skiers to the summit in 10 minutes. Then it challenges them with trails like the 1¾-mile (2.8-km) "Cat Dancer" or the popular bump run called "Geronimo". A favorite steep but well-kept trail is "Starfire".

The calendar at Keystone is packed with activities that meet a variety of skiers' interests and abilities. Recently, Olympic medalists Phil and Steve Mahre established their training center at Keystone. The week-long program is designed for everyone, from the never-ever to the expert racer. The gold and silver medalists are joined by their former coach as they present a training program utilizing exercises developed around natural skiing motions and using visualization as mental preparation. Included in the Mahre Training Center package is lodging, lift tickets, six days of ski instruction, meals and parties.

Cross-country fans of any level enter some of the most spectacular Rocky Mountain backcountry on the 20 miles (33 km) of prepared trails in the **Arapahoe National Forest**. Lessons on both cross-country and telemarking are offered through the Keystone Cross-Country Touring Center. For an extra-special experience, a moonlit cross-country tour, including dinner, is recommended. It will give that extra dose of romance to a winter vacation.

There's no lack of activities off the slopes. The outdoor skating center is the largest of its kind in the country and the season lasts from early December through mid-March. At the day's end, a horse-drawn sleigh takes guests to dinner at the old **Soda Creek Homestead**; advance reservations are required. Or, for the adventurous, snowmobile tours of the backcountry are available at **Tiger Run**, a few miles from Keystone.

Tired of the snow? The John Gardiner Tennis Center at Keystone offers two indoor courts year-round (12 more for outdoor play in summer), lessons, clinics and matches. A special vacation touch is presented by the Condominium Grocery Service. For your convenience, Keystone will do your shopping for you and have your condominium completely stocked with groceries and fresh produce when you arrive. The resort makes it literally impossible for you not to have a great and relaxing stay.

Information on a winter vacation in Keystone is available through the Keystone Resort Association or, if you want to check skiing conditions, telephone 303-468-4111 for a daily update.

A Skiing tradition: Historic **Breckenridge** presents a direct contrast with Keystone's modern buildings and conference facility; old Victorian homes and bright paint combine with the enthusiasm of the local community. A few years ago, Breckenridge was a downtrodden old mining town that just happened to be the site of Summit County's largest ski area. With an injection of capital from investors, such as the ski company and local businesses, Main Street nowadays fairly sparkles with life and personality. On the side streets, visitors will find a variety of hidden pleasures, from restaurants to lodges. Quaint is one way to describe Breckenridge today, but that implies it's a place to visit where there is no action. Not true: much of the excitement and enthusiasm of the Old West remain in this rejuvenated community.

Skiing events such as the World Freestyle Championships and the Mogul Challenge dot the calendar. But the highlight of the winter season is the Ullr Fest in January. Ullr, the Nordic god of snow, is honored in a week-long celebration which includes a parade that's second-to-none. It features inventive floats, and snow and ice sculptures line Main Street.

All are created by the townspeople, who dedicate themselves to making the event fun for visitors. Fireworks, crowning of the Ullr King and Queen, and a moonlight cross-country tour complete the activities.

Complementing the Ullr Fest is the World Freestyle Invitational, an event that brings freestyle ski competitors together for the greatest contest in the country in ballet skiing, moguls and aerials. The event garners national attention and is aired on television specials. Part of the fun is the celebrity ski race, where Breckenridge skiers rub elbows with stars from American television shows and even with players from the Denver Broncos football team.

You never need put on your skis to be part of the fun in Breckenridge, although you would be missing a lot if you didn't. **Maggie Pond** is excellent for ice skating, snowmobile tours are just around the corner, and the cross-country center offers 28 miles (45 km) of trails along with complete lessons, ski rental and "warming hut" facilities.

Once the skis are on, skiers can undertake helicopter trips into the Colorado backcountry, in addition to more than 1,526 acres (618 hectares) of skiing on the mountain. Powder helicopter skiing is not for the faint of heart; it's for those who enjoy the challenge of wilderness skiing in remote terrain. The rewards are excitement and solitude.

On Breckenridge's two mountains, Peaks 8 and 10 are 110 trails. Forty-seven percent of the slopes are rated for expert skiers alone, but there's no lack of terrain for intermediates and beginners. **Mach I** is the super mogul run that is the site of the Bump event in the Freestyle Championships and the Annual Breckenridge Mogul Challenge. Mach I has been judged to be one of the most difficult mogul courses on the International World Cup circuit – it's definitely not for the casual cruiser. But nearby Peak 9 rates 87 percent of its trails as beginner and intermediate. The challenge is to ski them all during one winter vacation while still having time for the other activities in the resort. Favorites among the intermediate skiers are "American" for friendly bump skiing and "Gold King" for those who prefer groomed trails.

Several special programs punctuate the Breckenridge season. Book three or more consecutive nights, and the fourth night and next-day's skiing is free. Ski Free is available through the Breckenridge Resort Association – an extremely popular program, to say the least.

A full ski school program includes the regular complement of lessons, a women's three-day skiing seminar and the Peak 8 Nursery and Junior Ski School which handles infants aged two months or older.

Historic charm in the Rockies: The Camel Sprint Series gives recreational skiers a chance to test their speeds on a safe and controlled track. It is the one time in the season when it's both safe and acceptable to go as fast as your legs and heart will allow.

True to the Old West flavor of the resort, the "Telemark" returns each spring. Skiers dress in 1880s costumes and compete on a 6-mile (10-km) course, moguls and in the classic telemark style.

Getting about as high as you can in the Rockies for the figure-eight competition in Horseshoe Bowl brings the ski season to a close. For the competition, two skiers start at the same point at an elevation of about 12,200 ft (3,720 meters) and cross each other's tracks, making a series of 8s as they ski down the fall line – almost a springtime tradition in the mountains.

Health clubs and Olympic workouts: Ski the Summit's final resort is **Copper Mountain**, nestled in Wheeler Flats at the upper end of Ten Mile Canyon. The image of Copper contrasts with that of Breckenridge. It looks more like a modern European resort with its tall, straight-walled buildings that maximize the minimal space. The village has recently developed into one in which guests can find all the customary goods and services, with the added advantage of being within a 30-minute drive of Vail and other Ski the Summit areas.

A new addition to Copper is the health club, which provides facilities in which to relax and soothe aching tired muscles, or to exercise for those who didn't get enough on the slopes. Jacuzzis, steam rooms, saunas, racket-ball courts, tennis courts, 25-yard lap pool, aerobics room, Nautilus, weight rooms and a staff masseuse complete the menu at the athletic club.

Copper now has one high-speed quad, six triple and nine double chair lifts, along with four surface 20 lifts that serve 75 trails. The on-mountain programs available to skiers are abundant, beginning with the Belly Button Babies (two months to two years) and the Belly Button Bakery where the kids cook and bake, play indoor and outdoor games, and do crafts. Once the kids reach six years of age, they move on to Junior Ranch and Senior Ranch. The learn-to-ski programs expand to intermediate and hot-shot, covering the entire mountain. Youngsters are supervised throughout the day.

For adults, there are Women's Skiing Seminars, Early Season Ski Clinics to hone rusty skills and all the usual lessons and value-conscious packages.

Copper Mountain is proud of its commitment and involvement with the US Ski Team. In November, the team arrives at Copper for early on-the-snow training, and is joined by recreational racers at the Salomon/Copper Mountain Recreational Race Camp. Copper hosts the US National Alpine Championships each year, bringing to town top competitors from around the world. Copper has hosted both the men's and women's team competition, and the commitment continues year-round to provide some of the finest racing and recreational skiing available in the state.

Copper is truly a family atmosphere; a self-contained resort that is large enough to provide challenge on the slopes and plenty of *après-ski* action, yet small enough to be intimate and comfortable; and a place where the entire family can be independent, yet very much together.

Cosmopolitan Vail: Vail is the largest single mountain ski resort, which says a lot but not the whole story. There's a complete village with more than 70 res-

Flying through the air on a frosty morning.

taurants and shops that literally take days to explore. About 22 years ago, Vail was nothing more than a green valley and sheep pastures intersected by Gore Creek and a highway. Vail Village streets now reflect an international flair dominated by Bavarian architecture. Where summer flowers fill the window boxes, winter finds them sparkling with lights and evergreen boughs. The cosmopolitan atmosphere is repeated throughout the diverse boutiques and punctuated with accents from around the world.

The broadest variety of housing can be found in **Vail** and **Lionshead villages**, from large hotels to pensions and intimate lodges to bed-and-breakfast. Depending on the level of service desired, guests can either check in for complete personal care at the **Marriott** or **Westin**, or rent a condominium or luxurious private home and be strictly on their own. Lodging information is available either directly through the hotels and lodges or through the Vail Resort Association toll-free numbers.

The largest single winter event is the American Ski Classic. Lasting for almost a week, the Classic includes World Cup Racing, which brings the top racers from around the world to compete for points in World Cup standings. In 1984, gold and silver medalists, Phil and Steve Mahre, raced in and retired in Vail after the slalom races that followed the Olympics.

Former President Gerald R. Ford, a skiing enthusiast himself, hosts the Jerry Ford Celebrity Cup, an event that draws notables from the worlds of sports, politics, media and screen to Vail. The third piece of the American Ski Classic is the Legends of Skiing, a unique race that features former Olympic and National Team greats from every Olympic skiing country. Olympians from the 1930s ski and share an easy camaraderie with those just off the circuit, then go on to captain the Celebrity Cup teams.

Come race every which way: American Ski Classic events are divided between Vail and Beaver Creek, just 10 miles (16 km) west. The entire community gets into the act with parades, fireworks, charity film showings and art displays that benefit the Jimmie Heuga Center for the Physically Challenged.

The final celebration takes shape in Mountain Madness, a wacky welcome to spring and joyous farewell to the snow. For two weeks, local residents and guests race in the Rental Cup or the Great Race – on cross-country and downhill skis, across swimming pools, on tricycles and other "vehicular conveyances", all done in ski boots. A treasure hunt, lasting the entire two weeks, offers prizes to those unraveling clues given by the local media and able to locate them on the mountain.

Special lodging rates are offered through the Vail Resort Association for Mountain Madness and two other value periods. Early December and the month of January are value periods during which snow conditions are generally good to exceptional, the crowds are small, and the essence of the resort abounds. Value seasons and Mountain Madness entice skiers away from the peak Christmas and President's Birthday weekend periods when the village and the mountain are crowded with vacationers.

All this can be found in the villages; the mountains have yet to be explored. In addition to Colorado's champagne powder, Vail is probably best known for the expansive **Back Bowls** – 780 acres (316 hectares) of uninterrupted vistas and ungroomed snow plunging from an elevation of 11,250 ft (3,430 meters). The steep consistent fall line entices powder hounds to line up at the top after a recent snowfall, awaiting the first signal from the ski patrol that signifies the bowls are open. Skiers are quickly swallowed up in the enormity of the naturally open terrain.

But for those not yet ready to tackle expert-only terrain, Vail has **Game Creek Bowl** – 10 sq. miles (25 sq. km) of skiing terrain. The longest run at Vail, **Riva Ridge**, begins at the mountain top on gentle slopes that build the ego. Then Riva pitches down toward **Tourist Trap** and becomes a pleasantly challenging advanced run that winds its way into the village. The western part of the mountain is served by a six-passenger gondola that towers above 200-ft (60-meter) trees, making an impact on the landscape. Over the entire mountain, 18 lifts serve slopes ranked 30 percent easiest, 40 percent more difficult and 30 percent most difficult.

The **Vail/Beaver Creek Ski School** is the largest in the world with more than 475 instructors, many of whom are multilingual. The school is noted as a leader in developing ski technique and methodology, and was the training and development ground for the American Teaching Method, now used by certified ski schools across the United States and recognized worldwide. The full array of ski school programs are presented with Super Classes for those who like lots of skiing, complemented with instruction and intensive workshops in powder, mogul skiing, racing and any discipline of particular interest.

"By the light of the silvery moon…": The cross-country center introduces novices to the serene sport of ski touring and polishes the skills of more accomplished "skinny skiers". Beginning on the golf course and, when technique allows, branching out to the numerous trails in the White River National Forest with their guides, the cross-country program is one of the largest in the country. Special features include the Gourmet Cross-Country Tour and a Moonlight Tour offered on full moons. For the Gourmet tour, skiers accompany their instructor into the backcountry and are treated to an exceptional meal prepared by the developer of the program.

Under a full moon, a lucky group takes a guided tour on **Shrine Pass** (or another location selected by the experienced guides). The crisp mountain air and moon-lit snow create an incomparable experience.

Beaver Creek, touted at its opening in 1980 as "the last resort", has become one of the most luxurious, yet affordable and approachable destinations in Colorado. The difficulty, time and investment involved in obtaining permits required to develop ski areas and the accompanying villages and facilities

The view at Crosscut Ranch, Montana.

caused the "last resort" designation to be assigned to Colorado's seventh largest ski area. True to detailed master plans, there are nine lifts, one quad, five triple and three double chairs. The triple and quad chair lifts are so efficient – getting skiers on the slopes and out of the lines – that a wait in a liftline is almost unheard of at Beaver Creek, even during peak season. The slope design takes advantage of Mother Nature's U-shaped valley. Few bottlenecks exist even where numbers of trails and several on-and-off mountain routes converge. Skiers get to the lifts and up the hill from locations close to their hotels.

Many skiers have called this a cozy mountain, one with an unhurried atmosphere, few crowds and a complete variety of terrain. At the top of the mountain, a beginner's area is set aside for skiers who have just learned to turn and stop. The views, consistent snow and a long scenic run back to the bottom make this an enjoyable run.

Intermediate terrain invites cruisers to ski much of the middle of the mountain and newly opened **Larkspur Bowl**, where one can find anything from moguls to the large, sweeping expanse of snow and seemingly endless turns to the valley in the bowl.

Slopes for the experts: For the experts, the "Birds of Prey" await. Some of the steepest, longest and most challenging slopes in the Rockies are **Peregrine, Goshawk** and **Golden Eagle**. While they are steep and long, the bumps have remained friendly and telemark skiers are frequently seen dancing through the moguls on Peregrine under chair nine – truly a delightful sight and one worth riding this chair for.

Centennial, a 2¾-mile (4.4-km) top-to-bottom run was designated as the downhill course for the 1976 Olympics when Beaver Creek was suggested as the site for Alpine events. Colorado voters vetoed the Olympic bid, which allowed planners to proceed at a deliberate pace to create the present mountain and village. "Centennial" is a delightful trail with relaxing gentle sections punctuated with steeper plunges. It twists and turns with the natural terrain to keep essentially all of the skiing in the fall-line.

The on-mountain gathering place is **Spruce Saddle**, an award-winning log-and-cedar building with spectacular views and a sunny deck crowded with sun worshippers on nice days. While at Spruce Saddle, sample lunch at **Rafters**, an inviting table service restaurant with delightful specialties such as baked apples stuffed with cheese and a mouth-watering dessert cart.

The Vail/Beaver Creek Ski School cross-country center is at the top of the mountain. Novice to expert cross-country skiers can strike off on set tracks across the top of the mountain. When ready to return to the village, they have their choice of riding the chair back down or skiing one of the intermediate or advanced trails under chair 12.

Once back in the village, a free horse-drawn sleigh takes skiers or shoppers back to their lodges.

The noted winter events in Beaver Creek compose the Mountain Man Winter Triathlon that sets competitors off on cross-country skis, snowshoes and then finally ice skates. The grueling course goes to the top of the mountain twice before its exhausting finale on Nottingham Lake in Avon.

Aspen: This town presents the skier with four completely separate ski mountains linked by shuttle bus service and a lift ticket that is good any day at **Aspen Mountain, Snowmass** and **Buttermilk**. Add $1 per day to add a fourth mountain, **Aspen Highland**. Four mountains at your disposal ensures plenty of skiing, from the face of "Bell" for powder hounds to numerous intermediate and beginner runs at Buttermilk, to the expansive "Big Burn" at Snowmass. One can stay at Aspen for weeks and never become bored.

Highlighting Aspen's calendar are Winterskol and the Subaru Aspen Winternationals. Winterskol is a five-day festival featuring a bevy of winter events including zang skiing contests, ice hockey, balloon races, snowshoe races, a torchlight parade that dances down the mountain, and the Winterskol Parade – probably the oldest winter parade in the

Rockies. Winterskol occurs in January, when lift tickets are discounted and most businesses offer tremendous savings on everything from meals and lodging to skiwear and furs.

Aspen has long been a major part of the international ski racing scene and the Winternational returns with World Cup Downhill and Giant Slalom events. Bill Johnson, the Olympic Gold Medalist, stopped in Aspen to thrill crowds on the Americas Downhill and is expected to return to capture the title again.

For those who are not yet afficionados of ski racing, Aspen has developed a unique "trailblazer" sign system that makes it easy to trace the path the World Champion racers take while also discovering the history of Aspen and World Cup Racing.

Although Aspen is one of the oldest resorts, it has not stopped growing; "Steep and Deep" has just been added to Snowmass. "Hanging Valley" and "Cirque" contrast 120 acres (48 hectares) of expert-only terrain. Those who don't feel the need for that kind of challenge should try the newly improved and expanded restaurants, such as **Ullrhof**, which includes more seating capacity, lockers and an accessory store with a woodburning stove to chase away the chill on cold days.

In Aspen, the mining town that experienced its first boom in 1880 when silver was discovered, and its second when the ski boom in the 1940s revived the dying community, one finds an upgrade and renovation boom going on. New hotels are being added and many lodge owners are pouring millions of dollars into improving their facilities. The historic **Jerome Hotel** received a $12 million injection for renovation and reopened after 14 months with a nightclub, formal dining room and cafe, and 105 rooms that reflect the personality of modern Aspen as well as the charm of the old hotel.

Getting to Aspen is easier than ever now that Grand Junction is a viable airline gateway. From Denver, one drives for about four hours via Interstate 70, or flies one of the small commuter

A time exposure of night skiers carrying torches.

airways. Weather conditions can sometimes delay flights into the mountain airport. From Grand Junction, skiers connect with ground transportation that takes about half as long as the drive from Denver, and no mountain passes to negotiate. Travel agents and tour operators have details on reaching Aspen via Grand Junction.

Steamboat Ski Area and **Steam Village** are where the skiers and cattle ranchers shake hands and say "howdy". A complementary relationship exists between the two very different enterprises and that gives Steamboat much of its personality. The ski area adjacent to the old ranching community, first opened in 1962, was called Storm Mountain. In 1964, the name was changed to Mount Werner in honor of Buddy Werner, an Olympic ski racer killed in an avalanche while filming a movie. Werner was raised in Steamboat, and the Werner family remains a vital part of the ski operation and the town.

The resort has responded to the growth of the ski industry with its own growth; 400 acres (160 hectares) of intermediate skiing has just opened in **Sunshine Bowls** graded slopes. This enticing terrain is adjacent to the already noted expert trails in Priest Creek that plunge from Sunshine Peak to the bottom of the Bowl. Steamboat sports a new restaurant, **Ragnar's**, that settles into the Rendezvous Saddle building. Ragnar's is named after Ragnar Omvedt, a Norwegian ski jumper who set a world record on Steamboat's historic Howelson Hill in 1915. Ski jumping played a large part in the development of the ski industry at Steamboat.

While the quiet atmosphere of the western winter is ever-present, constant energy is created by the numerous events at the ski mountain. Billy Kidd, another Olympic skier who makes his home in Steamboat, fills his race camps with eager recreational skiers for six and four-day sessions throughout the winter months.

Joining the new west and rodeo with today's ski resort is the Cowboy Downhill, now more than 10 years old. The Cowboy Downhill was developed when Larry Mahan, six-time All Round World Champion cowboy on the pro rodeo tour, and Billy Kidd invited several cowboys competing in Denver's National Western Stock Show for some post-rodeo skiing. Everyone had such a good time that the Cowboy Downhill developed into one of the greatest events of the Rocky Mountain winter.

The Winter Carnival in February is a traditional celebration of how skiing came to the valley. Ranchers, cowboys and visitors get together with a week of racing, ski jumping, sled races, cross-country/hot air ballooning, a parade and "ski jouring". The carnival began in 1913 when Carl Howelsen, "The Flying Norseman", arrived from Norway with skis strapped to his feet and got the local youngsters all excited about ski jumping. Carl convinced the locals that snow could be fun rather than just an annoyance for the ranchers. And they are still convinced.

The Steamboat Springs Stampede finishes off the year. The highlight event is the wacky Cardboard Classic in which competitors race in a "vehicle" made of cardboard, tape and glue. Lots of lodging, shopping and lift ticket bargains are available as are abundant spring snow and sunshine.

Ski options at Jackson Hole: Jackson Hole, Wyoming, is one of those ski mountains that skiers looking for the big challenge just can't stop talking about. Three thousand acres (1,215 hectares) of terrain is 2½ miles (4 km) wide and 4,139 ft (1,260 meters) from top to bottom. It regularly receives 38 ft (12 meters) of famous Rocky Mountain dry powder snow. The two mountains comprising Jackson Hole are served by one quad lift, five double chair lifts, one triple chair lift, two surface lifts, and a 2.4-mile (4-km) aerial tram that carries skiers from **Teton Village** at the base to the top of **Rendezvous Mountain** where experts find steep chutes and ridges filled with champagne powder.

Jackson Hole is well-known for its ski school and a wide variety of programs for recreational skiers and racers. Pepi Stiegler, the Olympic skier, directs the programs, including Star Test International's PSIA proficiency test, Children's SKIWee sponsored by SKI magazine, and Stiegler's racing camps that feature daily ski instruction, video taping and *après-ski* options such as tennis and racquetball.

Cross-country skiing abounds in the Jackson Hole area. At Teton Village adjacent to the lifts is the **Jackson Hole Karhu Cross-Country Ski Center**, and nearby are **Togwotee Mountain Lodge Center Grand Targhee, Teton Pines** and **Spring Creek Ranch Ski Touring Center**. Surrounding Jackson Hole, the backcountry and Grand Teton National Park are webbed with marked trails. An easy guide to the cross-country areas is available from the Jackson Hole Chamber of Commerce, together with information on lodging and restaurants for the resort towns of Teton Village and Jackson Hole.

Big sky country: Montana is known as Big Sky Country because of its vast size and frontier environment. The western part of the state is dotted with ski areas and charming hideaways for guests who prefer a vacation at a secluded spot with local flair. Some of the longer trails stretch for 3 miles (5 km), and the season in Montana lasts from mid-November through April at most ski areas. **Big Sky, Bridger Bowl, Big Mountain** and **Red Lodge** are the largest and most noted of Montana's ski areas, but 11 other areas round out the list.

Big Sky sports two gondolas, a triple chair and four double chairs serving 55 miles (88 km) of alpine trails. With a vertical drop of 2,800 ft (854 meters) and 400 inches (1,016 cm) of Rockies powder falling each year, Big Sky draws skiers who want to make the best of a ski vacation in a unique location.

Big Mountain has a vertical drop of 2,145 ft (654 meters) with 43 runs situated on 33 miles (53 km) of ski terrain. Nearer to Billings, Red Lodge offers 30 slopes from which to choose, covering 25 miles (40 km), and has a vertical drop of 2,016 ft (615 meters).

Much of the fun of skiing in Montana is staying at many of the ranches, lodges or country inns that open their doors to

eft,
eturning to
e warmth of
hut. **Right,**
St. Bernard
arries a
rink to
kiers in
ouble.

winter visitors. Many of the ranches provide family-style meals, horse or mule-drawn sleigh rides, snowmobile trips and vast cross-country trails upon which those taking a break from alpine skiing can really get away from it all for a day in the wilderness. Accommodation at the inns and ranches varies from single rooms without baths to fully-furnished condominiums. Advance reservations are recommended at most lodges especially in the winter months.

Up-market skiing at Deer Valley: The front of Deer Valley's trail map calls the resort "Unspoiled, Uncrowded and Uncommonly civilized", and truly it is. Touted as Utah's answer to Colorado's Beaver Creek in gentility, it is already known for the fine food that is offered all over the mountain. Where else can one find salmon *en croûte* at the ski area cafeteria? The **Snuggery** at mid-mountain **Silver Lake Lodge** and the **Huggery** at the base area **Snow Park Lodge** set the stage for some of the finest ski-area cuisine anywhere.

It's the above-and-beyond frills for

which Deer Valley is becoming famous: like the uniformed "ski valets" who unload the car and lead you to the slopes.

The village at Deer Valley presents guests with more luxurious choices such as **Stein Eriksen's Lodge**. Eriksen, an Olympic medalist, is Director of Skiing at the noteworthy resort. In addition to greeting guests at the lodge and attending to details, he escorts VIPs around the mountain with that famous Norwegian smile and effortless skiing style that has become his trademark.

Ski Utah makes its winter ultimate escapes incredibly easy. The organization offers information and booking routines for 15 winter resorts including the big, well-known areas like **Snowbird, Alta, Park City** and the smaller but no less enticing **Sundance, Powder Mountain** or **Brighton**, and the better known cross-country ski areas.

One of the greatest advantages that so many of the Utah resorts have is the proximity to the International Airport at Salt Lake City. Located on the end of the Great Basin, Salt Lake City provides a hub for additional lodging, restaurants and a metropolitan entertainment and activity center nearly at the base of the ski mountains. Working half day and arriving at a Utah resort in time for a few runs before the end of that day is entirely possible and a feature that more and more people are taking advantage of all the time.

Utah's skiers who want more than skiing within the area boundaries can opt for the Interconnect Adventure Tour. The five-area tour is modestly priced and takes the adventurers from Park City to Snowbird, Alta, Brighton and Solitude ski areas with the aid of a guide licensed by the United States Forest Service. Tour participants will ski some of the slopes within the individual resorts and then go out of bounds on the way to the next destination. The tours require skiers to be in good physical condition because hiking and skiing some ungroomed slopes is a regular part of the day. Shorter Interconnect Tours visiting four or three areas are available. All are subject to weather or snow condition cancellations. Groups are limited

Enjoying the famous "Cowboy Downhill" event.

to four to 14 skiers. Obtain information from Ski Utah, Inc.

Nestled just 31 miles (49 km) up Little Cottonwood Canyon from the Salt Lake International Airport are Snowbird and Alta resorts. Known worldwide for their breathtaking slopes and deep, deep powder. Snowbird boasts 500 inches (1,270 cm) of the white gold each season, stretching from mid-November right into mid-June when the weather permits. Serving the mountain are seven chair lifts and a 125-passenger tram that whisks skiers 2,900 ft (884 meters) up from the base over a distance of 8,395 ft (2,559 meters). The upper tram terminal perches at 11,000 ft (3,350 meters) in altitude and affords skiers a 3.3-mile (5-km) run through **Gad Valley** starting out from the summit in a spectacular bowl that challenges experts and then dropping into the intermediate trail, **Lower Bassackwards.**

Snowbird's slopes, steep and deep: The ski runs in Utah have gained the reputation of being electrifying and with good reason. With a vertical drop of 3,100 ft (945 meters) and 50 percent of the trails being rated advanced expert, the impression is realistic. Snowbird's slopes are steep, deep, sometimes wide and sometimes quite narrow but almost always exciting. But the resort doesn't cater only to the seasoned skier who is looking for more challenges. Thirty percent of the terrain is rated intermediate and 20 percent beginner, almost the perfect combination according to resort planners who insist that expert skiers command more acres of skiing because they cover ground more quickly than less experienced enthusiasts.

Sun Valley and the stars: Sun Valley, Idaho, holds the unique position of being the first American Ski Resort and for erecting the first chair lift in the United States in 1935. Sun Valley has attracted Hollywood starts since its beginning, and continues to do so.

The ski mountain now sports 16 chair lifts serving more than 70 runs. Slopeside lodging is available at **Warm Springs** and also at pretty **River Run**, near the Sun Valley complex.

A cowboy skier ropes himself a wild filly".

"Something Hidden, Go find it.
Go look behind the Ranges –
Something lost behind the Ranges.
Lost and waiting for you. Go!"
— From *The Explorer*
by Rudyard Kipling

The Rocky Mountains are known for the diversity of experience they offer. For the lover of sports or art, nature or culture, summer in the Continental Divide is a parade of festivals and happenings. If you want to arrange some extraordinary encounters with Rocky Mountain people, plan your journey through the Rockies to coincide with some of these events. The Rockies have become the summer festival territory of the United States with celebrations taking place everywhere. Lists of happenings in most areas, from environmental and cultural to athletic activities, are available from Chambers of Commerce and travel agencies.

Denver, Colorado's capital city, is teeming with events and festivals. The Denver Center for the Performing Arts has a wonderful theater company that stages both local and hit Broadway plays all year round. The Boettcher Concert Hall, which the *New York Times* has written can take anything a symphony orchestra can deliver, is the home of the well-known Denver Symphony Orchestra, and perhaps one of the best musical auditoriums in the world. Great performers are frequently known to stop here on national tour, for a bit of playing and a bit of skiing. Many exciting community outreach events occur during the year, such as the Festival Caravan which promotes greater understanding of different cultures.

In Denver, there are also many museums and art galleries that offer exceptional special events. Spending a few days in Denver gallery-hopping will expose you to some of the best art in the world.

Heading down south towards Durango –

Preceding pages: "Cowboy Downhill" ski contestants run the good race. **Left**, stop and pose for a portrait at the Renaissance Festival in Larkspur, Colorado. **Right**, dressing in period costume at the Renaissance Festival.

on probably one of the most beautiful roads in the country – you'll be taken through the San Juan Mountains and to the popular ski resorts of Aspen and Vail.

One of Aspen's biggest summertime attractions is the Aspen Music Festival, which includes chamber music and modern jazz and attracts world-renowned musicians.

Vail also has a series of exciting events. The Avon Hot Air Balloon Race in the middle of the Rocky Mountains is a visual delight. All through the summer, balloon races

are held in different areas in the Rockies. Del Norte in Southern Colorado has a balloon farm for the serious balloonists.

The Telluride Festivals: State Highway 145 winds its way down through the San Miguel Mountains and ends at Telluride, which is nestled 8,745 ft (2,665 meters) in the midst of the towering San Juans. It has been rediscovered by a new generation that appreciates its magnificent snowcapped mountain slopes. Telluride is a year-round resort. Several Rocky Mountain Festivals are held here, including the Dance Festival, the Wine Festival, the Bicycle Classic, the Jazz Festival, the Balloon Rally, the Chamber Music Festival, the Lunar Cup 4th of July Ski Race, the Hang Gliding Invitational and the well-known Telluride Blue Grass Festival. Film buffs who also like the mountains will enjoy the popular Telluride Film Festival held in the summer, which brings together film-makers, film stars, climbers, mountain men and outdoor enthusiasts.

The Telluride Blue Grass Festival is a spectacular event which was started in 1973 by a small, local blue grass band called "Fall Creek". According to *Esquire* magazine, Telluride has established itself as "the country's premiere progressive blue grass event." Thousands of country music lovers arrive for a weekend of the best blue grass music in the

Cash, The Band, New Grass Revival, Hot Rize and many others.

At the top of the list of visual experiences is the Winter Park Cool Water Revival held at Lake Granby in August. This windsurfing regatta lasts for an entire weekend. Located on Lake Granby, the setting is perfect for a host of colorful windsurfing events. The Great Lakes of Colorado include Grand Lake, the largest natural body of water in Colorado, Shadow Mountain Lake and the man-made Lake Granby. People from all over the United States come to sail here, as Grand Lake has the world's highest registered yacht anchorage and hosts the traditional Lipton Cup Race in August. There are several mari-

Rockies. The setting is a large field backdropped by the snow-peaked San Juans. It's a carnival with food stalls, craft booths and musicians playing on stage while people sit, stand, dance, talk and play frisbee.

All types of people pitch their tents on a field in town, and the city bustles with action. Little groups of musicians jam the street or the parking lots. The atmosphere is very casual and relaxed, and it allows country music fans to get together to appreciate the best professionals in the field. Throughout the years, this festival has hosted the finest blue grass musicians, including Leon Russell, Willie Nelson, John Hartford, Roseanne

nas and boat facilities, and you can bring your own boat or rent one. Classical sailing regattas are held regularly every summer.

The big bicycle event: Another historic event is the International Bicycle Classic. This is not just a bicycle race, but a strenuous climb through mountain towns like Vail and Aspen and desert towns like Grand Junction and Cheyenne, Wyoming. Bicycling an accmulated climb of 50,000 ft (15,240 meters), the energetic participants thrive on speed and danger.

The Classic began as a two-day event in Boulder in 1975, and was called the Red Zinger Bicycle Classic. Mo Siegel, president of Celestial Seasonings Herb Tea Company, wanted to show the entire world – or at least the people in Boulder – "that it was time for Americans to get out of their cars and get on to their bicycles." He saw the use of the bicycle as one way to deal with the shortage of world oil. Thus, the Red Zinger Bicycle Classic was born and named after Mo Siegel's brand of tea.

In 1980, the sponsorship of this Classic was transferred to the Adolph Coors Company based in Golden, Colorado. In 1989 Coors stopped sponsoring this event but spectators love the International Classic. During July and August, you can catch the race at Vail, Boulder, Aspen, Estes Park, Denver, or

most important exhibition race for women.

The Colorado Renaissance Festival, held on seven consecutive weekends in June and July, offers a trip back in time. Located at the base of the Rocky Mountains, in the shire of Larkspur, between Colorado Springs and Denver off Interstate 25, this is an event in which the whole family can experience the atmosphere of a 16th-century European marketplace, with nearly 200 craftspeople demonstrating and selling their wares to the curious public.

A colorful cast of village characters welcomes the public to the magic merriment of a fantasy kingdom. Entertainers include combat jousters, sword swallowers, belly

at the Colorado National Monument where a "Tour of the Moon" was added not too long ago. Write to International Bicycle Classic, 4885, Riverbend Road, Boulder, Colorado 80301, for information.

Package tours are available to see the entire 11-day Classic or just a part of it. In 1984, more than 30 international Olympic teams participated. Today, this 1,100-mile (1,800-km) event is the premiere men's cycling event in the United States and the world's

Left, the Blue Grass Festival at Telluride, Colorado. Above, the renowned International Bicycle Classic.

dancers and wandering players. The Celestial Seasonings Pavilion in Tumble Downs features music, madrigals, magic and merrymaking. Great Shakespearian actors roam the fairgrounds while witty young lasses force kisses on you. Nibble on turkey legs, tempura steak on a stake and spicy sausages. It's all fun, action-packed and continuous entertainment on 20 acres (8 hectares) of Renaissance Country.

Fort Hall was built by a Bostonian in 1784 for the purpose of trading with the Indians and the trappers. The building became the common boundary between British and American trappers west of the Rockies. During this time, the Shoshone and Bannock tribes were living in harmony. Though some tribes roamed the Fort Hall area, no connection between Fort Hall and the two tribes existed when the fort was established. Today, this reservation is the home of the Shoshone and the Bannocks, and the center of many Native American events. The trading post and shopping complex have beautiful and intricate buckskin and beadwork; it is some of the best craftmanship you'll see.

The Shoshone Bannock Festival features a variety of arts and crafts stalls selling exquisite Indian jewelry, leather goods, beadwork and other unusual Native American items. Hot dog and hamburger stands are plentiful,

but it's hard to top the authentic Navajo Tacos. When you attend this event, you can either stay at Pocatello and commute daily or camp out on the reservation in areas well-prepared for campers.

One of the biggest Native American pow-wows in the nation is held at this festival. Tribespeople dance into the night to the rhythm of drums. These events have a flavor all their own. Instead of the glamour and finesse that some of the other Rocky Mountain festivals demonstrate, a sincerity and simple, earthy feeling unite all the participants here.

Operas and rodeos: Central City Opera

Festival is one of Colorado's oldest summer festivals. This nationally famous festival takes place in the 1878 Opera House at the old gold mining town of Central City, 35 miles (56 km) west of Denver. For opera lovers, Colorado College at Colorado Springs hosts the Colorado Opera Festival in July. Another nationally important music festival is the Colorado Music Festival held at the 1896 Chautauque Auditorium in Boulder. For five summer-time weeks, a series of chamber music concerts is held. Also of interest are lectures, symposia, concerts, films and exhibits.

Wyoming is another Rocky Mountain state bursting with festivals and events. One of the most important is the rodeo, held throughout the state during the summer. A list of dates and locations can be obtained from the Chambers of Commerce. As far as rodeos go, the Big Daddy of 'em all is Cheyenne Frontier Days, which began in 1897 when 15,000 people cheered cowpony races, pitching and bucking broncos, a pony express and a battle between Sioux Indians and United States Cavalry. It was so successful, it lasted two days. Today, Frontier Days lasts 10 days. The world's best rodeo is combined with a fabulous mile-long parade, superstar entertainers, free breakfast, square dancing, Native American dancing and an excellent Old West Museum. More than 1,300 top professional cowboys compete for nearly $500,000 in prize money.

In Montana, too, you can join the locals in foot stompin' rodeos that go on almost every weekend during the summer, from the College National Finals Rodeo in Bozeman to the Wild Horse Stampede in Wolf Point. Another special happening is the State Fiddling Championship held every July in Polson, on the south shore of Flathead Lake and enjoy the music of the Montana Old Time Fiddlers Organization.

How does one choose the best festivals? The choices are unlimited, so plan your time carefully. The Rockies are a great place to begin your escape or to start an adventure. Every festival and event in the tall mountains will let you experience an unforgettable "Rocky Mountain High".

Left, Cheyenne father and daughter celebrate the old ways. **Right**, a Cheyenne dancer in full feather and flight.

NATIONAL PARKS

A trip to the well-preserved natural wonderlands known today as national parks readily conjures up images of the past. One can only imagine what took place before the white man arrived, before ski lodges, before paved highways carrying Winnebagos and windjammers, before tackleboxes and snowmobiles – it was a time when huge herds of buffalo roamed free amid towering mountains teeming with deer, elk, moose and grizzly bears.

The first people to live in this area were Native Americans who coexisted in harmony with the environment for centuries. But others eventually arrived to disrupt the peace. The Louisiana Purchase opened the way for American trappers to penetrate the Rocky Mountain region, and they took immediate advantage of the opportunity.

John Colter, a fur trapper, is believed to have been the first white man to enter the area which is now Yellowstone National Park. Working as a hunter for Lewis and Clark, Colter left the expedition as it returned to the United States. Joined by two trappers, Forest Hancock and Joseph Dixon, he turned once again to the wilderness for yet another winter.

In the spring of 1807, Colter met the keelboats of the trader Manuel Lisa, who was ascending the Missouri River to establish a trading post in Yellowstone, at the mouth of the Big Horn River. Colter was persuaded to return to the mountains to "Manuel's Fort", from where, in the winter of 1807–08, his epic journey began.

Colter's secret: Lisa, for whom Colter was then working, sent him out to drum up trade with the Native American tribes. He passed through Pryor's Gap, past a thermal region (near present-day Cody, Wyoming), crossed the mountains into Jackson Hole, and most likely journeyed across Teton Pass into the Teton Valley. Heading north up the Snake River, Colter entered the present boundaries of the park. He crossed the Conti-

Preceding pages: Snake River coils through the Grand Tetons; Bryce Canyon National Park. Below, Yellowstone Park view.

nental Divide eastward and, high up on this plateau, laid eyes on a vast expanse of water – the Yellowstone Lake. Following the Yellowstone River north, Colter discovered the Grand Canyon of Yellowstone and its two magnificent waterfalls. But for a time, the wonders of the Yellowstone region were Colter's secret, shared only with the Indians.

Three years later, Colter returned to St Louis and reported his discoveries. His accounts of the strange phenomena of the wild west were regarded with disbelief. Scoffers labeled him a "plain and fancy liar" and laughed at his descriptions of boiling hot springs, bubbling mud pools, and gushing geysers. They coined it "Colter's Hell", the name by which Yellowstone was known for many years. Although his stories were discounted by the public, Captain William Clark outlined Colter's course on the expedition's map, marking it "Colter's route in 1807".

Bridger's tall tales: Of the trappers who eventually entered the region, Jim Bridger became the most well-known.

At the end of a three-year trapping stint in Yellowstone country, Bridger also returned to St Louis. His incredible reports met with the same disbelief; newspaper editors called his stories too "preposterous" to print. Bridger, esteemed as a truthful man until his Yellowstone tales, figured since he was gaining a reputation as a liar, he might as well earn it. So in Paul Bunyan style, he spiced up his tales a bit.

"And a fellow can catch fish in an icy river," drawled Bridger, "pull it into a boiling pool, and cook his fish without ever taking it off the hook." He also told of an old Native American Medicine Man who cursed the region with instant death, transforming a flourishing forest into hard, cold stone. Today, Yellowstone visitors still admire those petrified trees along Specimen Ridge.

No serious exploration of Yellowstone occurred until several years after the days of Bridger and other early trappers. The 1849 gold rush brought a few fortune seekers to the area, but finding no gold, they pressed on to California. The decline of the fur trade led to the trappers' subsequent departure. Danger from Native Americans and a general lack of interest in exploration – especially during the predominating cold and snowy months – were good enough reasons for most to continue avoiding the area. The Civil War kept the government busy in the east, so official expeditions or geological surveys weren't conducted either. It became, once again, a nearly forgotten wilderness.

After Colter's initial penetration, the second important expedition to the Yellowstone region was the Cook-Folsom-Peterson Party in 1869; it was the first exploration based on curiosity rather than profit. The three explorers scouted the area, where they observed the geysers, hot pools, and other principal points of interest. But, as with Colter and Bridger, their reports of Yellowstone's wonders were never believed.

Lost and found: In 1870, however, the stories circulating were sufficient to warrant formation of the first official exploration party – the Washburn-Langford-Doane Expedition. The party was official insofar as the prominent men were given a five-man military escort. One of the members of the expedition, Nathaniel P. Langford, later served as the first superintendent of Yellowstone National Park.

In less than four weeks, the expedition discovered and reported on most of the sights about which John Colter and Jim Bridger had told tales 60 years earlier. The journey was marred by one unfortunate mishap. One member of the party, Truman C. Everts, was separated from the others and spent "37 days of peril" in the wilderness. Unassisted by today's park rangers, walkie-talkies, or the National Guard, the expedition turned into a search party. During the search, the team stumbled upon the area now designated the Upper Geyser Basin. With awe, they tagged the world-famous geyser with its present name, Old Faithful.

After some time, the loss of Everts to the wilderness turned the adventure sour, and the despondent crew headed home. To their surprise Everts returned safely, rescued by another party of explorers. Possibly out of sympathy for his hardships, a mountain was named after him – Mount Everts.

The nation's first National Park: A year later, in 1871, a scientific and military expedition led by Dr Ferdinand V. Hayden substantiated the reports of the previous expeditions. An official photographer, William H. Jackson, was taken along to record the wonders.

The Hayden Survey reports, along with the accounts of the Cook-Folsom-Peterson and Washburn-Langford-Doane expeditions, resulted in the wondrous Yellowstone country being brought to national attention and, subsequently, led to the Congressional bill that created the nation's first national park. Overwhelmingly passed by Congress in early 1872 and affixed with President Ulysses S. Grant's signature on March 1, 1872, the Yellowstone Park Act set aside more than 2 million acres (810,000 hectares) for the enjoyment of the public.

"Be it enacted by the Senate and House

Two young elk lock horns in a territorial contest.

of Representatives of the United States of America in Congress assembled, that the tract of land in the Territories of Montana and Wyoming, lying near the headwaters of the Yellowstone River…is hereby reserved and withdrawn from settlement, occupancy, or sale under the laws of the United States, and dedicated and set apart as a public park or pleasuring-ground for the benefit and enjoyment of the people."

For 14 years, Park supervision was in the hands of a series of five superintendents. Properly developing and preserving the Park was a monumental task. So, from 1886 to 1918, managing the Park became the US Army's responsibility. Abuses occuring under the attempted civilian management were finally brought under control. After 32 years of military law and order, a more mature attempt at civilian supervision was made.

The National Park Service: In 1916, Congress established the National Park Service "to promote and regulate the use of the…national parks, monuments, and reservations" to "conserve the scenery and the natural and historic objects and wildlife therein…by such means as will leave them unimpaired for the enjoyment of future generations." Today, the National Park Service actively assists more than 90 nations who have adopted the national park concept in establishing and expanding their own national park programs.

Currently, more than 340 areas in the United States National Park System are attended yearly by 300 million visitors. Sometimes, a summertime map navigator may become a bit confused for his road atlas reveals not only national parks, but also national forests, national monuments, national recreation areas, national historic sites and national landmarks. While national monuments generally consist of one outstanding feature and national forest resources are managed to produce a sustained yield, national parks stand alone as unrivaled vacation lands, unique areas – nature's grandest expressions – preserved for the purpose of enriching the lives and lifting the spirits of their visitors.

YELLOWSTONE NATIONAL PARK

"There is something in the wild romantic scenery of Yellowstone which I cannot describe; but the impressions made upon my mind while gazing from a high eminence on the surrounding landscape one evening as the sun was gently gliding behind the western mountain and casting its gigantic shadows across a vale were such as time can never efface from my memory…for my own part, I almost wished I could spend the remainder of my days in a place like this where happiness and contentment seemed to reign in wild romantic splendor." Such was the sentiment of Osborne Russell, who was a trapper in the region until late in the 1830s.

In the northwest corner of Wyoming sprawls the **Yellowstone National Park**, the nation's first and the largest of the national parks in the lower 48 states. It remains one of the most thrilling holiday attractions available, drawing millions of cosmopolitan visitors yearly.

In the summer of 1988 drought, high temperatures and wind combined to set the stage for dramatic forest fires affecting almost half the park. A large part of the Park seems to have recovered. It is green once more and looks little affected although it could take up to 100 years for the burned-out forest areas to return to their pre-fire condition.

The fires have sparked a new interest in the park, with some $1.5 million being spent to construct roadside and visitor center exhibits to help people understand the fires and fire ecology.

The effects of continual geological processes – building up and tearing down the landscape by radically different agents of fire and ice – are probably more visible today in Yellowstone than any other place in the world. Immense mountains uplifted from the sea, the aftermath of a succession of volcanic eruptions, against a backdrop of ice-etched and water-carved rocks and canyons: the vastness and variety of these attractions, each unique and outstanding, bewilders visitors and presents newcomers with a difficult decision – where to go, what to see, and what activities to plan. Before beginning your Yellowstone adventure, write to the National Park Service in Washington, DC for specific information.

Contained within Yellowstone's 3,472 sq. miles (8,992 sq. meters), more than 2 million acres (810,000 hectares), are hundreds of impressive sights. Take advantage of the many friendly visitor and interpretive centers in the Park.

The Yellowstone boundary creates a common bond between Montana, Idaho, and Wyoming, and the five separate entrances access attractions at all points of the compass.

In 1805, based on information received from the Indians, Lewis and Clark sent to President Thomas Jefferson a progress report which included a map on which "Yellow-Stone" appeared in English, thereby permanently naming the river as the Missouri River's principal tributary. Seven years before, full rendering of the river's name into English was made by explorer-geographer David Thompson, who had visited the Mandan towns near present-day Bismarck, North Dakota. The yellowish sandstone bluffs, conspicuous along the lower course of the river, most likely inspired the name that eventually lent itself to the entire Park. Yellowstone's glorious **Grand Canyon**, with its towering 100-ft (30-meter) cliffs, is a rainbow of colors. Highlighted by the **Upper and Lower Falls**, the canyon is considered the most photogenic region of the Park.

Thermal theater: Almost every visit to Yellowstone includes a stop in the **Upper Geyser** to witness world-famous **Old Faithful** spouting hourly. Although Old Faithful enjoys the limelight, Yellowstone's entire thermal theater is the most extensive area of geyser activity in the world, harboring more than 10,000 thermal features. Only in Iceland, New Zealand and Siberia are there thermal wonders comparable to what can be seen here.

Heat from the enormous reservoir of molten rock remains relatively close beneath the earth's surface, sustaining

Preceding pages: Mammoth Hot Springs, Yellowstone. Left, Clepsydra Geyser blows its top.

the spectacular hot water and steam phenomena. Though geysers, hot springs, mudpots and fumaroles are all hot springs technically, the only difference is the end result of their activity. A geyser erupts, a hot spring flows, a mudpot emits both water and steam, and a fumarole issues just steam.

The most spectacular features are the geysers, for which Yellowstone is justly famous. Yet it has earned its name as the most popular national park, not simply because of its displays, but because of its wildlife. As a wildlife sanctuary, Yellowstone is unparalleled, with untamed creatures roaming free in unspoiled surrounding. Yellowstone provides a perfect habitat for a variety of creatures, all essential to one another.

A wildlife extravaganza: Yellowstone's larger animals include the infamous bears, buffalo, elk, mule deer, pronghorn antelope, bighorn sheep, coyote and lynx. On rare occasions, wolf and mountain lion have been spotted. Birds such as the bald eagle, Canadian goose, osprey, rare trumpeter swan, California and ring bill gull, white pelican, a variety of ducks, and a host of other species share the wilderness with mountain whitefish, grayling and cut-throat trout – the only three game fish native to Yellowstone – and German brown, brook, lake and rainbow trout.

Due to early liberal feeding restrictions, the black bear (in colors varying from cinnamon to brown to black) and the occasional grizzly could be spotted easily along the roadside. In an effort to restore natural balances within Yellowstone, however, the major dumps, where bears were fed garbage from the hotels and inns, were closed in 1969. Bears could no longer depend on the dumps for food, and visitors no longer see them nearly as often.

Endless varieties of trees and profuse gardens of flowers (in season) provide a rich habitat for the Park's wildlife. Ninety percent of Yellowstone is forested, and a staggering variety of flowers populate this botanists' paradise. In spring and summer, it is hard to find a spot where flowers do not grow in abundance.

As if the terrific spectacle of the present were not enough, a frozen glimpse of the past has been dramatically preserved. A fascinating consequence of the volcanic era in Yellowstone is the fossil forests, an area covering more than 40 sq. miles (100 sq. km) running along the northeastern border of the Park. Trees stand amazingly erect in the same place and position in which they originally thrived.

Whether your mode of travel within the Park is bicycle or mobile home, and whether your accommodation includes room service at one of the comfortable lodges or a canopy of stars in the backwoods, Yellowstone National Park supplies a rich setting for a wide variety of activities. The regular Park season generally runs from the first week in May through Labor Day (first Monday in September). Limited services are available earlier and later in the year. Camping throughout the season is on a first-come, first-serve basis, with most campgrounds open between mid-June and mid-September. Check at the en-

The morning glory pool at Yellowstone.

trance gates for information on open campgrounds and available campsites upon your arrival at Yellowstone.

More than 100 miles (160 km) of trails lead to remote sections of the Park. Some are easy walks of a few hours, including self-guided nature trails, while others are strenuous hikes and climbs that require hiking skill and stamina.

With the exception of Lake Titicaca in the Andes in Peru, **Yellowstone Lake** is the largest lake in the world at this altitude of 7,731 ft (2,350 meters). Fishing licenses are required and can be obtained free of charge.

Permits are also required for all types of vessels. For launching larger vessels, marinas and ramps are available on Yellowstone and Lewis lakes. Other designated areas are reserved for canoes and row boats. **Shoshone Lake** is a favorite with canoeists.

For those visitors who want to get out on the water but can't bring their own crafts, the Park offers boat rides.

Yellowstone's breathtaking scenery naturally makes it a photographer's paradise. Tumbling waterfalls, steaming hot pools, rare wildlife, abounding fields of flowers – the splendor of summer in Yellowstone must be personally experienced to be truly appreciated. Yet some maintain that the quiet beauty of Yellowstone in winter is best. Hushed by a thick blanket of snow covering the landscape from early October until June, winter is truly another world – a silent world of unearthly shapes and contours where waterfalls freeze in mid-plunge and trees are wreathed with frost. Even as Yellowstone appears to be sleeping, the lively wilderness saga continues, and it can be witnessed only by the adventurous. Only snowshoes, cross-country skis, snowmobiles, or snow coaches allow first-hand access to the winterscape where elk patrol the white meadows, bison plow through deep snow, and Old Faithful remains true to its name. Whatever season attracts you to Yellowstone, the nation's first national park remains foremost with its unparalleled beauty, opportunity and natural enjoyment.

Yellowstone's most famous geyser, "Old Faithful".

The magnificent grizzly bear is rapidly becoming a creature of the past – a vanishing symbol of America's national heritage. The grizzly bear has acquired two popular reputations, as either a vicious killer or a cuddly "Gentle Ben". Fatal maulings receive so much media attention that an exaggerated impression has been created; the Gentle Ben image, on the other hand, is also unrealistic. The real grizzly rarely has been introduced to the American people. The truth about him lies somewhere between the two extremes.

The largest and most formidable of carnivorous North American animals, the grizzly is potentially dangerous. Fortunately, he minds his own business most of the time and doesn't allow himself to become addicted to panhandling as the more common black bear has done.

Their invulnerability and ferociousness in direct confrontation have long earned grizzlies the respect they deserve. Lewis and Clark provided early scientific reports on grizzly bears. Captain Lewis recorded: "…these bears being so hard to die rather intimidated us all; I must confess that I do not like the gentlemen and had rather fight two Indians than one bear."

The romantics look at him from a different point of view. "If bravery comes from the heart, his heart is very big for he is very brave," admired western artist Charles Russell.

In all fairness to the vanishing grizzly bear, we must admit that his brave self-defense of his own territory is responsible for his criminal reputation.

Of the thousands of grizzlies who once roamed freely throughout most of western North America, fewer than 1,000 have survived. They are limited to the wilderness areas of Montana, Wyoming and Idaho.

Complete extinction has taken place throughout most of the grizzly's historic range. It seems the grizzly and the Native American have shared a similar fate. Affectionately referred to by mountain men as Old Ephraim, the grizzly was firmly planted in

North America long before the first European ventured to these shores. Like Native Americans, grizzlies were marked for destruction by the same natural enemy, the white man, who exemplified the rolling wave of "civilization" that swept across the new frontier from coast to coast. To the nation's shame, the war cry of the western frontier armies became "the only good Indian is a dead Indian". Cattlemen and stockmen used the same cry against every grizzly.

The factor most responsible for the grizzly bear's destruction in the United States was the introduction of the domestic cattle industry into the grassy mountain valleys and open ranges west of the Great Plains. As the nation grew, the demand for beef also grew. Cattle were brought by the thousands into grizzly country, and most of them roamed free and wild. Grizzlies quite naturally cultivated a taste for beef. The slow-moving cattle were easy prey for the carnivorous bears, and the grizzly quickly became the cattleman's foremost predatory enemy. For most cattlemen, the new, improved high-powered repeating rifles and packs of trained hunting dogs made slaughtering every possible grizzly bear relatively safe and easy.

A large population of grizzlies still exists in Canada and Alaska, but this fails to pacify many in the United States. Aldo Leopold, for one, says, "Relegating grizzlies to Alaska is about like relegating happiness to heaven."

The advent of ultra-light backpacking equipment allows hardy campers to venture into the most remote recesses of the grizzly's dwindling domain. As the number of confrontations between grizzlies and recreationalists increases, Old Ephraim once again becomes a menace to human safety.

Overall knowledge of grizzlies is the best safety precaution when visiting bear country. Get tips from the local rangers on how to pack and store your food for camping so as not to attract unwanted visitors. Never go near a cub or you'll arouse the mother's wrath, and menstruating women should be prewarned not to go near a grizzly area. When you venture into these areas, remember that you're a foreigner in a king's domain, so good manners are in order.

Left, a grizzly, known for its slightly humped back, wanders through a mountain field.

TETON
NATIONAL PARK

Standing in northwest Wyoming, just south of Yellowstone National Park, are the majestic **Grand Teton Mountains**, the outstanding feature of the **Grand Teton National Park**. The mighty Teton mountain range is tiny as mountain ranges go, but because they "come from nowhere" and explode abruptly from the valley floor to a summit of almost 14,000 ft (4,265 meters), they are incredibly picturesque. The blue-gray pyramid-like Tetons are among the most noble creations of the American West. Soaring more than a mile (1.6 km) above the Sagebrush Flats and morainal lakes of Jackson Hole, the imposing Tetons are a striking example of the fault-block type of mountain formation (in contrast to the results of volcanic action in Yellowstone).

By geological standards, the Teton range is a young mountain range, the youngest in the Rocky Mountain sys-tem, and it's still growing. A series of upthrusts over a period of time progressively exposed this great block of the earth's crust. As the earth cracked along a north-south line, the outer crust faulted under tremendous pressure deep within. The western block tilted upward and the eastern block sank, accounting for the tremendously steep eastern face of the mountains and the gentle western slope.

For hundreds of years prior to the early 1800s, the Native Americans held undisputed dominion over Teton country. They frequently crossed the passes into the basins on warring expeditions or to hunt and fish, but they didn't stay long. The winters were too severe in Jackson Hole for permanent settlement and the land was left virtually untouched.

On his trek to Yellowstone country in 1807, the intrepid John Colter crossed the Teton range, probably making him the first white man to enter the area.

For the next few decades, known as the Fur Era, the Tetons became the center of activity for fur trappers and traders representing both American and

Horsepacking through the Teton Mountains.

British interests. By 1845, the trappers had left the Rockies, and – for the next four decades – the valleys near the Tetons were deserted except for a few wandering bands of Indians.

As the frontier closed in, several government expeditions passed through Teton country, naming many of the natural features. In the late 1880s, the first permanent settlers homesteaded the valley, augmenting their meager earnings by arranging summer lodgings for visitors and guiding dude and hunting parties. Setting apart Jackson Hole as a national park was discussed as early as 1890, but many of those interested in preservation owned ranches in the area which they felt should be protected. This distinguished the Teton situation from the Yellowstone, where no one had ever lived.

As Jackson Hole developed economically, socially and recreationally, certain individuals, societies and government groups kept alive their interest in the national park idea. The greatest single benefactor was John D. Rockefeller

Jr, who in 1925 purchased privately owned lands within the area to accomplish the shared purposes of those dedicated to preserving it.

Unaware of the operation at hand, Congress voted to create Grand Teton National Park on February 26, 1929. The Park was about one-third the size of today's Park, protecting only the immediate mountain range and very little of the valley floor. In 1949, the lands purchased by Rockefeller were conveyed by Jackson Hole Preserve, Inc. to the Secretary of the Interior as a gift to the people of the United States. The deed covered 33,455 acres (13,540 hectares) in Jackson Hole, and represented $2 million and nearly 25 years of tenacity and endless patience. The present-day Grand Teton National Park, created by a Congressional Act on September 14, 1950, combined the former Park with newly acquired land, expanding the Park to almost 500 sq. miles (1,300 sq. km).

One's first impression of Teton is naturally inspired by the looming Teton range, but it isn't the whole picture. There are also dozens of lakes shimmering like a row of jewels at the foot of the peaks. Hidden behind fringes of trees or up a short stretch of trail, most of them are reached only by leaving the highway behind. **Jackson Lake** is the largest body of water in the area. Marinas are available and sail boating is allowed only on Jackson Lake. Power boats are permitted on Jackson, Jenny and Phelps lakes; the others are reserved for noiseless hand-powered crafts.

The Grand Teton National Park and Jackson Hole have no monopoly on the **Snake River**, one of the cleanest left in the United States, although it extends 17 miles (27 km) south through Jackson Lake. Of its 1,000-mile (1,600-km) traverse from the Continental Divide near Yellowstone National Park to its confluence with the Columbia River near Pasco, Washington, just 40 miles (65 km) of the Snake River are spent in Teton country. Compared to the lakes, the Snake River harbors a wealth of aquatic life, due to the enriching quality of the abundant shoreline. It supports a plant complex which, combined with

A windstorm at the top of a Grand Teton peak.

countless insects, supplies food for the profuse fish population. The fish, in turn, become a tasty meal for more than skilful anglers. Herons, mergansers, eagles, ospreys, otters and other terrestrial predators also rely on the Park's aquatic food pyramid. Of the several varieties of game fish luring thousands of fishermen to the waters of the Tetons, the Snake River cut-throat trout – found only in the Snake's watershed – is unique. Fishing regulations within the Park conform to Wyoming's laws.

A highlight of Jackson Hole is a float trip on the Snake River, one of the best ways to experience the Park's wildlife and outstanding scenery. Local commercial operators conduct raft trips – either all-day or half-day scenic or exciting whitewater adventures. The Snake River regains its free-flowing character at the **Jackson Lake Dam**. This is the 27-mile (43-km) section of the river within the Park that is most appealing to floaters. On a float trip, you don't have to tote your backpack, watch the trail or mind your horse. You just watch the wildlife and the scenery as the guide recounts the local lore and nature identifications. As the Teton range glides by, you may see bald eagles, ospreys, moose, great blue herons, Canada geese, beaver, otters and a variety of ducks in the same primitive setting appreciated by the territory's earliest inhabitants. You can float the river in your own craft, but a permit is required – kayaks, inflatables and canoes are the best. For a truly exciting experience, whitewater excursions are available for the adventurous. A word of caution: do not underestimate the power of the Snake. Write the Park for information about hazards, regulations, equipment and best travel times for floating the Snake River.

To make best use of your time in Grand Teton National Park, stop first at the **Moose Visitor Center** (south end) or the **Colter Bay Visitor Center** and ask the rangers about Park activities and services. The National Park Service presents the Park's many features in movies, slide shows and talks at amphitheaters near the major campgrounds.

Snow can be seen on mountain tops all year long.

On the trail: Besides the museums and historical displays, great family activities like self-guided nature trails at **Jenny Lake** and **Colter Bay** are available. These are the shortest trails, from 1½ to 2 miles (0.8 to 3.2 km), just a fraction of the more than 200 miles (322 km) of hiking trails in the Park. The valley trails, running along the base of the Teton range to the lakes in front of the mountains, are shorter and less demanding than the mountain trails. But these valley trails will pique your interest and help you decide if you want to hike further into the mountains. Half-day and all-day hikes into the canyons between the Teton peaks are more difficult, requiring uphill and downhill efforts, but the rewards in mountain views, wild flowers and wildlife are worth it. For overnights in the backcountry, a free backcountry use permit is required.

Grand Teton National Park is considered one of the country's finest areas for general mountaineering, offering an exceptional range of climbing difficulty.

Ask a ranger: The **Jenny Lake Ranger Station** is the center for climbing information and registration in the Park. The National Park Service requires all climbers to register in person before climbing and to sign out afterwards. Climbing conditions are best from mid-July through late September.

Seasonal changes dominate the Park, bring warmth and life, winter and stillness in their turn. Winter weather in the Teton range is severe, bringing heavy snowfall, high winds and extreme temperatures. But winter activities gear up just the same in mid-December. One good snowstorm can turn Jackson Hole into a winter wonderland, covered with up to 7 ft (2 meters) of snow. As well as winter camping areas, lodging within the Park is available at **Flagg Ranch, Triangle X Ranch** and **Signal Mountain Lodge**. Nearby Jackson offers full tourist services year-round.

So, whether you are cruising down **John D. Rockefeller Jr Memorial Parkway** or scaling one of the peaks, the Grand Teton National Park is awesome from any angle.

split rail
ence frames
ie distant
iountains.

ROCKY MOUNTAIN NATIONAL PARK

In north central Colorado, the snow-mantled peaks of **Rocky Mountain National Park** rise high above fresh green alpine valleys and glistening lakes. With 71 peaks reaching over 12,000 ft (3,650 meters) and nearly 40 miles (64 km) of the Continental Divide running through it, the Park is often referred to as the "top of the continent". Any visitor to Rocky Mountain Natonal Park is immediately humbled by the magnitude and grandeur of the surrounding mountainscape.

Gigantic earth movements: The history of Rocky Mountain National Park is one of gigantic earth movements. Geologists confirm that a great sea once covered the area. Yet today's magnificent mountains, the smooth and gentle slopes on Trail Ridge, the U-shaped valleys, and the uptilted rock strata are fascinating evidence of the powerful forces of change in nature.

A unique feature of the Park is the marked differences found with the changing elevations. In an exhilarating trip over the 38-mile (62-km) Trail Ridge Road, you traverse a quantity of life zones equivalent in number to a round-trip of the Arctic Circle. The best evidence of these differences, besides visitors' difficulty in breathing comfortably at greater altitudes, is the diverse plant life.

At lower levels, open stands of ponderosa pine and juniper grow on the slopes facing the sun; on cooler northern slopes, the Douglas fir reaches skyward. Embellishing streamsides are blue spruces intermixed with dense stands of lodgepole pines. Groves of aspen appear here and there, and meadows and glades are speckled with wild flowers. Above 2,970 yards (2,715 meters), forests of sub-alpine fir take over. Gaps in these cool, dark forests produce wild flower gardens of rare luxurious beauty where the Colorado columbine reigns. Grotesque, twisted trees hug the ground at the upper edges of this zone. One-

Alpine tundra in Rocky Mountain National Park.

third of the Park is actually above the treeline, where trees disappear and the harsh, fragile world of alpine tundra predominates. More than one-quarter of the plants here can also be found in the Arctic.

The modern Ute and Arapahoe were the most recent Native American inhabitants of the Rocky Mountain National Park region. Several thousand years earlier, other tribes – of whom little is known – also used the region for hunting. Meadows and hills teemed with the elk, antelope, bighorn sheep, bear, deer, beaver and other game. Winters were apparently too cold for these semi-nomadic peoples, and no one tribe claimed the land as home.

Settlers arrived: In the early 1800s, after the United States acquired the region through the Louisiana Purchase, white men began tentatively exploring this country. Explorers, adventurers and famous mountain men trappers passed through the Park. In 1806, Lt. Zebulon Pike's expedition was the first to see and record Long's Peak, the highest mountain in the Park, named for Colonel S.H. Long who led a party along the foot of the mountain 14 years later. However, he never actually climbed it himself.

The first white man to live in Rocky Mountain was Joel Estes. In 1860, Estes settled his entire family in the grassy meadows of the forest-rimmed valley which now bears his name; they lived there for six years.

Estes Park and parts of Rocky Mountain National Park are the only areas in the United States that were once the private hunting preserve of a European nobleman. The Irish Earl of Dunraven was so impressed by the scenery and abundance of game on his 1872–73 hunting trips that he ordered his agent to buy the place. At one time, he owned or controlled about 15,000 acres (6,070 hectares). Other settlers disagreed with the earl's notion that the Park was his own private domain. Court settlements stemming from charges of fraudulent land-grabbing methods reduced the earl's holdings to 8,000

ild flowers
rpet the
ountain
opes.

acres (3,240 hectares). In 1906, he sold his remaining land to two men, one of whom was F.O. Stanley – of Stanley Steamer fame – who also built the sparkling white Stanley Hotel, which has overlooked Estes Park since 1910 from its grassy knoll north of town.

Establishment of Rocky Mountain as a National Park is historically linked with the name of one man – Enos A. Mills, the "father" of the Park and a famous naturalist. At his own expense, he spent seven years promoting the idea of a national park, making many trips from Colorado to Washington, New York, and other centers of influence. His enthusiasm, reports and lectures laid the groundwork that eventually led to legislation setting aside the area as a national park in 1915.

By the mid-1920s it was apparent that the Fall River Road, which first opened to traffic in September 1920, was quickly becoming inadequate. The views from the road on the east side were restricted by large rocks and trees and the west side traversed a series of such hair-raising switchbacks that the pleasure of the view was substantially diminished. Furthermore, the snow-removal problem kept the Park superintendent up many spring nights worrying about whether the road would be cleared by mid-June for the tourist season.

The National Park Service began a determined search for an alternate route in 1926, one which would provide moderate grades, gentle curves, few places of heavy snow accumulation, and, most importantly, unparalleled views of spectacular scenery.

Almost immediately, the search narrowed to Trail Ridge, which derived its name from the Ute Trail traversing its entire length. The trail, traveled by both Ute and Arapahoe Indians, was used to cross from Middle Park through Estes Park, where game was particularly abundant, to the high plains lying to the east of Front Range. The trail was also used by miners traveling across the divide to Lulu City and other mines in the Colorado Valley as early as the 1880s. And, with the coming of the 20th century, the

The Stanley Hotel in Estes, Colorado.

trail was used increasingly by vacationers traveling between Estes Park and Grand Lake on foot or horseback.

Visiting requirements: Stop at one of the four Rocky Mountain visitors' centers and become acquainted with the Park. The **Headquarters Visitor Center** on the east side and the **Grand Lake Visitor Center** on the west side are open all the year round. Guided walks, campfire talks, and many other services begin in early June and extend into September.

Rocky Mountain is a park for hikers. More than 300 miles (480 km) of trails provide access to the Park's remote sections so you can get away from the crowds and savor the streams, meadows, mountains and wildlife. For detailed information on elevations, lakes, and hiking trails, purchase a US Geological Survey topographical map or other guide at any visitor counter. To remain overnight in the backcountry, you will need a backcountry permit, available free at Headquarters or the West Unit Office. Some areas are closed to overnight camping and danger from avalanches exists, so plan your trip carefully; check with park rangers for the latest information on areas in which you plan to travel. Rangers can also suggest the most lightly used trails and what to watch for along the way.

You won't see any wolves or grizzly bears; they are already extinct in Colorado. Common larger animals remaining are elk, deer, bighorn sheep, coyote, beaver and a few black bears. And, of course, many varieties of birds abound.

Park mountain season: Some 3 million people come to Rocky Mountain National Park each year, and many of them can testify to how difficult it is to acquire a campsite during the peak summer season. A beautiful time of year to consider a trip to Rocky Mountain National Park is in September or October when the weather is pleasant, the aspens are golden, and the crowds are gone.

Weather is a concern to everyone here, for weather determines what you can do, where you can go, and how long you can stay. Primarily due to differences in altitude, slope and exposure, the high country of Rocky Mountain National Park produces a variable weather pattern. Another consideration is the drastic difference between daytime and night-time temperatures. Summer days reach well into the 80s (26°C) and drop into the 40s (4°C) at night.

The Continental Divide runs along the crest of a range of high peaks in a northwest to southeast direction through the center of the Park. Because of this, there are two distinct weather patterns. One is typical of the east side (Estes park) and the other of the west side (Grand Lake).

The cold waters of the high Rocky Mountains may not produce large fish, but you just can't beat the mountain scenery as a soothing fishing environment. Remember, though, you must have a valid Colorado fishing license, and the use of live bait is prohibited. Some streams and lakes are closed to protect the greenback cut-throat trout, which is being reintroduced into its natural habitat. So check with the nearest ranger station before going fishing.

For the climber, Rocky Mountain National Park offers a variety of challenging ascents throughout the year. A Park concessionaire operates a climbing school and guide service providing mountaineering instruction. For more information and details, contact Park headquarters.

Horses and guides can be hired at two locations inside the Park on the east side or from a number of liveries outside the east and west Park boundaries during the summer season.

Winter means snow in the Rockies and snow means skiing – cross-country skiing in the lower valleys, winter mountaineering in the high country, and downhill skiing at **Hidden Valley.** Access roads from the east are kept open, providing winter travelers with a panorama of the high mountains.

Most travelers to Rocky Mountain National Park stay pretty close to the Trail Ridge Road, but do take time to get to know the lesser-known parts of the Park. There is much to see, to do, to ponder and to appreciate here at the "top of the continent".

UTAH'S NATIONAL PARKS

Located within a 200-mile (320-km) circle, each of Utah's five national parks exhibits a flavor and personality of its own. Though the geological forces working in each park are identical, the effects are not.

Zion National Park: Powerful upheavals combined with the erosive forces of wind, rain, frost, and the **Virgin River** have cut through Navajo sandstone creating what is now **Zion National Park**. Zion is the grandfather of Utah's national parks and one of the nation's oldest. It contains some of the most colorful, deep, narrow canyons, sheer rock walls and unique formations in the plateau country of southern Utah. Vividly colored cliffs tower above the scenic route along the floor of Zion Canyon. This narrow, deep canyon is the centerpiece of the Park.

On most days, the Virgin River winds peacefully through the canyon. Frémont cottonwoods, willows and velvet ashes along its banks provide shady spots for picnics or short walks. Mule deer and a wide variety of birds seek refuge from summer's extreme midday heat beneath this canopy. Other wildlife, including ringtail cats, bobcats, foxes, rock squirrels and cottontails, rest under jagged rocky ledges.

Most of the rock formations can be seen from roads which pass through the Park; however, the best way to view Zion is on foot or horseback. Self-guided trails lead to the major formations. Among the most popular is the 1-mile (1.6-km) trail, **Gateway to the Narrows**, beginning at the **Temple of Sinawava**. Arrangements for guided horsepack trips are made at **Zion Lodge.**

Three campgrounds are located within Zion. The visitor center, at the south entrance of the Park, is open year-round. In addition, the **Zion Canyon Scenic Drive**, the **Zion-Mount Carmel Highway** and the **Kolob Canyons Road** are open all year. Zion's roads introduce you to the Park's spectacular cliff-and-canyon landscape. Once within Zion, you can drive, bike, hike or take the guided tram tour (mid-March to mid-October) depending on your time and vacation interests.

The visitors' center at the north end of the Park is also open year-round. Here, useful information is available free, as well as interesting exhibits and a slide program. The Park also offers a variety of interpretive programs in summer and fall, including human and natural history talks, campfire programs, view talks, guided nature walks, and special interest walks. Camping spots are available year-round in the Park; however, drinking water is available only during the summer months. Accommodation and services can be obtained within the Park and the surrounding towns.

Capitol Reef National Park: In the slickrock country of south central Utah lies **Capitol Reef National Park**, an area where water has cut monoliths, arches and mazes of canyons out of a sandstone-and-shale desert. Massive gorges, scarps and artifacts of the Columbian Indians of the Frémont Culture are contained

here. From May through September, you can join a Park naturalist on a walk or attend informative evening campfire programs. The main visitors' center, as well as the Capitol Reef's two campgrounds, are open year-round.

The term "reef" as applied to land formations means a ridge of rock that is a barrier. Capitol Reef was named for one of its high points: **Capitol Dome**, which resembles the dome of the US Capitol. The Park has been penetrated and explored only in the past 100 years and much of it still remains a rugged wilderness.

The domes of Capitol Reef are part of **Waterpocket Fold**, a 100-mile-long (160-km) bulge in the earth's crust which contains pockets eroded into the rock that catch thousands of gallons of water each rainfall. The layer upon layer of rock was, once, a tidal flat whose ripple marks are now hardened into stone. At another time, dunes drifted across the land, eventually consolidated into crisscrossing beds of sandstone.

The most spectacular experiences are off the main highway on graded or dirt roads. Marked roads lead to ancient petroglyphs, waterpockets and magnificent overlooks. The Park's remote sections are accessible only over rough backcountry roads. Spring and fall are ideal for backcountry hiking and camping because of the mild temperatures.

Arches National Park: The largest concentration and greatest collection of natural stone arches in the world lies on the **Colorado Plateau** in southeastern Utah's red rock country. All stages of arch formation and decay are found in **Arches National Park**. The forces of wind, water and time have carved the incredible arches within the 115-sq.-mile (300-sq.-km) Park.

Arches National Park's trademark is **Delicate Arch**, an isolated rocky remnant standing on the brink of a canyon, with the white-capped LaSal Mountains as a backdrop. Spires, pinnacles, and balanced rocks perched atop seemingly inadequate bases vie with the arches as scenic spectacles. Early explorers thought the huge arches – **Landscape**

"Triple Arch" at Arches National Park dwarfs visitors below.

Arch is the world-record-holder with a span of 291 ft (88 meters) – and monoliths were remnants of a lost culture, like Stonehenge in England.

Many of the more than 90 sandstone arches are seen from the paved roads running through the Park, but, to properly appreciate their magnificence, leave your car and take a short walk along the well-marked footpaths.

At the visitors' center, you can see a color slide orientation program, the geology museum, history exhibits and other maps and publications. Ask also about the popular naturalist-led Fiery Furnace Walk and obtain a self-guiding tour booklet which includes information coordinated with numbered stops along the Park road.

Bryce Canyon National Park: Unlike Zion, the mood in **Bryce Canyon**, located 50 miles (80 km) northeast of Zion, is light and lacy. Delicate rocky pinnacles and spires are colored in pink, white and rust shades.

Though called a canyon, Bryce Canyon is actually a series of "breaks" in 12 large amphitheaters. These breaks plunge down 1,000 ft (305 meters) in multicolored layers of limestone. The many shapes and forms in stone conjure all sorts of images: walls, windows, minarets, gables, pagodas, pedestals and temples. Photographs usually emphasize the otherworldly magnificence of Bryce Canyon. As light shifts with cloud movements or as the sun rises or sets, the changing scenery passes before you in vivid color.

The forests and meadows of Bryce Canyon support a remarkable diversity of plant, animal and bird life. Three distinctive plant communities thrive here – the piñon junipers in the canyon, the ponderosa pine forests on the plateau in the main park area, and the fir spruce forest at Rainbow Point, the highest elevation in the Park.

Mule deer are the largest mammals at Bryce Canyon. They can be seen on summer mornings and in the evenings in meadows and along park roads. Cougars, also called pumas and mountain lions, are the most secretive animals in

A panoramic view of Bryce Canyon National Park.

the area. A huge rodent population, together with jackrabbits and cottontails, is preyed upon by small populations of night hunters including badger, skunk, bobcat, weasel, ringtailed cat, gray fox and coyote.

More than 164 species of birds, ranging from tiny swifts to golden eagles, visit Bryce Canyon annually. Meadowlarks, bluebirds and robins are active in meadow areas.

The best time to view wildlife is at dusk, dawn and after dark. The Bryce Canyon visitors' center is open year-round. The park has two campgrounds. Part of one is open all year.

Canyonlands National Park: Driving to **Canyonlands** is an adventure in itself. Since the Park is located a vast distance from anywhere, gas is hard to come by. The closest service station is 60 miles (96 km) away and water is difficult to acquire. Piped water is available only near the campground in the Needles district; anywhere else in the Park, you'd better provide your own or be prepared to get mighty thirsty. Visitors should

also contact rangers at north and south entrance information centers for advice on road conditions.

Hiking, jeeping or scenic flights are great ways to explore the rugged wilderness of Canyonlands; but, the ultimate recreational experience is an unforgettable river ride down either the **Green** or **Colorado river** and through **Cataract Canyon**. Commercially operated float trips, led by licensed guides, are the most popular. Guides are also available in nearby communities for overland trips into the more remote areas. Primitive campsites are located in four-wheel-drive areas of the Park.

In southeastern Utah, the Colorado and Green rivers merge midway in Canyonlands National Park to form the wildest river on the continent. Entrenched in twisting ravines, they cut deep into the earth, almost 1,500 ft (455 meters), creating the spectacular canyons responsible for the Park's name. The outstanding quality of Canyonlands is its variety of form and color – the combined effects of substance, time, and erosion.

The desert lands look desolate and empty, but are occupied by plentiful plant and animal life. Bighorn sheep, mule deer, cougars, bobcats, coyotes, foxes and pronghorn are at home here, as well as rodents in enormous variety and numbers. Along the rivers are found beaver, shorebirds, ducks and other wetland animals.

Bird life in Canyonlands is especially diverse because of the wide range of habitats. Totally different conditions may occur within very short distances, and birdwatchers find a rich variety of species throughout the year.

Paved and graded state roads allow access for passenger cars to the Park's overlook areas and some interior areas, but Canyonlands is basically a paradise for four-wheelers and backpackers. Much of the Park's 337,570 acres (136,600 hectares) is still unexplored and provides innumerable opportunities for adventure.

Take your time exploring and be prepared for the astonishing scale that is so special in Utah's National Parks.

Left, a way of life in Capitol Reef National Park. **Right**, erosion patterns can be seen clearly in the rocks of Zion.

The very word "tundra" conjures an image of coldness, flatness, desert land or even waste land. The word really describes a kind of vegetation, an area with a specifically different ecosystem; it defines the land beyond the tree limit, whether in the North Pole or in the mountains. "Alpine Tundra" is delicate mountain land above the timberline in the Arctic regions of the North and South Pole. In both these areas, the vegetation and climate are similar. The flower-rich meadowland, which grows beyond the limit of trees,

mood of elation. The thin air holds less heat, making it about 30 degrees cooler than in the valley. Sunglasses, sunburn cream and plenty of warm clothing and good hiking boots are essential equipment if you plan to explore the tundra grasslands.

In "Lilliput" land: Tiny wild flowers struggle to survive under the severe weather conditions of cold, wind, snow and strong sun. Daisies in your garden may grow to be 3 feet (1 meter) tall, but here the same plant toils almost vainly to reach a height of about ⅓

is similar to a miniature "forest". The mammoth sky and towering mountains contrast significantly with the delicate microscopic tundra flowers.

In alpine tundra country, the contrast of the snow-capped mountains and the sky at this high altitude is intense. It's a deserted area with no trees, very few animals and nothing man-made – just you, the boulders and the mountains. Since there's twice as much ultra-violet radiation and 25 percent more light, the dazzling brightness confuses your perspective of scale, making distant mountains look much closer and more defined. The light gives the alpine tundra a

inch (1 cm) at full term. It's magical to come across one of these tundra grasslands – like being in Lilliput, where everything is so perfectly miniaturized. You will have to bend down low or even crawl on your belly to see up-close the tiny forest that exists at the tips of your toes.

Tundra is composed of various dwarfed shrubs, sedges, mosses, grasses and flowering plants. Even though these stunted living things can withstand rigorous and bitter winters accompanied by stormy summers, they are extremely fragile and delicate and should not be trampled. Sometimes, hundreds of years are required to achieve the growth you see. Flower buds begin growing a few years ahead to get a full bloom. They are usually well-formed by the end of the summer to protect themselves when the harsh Rocky Mountain winter sets in.

The plants are small and stay low to the ground. They can dodge the mountain wind, though they are still exposed to severe winters. As a group, alpine tundra have fewer and smaller leaves and fewer flowers. The grasslands themselves are spotty, the growth is thick in some areas and desert-like in others. Sedge turfs, however, are like thick, lush rugs and spaced sporadically over an area. The alpine flower, although it is so small, sometimes looks oversized in com-

parison with its leaves, because growth is only stunted at that portion of the plant below its flower.

The meadows abound in the Rocky Mountain region. Trailridge Road in the Rocky Mountain National Park has a tremendous view of tundra slopes, and just a few meters from the main road in the Rocky Mountain National Park are fields of tundra flowers. The Native Americans used this ridge as an east-west traverse across the Colorado mountains in the summer. The trail

Left, wild flowers are everywhere. **Above**, on the wagon in the Rockies.

is still clear, even though it as been unused for so many years. Tundra vegetation takes a very long time to recover from that type of traveling. More than a million people visit Trailridge Road each summer, and the visitor-pressure is hard on alpine tundra plants. Keep in mind that the plants are extremely delicate; if you step on them, they will be permanently damaged.

Summer in the tundra: As the growing season is short, the summer is a good time to enjoy the alpine tundra. When the sky is blue during July and August, the tundra is fresh, bright and beautiful, truly a visual delight. Some of the other easily accessible areas in the Rockies where you will see alpine tundra in summer are Independence Pass, the road from Red Lodge to Cook City in Montana, the northern entrance to Yellowstone, and most of the forests whose mountains rise above the timberline.

In these high elevations, few animals choose this environment for their home. Most of the larger animals leave the mountains during the winter, as grazing is poor. Smaller animals who have adapted to the harsh climate and stay through the year are the pocket gopher, meadow mole, mouse, shrew, marmot, pika and weasel.

A common small animal is the yellow-bellied marmot, a large rodent that looks like a woodchuck. On scenic turnoffs, you will spot these 2-ft-long (½ meter), 10-lb (5 kg) creatures being trained by tourists to beg for handouts. Although feeding them is not, as yet, prohibited, it interrupts their natural feeding cycle and can be harmful to them. Their long front teeth can be detrimental to you. Other friendly creatures, such as rock rabbit, chipmunk and pine squirrel also roam the tundra.

Most of the alpine areas do not have paved roads, trails or easy accessibility – one way in which the alpine tundra has been preserved. With the development of mountain tourism in modern times, trailbikes, snowmobiles, jeeps and four-wheeled vehicles have disrupted the peaceful tundra world. During winter and fall, the most delicate stages of the alpine plants, vehicle tracking can do permanent damage. Conservationists today fear the alpine tundra may become endangered. It would be sad if these tiny yet tenacious flowers were destroyed by the very people who come here to enjoy them.

NATIONAL MONUMENTS

The nationally preserved areas we know as National Parks and Monuments offer visitors a new perspective. These places, where nature still thrives, ensure that forthcoming generations will be able to enjoy these "islands of hope". National Monuments in the United States are unique places set aside for the preservation of one particular outstanding feature. Fifteen National Monuments located in the Rockies highlight both geologically and historically spectacular sights. All are worth a visit and a few are highlighted here.

North America's tallest sand dunes are preserved at the **Great Sand Dunes National Monument**. The Dunes are piled at the foot of the Sangre de Cristo Mountains, located in the San Luis Valley in South Central Colorado. A geological and recreational wonder, the Sand Dunes are formed as winds heap up billions of sand grains, building low sand hills against the mountains.

The essence of this place is to be found in the contrast of light and shadow, desert and forest, sky and dune, valley and mountain. Whether jumping off a dune peak, relaxing in the sand, or watching the sun go down behind the San Juans, visitors find the Sand Dunes truly magnificent.

In west-central Colorado, nature has sculpted 18,000 acres (7,285 hectares) of towering monoliths and strangely beautiful rock formations. Here in the **Uncompahgre Highlands**, the earth's crust has been worn down by constant erosion. Dinosaur bones, petrified logs, colorful stones and prehistoric Native American artifacts have been discovered in the canyon floors. The 22-mile (35-km) **Rim Rock Drive** goes around the walls of **Red, Ute, No Thoroughfare** and **Monument Canyons** and a scenic tour of the landscape.

At **Florissant Fossil Beds National Monument**, 40 miles (64 km) west of Colorado Springs, remains of fossil bones can be seen embedded in the rock. **Dinosaur National Monument** is located in the northeast corner of Colorado and stretches into the edge of Utah. Fossilized dinosaur remains are to be found here. The Quarry Visitors' Center, 20 miles (32 km) east of Vernal Utah, features a world-famous display of dinosaur fossils. The Center is open daily, all year round.

Located 23 miles (37 km) east of Cedar City, Utah, is **Cedar Breaks National Monument**, a natural ampitheater with limestone formations, mountain meadows, alpine flowers and picturesque scenery. A 6-mile (10-km) paved rim road encircles the fields and forests, affording numerous vistas of the Breaks.

One of the seven natural wonders of the world, **Rainbow Bridge National Monument** in Utah is the largest natural rock bridge on earth. The bridge reaches 290 ft (90 meters) in height and 270 ft (85 meters) across. Rainbow Bridge can be reached by foot or horseback, but the best approach to the monument is by boat on Lake Powell. Take the 50-mile (80-km) water route from Wahweep Marina to the landing in Bridge Canyon and walk half a mile (1 km) up to the bridge.

The three sandstone bridges (Kachina, Sipapu and Owachomo) forming **Natural Bridges National Monument** can be seen along a 8-mile (13-km) paved road 42 miles (67 km) west of Blanding, Utah. Museum exhibits and educational information are available at the visitors' center. A large photovoltaic solar system was installed to provide electricity to the monument's facilities. The system's 96 solar panels produce 130 HP (100 kilowatts) of electricity at peak power.

In south central Idaho, immense lava fields studded with cinder cones and huge central depressions form **Craters of the Moon National Monument**. The first US astronauts practiced their "moon walk" on this amazing landscape that resembles lunar craters. The 86-sq.-mile (220-sq.-km) volcanic National Monument is open for exploration. Naturalists at the visitors' center are also available to help you get acquainted with the area.

Big Hole National Monument, 12 miles (20 km) west of Wisdom, Montana, marks the site of a surprise attack on Chief Joseph and his Nez Perce tribe who evaded the army by setting fires and forcing the soldiers to retreat. The Monument is open from Labor Day to Memorial Day, when you can tour the battlefield and visit the Museum.

Another site history buffs will appreciate is the famed **Custer Battlefield National Monument**, 15 miles (24 km) from Hardin, Montana. Known as "Custer's Last Stand", the 1876 battle between Sioux and Cheyenne warriors and Lt. Col. George Armstrong Custer's troop of 225 men is the most famous Indian battle in US history. Walking along the bluffs that concealed Native American warriors from Custer's troops you will see the memorial graveyard of the unfortunate Seventh Cavalry.

In southwest Wyoming, the **Fossil Butte National Monument** proves that this part of the country was under water at one time. Rising 7,500 ft (2,285 meters) from Twin Creek Valley is a concentration of fossilized freshwater fish preserved in sandstone; this unique find became a National Monument in 1972.

Northeast Wyoming's **Devil's Tower National Monument** is a unique formation rising 1,280 ft (390 meters) above Belle Fourche River. The tower itself is 600 ft (182 meters) tall and is composed of phonolite, a volcanic rock, that rings when struck. It can be seen for nearly 100 miles (160 km) before reaching it. The Sioux Indians called the tower "Mapo Tipi" meaning "Bear Lodge". It is said that three young maidens were attacked by grizzly bears while picking flowers. The girls climbed on top of a large boulder for protection. (A sympathetic god had allowed the rock to grow.) The persistent bears never reached the top, but their claw prints can be seen as vertical grooves along the tower. After the bears left, the damsels lowered themselves from the rock with ropes of flowers. The famous chief, Sitting Bull, is said to have prayed atop "Mapo Tipi" many times for victory over the whites.

Great Sand Dunes National Monument (CO).

If you are like most travelers, you will enjoy taking home the reminders and evocative images which photographs of your trip can bring to mind. The Rockies cover a spectacularly varied region and there are endless possibilities for capturing on film scenery, wildlife and natural phenomena. Be prepared for this land of challenges, use your imagination creatively, and keep the following photo tips in mind when shooting in the Rockies.

Landscapes: Decide whether your photo

Wildlife: Keep your camera ready, stay at a safe, unobtrusive distance and be patient. A fixed telephoto or zoom lens would be ideal. In your car, a small bean-bag over the door frame (window open) makes a good lens support.

Best light: At dawn and dusk, when most animals feed.

Exposure: Set ahead of time (use a higher shutter speed (1/250th) and a wider aperture (f-8) to free yourself to concentrate on your subject.

will be wide angle or telephoto, or both. Choose a center of interest and compose the shot to accent that subject. (It is more interesting if you avoid always centering horizon and subjects.)

Best light: Sunrise, late afternoon and sunset. Side lighting is an excellent way to maximize drama. Be careful to avoid looking at the sun through the camera lens – it can cause eye damage.

Snow: Automatic light meters tend to underexpose snow and ice. Open the aperture a stop or two to compensate. If optical lens flare is an undesired effect, make sure the sun is not in the lens.

Wild flowers: Focus is critical when you are photographing delicate alpine wild flowers – and the depth of field gets shallower the closer you get to your subject. Use a macro lens for extreme closeups. A tripod isn't necessary if the wind is calm and the light adequate.

Best light: Early morning, late afternoon and shade. Remember, you can make your own shade!

People and events: For candid and action shots, pre-set exposure and approximate focus on your telephoto lens. Then browse, ready to catch an interesting face unaware. For a studied pose, windowlight and shade provide good portrait lighting. Indoors or out, use a portable flash when possible to ensure adequate lighting of your subject.

Architecture: Tilting up will cause distortion; when photographing monuments or buildings, you should try to keep your camera parallel to the ground. When possible, find a spot higher than the base of the building, and shoot from there.

Best light: Afternoon or morning. Accent the facade by throwing one side of the building in shade.

Overcast conditions: This is a great solution to taking portraits when you do not happen to have a flash at hand. Many subjects which do not photograph very well in sunlight can

Storms: The breaking or clearing of a storm brings forth the elusive rainbow. If you are patient, the resulting photograph will be highly dramatic.

Fog: Take advantage of this condition. For some cities and landscapes, fog is an essential part of the local flavor; forests particularly take on a new dimension in fog.

Night shots: To photograph night fairs, festivals or floodlit buildings, bracket from ½ second to 1/125 second exposure at a wide aperture (f-L 1.5). Cities are best photographed just after the sun has set. When shooting landscapes lit by the full moon, use a tripod and try 30-second, one-minute, two-minute, and four-minute exposures.

make excellent subjects when shot under overcast skies.

Rain: You can capture raindrops during the daylight when the background is dark, or illustrate the reflecting neon signs in wet city streets at night. In rainy weather, always carry an umbrella to protect your equipment, or put the camera in a loose plastic bag, with an open hole around the filter, with the lens poking through.

Left, focus close-up with a powerful lens to capture the alpine tundra. Above, Yellowstone Canyon provides the ideal view for aspiring and professional photographers.

Aerial: A small plane or helicopter, with the door removed or window opened is a successful way to photograph. If you plan to shoot through windows, be sure to clean them before leaving the ground, and shoot out of the shady side of the plane. Use a high shutter speed (1/250 or 1/500) and focus on infinity. Slower films (ASA 64 or 100) give best results. Use your body to absorb any vibrations and remember to keep your horizon straight.

Rivers and waterfalls: Long exposures (¹/₈ second or longer) produce a fluid motion image when shooting fast-moving water. Use a tripod at slow shutter speeds.

COLORADO'S FRONT RANGE

The Continental Divide, which runs the length of two vast continents, is an effective population and weather barrier. Nowhere is this better demonstrated than in the Rockies of Colorado. The Front Range, as the eastern slope of the Rockies in Colorado is called, is where the mountains end and the plains begin. The Front Range is a booming megalopolis that extends from Pueblo in the south, through the cities of Colorado Springs, Denver, Boulder, Longmont, Greeley and Fort Collins, near the Wyoming border. As soon as the foothills begin to rise to the west this densely settled area gives way to huge expanses of wilderness and small mountain towns.

Though Denver is a mile (1.6 km) high, the weather is considerably balmier there than it is just a few miles away, up in the mountains. Most of the storms that regularly drop a foot or two of glistening powder snow on the ski slopes have used up all their moisture in the mountains by the time they reach the Front Range. Denver receives only 8 to 15 inches (38 cm) of precipitation each year, about the same as Los Angeles, and has as many sunny days a year (over 300) as Miami. Summers can be hot, but the low humidity keeps it relatively comfortable.

Tent town: The white man's history of settlement on the Front Range is little more than a century old. Lieutenant Zebulon Pike got part-way up the peak named after him in 1806, but he and his men followed the eastern slope of the Rockies south, never really broaching the mountains. In 1849, when hundreds of people were migrating west in the Gold Rush to California, Denver was still a quiet valley belonging to the Ute Indians and a handful of itinerant mountain men. A few of the mountain men, such as Jedediah Smith and Bill Williams, had penetrated the Colorado Rockies while they were trapping beaver, but most of the trapping expeditions and explorations were concentrated to the north in the Wind River Range of Wyoming.

The first gold strike at Cherry Creek in 1859 attracted enough miners to create a small tent town where Denver now stands, but it was the rich lode found at Clear Creek a year later that brought 15,000 people to the area in a matter of months, and over 50,000 within a year, in the famous "Pike's Peak or Bust" gold rush. These immigrants eventually settled along the length of the Front Range in Colorado, and from there made forays into the mountain widernesses to look for the golden ore that would make them rich.

Growing pains: It took only a few years for ambitious Denverites to create a reasonably well-governed, though somewhat wild city, complete with a mayor, aldermen, police and street commissioner. A commercial section of the city was established around what is Larimer Square today, and a residential section was built, complete with ornate Victorian homes. After a fire in 1863, wooden buildings were forbidden, and impressive brick structures replaced

Preceding pages: Denver's downtown Civic Center. Left, Denver is the metropolitan center of the Rockies. Below, "Unsinkable Molly Brown's" house.

them. But in spite of the enthusiasm of the town fathers, the Denver area went through a major slump for nearly a decade after the first gold strike. Colorado was too isolated, the ore was too difficult to get out of the mountains for refining, the necessary milling machinery too expensive to import, and marauding Native Americans were scaring away many potential settlers. The Native Americans were taken care of by a series of massacres that all but exterminated the Rocky Mountain tribes.

The problem of isolation was finally solved when the Denver Pacific and Union Pacific railway lines were completed in 1870. These branches from Kansas City and Cheyenne created another, though smaller, boom in Denver when towns sprang up along the line. These first railway lines fueled further entrepreneurship, and by the early 1880s, the Denver, Rio Grande and Sante Fe railroads had laid nearly 2,000 miles of regional track along the Front Range and into the mountains.

It was the discovery of silver in Lead-ville that put Colorado back on the map for another decade. Those mines, which earned $11.5 million in 1880, and others that opened up on the Western Slope attracted another wave of immigrants to the area. Denver, the gateway to the Rockies, reaped many benefits from the silver rush. Other industries grew as well. Huge stands of timber were cut for building mine shafts, and coal was mined in great quantities to fuel locomotives and warm homes. Once the Easterners learned how to use irrigation ditches, agriculture thrived in Greeley, Longmont and Fort Collins. Cattle ranching became established in eastern Colorado. The University of Colorado was organized in 1877, to be followed by Colorado Agricultural College, the University of Denver, and the Colorado School of Mines. Pueblo became a center for smelting. These were the industries that continued to carry Colorado economically through the 1950s.

Early sightseers: Thanks to the railroad, the Rockies attracted tourists early on. An estimated 200,000 people traveled

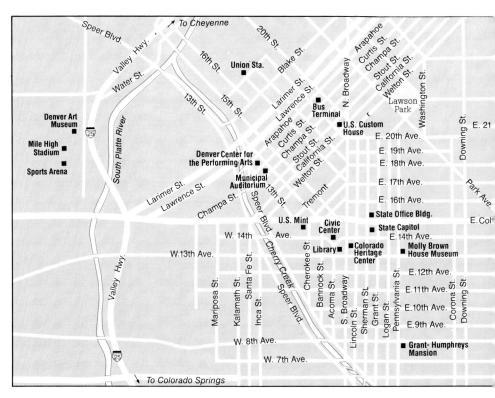

to Colorado in 1878 to see its scenic wonders. Among the more popular spots were Idaho Springs, which had a first-class hotel and hot springs for the health-oriented; the Hotel de Paris and a scenic narrow-gauge railway trip in Georgetown; the Stanley Hotel in Estes Park; and the famous health spa of Colorado Springs, with its sumptuous Broadmoor Hotel, wealthy clientele, and invigorating mineral hot springs. In fact, the dry, crisp mountain air and numerous hot springs made Colorado a major destination for tuberculosis victims and others with respiratory illnesses. Dude ranches also thrived, and to lure ever more visitors, Colorado's business community dreamt up large numbers of celebrations and festivals.

With the Silver Panic of 1893, the Front Range went through yet another slump but was once again bailed out by the discovery of gold at Cripple Creek – the richest strike ever made in the United States. By this time the town fathers of Denver had learned the value of boosterism, and they poured their new wealth into parks, trees, fountains, statues, curbed streets, a capitol building, and a civic center – the wild, muddy, disreputable boom town was becoming respectable.

Mile-high city: Through the early part of the 20th century, until after World War II, Denver was little more than a sprawling cow town – quiet and stable, with little of the growth, glitter, and glamour of a big city. When the energy boom hit, Denver turned out to be in the perfect location to take advantage of it. In addition to being the geographical headquarters for the West's massive coal reserves and oil shale deposits, the climate was good, and there was plenty of room for housing and industry. It wasn't long before the Front Range became a leading area for solar research, thermal power and wind power. Many oil exploration companies moved their headquarters to the growing city, along with major corporations such as IBM, Kodak, John Mansville, and Frito Lay. The latest boom has been in the hi-tech industries, turning the Front Range into

The fabulous Arts Center Mall.

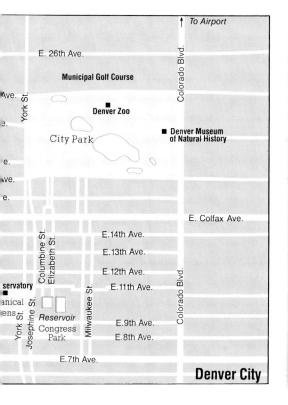

Denver City

the Silicon Valley of the Rockies. The federal government has a huge complex in west Denver, giving the city the second highest number of federal employees in the nation.

All this meant tremendous growth for Denver from the mid-70s to the mid-80s. By the late 1980s, Denver was in a mild recession although a new $126 million convention center and the world's largest airport show the city's optimism for the future – a 30 percent increase in population, 16 new skyscrapers, and a sense of cultural and economic well-being. The majority of the people who have moved to the Denver metro area are young and well-educated – Colorado's capital city has one of the youngest median ages and highest percentage of college graduates in the United States.

Garden greens: For the most part, Denver is an easy and pleasant city to live in. Parks were built in abundance from the very beginning and, as a result, there are 205 of them in Denver alone, and 20,000 acres (8,000 hectares) of

mountain parks are operated by the city. Cherry Creek and the South Platte River, which run through the heart of Denver, are lined with bicycling and jogging trails. Pedestrian skywalks and bridges make it possible to get around the downtown area without fighting traffic.

Most people en route to the Rockies at least drive through Denver, but it's well worth it to stop and spend a couple of days exploring the city itself. There's no better place to begin to get a sense of the history and development of the Rocky Mountains than Denver. The downtown area is spanking new, clean, and full of exciting shops and museums. The mountains that keep Denver's climate mild also create weather patterns that allow air to settle into the valley. That, coupled with the city's high altitude, creates a high level of carbon monoxide, a colorless, odorless gas. The city government has gone to great lengths to encourage residents and visitors to take public transportation, walk, ride bicycles – anything but drive a car. Free shuttle buses leave both ends of the 16th **Denver city skyline.**

Street Mall (at a mile, one of the longest pedestrian malls in the country) about every 90 seconds, putting the entire downtown area within easy walking distance.

A walk downtown: The best place to begin a tour of a capitol city is, of course, the **State Capitol** building. On the 13th step is a marker informing you that you are exactly one mile high. Denver calls itself the Mile-High City for obvious geographical reasons, but after a few days there it will become apparent that the young city is as high on itself and as full of itself as a college freshman. Ninety-three steps up into the Capitol rotunda is an open-air deck with fabulous views of the city and the Front Range. On a clear day it's possible to see the Rockies from the Wyoming border south to Pike's Peak, a distance of about 150 miles (240 km).

This view will also give a good feel for the layout of the city, which can be confusing at first. Outside of the downtown area, the streets run north-south and east-west like most cities, but sud-denly in the downtown area they seem to go every which way. It's thought that when General Larimer laid out the city streets in 1858, he pointed them at Long's Peak, which rises 14,000 ft (4,000 meters) to the northwest, giving them a northwest-southeast orientation. The impressive building with the white pillars directly in front of the Capitol is Denver's **City and County Building**. In a tradition that goes back to the turn of the century, the Christmas lighting display on and around the City and County Building rivals anything in the world. Between the Capitol and the City and County Building lies **Civic Center Park**, with large expanses of green lawns, gardens and shade trees – a nice place to rest the feet and stroll.

A short detour to the east of the State Capitol building is the **Molly Brown House and Museum**, an outstanding example of the way the upper middle classes lived at the turn of the century. Molly Tobin followed her brother to Leadville in 1884, where she met and married J. J. Brown. It was after the

Wintertime in Georgetown.

Browns moved to Denver that Molly sailed on the ill-fated voyage of the *Titanic*. According to legend she herded a group of immigrant women and children into a lifeboat. Dressed in a chinchilla cape and waving a small pistol she always carried, she kept the men at the oars rowing until rescue ships arrived, earning herself the nickname of "The Unsinkable Molly Brown". Between the 13th and 8th avenues on or just off Pennsylvania Street are more than 40 historical houses and mansions dating from the turn of the century.

Museums and dioramas: Going back to the State Capitol area, a block south of the Civic Center Park is the **Colorado History Museum** which details Colorado's colorful past from the ancient Anasazi Indians, who lived at Mesa Verde, to the space-age skyscrapers that tower above the city. The highlight of the museum is the dioramas depicting old forts, Native Americans on a buffalo hunt, gold mining, and a particularly large and superbly crafted one of Denver as it appeared in 1860 before it was destroyed by fire and flood. This is also the place to see some of the finest old glass plate photographs ever taken of the West, in the collection of William Henry Jackson's work.

Heading west, around the Denver Public Library, is the **Denver Art Museum** designed by Gio Ponti of Italy. The 28-sided structure with a Corning gray glass tile "skin" and fortress-like roof is a work of art itself. It houses what may be the finest collection of Native American art in the world, as well as a complete range of other art exhibits. For those with a penchant for money and museums, this walking tour can be continued to the west and north, back towards the 16th Street Mall, to the **United States Mint** (free tours but no free samples), the **Denver Firefighters Museum** and the **Trianon Art Museum and Gallery**, which has a fine collection of 18th- and 19th-century furniture and art from all over the world.

At 17th and Tremont streets is the triangular **Brown Palace Hotel**, a *grande dame* hotel built in 1892. Even if

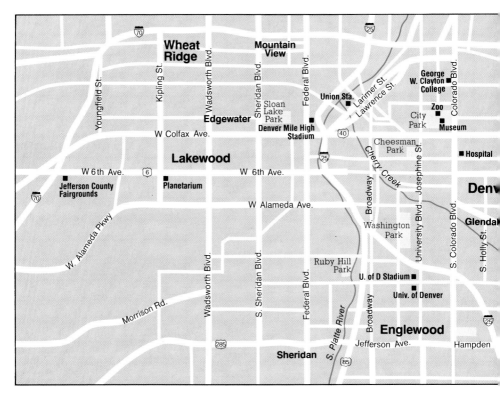

you don't stay there, it's worth a look at the nine-story atrium, topped by a Tiffany stained-glass window, and the sumptuous lobby. You can still see the entrance to a tunnel that once led across the street to Denver's fanciest bordello and gambling hall, the Navarre. The tunnel was constructed so that Denver's finest couldn't be spotted entering that notorious den of iniquity. The Navarre now houses the new **Museum of Western Art**, a treasure trove of paintings and sculptures by such renowned western artists as O'Keefe, Remington, Russell, Moran and Bierstadt.

Street mall shopping: The 16th Street Mall is the place for shopping, even if just window shopping, and perhaps some espresso at an outdoor cafe. Denver is justifiably proud of the new glass-enclosed **Tabor Center**, an architectural triumph filled with fancy shops and restaurants. Street musicians, jugglers, fountains, banners, hanging plants and brick walkways give the whole area a festive air. At the north end of the mall is the historical **Larimer Square**, where

it all began in Denver. There are 18 renovated Victorian buildings, gas lamps, and an atmosphere reminiscent of Denver's early days. Larimer Square's Oktoberfest is a rollicking festival patterned after the one in Munich.

Yet another centerpiece of a glittering and sophisticated new Denver is the **Center for the Performing Arts**, the most complete performing arts center in the country, located a few blocks southwest of Larimer Square. The space age architecture is dazzling, and the **Boetteher Concert Hall** in-the-round is the first of its kind in the United States. The complex is larger than Lincoln Center in New York City. It houses four theaters, the nation's largest resident acting company, a film center, and one of the most advanced recording and voice research centers in the world.

Other roadside attractions: Three miles (4½ km) east of downtown Denver is the outstanding **Museum of Natural History**. As expected in a natural history museum, there are dozens of dioramas of animals from all over the world,

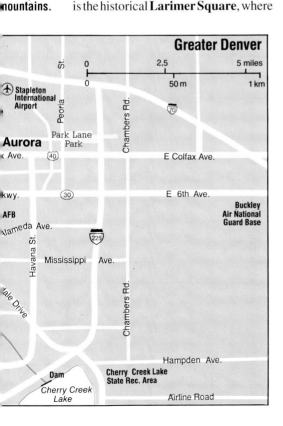

Greater Denver

including many Colorado species. But for kids – both old and young – the **Gates Planetarium** and the new IMAX **Theater** are a special treat. You don't just look at solar systems and galaxies in the planetarium, you travel to them. If that doesn't take you far enough into space, stick around for one of the laser light shows. In the IMAX Theater are 30 specially designed speakers, the biggest movie projector made, and a large story screen, all of which combine to make you see, hear and feel the movies as if you were actually there – heaven on earth for movie buffs and hi-techno-philes. Across City Park from the museum is **Denver's Zoo.**

For plant lovers the **Denver Botanic Gardens** have a nice selection of orchids and tropical plants as well as many special outdoor gardens. The Rock Alpine Garden is a great place to get a head start on identifying some of the plants you'll be seeing in the mountains.

Denver also has its share of amusement parks. **Elitch Gardens**, east of downtown, is the oldest and biggest, with a roller coaster rated among the nation's top 10, a beautiful old carousel, and a summer stock theater named the **Elitch Theater Company**. It's a pretty place, with plenty of flower gardens, fountains and pools. Others include **Lakeside Amusement Park**, north of Elitch, and **Heritage Square** in Golden, 12 miles (19 km) west of Denver, which has a reconstructed Colorado city from the 1870s, a narrow-gauge railroad and an alpine slide.

Coloradans, and Denverites in particular, are loyal and often fanatical fans of the Denver Bronco football team, which plays its home games in **Mile High Stadium**, located just west of the downtown area off Colfax Avenue. In fact, thanks to sellout attendance, lusty Colorado vocal cords, and inadvertently good acoustics, the stadium has the highest recorded crowd noise level in the country. For sports fans, there is **MacNichols Arena** where the Nuggets play basketball and the Flames play hockey, two dog racking tracks, and a horse racing track.

The fact that Denver is a major trade center for ranching is never more evident than in January when the National Western Stock Show brings thousands of cowboys into town for 10 days of rodeo, exhibits, shows and auctions.

Denver after dark: There are more than 2,000 restaurants in Denver, and, as in any big city, there's a little bit of everything and a few regional specialties. Steak is the most obvious specialty, but buffalo and venison are also frequently found on menus. Rocky Mountain rainbow trout is especially good provided it's fresh – be sure to ask before ordering. Mexican food is Denver's international specialty, but the best authentic Mexican food is often found in unlikely looking neighborhood dives rather than the slick, downtown spots.

It's easy to dance the night away in Denver, thanks to an unusual zoning situation in **Glendale**, southeast of downtown Denver, that has a concentrated cluster of discos, saloons and restaurants in an area served by one vast parking lot. Live club bands playing rock, country and swing, they're all

Left, the Hotel Imperial in Cripple Creek has a western atmosphere. **Below**, gliders near Pike's Peak.

there, from the glitter to the funk, with some uniquely Denver touches like two outdoor volleyball courts. Some other spots in the Denver metro area with a concentration of nightlife can be found along East Hampden Boulevard, South Parker Road, South Monaco Boulevard, and on East and West Colfax.

Outdoor concerts are something special at **Red Rocks Amphitheatre**, 12 miles (19 km) west of Denver. The 8,000 seats are built into a natural amphitheater of red rock walls that rise 400 ft (122 meters) on two sides, with a great view of Denver on a third side. Most of the top-name artists featured play pop, rock and country and western, but the surrounding sandstone has also reverberated with the sounds of classical music and jazz.

South of Denver: The southernmost city in the Front Range is **Pueblo**, about 100 miles (160 km) south of Denver. This diminutive little city began its life as a trading post, conveniently located at the confluence of a number of trails coming out of the mountains and at the conflu-

ence of the Arkansas and Fountain rivers. Before New Mexico became a part of the United States, it was also the first watering-hole north of the border, not far from Taos. When the Rio Grande railroad was routed through Pueblo, it became one of the largest ore smelting towns in the country, and to this day it remains a large industrial city with the Colorado Fuel and Iron Mills (CF&I) the largest employer in the county. Pueblo is also a trading center for the agricultural and ranching areas which surround it, but it remains something of a political, social and economic backwash. It's here that the adobe buildings of the southwest begin to appear, evidence of a large Hispanic population that increases as one goes south.

The high point of the year in Pueblo is the Colorado State Fair, held for 10 days in the last week of August through Labor Day. Thousands of people from all over the West come for the rodeo, horse racing and all the other attractions that go along with a state fair.

Sangre de Cristo: There are some beautiful drives through the San Juan mountains to the east and south of Pueblo. At Walsenburg, south of Pueblo, State Highway 160 follows the Cucharas River, then forks. State 12 to the south continues along the river, through a series of mountain valleys, the small Spanish village of La Veta, over Cucharas Pass, and back down into arid lowlands. State 160 heads for **Great Sand Dunes National Monument**, an anomaly in the verdant San Luis Valley. The 10-mile (16-km) stretch of multihued, shifting sand can be explored either by foot or by jeep. **Medano Creek**, which flows along the east side of the dunes, is a particularly pleasant spot to hike or just cool the feet.

From Walsenburg it's possible to head for Pueblo, Colorado Springs or Denver by back roads. One of the most scenic roads is via State 69, which goes northwest through the Huerfano River Valley and the San Isabel National Forest. (Ask at Walsenburg first about the road, since a section of it is gravel.) Just outside of Gardner is Gardner Cone, a large standing rock surrounded on two sides by

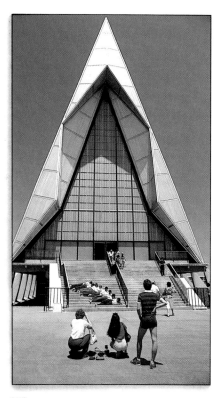

Families pose at the Air Force Academy chapel.

piñon trees. The sweet, rich piñon nuts which ripen in the fall are a delicacy. From Gardner the road climbs to **Promontory Divide** with magnificent views of Crestone Peak and the Crestone Needles, part of the Sangre de Cristo (Blood of Christ) mountain range. To the north is the green **Wet Mountain Valley**. The valleys on either side of this divide provide a study in cultural contrasts: the Huerfano river valley is largely Hispanic, with adobe buildings. In the Wet Mountain Valley, which was settled by Europeans, mostly Germans, are white wooden farmhouses and red barns.

At **Westcliffe**, a classic Western ranching town, turn east on to State 96. Silver Cliff was once Colorado's third largest town, but faded as quickly as it grew in the boom-and-bust mining days. This route goes back to Pueblo, or take State 67 north to Florence and Canon City (covered in the "Canyon Country" chapter of this guide).

Colorado Springs: Until World War II, Colorado Springs was a pretty and wealthy little town. Then business lead-

ers decided the bloom might eventually fade from the tourist rose and invited the military to settle there, luring them with 35,000 free acres (14,000 hectares). The military came in full force, first with **Fort Carson**, then with **Ent Air Force Base,** headquarters of the North American Air Defense Command, which dug itself into a massive and expensive cave in the side of Cheyenne Mountain. The last military branch to move in was the **Air Force Academy**, which, for the military, is unusually imaginative architecturally. One of the highlights of the Air Force Base is the falcon training. Beautiful falcons are raised (some from eggs) and trained by cadets. They perform often at the football games. Visitors can tour some of the buildings of the academy and watch the Cadet Wing march to lunch every weekday at noon.

Today Colorado Springs is an odd combination of unchecked urban sprawl, tourist traps, old castles and mansions, and lovely, exclusive neighborhoods. There are literally dozens of attractions from the **Hall of the Presidents Wax**

wo Air Force adets show ow to train lcons.

Museum and the **Cheyenne Mountain Zoo** to the **American Numismatic Museum** (of old coins, medals, etc.) and Flying W. Chuckwagon Supper and Western Show. The **Van Briggle Pottery Studio** conducts pottery demonstrations and tours of the studio throughout the day. **Seven Falls** and the **Western Museum of Mining and Industry** are two attractions that should also be included in your itinerary. The high points of the natural attractions include the **Garden of the Gods**, 700 acres (280 hectares) of huge standing rocks the Utes believed were invading giants turned to stone by the Great Manitou, and of course **Pike's Peak.**

Pike's Peak Country: Cripple Creek and Colorado Springs can be approahed from Canon City by a dirt road that's a continuation of State 67 – ask first in Canon City about road conditions, though. On the backside of **Pike's Peak**, nestled in a valley created by a long-extinct volcano, is one of Colorado's most famous towns. **Cripple Creek** was the site of one of the largest gold strikes in the world and once supported a population of about 50,000. It now hovers between the status of a ghost town and a tourist attraction, uncertain of its identity but possessing a quiet charm. Some of the residents still remember the old mining days, others have moved there for the small-town atmosphere and the beauty of the surrounding mountains.

A narrow-gauge train passes through the deserted mining camps that surround Cripple Creek, on its way to Anaconda, one of the largest of the old mines. At the Mollie Kathleen gold mine it's possible to descend 1,000 ft (300 meters) in a miner's cage, to see the conditions the early miners worked in and the equipment they used. There's still plenty of gold around too. A couple of places in Cripple Creek give gold panning lessons – you never know, you might strike it rich!

The **Imperial Hotel** is a good reason to spend the night in Cripple Creek. The only original Cripple Creek hotel still standing, the Imperial has many of its original furnishings. But the high point **Waterplay in the hot springs of Colorado.**

of a stay there is the **Victorian Melodrama Theatre** (when the villain appears the audience hisses), one of the best in the country.

Like so many Rocky Mountain towns, **Colorado Springs** began as a mining town, but it soon became Colorado's first and finest destination resort, a haven for the wealthy seeking health and beauty or a cure for respiratory illnesses in the dry mountain air and hot mineral springs at the "Saratoga of the West". Railroad magnate William Jackson Palmer literally created the town in the 1870s, envisioning it as a Utopia inhabited by teetotaling, well-to-do, educated citizens. Thanks to some judicious advertising there was a healthy English population in the town, giving it snob appeal. By the early 1900s the town had begun to open its door to tourists of all classes, a change initiated through the efforts of Spencer Penrose, a wealthy developer and one-man chamber of commerce. In the span of a decade he had an auto road and a cog railway built to the top of Pike's Peak; constructed

the Cheyenne Mountain Highway; bought and renovated the Broadmoor Hotel and Casino; built a zoo, a polo field, an indoor arena and donated libraries and civic buildings.

Manitou Springs is an old spa town perched in a valley above Colorado Springs, near the mineral springs whose name it bears. Many of its houses and streets hug the steep hillsides, and much of the original Victorian architecture remains. In terms of attractions, Manitou Springs is essentially an extension of Colorado Springs, with its **Buffalo Bill Wax Museum, Miramont Castle, Cave of the Winds** and the cable car ride to the top of **Mount Manitou**. The cog railway to the top of Pike's Peak begins at Manitou Springs.

There are two back roads through the mountains from Colorado Springs to Denver, both very scenic. Either continue on State 67 or on narrow, winding State 24 then north on State 285, which is a major road.

North and west of Denver: The metropolis of the Front Range in Colorado

ountain
affic twists
rough a
cky pass.

extends north from Denver to Fort Collins, only about 50 miles (80 km) from the Wyoming border and Cheyenne. **Golden,** just west of Denver, is best known for the **Coors Brewery**. Free tours – and samples – are available. Above Golden on Lookout Mountain is **Buffalo Bill Cody's Grave and Museum**, with lots of interesting memorabilia and history, and excellent views of Denver. Railroad buffs will enjoy the **Colorado Railroad Museum**, also located in Golden. Nearby **Evergreen** is a quiet, attractive little town, mainly catering to people who have second homes there, including a few celebrities. **Evergreen Lake** is a pleasant place for swimming and boating in the summer and ice-skating in the winter.

One of the most scenic loop drives in Colorado begins in Golden on State 6, which winds up Clear Creek Canyon along an old railroad bed and through many short, dark tunnels. State 119, which branches off to the right leads to Central City and a back road to Boulder through Rollinsville and Nederland.

Central City is one of the best preserved of the old Rocky Mountain mining towns. The huge strike there was nearly Denver's undoing when most of the population dropped whatever they were doing to head for the "richest square mile on earth". Many of those who struck it rich built the impressive and picturesque stone and brick buildings that still perch on the sides of the narrow valley. The narrow streets, plank sidewalks and beautifully renovated buildings are very effective in taking the traveler back in time. The **Teller House**, where President Grant, Oscar Wilde, Baron de Rothschild and a host of other rich and famous names once stayed, is a Historic Landmark hotel and a great place to spend the night or just to have a good meal at very reasonable prices. Don't miss the famous **Face Bar**, featuring Madeleine's face on the bar room floor. The Opera House next door has a dinner theater during the winter months, and in July an opera company with some outstanding productions does a short season there.

The Garden of the Gods, Manitou Springs.

True to the rollicking Rocky Mountain spirit, Central City holds a no-holds-barred celebration in June called Madam Lou Bunch Day in honor of the "sporting house girls" of a bygone era. The Original Bed Race is held on Main Street, and in the evening locals and visitors alike don their finest attire for the Madam and Miners Ball.

Backtracking to Interstate 70, **Idaho Springs** was first a mining town, then a health spa, centered around the hot springs which once brought Ute Indians from near and far. The **Indian Springs Resort** is the place to enjoy the healing hot water of the springs, which are funneled through two tunnels underneath the hotel, one for men and one for women. It's also possible to rent a private bath. The hotel is not fancy, the rates are low, and there are often good country bands playing there on the weekends.

About 20 miles (32 km) west of Idaho Spring off I-70 is **Georgetown**, yet another well-preserved old mining town with quiet, narrow streets, well-preserved Victorian buildings and a host of gift shops. The narrow-gauge railway, the Georgetown loop, runs a precipitous route between Georgetown and Silver Plume, and it is among the best of the narrow-gauge rides in the state. A narrow, switchbacking road just north of town (not for the faint of heart) leads up to **Guanella Pass** through a number of Rocky Mountain life zones from lush green meadows and aspen groves, through conifer forests, to the sparse vegetation of the alpine tundra at the top. This is an excellent drive for plant lovers and for day hikes to the surrounding peaks.

Boulder: Until just a few decades ago, Boulder was a quiet little university town with few paved roads and lots of scenic views. Then the natural beauty of the setting and the convenience of a large university attracted NCAR (the National Center for Atmospheric Research), IBM, the Ball Corporation, Rockwell International and a dozen other large, clean-industry corporations. Neodata Services takes care of

Window shopping in Central City.

subscriptions for dozens of national magazines. Many medium-sized hi-tech electronics firms have located in Boulder, and the city is overflowing with small publishing houses. Celestial Seasonings went from a home-style operation to a major corporation in less than five years and radically changed the tea-drinking habits of Americans.

Boulder is also a cross-section of the West in that it's perceived as a place of opportunity and a young, energetic, optimistic town. The prevailing open-minded attitudes of the populace have encouraged the growth of holistic health clinics, health food stores and other hall-marks of alternative lifestyles which proliferate and thrive in Boulder along-side a passion for the latest in hi-tech, from electronics to bicycle parts.

The arts thrive in Boulder. The Colo-rado Music Festival sponsors classical concerts in the outdoor amphitheater at **Chautauqua** every summer, but there is also a year-round philharmonic orches-tra, half a dozen theaters including the university-sponsored Shakespeare Fes-tival in the summer, a mime school, bands, chamber choirs, a center for the visual arts, and dozens of galleries – the **White Horse Gallery** is nationally known for its collection of Native Ameri-can and Western art.

Back at Idaho Springs is State 40, one end of the famous **Peak to Peak High-way**, a long and spectacular road over Berthoud Pass, past Berthoud Ski Area, Winter Park Ski Area, through Granby and past the Great Lakes of Colorado – **Grand Lake, Shadow Mountain**, and **Granby Reservoir** (see "Mountain Towns" for more details). From Granby the road becomes State 34 and follows the North Fork of the Colorado River through the green and lovely Kawuneeche Valley, up to Rocky Mountain National Park and Trail Ridge Road, the highest paved road in America. From there the road descends to Estes Park, back to the Front Range.

Estes Park is the gateway to Rocky Mountain National Park, a busy little Western town in the summer. The beauty of the valley, which is surrounded by the snowcapped peaks of the Continental Divide, is unmatched. In the late 1800s the Earl of Dunraven purchased the Estes Park valley with hopes of making it a big game hunting park and preserving its natural beauty. His dream didn't come true, but a few years later, thanks largely to the strenuous efforts of naturalist Enos Mills, **Rocky Mountain National Park** (for details, see the "Rocky Mountain National Park" chapter) was officially established. On winter weekends hundreds of Coloradans head for Estes Park and the mountains above for cross-country skiing.

A pleasant stop en route to Wyoming is **Fort Collins**, a busy, pretty, unspoiled little city that did indeed begin as a fort. But for most of its life, Fort Collins has been a prosperous agricultural and university city. The sugar beet industry first put it on the map and **Colorado State University** adds a touch of sophistication.

From old-time music halls and min-ing towns, to bustling cities, you'll find it all in Colorado's Front Range – the most exciting part of the state.

Below, Garden of the Gods in Colorado Springs. Right, canoeing on Grand Lake.

COLORADO MOUNTAIN TOWNS

The Continental Divide and its mountain ranges occupy two-thirds of the state of Colorado, making most communities on the western slope mountain towns. The following tour will encompass the highlights – the most picturesque, historically interesting and scenic mountain towns of Colorado, as well as some particularly panoramic back roads.

Back roads are for the adventurous – dirt or gravel roads in the Rockies should be approached with caution. Ruts, washboards and washouts can be rough on any vehicle. Sturdiness, reliability and reasonably high axles are a must for all of the back roads mentioned in this section. High water at creek crossings and mud slides can also be a problem. Ask locally before traveling on them and start off with a full tank of gas.

There's a certain amount of etiquette involved in traveling on back roads; uphill vehicles have the right of way on narrow roads; closed gates should always be securely refastened; slow down for horseback riders and hikers – some horses aren't used to traffic, and nobody likes to eat the dust raised by cars.

Never drive off the road; alpine tundra and meadows are delicate and may take decades to recover from tire scars. It's illegal to pick columbine flowers; they're on the endangered species list, and besides, they wilt almost immediately after picking and so will you when you could be fined $300 for doing so.

The Great Lakes of Colorado: One of the best ways to begin a tour of the Colorado Rockies is with Rocky Mountain National Park (dealt with in detail in the National Parks section).

Granby and its surrounding lakes are the southwestern gateway to the park. The log buildings around the lakes are mostly summer homes. At one time, Granby was a year-round supply depot for miners prospecting in the surrounding mountains. Grand Lake, Shadow Mountain Reservoir, Lake Granby and

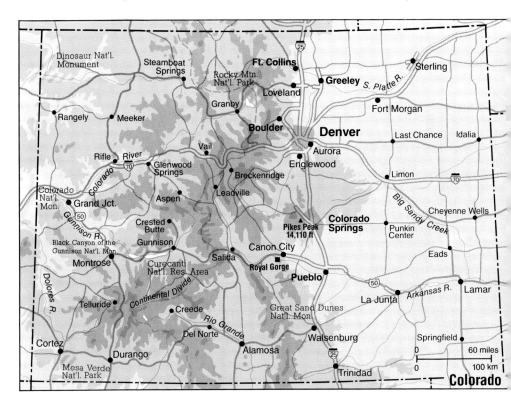

the Willow Creek Reservoir are a series of interconnected lakes known as the "Great Lakes of Colorado".

Grand Lake, the highest yacht anchorage in the United States, is dotted with boats all summer and, frequently, a regatta of some sort is going on, sponsored by the local yacht club. Windsurfer, sailboat and motorboat rentals are available.

A number of legends haunt Grand Lake, which is called Spirit Lake by the Utes. According to one legend, when the Utes were attacked by the Cheyenne and Arapahoes, they sent their women and children out to the middle of the lake on a large raft for safekeeping. During one great battle, the Utes won, but a violent thunderstorm created a maelstrom of wind and waves on the lake, drowning all the women and children. The mists that rise on the lake are, legend says, the restless spirits of those women and children.

South of Granby, US Highway 40 goes either southeast to the ski area of Winter Park, or northwest through Hot Sulphur Springs to Steamboat Springs. This is a spectacular drive, first along the uppermost reaches of the great Colorado River, past the mining and ranching town of Kremmling, then a steady climb up and over Rabbit Ears Pass (look for the rock formation that gave the pass its name) to descend into the Yampa Valley and Steamboat.

Cowboy country: Steamboat Springs is a divided town in more ways than one. At one end is the ski mountain and the dense clusters of condominiums and shops that surround the base. A few miles down the road, one arrives in Steamboat Springs proper, a genuine one-street western town with the attendant cowboys, farmers and saloons.

A series of ads sponsored by a condominium development company which included the promise that they would "take the cowboy hat off Steamboat" was met with little enthusiasm by locals and visitors – Steamboat's cowboy image is an integral part of its charm.

Seasonal celebrations, such as the Winter Carnival during the second week

of February, have the usual resort-style parades and races, but are particularly fun because of enthusiastic local participation in such events as a cross-country skiing and muzzle loading biathalon, and ski-joring contests down Main Street in which the contestant on skis is towed by a galloping horse.

Winter and summer, something's always happening at the city recreation complex on the edge of town, which has a ski jumping complex, ice-skating rink, rodeo grounds, tennis courts, softball, rugby and soccer fields and a racetrack. A ride up the gondola at the ski area provides panoramic views of the mountains to the north and east, and the Flat Tops Wilderness to the southwest.

Good jumping-off points for hikers are to the north at Slavonia or at the South Fork of the Elk campgrounds at the edge of the Zirkel Wilderness, **Hahns Peak Village**, 24 miles (40 km) north on State Highway 129, is an old gold mining camp that was once the Routt County seat. Nearby are a host of campgrounds and **Steamboat Lake**, which is apt to be dotted with colorful sails in the summer. The Yampa and Elk rivers provide good fishing, kayaking and tubing. **Fish Creek Falls** is a 283-ft-high (85-meter) series of waterfalls. To get there, take Third Street to Fish Creek Falls Road, then drive 4 miles (6 km) east. As the name indicates there are a number of hot springs around Steamboat. Ask at the Chamber of Commerce for those that are open to the public.

South of Steamboat, State 131 winds along the Yampa River through a beautiful ranching valley. **Oak Creek** used to be inhabited by a large hippie population that mingled somewhat uneasily with retired miners and ranchers. **Phippsburg** is an old railroad town with a good café. Stop in at the Antlers Café & Bar in **Yampa** for a dyed-in-the-wool taste of the Old West. This used to be a major stage stop between Wolcott and Steamboat, and is now a local hangout, complete with a stuffed golden eagle, old oil paintings, and a bar that's seen a lot of history go by. Farther down the road at **Toponas** is another relic, a

Windsurfers head their sails into the wind.

general store called the People's Store.

At Toponas the road forks, and State 134 heads back east over Gore Pass. The pass and the Gore Range were named after Sir George Gore, an Irish nobleman who hired mountain man and scout Jim Bridger to lead one of the earliest hunting parties in Colorado in 1855. The party consisted of more than 40 men, and a long parade of carts, wagons, horses, dogs and oxen. Unfortunately, Gore's name was fitting, for he and his party reputedly killed uncounted thousands of buffalo, bear, deer, elk and antelope. The Ute Indians were almost driven to kill Gore, so worried were they that their winter meat supply would be depleted by his careless and bloody killing spree.

Summit County and beyond: The Gore Range continues south to the Summit County area, which can be reached either by continuing south on State 131 or by heading south at Kremmling on State 9. **Summit County** is a series of valleys off Interstate 70 between the Eisenhower tunnel and Vail pass, encom-

passing the resorts of **Dillon, Keystone, Breckenridge** and **Copper Mountain.**

The town of Dillon grew up around **Dillon Reservoir**, one of the largest bodies of water in Colorado and another haven for boating fans. Keystone and Copper Mountain grew up around the ski areas that rise above them.

Breckenridge bills itself as the "oldest authentic Victorian mining town in Colorado". The town does indeed have many colorfully restored Victorian homes, shops and western saloons, surrounded by modern hotels and condominiums that fill up during the winter. Breckenridge also has hiking, horse riding and festivals that bring so many people to the Rockies in the summer.

When Colorado was made a state in 1876, Breckenridge was somehow left out of the process. The miffed town elders finally decided to become an official part of the state and the country in 1936, on the condition that the town be a "free and independent kingdom three days each year". And so, for three days every August, visitors and residents of

.ate season
snow on the
Red Mountain
Pass from
Ouray to
Silverton.

Breckenridge are in "no-man's land" – naturally there's a parade, barbecue and dance to celebrate the event.

Two roads head south out of Breckenridge, both scenic and historic drives. One is gravel, crossing the Continental Divide at Boreas Pass, where it drops into South Park. Many remnants of the mining days are visible on this road, which used to be a major stage route and narrow-gauge railroad track. State 9 is the other road, crossing the Continental Divide at Hoosier Pass, then dropping down into Alma and Fairplay. Mount Silverheels is named after a dance-hall girl who bravely nursed the miners of Alma through a smallpox epidemic, when nobody else would come to help, before she mysteriously disappeared.

State 9 follows the South Platte River into **Fairplay**, a small town of log cabins whose local hero is a burro named Prunes. Burros were indispensable workers and companions to early miners. Prunes lived in Fairplay for all of his 63 years, and when he died, a monument was built in his honor. When his owner died a few years later, he was buried next to his burro.

During the last weekend of July, the town of Fairplay sponsors the World Championship Pack Burro Race over Mosquito Pass. This hilarious event is publicized by a bumper sticker that says, "Get your Ass Over the Pass." The **South Park City Museum** in Fairplay is a street of old buildings preserved from the days when Fairplay was a boom town, complete with a general store stocked with patent medicines.

The roads to Leadville: From the Fairplay area, there are two ways to Leadville. The back way is over Weston Pass, a beautiful drive, but it can be impassable at times, so check before trying. The other road is US 285, which goes through South Park Valley to Buena Vista, then north on US 24 along the Arkansas River and past the Collegiate Range to the west. Every year, alumni groups gather to climb their respective peaks – Yale, Harvard, Princeton, Columbia – but one doesn't have to be an Ivy Leaguer to enjoy this magnificent section of the Sawatch Range.

South of Buena Vista is Salida, and on the other side of Poncha Pass is the San Luis Valley, flanked on one side by the Sangre de Cristo (Blood of Christ) mountains and on the other the San Juans. The **San Luis Valley** is a long, flat, rich ranching area with the protective mountains rising steeply on either side. **Salida** is a pretty little town, but the drive between Monarch Pass, west on Highway 50 and Salida is one of the most scenic anywhere.

The halcyon days of **Leadville** are in the past. It was once, thanks to its abundant gold mines, one of Colorado's biggest, richest, busiest cities. Mining magnate H.A.W. Tabor spent fortunes erecting the still-standing stone buildings; presidents, royalty and celebrities walked the streets; railroad and stage lines were busy and profitable.

Active or even semi-active mining towns are not really pretty places, and Leadville is no exception. Huge slag piles, crude shacks and surrounding mountains denuded of timber do not contribute to the charm of a town. But

Left, season's greetings from Keystone, Colorado. Right, a snow bunny checks out the skiing action.

the panoramas from the town are breathtaking. Leadville is trying hard to recapture its past, and has a number of museums worth stopping to see, among them **Healy House** and the **Dexter Cabin**. The **Matchless Cabin** is a sad reminder of the woman who inspired the opera *The Ballad of Baby Doe.* Leadville is still a mining town, but, these days, most of the digging activity takes place 12 miles (19 km) north at the huge Climax molybdenum mines.

Vail village: Vail is reached by heading north on US 24 from Leadville over Tennessee Pass. **Vail** and the nearby newer towns of Avon and Beaver Creek were built purely for their fabulous skiing – there is still nothing in the United States that compares to Vail's back ski bowls. The modern little village of Vail has grown from a wide spot in the road to a chic resort that attracts celebrities and money like a magnet.

Though the usual Rocky Mountain outdoor attractions are better found elsewhere in the summer, Vail has made up for it with two months packed with glamorous events. The Summer Vail Kick-Off Celebration during the first week in June does just that, with gondola rides to the top of the mountain, lawn parties, barbecues, music, golf and tennis matches. The fun and glitter continues throughout the summer with "It's a Small World", a convocation of puppeteers from around the world; the International Bicycle Classic; a Pro-Celebrity Tennis Classic at Beaver Creek; a Big Band Swing Festival and much, much more.

Into the heart of the Rockies: To reach Aspen from Leadville, head south on State 82, which passes Twin Lakes, then heads up and over the Continental Divide via Independence Pass. For those with a fascination for wolves, the **Inn at Twin Lakes** serves hearty, basic meals and is home to a few wolves, which are sometimes chained to the bar inside.

The name **Aspen** is universally recognized enough to have deserved a special chapter of its own (see "The Aspen Mystique" which follows). A half-dozen campgrounds and trail heads veer off State 82 as it winds its tortuous way

down into the Roaring Fork Valley from Independence Pass. The Grottoes and the Devil's Punch Bowl, strange formations and caves carved out of the rock by the Roaring Fork River, are great places at which to picnic and swim (the Devil's Punch Bowl can, however, be dangerous at high water).

Once in Aspen, hikers can head out in almost any direction to find unpopulated trails, streams jumping with rainbow trout, hanging lakes and challenging rock faces. The **Maroon Bells,** twin peaks towering above a small lake, is one of the most photographed scenes in the Rockies. Reservations must be made well in advance for a space at the Maroon Bells campgrounds.

Behind the Bells is a vast wilderness area that would take months to explore thoroughly on foot. On the other side of the Elk Range, to the west, is Castle Creek. At the end of this road is **Ashcroft**, an old ghost town that has groomed cross-country trails in the winter. The **Pink Creek Cookhouse** at Ashcroft serves simple but superb lunches for

Summertime street corner.

very reasonable prices. For a day hike in Aspen, nothing beats **Hunter Creek**, a hanging valley and ghost town just east of Red Mountain.

Heading west out of Aspen on State 82, turn left at Carbondale, where Mount Sopris rises majestically out of the valley. Here State 133 winds south and west alongside the Crystal River. Across the river is an old railroad bed with occasional chunks of marble scattered along it. These are droppings from the mine at Marble.

But first there's **Redstone**. This little town began as a somewhat eccentric Utopian community, envisioned by a mining magnate who built the nearby **Redstone Castle**. His dream was a company town where everyone would share and nobody would ever go hungry – while he, as feudal lord, ruled from his castle. The castle is open for tours and is reported to be haunted. The **Redstone Inn** has been renovated and serves excellent food.

Still on State Highway 133: Farther up the road, **Marble** once had a population of 2,000, and supplied the marble for the Lincoln Memorial and the Tomb of the Unknown Soldier in Washington DC. The handful of log cabins there now are summer refuges, and nearby is the base for an Outward Bound school. The marble mine, a few miles away, is a surrealistic, cavernous, echoing hole in the mountain, worth taking the trouble to hike up to.

Continuing on State 133, the road winds up and over McClure Pass, and eventually into a valley that, blessed with warm weather and rich soil, produces some of the tastiest peaches in the world. Paonia, Delta and Hotchkiss are filled with fields and fruit orchards – this is the place to stock up on cherries, apples, peaches and vegetables.

The dirt road over Schofield Pass, from Marble to Crested Butte, is strictly for four-wheel-drive vehicles and even then, is often impassable. From Paonia, there's a reasonably well-maintained dirt road that goes over Kebler Pass and then east into Crested Butte, or continues south to Gunnison over Ohio Pass.

Maroon Bells Peak, Colorado.

Crested Butte is one of the few ski resorts that has retained much of its small-town atmosphere, thanks to its isolated location. As the crow flies, it's just over the Continental Divide from Aspen, but by car, Crested Butte is a long way from anywhere. Best known for the copious amounts of powder that fall on its slopes in the winter, it also offers all the requisite Rocky Mountain attractions during the summer.

Crested Butte drew national attention a few years back, when a large mining company decided to move in and extract valuable molybdenum from Mount Evans which towers above the town and gives it a name. Knowing that Crested Butte would never be the same with a gigantic bite taken out of the mountain and massive slag piles heaped up below, a grassroots movement was organized. Money and expertise poured in from all over the state and the nation, and after a long and tedious battle, the mountain stayed intact.

At the top of the world: Heading south now, and skipping past Gunnison which is covered elsewhere (see Canyon Country), are the idyllic mountain towns of Ouray, Telluride and Silverton. **Ouray**, named after a Chief of the Utes, is a high mountain valley with steep mountainsides rising all around it. The town is small, friendly and quaint, with a couple of hot springs to soak in. The **Beaumont Hotel, Wright's Opera Hall**, the **Elk Lodge** and the **Western Hotel** are all buildings of historical value.

The surrounding mountains hold some of the most spectacular hiking and jeeping country in the Rockies. A good day hike is up the trails of **Box Canyon**, along Canyon Creek, which plunges dramatically down to the valley in a series of waterfalls.

South of Ouray, along the "Million Dollar Highway" (named for the low-grade ores that it was found to be paved with after the fact) and over Red Mountain Pass, is **Silverton**, supposedly named when a miner claimed that "we might not have much else, but we got a ton of silver!" It is famous for the narrow-gauge railroad that transports people between Silverton and Durango. The coal-fired locomotives chug and puff along the Animas River on the same line that was once used to haul $300 million in silver and gold out of the mountains.

Telluride is another ski resort that has remained small and charming because of its remote location. The steep, narrow valley, with snow-capped peaks at one end, is reminiscent of Switzerland. There are beautifully restored old buildings and plenty of friendly local bars. The bank in Telluride once had the dubious distinction of being robbed by Butch Cassidy.

At the end of the valley, a steep switchbacking road that eventually becomes very rough leads up to **Bridal Veil Falls**, which plummets dramatically off a cliff. Another spectacular waterfall cascades in **Bear Creek Canyon**. Telluride's ski slopes haven't earned it as much renown as its summer events have. The Telluride Jazz Festival, Blue Grass Festival and Film Festival are internationally known and well-attended events. Reservations are needed and tickets bought months in advance.

Left, Lake Dillon, Colorado. **Right**, a January day at the Snowmass ski resort.

196

Aspen has a glamor and mystique all its own. This special quality is more than the jetsetters and celebrities who make it their second home, more than the strict zoning regulations which have kept out the "shake-and-bake Bavarian village" look of other resorts. There's something special about the valley itself that has been inspiring philosophical visionaries and bartenders alike to settle in Aspen for more than a hundred years.

How long the Ute Indians lived in the Roaring Fork Valley before the white man

the Front Range of Colorado, now became a silver rush that began to populate the rest of the state. Leadville was already a well-established town when the first strike in the Roaring Fork Valley was made near Independence Pass (where the ghost town of Independence still stands). Even today, the road over Independence Pass from Leadville is tortuous and high enough to be closed most of the year. In Frank L. Wentworth's book, *Aspen on the Roaring Fork*, is a description of one resourceful settler's trip over the pass.

made his appearance is not known, but they fought to keep it, killing 11 of the valley's first settlers (who named it Ute City) and an army troop investigating the attack. But the lure of rich silver veins overcame the fear of Indian attacks, and the miners quickly edged them out by sheer force of numbers and a series of massacres.

The Sherman Silver Purchase Act in 1878 inspired settlers to risk the wrath of Native Americans and explore the Rockies of western Colorado. Under the act, the federal Treasury Department bought silver every month and had it coined into silver dollars. The rush for gold, that originally populated

Henry Gillespie asked Henry Staats to assess some of his claims in Aspen, but was afraid the trip from Leadville might be impossible because the snow was so deep. He reported that many people were on the trail to Aspen, and some of them had been trying to get there for three weeks. Staats assured Gillespie he could reach the town in three days.

He had five wooden boats made which he and his men pulled up and over the pass. "Then, we began to get into the crowd of people trying to get to Aspen. There was not a man among them realized that night was the time to travel over soft snow. There were over a hundred men along that trail in 10 or

12 mile rigs of all kinds, sleds, snow-shoes, pieces of tin and baggage of all descriptions. About one-half of the outfits were going back to Twin Lakes to get more grub. The trail looked like a herd of cattle had passed over it. We made camp, borrowed two or three frying pans and made up enough bread to last us through.

"Word was passed around that we traveled at night, so quite a number waited until we got ready about 10 or 11 o'clock. We struck bare ground about 10 miles down the trail and had hard sledding from there on."

As so often happened in the early mining towns, most prospectors staked claims, then sold out to wealthy Easterners, who had the

as well), Wheeler virtually took over the fledgling town of Ute City. He surveyed the mining camp, laid out a townsite, renamed it Aspen after the trees on the surrounding mountainsides, staked out many claims, then went on a lecture tour to promote the many virtues of Aspen.

Men like Jerome B. Wheeler (no relation to Clark Wheeler), President of Macy's in New York, saw long-term potential in the town and put as much into it as he got out of it. Wheeler was lucky enough to be a partner in one of Aspen's richest mines, the Mollie Gibson. With that bonanza, he built a smelter, a bank, an opera house and a hotel. He was also involved in a marble quarry, coal and

capital to open a mine. Many of the street and building names in Aspen are reminders of these early developers and promoters.

Gillespie went to Washington to drum support for mail service, a telegraph line and a road into town. B. Clark Wheeler made a 17-day trek over the pass on snowshoes after hearing rumors of the rich veins of silver in the valley. Being a natural leader and promoter (many said a swindler and claim jumper

Preceding pages: nightlife in Aspen, Colorado. Left, a solitary skier slides on the slopes. Above, in the late 1800s, Aspen was a sophisticated and wealthy town.

iron mines and a ranch. By 1889, Aspen boasted a population of 8,000, the most advanced mining equipment available, 10 churches, two schools, two railroads, three daily newspapers, and a county courthouse. Handsome brick buildings housed shops, and splendid Victorian homes lined the streets of the residential areas. Even then, Aspen had a certain panache, a sense of sophistication. The wives of the silver barons formed a literary and a temperance society. Their husbands built polo grounds and a race track. D.R.C. Brown, father of one of the founders of the Aspen Skiing Corporation, started an electric company, making Aspen the first town in Colorado with electric street lights.

The silver dream: For all of its respectability, however, Aspen was still a mining town. The miners worked shifts around-the-clock; in fact, it was torch-bearing miners coming off a late shift on Aspen Mountain who started Aspen's tradition of skiing down the mountain in torchlight parades. Plenty of saloons catered to the miners, and a rowdy, lucrative red-light district flourished on Durant Avenue.

When the US government repealed the Sherman Act and de-monetized silver in 1893, Aspen was the largest silver camp in the world and the busiest town between Denver and Salt Lake City. Because the

town was completely dependent on silver for its economic well-being, most of the mines shut down, banks and businesses closed, and the population decreased by 1,000 almost overnight. People continued to leave steadily over the next few decades, and by 1930, fewer than 600 people lived in the sleepy little town. It was a shadow of its former self, with rows of empty houses available almost for the taking.

Three young dreamers named Ted Ryan, Tom Flynn and Billy Fiske saw the potential for developing skiing as a recreational sport in Aspen in 1936. They built a lodge below Mount Hayden, part of the ridge between

Castle and Maroon creeks. While Flynn was touring the country to raise money for a ski lift, tourists were coming to ski, climbing the high mountains under their own power. Famous European skier Andre Roch moved to town, formed the Aspen Ski Club, and began to give lessons. By 1938, a crude WPA-built tow was taking the first of Aspen's recreational skiers up the by-now well-known Aspen Mountain.

World War II put a stop to the early dreams of Aspenites. Billy Fiske became a pilot and was shot down and killed. His death ended the development of Mount Hayden as a ski resort. But as fate would have it, the US Army's 10th Mountain Infantry Division ski troops trained at Camp Hale near Leadville. Word quickly got around that Aspen was a lively little town with good skiing, and many went there on leave. Among those to return to Aspen after the war with big plans were Freidl Pfeifer and Steve Knowlton, who ran the Golden Horn restaurant for many years. Pfeifer joined forces with Chicago businessman Walter Paepcke to lease D.R.C. Brown's mining claims on Aspen Mountain, and the Aspen Skiing Corporation was born.

Meanwhile, Walter Paepcke and his wife, Elizabeth, had even more grandiose plans, which, ultimately, were to make Aspen the cultural mecca it is today. Paepcke was not only an astute and highly successful businessman, but an intellectual and a visionary as well. He formed the Aspen Company and bought real estate, including the Hotel Jerome and the Wheeler Opera House. The Jerome was modernized and the Opera House was opulently refurbished under the direction of Bauhaus designer Herbert Bayer. Paepcke wrote to potential investors, "Definite plans are underway to provide opportunities for man's complete life – to earn a livelihood, to enjoy facilities at hand for his enjoyment of art, music and education." Aspen's mandate hasn't changed since Walter Paepcke wrote that in the late 1940s.

Oil-rich Texans and New York City socialites followed the celebrities, and the drug dealers followed the money. And yet, the fast lane is a very small part of what Aspen is all about. One may catch a glimpse of a Kennedy on the chair lift, or bump into actor Robert Wagner grocery shopping at City Market, but the jetset is actually there infrequently and plays a very small part in the day-to-day life of what is basically a local community.

Though drug dealers are arrested with some frequency, the actual crime rate is extremely low. Most Aspen residents with families feel there's no better place to bring up a child, with the excellent school system, the emphasis on outdoor recreation and fitness, and the cultural events available.

Nevertheless, like all resort communities, there are places to see and be seen, and certain rules of etiquette. Little Nells and The Tippler are *après ski* favorites for both tourists and locals. Abetones, Andres and the Ute City Banque have never gotten rave reviews for their very expensive food, but the ambience is all glamor and glitter for the *après ski* crowd. Locals tend to favor the Hotel Jerome Bar, Little Annies (the barbecue is excellent), and the Red Onion. Andre's disco and The Paragon are hot spots after dinner. The Crystal Palace has long been famous for its hilarious dinner show routines and excellent food.

The International Design Conference, held in the music tent in mid-June, is the first event in Aspen to signal the coming of summer. Designers of everything imaginable – shoes and race cars, buildings and computers, movies and graphics – come from all over the world to attend a week's worth of lectures, seminars and special events. A few weeks later, the Music Festival begins.

Aspen is a seasonal town. Though it can accommodate up to 30,000 visitors, the permanent population hovers around 13,000. In winter and summer, the streets are filled with cars and pedestrians; there are waiting lines at restaurants; and hotels and lodges are fully booked. In spring, the town is almost deserted, and for good reason – spring is mud season in the Rockies. Fall used to be off-season too, a gloriously peaceful season of warm Indian summer days, crisp nights, and golden mountainsides of aspen trees. Now the rest of the world is catching on. The Aspen Film Festival in September is gaining a national reputation for picking the best of the independently made films of the year. An Art Cart Derby, sponsored by the Aspen Center for the Visual Arts, features zany designs on wheels and a death-defying race

down a street below Aspen Mountain. There's a County Fair in Snowmass and a rodeo, and a group of people who don red jackets and black hats and jump over fences on horseback, chasing hounds who are chasing coyotes – Aspen's version of the English fox hunt.

Snowmass: Snowmass Village, located in the Brush Creek Valley about 10 miles (16 km) southwest of Aspen, was incorporated as a town in 1967. It has done nothing but grow ever since, sprouting condominiums, fancy homes on the ski slopes, hotels, lodges, shops and restaurants at an astounding rate. Its success is due to its plethora of excellent intermediate ski runs, its determination to cater to families, and the marketing and

business acumen of the Snowmass Company, its major development company. The success of Snowmass is also due, in part, to its proximity to Aspen, something the little village may be forever trying to get over.

Soon after its beginning in 1950, the Aspen Music Festival expanded to include a summer music school and quickly attracted the most famous names in the world of classical music. From June through August, strains of music can be heard everywhere in Aspen – on the mall, where student groups play and pass the hat; and in the famous tent of the west end of town, where concerts are held most afternoons and evenings. While

<u>Left</u>, Windstar's founder and singer John Denver. <u>Above</u>, a magician/bartender in Snowmass entertains his patrons.

connoisseurs will want to buy a ticket and listen to concerts inside the tent, dozens of people always bring blankets and picnic baskets to enjoy the music and sunshine for free on the grass outside the tent.

Summer also brings Ballet Aspen, whose winter home is Salt Lake City, to leap and plié gracefully through the all-too-short warm months. As the ballet company has grown, toured and attracted international renown over the years, it has also spawned a school in nearby Snowmass.

For theater lovers, there is the Aspen Playwrights' Conference. Hosted by the Pilgrim Theater Company, this event gives new playwrights the opportunity to stage their

4th of July is always wild and crazy, with an Independence Day parade down Main Street and any number of peripheral goings-on, including fireworks against the backdrop of Aspen Mountain. On Halloween, the mall and every bar in Aspen overflows with costumed revelers out to see and be seen – in disguise. Winterskol is a mid-winter celebration in January, complete with ski races, parades, costumes, balls, contests and whatever else the Chamber of Commerce can dream up to give one and all a good time.

One of the treasures of Snowmass is the **Anderson Ranch**, which offers summer classes, seminars and workshops in a range of arts, from pottery and photography to

works, under the critical eye of well-known directors.

Aspen bursts at the seams with events during the summer, with crafts fairs; rodeos and rock concerts; balloon, sailboat, bicycle and running races; horse shows and polo matches; tennis, golf, softball and volleyball tournaments. It seems everyone is outdoors, riding horses, hiking, rock climbing, hang gliding, kayaking, fishing, jeeping – or just sitting in the mall soaking up the sun and watching the world go by. Local nightclubs feature everything from folk, jazz and country to disco, rock and punk.

Aspen also has its special holidays. The

woodworking and print making, taught by internationally known artists. Visitors can shop at the Ranch's gallery, and attend a variety of exhibitions held throughout the summer. Snowmass has also put itself on the map with the Snowmass Balloon Races, held in the early summer. The sight of dozens of balloons rising in the dawn light against the dramatic backdrop of the Rockies is a photographer's dream.

Farther west, in Old Snowmass, is Windstar, a place, an organization, a vision that only Aspen and the 1970s could have produced. With John Denver as a figurehead and financial supporter, Buckminster Fuller as a mentor, and Amory Lovins as a nearby resident, Windstar thinks of itself as the new Aspen Institute, dedicated to solving problems relating to alternative forms of energy, building, heating and growing food. They also have classes, seminars and workshops.

Because of the scarcity of inexpensive housing in Aspen, thousands of people who consider themselves Aspenites have migrated to the bedroom communities of Basalt, El Jebel and Carbondale. But Aspen remains the pot of gold at the end of the rainbow, a magical valley filled with people determined to keep it that way. The jetset and those who follow in their wake are fickle, and will probably move on, but Aspen will always have its great skiing, its charm, sophistication, roaring river, and the mountainsides of whispering aspen trees that inspired its name.

The Goethe Bicentennial in 1949 was the event that brought Aspen international attention. Patterned after the Salzburg Music Festival, and dreamt up by Paepcke and a group at the University of Chicago, it attracted scholars, philosophers and social and cultural leaders from all over the world, including Albert Schweitzer, Thornton Wilder, Jose Ortega y Gasset, Arthur Rubinstein, Gregor Piatigorsky, Dimitri Mitropoulous and Bruno Walter. Some of Aspen's most enduring and successful institutions were born out of the Goethe Bicentennial: the Aspen Institute for Humanistic Studies, a "think tank" for intellectual, political and cultural leaders; the International Design Conference; and the Aspen Music Festival.

Fur coat and cocaine crowd: Through the 1950s and 1960s, Aspen continued to grow. Ski bums flocked into the valley, living six to a shack and working three jobs so they could take advantage of Aspen's fabulous skiing. Aspen Highlands, Buttermilk and Snowmass gave the small valley three choices of ski mountains. Shops, restaurants, condominiums, and expensive homes proliferated. Those who loved the small-town atmosphere of Aspen saw the writing on the wall and elected "slow-growth" candidates to run the city and county. Building heights were restricted, neon and billboards were banned and strict zoning controls were adopted. The

Holiday Inn was relegated to a spot outside the city limits (it's been turned into condos), and McDonald's was only recently allowed to operate. The stringent growth controls successfully limited the number of people who moved into the valley, but it also made property values shoot up to the out-of-control level, until buying a home became out of the question for most residents.

Somewhere along the way, the jetset – the fur coat, cocaine and "the second home" crowd – decided that Aspen was the place in which to be, and gave the town a reputation for drugs, sex and life in the fast lane. It's hard to deny that such an element does exist – in fact, it would be naive to do so. One only

has to drive by the rows of Lear jets parked at the airport, or look up at the multi-million dollar homes in Starwood, an exclusive residential area on a mesa west of town that is home to celebrities such as John Denver and Jill St John. Other part-time residents include Jack Nicholson, Don Henley and Glen Fry of Eagles fame, Jimmy Buffet, and journalist Hunter Thompson, one of the few genuine long-time celebrity residents. Hack journalists and marketing executives have thrived on this image. It would also be naive to say that Aspen, which has had a car, a pulp novel and a soft drink named after it, hasn't thrived on all this economically.

Left, Aspen music-lovers under the tent. **Right**, a wagon full of fun-lovers celebrating Aspen's Winterskol Festival.

Avenue once housed the Smelter National Bank, and parts of the bank's vaults, which extended through the upper two floors, are still visible.

The **Strater Hotel** at Seventh Street and Main Avenue has been housing notables since 1887. Its Victorian architecture is enhanced with furnishings collected from 100 years ago. The scantily clad ladies with their net stockings and plumed hats who serve in the hotel's bar, the **Diamond Bell**, could be stepping right out of the last century. The hotel, just a block from the railroad depot, also includes the **Diamond Circle Theater**. The Diamond Circle and the **Abbey Theater**, also within a block of the train station, have nightly presentations during the summer months which include everything from serious drama to monologues to international dancing demonstrations and the tourist's favorite, vaudeville.

The **Fine Arts Auditorium** at Fort Lewis College also stages many productions from near at hand and far away. The Four Corners Opera Association performs during the summer months.

Scattered among those history-rich buildings are the Irish pubs: **Clancy's** and **Father Murphy's**; the Mexican cantinas: **Griegos** and **Franciscos**. Durango has a reputation for its fine restaurants and interesting lounges. Both **The Palace** and **Sweeneys** enjoy an international reputation.

Art selection: Like restaurants, art galleries abound. **Gallerie Marguerite** houses outstanding Western oils. **Earthen Vessel** specializes in colorful Colorado-made pottery and **Termar Gallery** displays fine art, prints, sculpture, pottery and jewelry, the work of both national and local artists.

If one could manage a visit to every art gallery in the Rocky Mountain region, among the most memorable would be Durango's **Toh-Atin Gallery**. At 145 W. 9th Street, the gallery has a reputation for handling the finest in handmade Native American art and crafts. Handwoven Navajo tapestries adorn the walls. Cases of handmade silver and gold jewelry with turquoise, shell, coral

razing
eneath the
an Juans in
idgeway.

and jet display the talents of artists such as Andy Kirk, Jimmie King Jr, Preston Monogye, Mary Marie, Jimmie Harrison and Ben Nighthorse Campbell.

Gallery owner H. Jackson Clark has been collecting Navajo weaving since 1957. Not only is he recognized as one of the most knowledgeable men in the field, but his collection, much of which hangs in the **United Bank of Durango** on Main Avenue, is one of the most extensive in the world and represents three centuries of Navajo weaving, all accurately dated and documented.

Trimble Springs, begun in 1882 a few miles north of town in the Animas Valley, was an internationally known health resort with visitors claiming "miraculous" cures from bathing in the naturally hot mineral waters. It burned to rubble in the late 1950s.

The first liquor reportedly was brought into the area by wagons from Santa Fe, New Mexico. Like most places where men do hard physical labor, saloons sprang up overnight, some of which were fronts for brothels and gambling houses. Right after the saloons came the churches. The first minister in Durango, the Rev. Mr C.M. Hogue, an ex-gambler and a Texan, was converted, and reportedly jumped on a gambling table in a local drinking establishment one night. Just before he called the gamblers to prayer he asked for a cut of the take to finance a new church.

That church, **St Mark's Episcopal**, opened its doors on February 1, 1881, and is still going strong. A year later, the Catholic Sisters of Mercy arrived and opened a school and a hospital, both of which survive as **St Columba School** and **Mercy Medical Center.**

Like many western towns quickly built of lumber and heated with wood fires, Durango experienced a disastrous fire in 1889. The prominence of brick and sandstone buildings seen today stems from knowledge gained from that fire.

A natural movie set: *Small Town Vamp* was the first of about 45 major movie and television shows filmed in the Durango area. That first film was shot by the late Jim Jarvis, a local man. The **Durango portrait parlor.**

film *Around the World in 80 Days* saw the narrow-gauge railroad in action. Perhaps the best known movie filmed in the area was *Butch Cassidy and the Sundance Kid*, starring Robert Redford and Paul Newman. The shot of the two of them jumping into the river was filmed at the Trimble Lane bridge over the Animas River.

Adding cultural and academic interest to the community is **Fort Lewis College**. It had its beginning as a military fort southwest of Durango during the last century. The site became a normal and industrial training school for Native Americans. The school taught agriculture and industrial arts from 1911 to 1927, when the state legislature authorized two years of college courses to be taught. In 1933, high school classes were dropped and the school became a junior college. In 1956, moving the campus from its rural setting to the mesa east of town spawned more controversy than the original 1881 shootout. In 1962, Fort Lewis became a four-year baccalaureat degree-granting college. It

currently has around 3,500 students. The campus joins the city's 18-hole golf course and the Chapman Hill ski slope.

Durango's two major celebrations each year draw participants and onlookers from nearby and far away. The Navajo Trail Fiesta is in late July or early August, and Snowdown takes place on the last weekend in January. The first began in 1935, the latter in 1979. The fiesta includes parades, rodeos and usually horse racing. It draws bullriders, barrel racers and horse fanciers of all kinds. Snowdown activities range from a bartenders' contest to serious winter sport competition, including cross-country and downhill skiing.

Visitors who arrive in Durango on Halloween may feel as if they have arrived in the Land of Oz. Six blocks of Main Avenue are blocked off for the evening's festivities, which find as many as 5,000 people – that's nearly half the town's population – parading in the most outlandish and creative costumes seen anywhere. It is not uncommon for participants to work on their costumes throughout the year.

The summer arts fair at the **Old High School Park** on Main Avenue the second weekend in August, has artists and craftspersons from all over the southwest, working at, displaying and selling their creations.

One of the favorite souvenirs that many tourists take away with them is an old-time photograph of themselves in the costume of a trapper, sheriff, brothel madam or saloon girl with props like guns, parasols, furs and garters. Two such studios operate on Main Avenue.

At an elevation of 6,500 ft (2,000 meters), Durango's surrounding geography provides the natural setting for river rafting, hiking, mountain climbing, hunting, fishing and skiing.

One-and-a-half million tourists annually make Durango seem like something more than a small town. But it really isn't. In more than 100 years, only 9,000 people have increased the population. It would be a challenge to find such a small place that is such a bubbling melting-pot of historical, current and anticipated events.

utdoor life
Silverton.

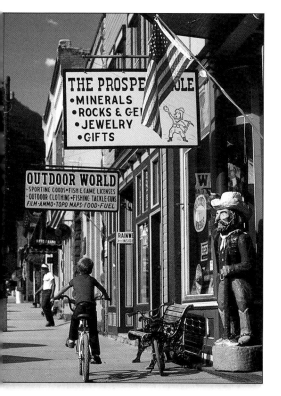

COLORADO'S CANYON COUNTRY

The **Royal Gorge**, 8 miles (13 km) west of Canon City, draws more tourists to Colorado than any other attraction. And only 170 miles (274 km) on US Highway 50, over the beautiful Monarch Pass is the **Black Canyon of the Gunnison**. It is 8 miles east of Montrose.

Both are mighty testaments to the powers of erosion. The canyons, great gashes in the earth's surface, were a minimum of 2 million years in the making. The Gunnison River cut the Black Canyon. The Royal Gorge was formed by the Arkansas River, one of America's longest rivers, traveling 1,400 miles (2,250 km) without any major tributaries. Years of rushing water, carrying tumbling boulders, cut through solid granite leaving the Royal Gorge in a class by itself. The Gunnison River drops 95 ft (29 meters) each mile and cuts the 2,000 ft (610 meters) deep canyon that is 1,100 ft (335 meters) wide at the top and only 40 ft (12 meters) wide at the bottom. The Black Canyon takes its name from the narrowness and steepness of its walls which the sun rarely hits, thus creating the "black" effect.

Because the canyon walls are so deep with little sunlight, plant life is sparse. And because there is little plant life, there are few animals. Various lichens and mosses grow on the rocks and oakfern and woodsiafern are found under damp overhangs. Douglas fir and aspen grow in a few places in the canyon.

Brown and rainbow trout, flannelmouth sucker and squawfish swim the Gunnison, and anglers can try their luck as long as they possess a Colorado fishing license.

Dinosaurs used to tread: Original inhabitants of the Royal Gorge were the dinosaurs. This area for fossil remains is one of the richest in North America. Since firearms are not allowed in Royal Gorge Park, mule deer, chipmunks and squirrels are tame and beg handouts of food from visitors. Other animals which can be seen and often photographed are ski skunks, coyotes, bobcats, cougar, porcupines and pronghorn antelope. But what most people come to the Royal Gorge to see is the world's highest suspension bridge from which they can view the Arkansas River, over 1,000 ft (300 meters) below. Construction began in 1929. A construction crew of 80 men worked from either side of the rim, first building concrete abutments which would serve as bases for the steel towers supporting the main suspension cables. After completion of the towers, steel cables were lowered from either side of the canyon, the ends spliced and the cable pulled back up on top. These served as the "carry cables" to allow the stringing of the rest of the cable work. Cables completed, the steel collars were clamped around the wires and suspender rods were attached to support the steel girders which serve as a floor for the bridge deck. Finishing the job required laying wood deck and fastening the 1,300 planks to the sides of the bridge. Protective side railings were bolted in place, the wire fencing fastened to the railing, and the highway approaches made ready.

receding ages: sheep ranching is still big business. **Left**, the Black Canyon of the Gunnison. **right**, bridge spanning the Royal Gorge.

Despite the fact that the laborers were inexperienced at this kind of construction, the job was finished in five months with no fatalities. Stabilizing wind and guy cables were added later. Without these, the bridge would not have been able to withstand the gusty winds that roar down the canyon.

Shortly after the bridge was completed an increase in visitors who longed to see the gorge from the bottom, encouraged the building of the incline railway. It is the world's steepest and was built from the top down. Special hoist machinery and automatic safety devices lower and raise the specially constructed cars. The incline railway was opened in 1931 and has been upgraded several times since. Visitors can watch a 25-minute multi-media show, introduced in 1988, at the Royal Gorge Plaza on the South side of the bridge.

The latest engineering marvel at Royal Gorge is the spectacular aerial tramway. Passengers may board at the main terminal near the visitors' center and are treated to spectacular views as they travel suspended above the canyon. The tramway is 1,178 ft (360 meters) above the canyon floor and 2,200 ft (670 meters) in length. The car holds 35 passengers. It cost $350,000 and was completed in June 1969.

Railroad wars: Rail buffs thrill at the famous Royal Gorge rail war fought between the Denver and Rio Grande and Santa Fe Railroads. Each company surveyed the canyon floor, wanting to extend their lines westward. Both lines flew into action when silver was discovered at Leadville and the town boomed overnight. The problem was that the canyon is too narrow to accommodate more than one rail line.

For several days, armed railroad workers laid track during the day and dynamited the efforts of the other crews during the night. Shots were exchanged, but no one was killed, although several arrests were made. The war was taken to the courts for settlement. The final agreement came on December 20, 1879. The Santa Fe was ordered to stay out of Denver and Leadville for 10 years, and the Rio Grande was ordered to pay the

Santa Fe $1.4 million for the construction they had completed in the Royal Gorge. The Rio Grande tracks were completed to Leadville in July of 1880, and a new gateway to the West was finally opened.

A visit to the Royal Gorge is best during the first weekend in May when Canon City's Blossom and Music Festival is held, and the valley's cherry and apple trees are sporting the best of their springtime blossoms. At this time of year the Arkansas River also offers some of the best of the West's whitewater river rafting.

Around the rim of the Royal Gorge runs the **Royal Gorge Scenic Narrow-Gauge Railway**. The 30-minute narrated trip covers 3 miles and allows riders a glimpse of wild flowers, cactus and an occasional deer. It stops at the brink of the gorge for a view of the canyon and the world-famous bridge that spans it.

Buckskin Joe, an authentic Wild west boom town which has served as a movie location for many western films, is an-

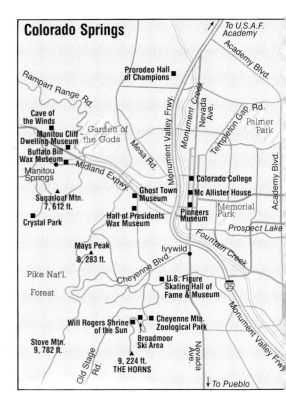

218

other feature of the Royal Gorge. Visitors here can ride a stagecoach, and watch nine gunfights each day. The **Silver Dollar Saloon** features live country music and the **Lincoln Theatre** has magic shows.

While the Black Canyon is administered by the National Park Service, the Royal Gorge is operated and maintained by the Royal Gorge Company, a Colorado Corporation under a lease agreement with Canon City, which derives a substantial portion of its municipal revenue from the park.

The Black Canyon: What the Royal Gorge is to the engineer, the Black Canyon is to the geologist and naturalist. A 13-mile (21-km) automobile field trip begins at Tomichi Point. From here, one can get a view of the entire length of the canyon which begins 40 miles (64 km) to the east. The distant flat-topped skyline is made of volcanic rock formed 2 million years ago.

Gunnison Point Overlook is near the visitors' center. The overlook to the right of the center is a 1.1-billion-year-old pegmatite dike (igneous rock injected while molten into a fissure). Because dikes are harder than surround schists (metamorphic crystalline rock), they weather more slowly and jut out into the canyon. Two thousand feet (610 meters) below is the Gunnison River.

The different rock colors of the inner gorge are striking. The pink streaks are pegmatites, which is a coarse variety of granite. The dark rocks are gneisses (foliated metamorphic rock similar to granite) and schists. Several mountains ranges were formed between 1.75 and 1.1 billion years ago making the rocks of this inner canyon the "roots" of these mountains.

Rocks and springs: The hills on the North Rim of the Black Canyon are made of sedimentary rocks of Morrison and Dakota sandstone. The **West Elk Mountains** are northeast. **Rock Point** is a large pegmatite with **Echo Canyon** just to the right. The Reverend Mark Warner gave Echo Canyon its name when he noticed how his voice rebounded off the walls as he spoke. It was Warner who was primarily responsible for having the area designated a National Monument in 1933.

Lion's Spring, one of the few spots of running water on the South Rim, gets it's name from the Montrose Lions' Club which helped establish the monument. This is a great place to watch for deer at dawn and dusk.

Cedar Point has an excellent self-guided nature trail. From here, one can also see Colorado's highest cliff, the "Painted Wall". The "paintings" are in fact colorful pegmatites, 2,400 ft (732 meters) high.

High Point offers an excellent view of the surrounding country. To the south are the **San Juans** and to the north is the **Grand Mesa**. East are the West Elks and to the west, the canyon country of the **Uncompahgre Plateau**. Uncompahgre has been translated from the Ute Indian language as "land where the red light shines on the water".

Both public and private campsites are prevalent in Black Canyon country from primitive to fully equipped, although they may get busy at times.

he
latchless
line,
olorado.

WYOMING WILDERNESS

Welcome to the Wyoming wilderness. The land of snowcapped peaks, crystal-clear lakes, lush green meadows and timbered slopes where early explorers hunted for game and trapped for fur. In summer, wild flowers carpet the landscape with a spectrum of color. Various kinds of flowers, including wild geranium, aster, fairy slipper, larkspur and brown-eyed Susan are abundant in the wilderness. In fall, aspen trees color the hillsides with hues of red and gold. The National Forest Service of Wyoming has set aside seven mammoth wilderness areas of virgin beauty, permitting no woodcutter's axe to fall, no permanent dwelling to change the scenery, no human civilization to crowd the wilderness. The untouched forest land is all we have to represent the last frontier – this land has been purposely preserved from industrial tourism.

Rugged mountains, big game as the

Native Americans knew it, bald eagles and sand pipers, trout and perch wait to be discovered. Bird-watchers spy sharp tail sage, blue and Franklin grouse and, in season, partridge, pheasant, wild turkey, ducks and Canadian geese.

Your route into these natural wilderness areas is often primitive. The easiest way is to use your own transportation up to the point where you'll have to hike or go on horseback. From thereon, it will be like the days of Lewis and Clark.

A trip to the wilderness requires careful planning. Essential are reliable maps, lists of horsepackers and outfitters, good guidebooks (one on birds or plants, if you are interested), along with a list of accommodation from the Wyoming Travel Commission, and brochures from the National Parks and National Forest Service. Clothing, camping gear, food, cooking equipment and climbing apparel need to be organized before starting your adventure. The luxury of camping at the spot of your choice in the wilderness is very special, but you must come prepared if you want to enjoy this freedom.

Medicine Bow dream: One of the most beautiful wilderness areas in the Rockies is the **Medicine Bow Range and National Forest** – the very essence of a nature lover's dream. Located in the southeast corner of Wyoming, Medicine Bow is an exceptional area, accessible and ideal for hiking, climbing and riding, with great fishing, hunting and camping. You can definitely experience the "in-heart feeling" of the real wilderness in the wild scenic **Snowy Range**. You should make a detour on State Highway 130 to go through this range. President Roosevelt declared the area a National Forest in 1902, and today it has expanded to cover an area of 3 million acres (1.2 million hectares).

The forest lies along the **Medicine Bow Range** (also called the Snowy Range) and extends from the Colorado/Wyoming border to the sagebrush-covered Great Plains. These rugged mountain slopes are covered with a variety of pines, fir and aspen. In higher elevations, the mountains are dotted with hundreds of bodies of water ranging from large lakes to potholes: a direct result of glacial activity. The larger lakes are a paradise for fishermen as they are loaded with a variety of trout.

Historically, Medicine Bow was a place where friendly Native American tribes would meet regularly in one of the mountain valleys to collect mahogany, from which the best bows were made. At these meetings, the tribes would also "make medicine" during ceremonial pow-wows that were held for the purpose of healing. Bow and medicine making soon merged to become "Medicine Bow", the name for both the forest and the range.

Trappers visited the area as early as 1810. However, this range became best-known through Owen Wister's western novel, *The Virginian*. More recently, the name "Medicine Bow Range" hit the headlines when a United Airlines plane crashed into the mountain ridge called Disaster Wall, killing 63 passengers and crew members.

In mid-summer, silvery remnants of the previous winter's blizzard still glis-ten on the 12,000-ft (3,660-meter) moun-tain peaks. Incredible rock formations are seen along **Middle Crow Creek**, where the strange landscape is called "The Devil's Playground", "Turtle Rock" and "Vedawoo Glen". Camping, picnicking, fishing, snow-mobiling and downhill skiing are the most common action sports to be found in areas closest to the roads and camping spots. Non-motorized activities include backpacking, horsepacking, hiking and cross-country skiing. This forest is a wildlife lover's haven with its elk, deer, antelope and bighorn sheep. Black bear and mountain lions have also been spot-ted in this area. Watch out for chip-munks and squirrels – these frisky crea-tures will steal any food supplies that are not properly concealed.

Primitive recreation: This range's brief history as a climber's dream began after World War II, when the 10th mountain division of the University of Wyoming veterans appeared. More recently, climb-ers from other areas of the Rockies have realized that the range is an excellent

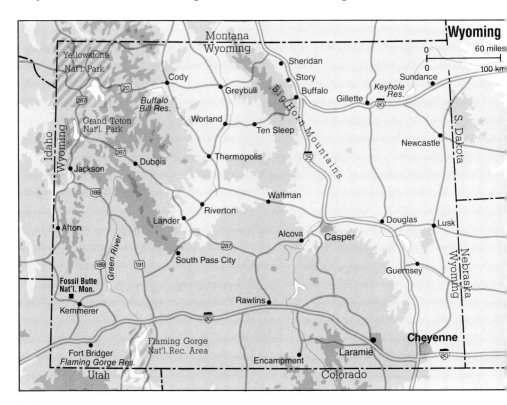

location for rock climbing practice. During the removal of bodies from a 1955 plane crash, many new climbing routes were created. The climbing cliffs are situated not more than a half-mile from the campgrounds.

Other primitive recreational experiences in Wyoming include **Snake River, Gros Ventre, Shoshore National Forest, Big Horn National Forest,** the **Salt River Range** and the **Wyoming Range**. The Salt River and Wyoming ranges form the western half of the **Bridger National Forest**. They are not very well-known, as they have yet to be more thoroughly explored. The Gros Ventre Range, used by the Arapahoe Indians and the French trappers, forms the eastern boundary of Jackson and is adjacent to the **Teton Range** on the west side. Creating a horseshoe shape in the eastern flange of the Bridger National Forest is the **Wind River Range**. This area of the Rockies was called the "shining mountains" because of the high mounds of granite, polished by glaciers, that gleamed in the bright sunlight. The Bridger Wilderness, northeast of Pinedale, contains areas of scenic beauty in the Wind River Range, including 1,300 lakes teeming with fish, that speckle the rugged landscape. In 1973, the Bridger Wilderness merged with the Teton National Forest. Presently called the **Bridger-Teton National Forest**, it is the largest forest in the 48 states and covers 3.5 million acres (1.4 million hectares), including the Wind River Range. Wildlife varies from grizzly and moose to beautiful birds. But be wary: grizzly and moose are dangerous if approached. Before winter sets in, multitudes of elk relocate from the mountain tops to the **National Elk Refuge**, north of Jackson Hole. The five main entrances to this area – **Green River Lakes, New Fork Lake, Elkhart Park, Big Sandy Lake** and **Boulder Lake** – provide easy access for short trips from one entrance to another.

Wind River Reservation: Seven of the largest glaciers in the continental United States are in the Wind River area. In the southern part of the range, most of the glaciers fell back leaving vertical ice-carved walls. North of the highway, up the Wind River Valley, is the scenic **Pinedale Buttes**, a spectacular formation that rises majestically above the land.

The Wind River Reservation, Wyoming's only reservation, has more than 2 million acres (¾ million hectares) of land that is home to the Eastern Shoshones and the Northern Arapahoes. Chief Washakie and the Shoshones called this area the "valley of the warm winds" for the constant winds that gusted down the valley, shaking man and horse, and filling their eyes with dust and sand. Chief Washakie knew what he was doing when he asked that the land be given to his people "for as long as the grass grows and the river shall flow". He loved his people, and he had the wisdom to foresee the effect of the white man's invasion of the Rockies. The Shoshones served as scouts for the US army and were not involved in the Indian wars. As a result of the chief's foresight, the Shoshones received the Wind River Reservation without bloodshed, in a

Dogsledding is a popular winter sport.

treaty signed at Fort Bridger in 1868. The reservation is the burial site for Sacagawea, the Shoshone guide who accompanied Lewis and Clark in their expedition to Yellowstone. She was buried west of Fort Washakie. Chief Washakie died at 102 years of age. He was the first Indian chief to be given military honors at his funeral, and he was buried in the old military cemetery along the Wind River.

Among the many recreation areas in the Rockies, the **Big Horn Canyon Recreational Area** and the **Flaming Gorge Recreational Area** have historic sights, scenic overlooks and a variety of wildlife. From **Yellowtail Dam** across the **Big Horn River** in Montana through 47 miles (76 km) of the **Big Horn Lake**, the Big Horn Canyon Recreational Area is truly spectacular. Elk, mule deer, black bear, grouse and other birds roam this territory. The **Big Horn Mountain Range** provides a beautiful backdrop for this wilderness. The Crow Indians were Big Horn's earliest inhabitants.

The wide lake and steep canyons are the main features of this recreational area. The visitors' center is located on the eastern edge of Lovell, and boat cruises are available at **Horseshoe Bend**. Boaters enjoy the multicolored canyon, majestic scenery and excellent fishing this area has to offer. Driving around the reservoir, you can look across the border and see the **Pryor Wild Horse Range** where the last herds of horses stampede through the wilderness.

Life in Flaming Gorge: The Flaming Gorge Recreational Area is reached from Interstate 80 by turning south on State 530 at the quaint town of **Green River**. You will have a quiet and satisfying time in these silent mountains with their beautiful red bluffs. The petroglyphs and other artifacts suggest that Native Americans hunted game near Flaming Gorge for centuries. During the early 1800s, men first came to Green River while searching for beaver. Flaming Gorge was named by Major John Wesley Powell, who led a two-man expedition down the Green River to the Colorado

A winter thaw forms pools at the base of Medicine Bow.

River and through the Grand Canyon. In 1870, ranchers moved to the valleys near the area. But life in the desert amidst grubbing sagebrush was difficult, and these early pioneers gave up the struggle and moved on. However, fugitives like Butch Cassidy and others used the isolated valleys along the Green River as a refuge on many occasions.

The roads were primitive across the Eastern Utina Range when the construction of **Flaming Gorge Dam** commenced. In 1964, the 66 sq. mile (170 sq. km) dam was completed, creating a wonderful recreation area. The dam, impounding the waters of the Green River, produces hydroelectric power and supplies water to the mountain valleys and cities in Utah, Wyoming and Colorado.

In recent years, people have come to appreciate the desert for its own natural beauty. You can see areas where rock has been stripped bare to expose the earth's strata. You can also see effects of the powerful geological forces that shaped the earth over the centuries. There are two easily identifiable areas of the Flaming Gorge – the mountainous areas of Utah composed of canyons, forests and benches, and the desert area of Wyoming with its rolling hills, desert brush and shale badlands. The Green River is the pulse of the Flaming Gorge, flowing through the Utina Range and giving fresh life to the forests lying in the Gorge.

Some of the recreational activities available in this area include rafting down the Green River, and boating and waterskiing on **Flaming Gorge Lake**. The reservoir is open to fishing all year long. In summer, fishing from a boat or off the shore is popular, while in winter, ice-fishing is the most common sport. The dam contains some of the best trout known, but do keep in mind that a license is required to fish in the dam. Camping facilities are available from primitive, earthy cabins to modern government campgrounds. Take the time to enjoy and appreciate the clean air, the multitude of stars winking in the clear night sky, the silent mountains and the red desert.

Herds of elk are a common sight in the Rockies.

JACKSON HOLE

"**Jackson's Hole**" was the name given in the early 1800s to the valley nestled at the foot of the Tetons, with one of the most awe-inspiring views in America. The well-known town of **Jackson** is located in the southern end of the valley and **Grand Teton National Park** lies to the north. The valley is a land of obvious beauty, teeming with wildlife – a unique paradise protected naturally by the mountains surrounding it.

John Colter was actually the first trapper to discover the wonders of Jackson Hole in 1807. Early trappers referred to the valleys in the Rocky Mountain country as "holes". William Sublette named this one for his partner, David Jackson – they were only two of a group of adventurous mountain men who frequented the region, trapping beaver, trading with the Native Americans and selling skins at the yearly rendezvous. The valley is guarded by mountains – the Tetons to the west, the Yellowstone to the north, the Absarokas to the northeast, the Mount Leidy Highlands to the east, the Gros Ventres to the southeast, and the Hoback and Snake River Range to the south.

The Teton Range is comparatively young, much younger than the Rocky Mountains. The Teton Mountains were formed about 10 million years ago, but the rocks that comprise them are closer to 2 billion years old. Geologists say that volcanic activity beneath the present-day Tetons resulted in an outward flow of lava creating an imbalance in the earth's crust. This set the stage for the faulting that created the mountains. As the Teton and Gros Ventre ranges began to rise, Jackson Hole simultaneously started to sink.

Before 1889, when the first permanent settlers arrived in Jackson Hole, the 50-mile-long (80-km) valley was known only to trappers and explorers. It is said that one of the reasons the valley was especially attractive to them was because they felt safe from attack here. By 1840, the fur trade's best days were over and most of the big companies,

such as the one owned by Jedediah Smith, William Sublette and David Jackson, were dissolved. Teton country was then deserted for about 20 years except for the bands of Native Americans who rode in to hunt and fish.

Famous outlaws: Unbelievable stories told by mountain men of the wonders of Jackson Hole country were confirmed in the early 1870s by scientific expeditions, such as the Hayden party which filed the first reports on Teton fossils, geology and mammals. These expeditions introduced the public to an unknown part of the West.

The years following the Civil War were famous for widespread lawlessness in Teton country. For more than a quarter century, Jackson Hole was one of the most famous outlaw hideouts in the nation. Butch Cassidy and Teton Jackson supposedly visited here. Stealing horses and robbing trains was a full-time and profitable business in their day, and Jackson Hole was almost impenetrable, whether hiding a herd of animals until their brands could be

changed or stashing loot until it "cooled".

The valley became famous for big game hunting early in the 20th century. Cattle ranchers often "boarded" guests and provided them with guide service, creating today's dude ranching. Word spread quickly of Jackson's beauty as a vacation spot and tourism soon became its economic base.

The town of Jackson is 12 miles (20 km) south of the entrance to Grand Teton National Park, in the southern end of Jackson Hole (the valley). A full-facility Information Center is located in Jackson on the north end of town. The **Jackson Hole National Monument** (the quarter of a million acres of land to the east of the boundaries of Grand Teton National Park), added to the park in 1950, establishes the borders that exist today. Open up all your senses, feel the majesty of the Tetons, breathe the mountain air – then you'll know the real story of Jackson Hole.

Spirit of the Old West: Jackson town was established in 1897. Some of the white clapboard houses were brought over Teton Pass west of town piece by piece in horsedrawn wagons and a number of the buildings surrounding the town square are originals. The spirit of the Old West is maintained everywhere. Stagecoach rides and boardwalks around town contribute to the feeling of nostalgia. Men and women alike dress in cowboy attire – jeans, boots and cowboy hats. Saddle horses are tied along Main Street. For almost 30 years, every summer evening at 6.30, the Wild West has returned to Jackson. Tourists line the curbs to witness an old-time shootout between outlaw and posse.

Jackson Hole is the birthplace of the western story. The valley and its legends inspired Owen Wister to write *The Virginian* – and it also served as the setting for the movie *Shane*, which still has summer showings in Jackson Hole.

Jackson is known, too, for its shops and art galleries. A number of well-known artists make their homes there, and local artists exhibit their works at local craft fairs every year. Whether watching famous artists at work or cre-

Stagecoach tours in Jackson.

ating canvases in your own mind, you will find Jackson full of things to do. There are symphony orchestra performances, a Fine Arts Festival, and playhouses for summer stock theater.

Buffalo are sometimes spotted along the Snake River near Moran Junction. Mule deer are mostly seen by the traveler who hikes the mountain trails. In the summer the deer prefer the lower slopes: in spring and fall, they move between the mountain slopes and their wintering grounds south of Jackson.

In spring, moose often feed in open ponds. Many browse in the Willow Flats close to Jackson Lodge. In summer, they move into the spruce and cottonwood forests along the river bottoms. In fall and winter, the moose move into open country where they can be easily observed. Moose are animals of unpredictable temperament, and observers should exercise caution, especially with moose cows and their calves.

Elk are more shy than moose, and more difficult to see. They usually rest in deep forest during midday, so the early morning and late afternoon are the best times to observe this member of the deer family in the open.

The **National Elk Refuge**, one of six major wildlife refuge areas in Wyoming where visitors can watch animals and birds in their natural surroundings, was established in 1912 when nearly 20,000 elk in the Jackson Hole region were starving during a severe winter. Residents of the valley raised $1,000 to buy hay for them, and the Wyoming State Legislature appropriated $5,000 for additional feed. Congress then set aside 1,000 acres (405 hectares) as a winter refuge for elk. The area has been enlarged since that time, partly by over 1,700 acres (680 hectares) bought and donated by the Izaak Walton League and partly through later land acquisitions of the Federal Government. Elk migrate on to the refuge in late October and November, and they leave the refuge for the summer in early May. Visitors may take sleigh rides among the elk from mid-December to early April, 10 a.m. until 4 p.m.

A family portrait in front of an arch made of deer antlers.

The **Bridger Teton National Forest** encompasses three sides of Jackson Hole. Its 3½ million acres (1.4 million hectares) and seven ranger districts are supervised from the Jackson Hole headquarters.

A visit to **Yellowstone National Park** is an opportunity to see a variety of wildlife. Year-round accommodation is available south of Yellowstone in the Jackson Hole area.

A study in contrasts – red rock, green forests and snowcapped summits mirrored in clear lakes vie for attention in Jackson Hole. No matter the season, the silent splendor of Jackson Hole will make any traveler's vacation a memorable one.

The **Moose Visitor Center** is open from 8 a.m. to 7 p.m. daily. An Information Center is operated by the National Park Service. The Teton County Historical Center in Jackson has exhibits which illustrate the mountain man fur-trade era in Jackson Hole.

The **Colter Bay Visitor Center**, open from 8 a.m. to 7 p.m., houses the **Indian Arts Museum**, where the David T. Vernon Indian art collection is featured in exhibit rooms.

The outdoor life: As the early mountain men discovered, camping is a good way to experience Jackson Hole. Campsites abound throughout the region in Teton County, Grand Teton National Park, and Bridger-Teton National Forest. Be sure to take along your insect repellent, though. There are times when Wyoming seems to contain every biting insect known to entomological science from green-eyed horseflies to humming swarms of mosquitoes.

Whether boating, rafting, wading, swimming, canoeing, fishing – Jackson Hole is a watersports paradise. Paddle on a crystal clear mountain lake, or thrill to a whitewater trip through one of the canyons of the Snake River. Jackson Hole's lakes (**Jenny, Leigh** or **Jackson**) yield Mackinaw trout up to 50 lbs (23 kg), or snag a native cut-throat trout in one of the fine streams (**Hoback**, **Buffalo** or **Snake rivers**).

Modes of transportation are as varied as the tourists themselves – take a sleigh ride through the National Elk Refuge and see the cutter races in January and February or view the scenery from a helicopter, glider or hot air balloon. Ski (downhill or cross-country) or snowmobile any of the three major ski areas (**Grand Targhee Ski Resort, Jackson Hole Ski Resort** and **Snow King Ski Area**). Ride the Jackson Hole Aerial Tram, the Snow King Mountain chairlift, or the Alpine Slide – they'll whisk you away for a breathtaking view.

Autumn in Jackson Hole beckons the big game hunter. Sports enthusiasts from around the world flock to the area when the hunting season opens to stalk the country's largest herds of elk and moose. Hunters will also find mule deer, mountain sheep and black bear.

Seeing the wildlife is as exciting as hunting it. A pair of binoculars, a little knowledge of animal habits, and "taking your time" can reap thrilling rewards. But remember that these are wild animals and can cause severe injury. Keep your distance and enjoy all that Jackson Hole has to offer.

Left, a mountain meadow. **Right**, The National Elk Refuge, Jackson.

CODY COUNTRY, WYOMING

Yellowstone, America's first national park, attracts millions of visitors each year. It is one of the few pristine and pure environments left: wild animals roam freely in the vast forests, and the waterfalls spill into rivers filled with trout that make some of the best fishing in the country.

One of the best kept secrets of this spectacular area is the **East Yellowstone/Wapiti Valley** connecting the East Gate of Yellowstone National Park and **Cody,** Wyoming. A vast magnificent view includes the **Shoshone National Forest**, America's first wilderness area to be designated a national forest. The traveler is hard pressed to watch the road ahead with his attention being caught by the forest surrounding him on all sides and eagles soaring above the majestic mountains and meadows. Tall stands of pine trees protect herds of deer, elk, moose and the occasional bears. Buffalo herds wander outside the Park boundaries to graze in the valley.

Several campgrounds tucked into the forest area invite the traveler to stop long enough to gather memories from a world that has existed for eons and has somehow survived here in this Wyoming land. A stop along this primitive area is an ideal opportunity to regain one's senses: campers are free to hike, backpack, take advantage of photographic skills, or simply lean back against a shady pine tree, and watch the river flow by or observe the wildlife in its natural habitat.

The Shoshone River follows the road into Cody, Wyoming, changing from raging, white water into flowing contentment. There are many places along the river banks where you can watch the trout jump and beavers building their dams. Several times a day, river floaters in rubber rafts can be seen riding the currents, and the traveler is torn between breathing in his surroundings or hurrying into Cody in order to arrange his own river trip.

As the road leads out of the dense forest land, the valley widens and color is rampant as red rock formations stir the imagination. Formations named Holy City, Laughing Pig, Elephant Rock and Ptarmigan look down from great heights and are met by stands of pines and breathtaking valleys. Sprinkled along this roadway between Yellowstone Park and Cody are guest ranches and lodges where rustic comfort is available. Many of the guest lodges are hidden from view so travelers must watch for signs indicating where they may be found. Accommodations are modern but manage to combine convenience with western flavor.

Ride the range: A stay in a guest ranch or lodge in the Wapiti Valley or any other scenic area surrounding Cody is an opportunity to get away from a crowded and fast-paced world that is oftentimes saturated with pollution. Here in this Wyoming country is vast uncluttered space, clear clean skies, and water so pure you can drink from the running rivers and waterfalls. The ranches and lodges offer horseback rides into the

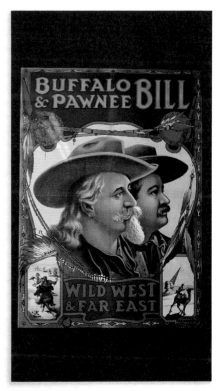

wilderness, camping, cookouts, hikes and backpacking and huge 'n' hearty homecooked meals three times a day. Not the least of the pleasures of the world is at day's end when one can gaze into cloudless star-filled skies and see galaxies and sparkling constellations with complete clarity.

The ranches are run by cowboys and cowgirls who are not much different from their predecessors at the turn of the century. These people have the same skills and heartiness of the frontier days, and they work from sunup to sundown caring for the horses and cattle, fencing the rangeland, and keeping the buildings in top condition. On their days off, the ranch hands head into Cody where they can kick up their heels in a western nightspot called **Cassie's** or compare stories and dreams with their contemporaries at the **Silver Lounge** or the **Proud Cut Saloon** across the street.

William F. ("Buffalo Bill") Cody was the founding father of the town of Cody and his influence is still strongly felt. Buffalo Bill first entered the area in the 1870s and saw its tremendous development possibilities. He returned with friends and named the site Cody in 1895. By 1902, the town was incorporated and Colonel Cody opened **Irma Hotel**, named after his daughter. The Irma Hotel, now a historic landmark, is still a gathering place for the community and an attraction for visitors.

Western memorablia: After the Colonel's death, an association was formed to preserve his memory and to immortalize his contributions to the setting of this portion of the frontier. Gertrude Vanderbilt Whitney was commissioned to do a historic sized sculpture. The sculpture is named *The Scout* and was dedicated in 1924. It sits on the west edge of Cody and was the beginning of a tribute to the American frontier heritage that has today become the well-known and fascinating **Buffalo Bill Historical Center.**

The Historical Center, a four-part museum, is usually a complete surprise to visitors who have not made the trip to Cody especially to see it. It sits with the

Artist Charles Russell captured the Wild West in *The Jerkline*.

Rocky Mountains as a background and has no resemblance to the original log cabin that sufficed at the beginning of this memorial effort. It is a huge modern structure built, for the most part, of rock and is composed of four separate museums – truly the Center of the West. The four sections are **The Plains Indian Museum, The Whitney Gallery of Western Art, The Winchester Arms Museum** and **The Buffalo Bill Museum**. Together, there are over 100,000 square feet of exhibit space.

Throughout the summer season, you can see tour groups from all over the world in the Historical Center, as well as an occasional celebrity. Writers and television personalities have found it a fascinating institution on which to focus because of its rare and diverse collections of western memorabilia. Visitors should allow a minimum of three hours to tour the Center – a week would be even better! Also during the summer months, there is a special exhibition, usually featuring the most famous western artists in history.

The Plains Indian Museum, guardian of cultures, traditions, customs and the creativity of the plains area tribes of the United States, is a wondrous world that one cannot see without a deepening understanding, appreciation and awe. The Whitney Gallery of Western Art is one of the major Western art museums in America and displays artworks by great artists including Bierstadt, Miller, Moran, Catlin, Sharp, Remington and Russell to name but a few. Remington and Russell are well known as western artists and their work is often compared. The Winchester Arms Museum, one of the most prestigious of its kind in the world today, has over 5,500 firearms and projectile weapons and is perhaps the most complete documentation of weaponry in the world. The collection was started by Oliver Winchester in 1860 and moved to Cody in 1975. The Buffalo Bill Museum displays hundreds of items that belonged to its namesake as well as memorabilia, artifacts, artworks and photographs, illustrating the development of the American West.

Sioux Indian dress patterns, c. 1860.

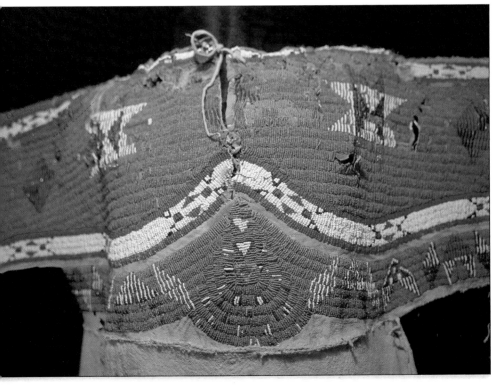

The visitor is treated to the memorabilia from Annie Oakley's days to Buffalo Bill's Wild West show. The sum offers an educational opportunity that is unsurpassed. It is doubtful that such rare and complete collections of Western American history can be found anywhere else in the world.

Carnivals and celebrations at Cody: Those looking for replicas of early western frontier towns will be disappointed, as Cody has remained untouched by a plastic facade. Cody is a small community and its residents have chosen to call it home for personal reasons: year round outdoor recreation, spectacular scenery and fresh open spaces – luxuries in today's fast-paced world. They drive 2 miles (3 km) out of the city limits and can be completely alone, or they can go downtown and be surrounded by friends. With the abundance of wildlife nearby, game hunting is excellent in the Cody area. Fishing is also rewarding.

In the summertime, this otherwise quiet community has an entirely different atmosphere. Visitors from all over the world come to Cody to take part in the unique attractions and enjoy the natural environment. Cody boasts that it is the Rodeo Capital of the World. Other towns may claim the same distinction but Cody does offer a rodeo every night of the summer which is PRCA sanctioned. And the cowboys and cowgirls who ride in the Cody rodeo are serious competitors: many of those riders go on to become the best in the business.

June is a great month to visit Cody. The weather is usually ideal and there are special events sponsored by the Buffalo Bill Historical Center. One such is The Frontier Festival held on the north lawn of the Historical Center. People bring their special skills and wares to the Festival and spend two days demonstrating and selling arts, crafts and foods authentic to the turn of the century. Demonstrations on spinning, weaving, saddle making, hide tanning, log hewing, Indian beadwork and the preparation of frontier foods, can be watched from booths all arranged within

Crow Indian headdress, c. 1830.

the Festival area. Throughout the Festival, entertainment is provided by groups who specialize in traditional western music and contests are held between outfitters as they race, pack saddles, and shoe horses.

An Indian pow-wow is another exciting June event. Participants invited from Plains tribes all over the United States and Canada compete throughout the day in a variety of singing and dancing competitions. All entrants wear traditional tribal clothing and make a day that is entertaining and educational.

On July 4, Cody holds a celebration that attracts thousands of visitors. The Stampede Days begin in the mornings with a parade down the main street. After lunch, contestants compete for championship titles at the Stampede Rodeos. Families enjoy picnics and parties, and the city park fills with crowds who come to take part in the entertainment. The day finishes with a bang, as the firework display lights up skies.

Throughout the summers in Cody, the days may begin with a river float down the Shoshone River in the Wapiti East Yellowstone Valley. Then it's on to **Old Trail Town**, which has been widely publicized by media such as *Good Morning America* and *National Geographic*, and is also a must-see on your vacation. Every building in Trail Town remains as it was originally. They have only been moved to Trail Town to be preserved for future generations; they make up a complete town, being furnished authentically from the livery stable and saloon, to the cabins that were lived in by famous frontiersmen.

Throughout the world, people value the legend of America's West. For the most part, that lifestyle, with its attitudes, recreational opportunities and open spaces, is a thing of the past. Replicas and imitations can frequently be found as recreations of a past era, but Wyoming and the Cody Country are alive and well. So load your camera and bring lots of extra film, gather your casual clothing for action or relaxing, and show your zest for "cowboy country" as it is today.

Buffalo Bill with his Indian friends, Red Cloud and American Horse.

SURGEON GENERAL HAS DETERMINED THAT CIGARETTE SMOKING IS DANGEROUS TO YOUR HEALTH.

CHEYENNE

CHEYENNE, WYOMING

On the sun-swept prairie where the plains meet the mountains, Cheyenne, the capital of Wyoming, had its humble but hardly modest beginnings in 1867 when the Union Pacific Railroad tracks were laid through this site on its way to the West Coast. The city was named after the Indian tribe "Shey-ah-nah" who roamed these territories and occupied the present-day southeastern part of Wyoming. The railroad brought all types of characters to Cheyenne and most of them never left. It was a wild frontier town possessing over 60 saloons and by 1868, 300 businesses were supported by hunters, trappers, railroad men, laborers, artists, engineers, Sioux, Pawnee and Cheyenne Indians, gamblers, musicians, promoters and gunmen. The only law enforcement for this unruly community known as "Hell on Wheels" was a gunny sack hooded "vigilance committee". Their nightly activities (which included some lynchings) subdued some of the law-breaking and motivated the more trustworthy citizens to elect a real sheriff. Some of the realities of early Cheyenne were cheap liquor, good pay and high stakes for gamblers, confidence men, shady promoters and robbers.

Grenville Dodge, Railroad Surveyor General, after surveying the town site organized his first camp on Crow Creek in west Cheyenne. This camp, ideally situated at the junction of many major routes, had direct access to military activities throughout the region. Soldiers and workers alike were recovering from a four-year war, and had become familiar with quick decisions and instant action. White ruffians, angry Native Americans and straying bullets made death a common affair. The cemetery was as important as the saloon, and the bad folks and workers were "dying to get in". In 1868, a reorganized vigilance committee assumed a strong stand by taking law and order into their own hands. They passed severe judgment on most matters; 12 men received death

penalties the first year. As the railroad moved West, it took some of the transient population with it. Cheyenne continued to evolve into a flourishing town and a thriving depot for army supplies.

An important contribution to the progress and development of Cheyenne's economy was the booming livestock industry. In the early 1800s, due to cattle raising, Cheyenne was the most wealthy per capita city in the world. It was during the height of her economic development that the world famous "Cheyenne Club" was built. In this exclusive club the cuisine of the imported chef was known from coast to coast. The club was luxuriously furnished in English style and had many wealthy members who spent their summers in Cheyenne and their winters in Europe. One of the most notorious paintings in the state, Paul Potter's *Bull* finished by Nesker in 1885, which hangs in the reception room of the Chamber of Commerce, is said to have been the cause of the dismissal of one Cheyenne Club prominent member. The member, a

wealthy cattle owner, shot a hole through the painted bull's front leg because he considered the painting a travesty on Wyoming livestock.

Most of the members were well-to-do cattlemen who spent time in the "Cheyenne Club" sipping rich wine and determining policies that affected the cattle empire throughout the West. The rich, nutritious grasslands that surrounded Cheyenne were the main reason that some ranchers started sheep ranching in 1890. In the northwest corner of Cheyenne is the site of the Old Court House where Tom Horn was hung in 1903. As sheep ranching became a threat to the cattlemen, a major feud developed. Horn, a range detective, was hired by wealthy cattlemen to do away with rustlers and other trouble makers, namely the sheep ranchers. It is said that he was suspected of killing many offenders before he was convicted for killing 13-year-old Willie Nickell. Horn was promised $500 to kill the rancher Nickell, but acccidentally killed his son instead. Horn was held in jail for many weeks prior to the execution. As the hanging day drew nearer, the "cattleman-sheepman range feud" was building up and Horn escaped jail. Rumors spread that the cattlemen were "fixing things" so Horn could escape before the hanging. After the hanging, Nickell had insisted that he should see the body but he was refused permission by the county attorney saying that it could cause a riot. This led many to believe that the law had been bought and, like some American "bad guy" celebrities, Tom Horn had been seen in various parts of Wyoming since he was hanged. While cattlemen held their own for a while, sheep interests eventually took over bringing much prosperity to the state. Today sheep farming is vital to Wyoming's economy making her sheep industry the second largest in the country.

"The Magic City of the Plains": During the late 1800s, Cheyenne was known as "The Magic City of the Plains". In the history of Cheyenne, transportation played an important role. In 1870, beef was shipped to Europe for the armies

The Anoka High School band in front of the Cheyenne Capitol.

fighting in the Franco-Prussian War. There was a time in Cheyenne when over 200 wagons had engaged more than 400 men to operate the daily Cheyenne-Dreadwood Stage Line. The Stage Line carried mail, gold bullion that was discovered in the Black Hills and, of course, passengers. In 1875, the gold outfitting prospectors and miners came to Cheyenne with long string teams hauling mining machinery, provisions and thousands of passengers.

Diverse activity and a versatile population created a busy social life in Cheyenne. The Opera House featured many Broadway productions on their way to San Francisco. Lavish balls, parties, dramas, literary and musical functions, and art exhibits added to the cultural life of the community, which far surpassed many other cities of that size in the East.

This highly developed cultural life still exists in Cheyenne. There is an active symphony theater, concerts, museums, art shows and many musical and cultural organizations. Cheyenne caters to the university population of Laramie which is only 50 miles (80 km) from here. The Cheyenne gunslingers bring the old West to life with reenactments of gunfights and other activities all through the summer (daily except Sundays) in the Old Town Plaza in downtown Cheyenne. Melodramas complete with olio acts are performed twice every night from mid-June through mid-August at the Atlas Theater.

The last week of July brings the Cheyenne Frontier Days, the year's most spectacular event and "The Big Daddy of 'em all". This event has been called "where the pavement ends and the West begins," "honest to goodness, bronc stompin', jumping up and down Western family fun". The city comes alive in the true Western fashion. Boots, cowboy hats, blue jeans, western shirts…the spectrum of attire here varies from the conventional to high fashion designer outfits. You can capture the magnetism and flavor of this place in its heyday. The early Frontier Days which started in 1897 were held on the prairies north

Square dancers whoop it up during Cheyenne Frontier Days.

of town. The spectators usually came equipped with their umbrellas to avoid the rain and to shoo away bucking broncos or steers.

Nowadays, before the celebration, Cheyenne natives dress up in big hats, high-heeled boots, and western shirts. Native Americans congregate from different parts of the country to participate in the Indian Village and Plains Indian Dancing which is the most colorful part of the event.

Cheyenne Frontier Days Rodeo is claimed to be the largest outdoor rodeo in the world, attracting the best rodeo performers with its high prize money of nearly half a million dollars. Every rodeo cowboy covets the Frontier Days trophy buckle which is awarded to the cowboy with the best performance. Each afternoon during this event the world's best cowboys compete for the grand payday against some of the nation's wildest stock. Thousands of fans and spectators thrill as cowboys and cowgirls, professional and amateur, compete with wild-eyed brahma bulls,

the roughest, meanest, and largest animals in the show. Press from all over the world come to cover the event. Special press areas (press box at the roof top) and a portion of the arena are reserved for international writers and photographers. Every once in a while press photographers have to run for the fence to avoid the attack of an angry charging brahma bull. The atmosphere is exciting, the action wild and fun-packed. Some of the other special events at the rodeo are bull riding, saddle bronc, calf roping, steer roping, steer wrestling, chuckwagon racing, bull fighting, pony races, wild horse races, and the naming of the all-round cowboy to the competitor who wins the most points in the individual events.

Every one of the Cheyenne Frontier Days Rodeos (except the first one) began with a big parade. An elaborate spectacle was held in 1898 when Buffalo Bill himself led the grand parade with his Wild West Show. For a number of years after that, the parade emphasis died down, with the exception of **Railway station in Cheyenne.**

Theodore Roosevelt's visit in 1910, and when the event celebrated its Silver Anniversary in 1921. In 1925, the Frontier Committee started improving the parade and introduced the theme "Evolution of Transportation" which is still maintained.

Today the Frontier Days Parade is an incredible experience and possibly one of the best parades in the country. The same parade is watched by thousands as it goes through Cheyenne on four different days. The parade boasts of having the largest collection of horse-drawn vehicles in the world. The pageant features the progress of transportation in the United States since 1860. On display are prairie schooners, stagecoaches, lumber wagons, freight wagons, express wagons, carryalls, surreys, single buggies, antique cars, high wheel bicycles, dogcarts, miniature passenger trains, racing gigs and many other modes tracing the "evolution of transportation". The parade is further enhanced with historic floats, marching bands, equestrians, baton twirlers, rodeo queens, Plains Indian dancers, and many other colorful groups.

The Frontier Days carnival has a wide variety of rides in the midway area of the fairgrounds. This goes on all nine days of the Rodeo. Concessions, games, and all types of merchandise from turquoise jewelry to western hats and belts are available. Every night some of the best country entertainment in the States performs on the fairgrounds. Other family fun includes events like chili cook-offs, free pancake breakfasts and square dancing. The Old West Museum, the Governor's invitational art show and sale and the Indian Village make this nine-day nonstop adventure one that is fun, educational, and cultural.

The State Capitol: The **Union Pacific Railroad Depot** in downtown Cheyenne is worth a visit. This mellow old building is uniquely designed and still serves as the Union Pacific Station. At the far end of the street is the **State Capitol** with its sparkling gold leaf dome; it can be seen from anywhere in the city. Though the first territorial government

Two bison fight it out on the open range.

met in Cheyenne, it did not have a permanent building for the legislative until 1888. In April of 1890, three months before Wyoming was admitted into the Union as a state, this French Renaissance capitol building was completed. The capitol occupies two full city blocks and is a part of a 14-acre (6-hectare) complex of Wyoming state buildings and offices.

Within the confines of the capitol, the history of Wyoming comes to life. It was here that the first woman governor in the United States (Mrs) Nellis Taylor Ross was elected. (She later became the first woman director of the United States Mint.) The first woman justice-of-the-peace in America, Esther Hobart Morris, a Wyoming native, has her statue in front of the capitol.

In the summertime on weekdays, guided tours of the capitol begin every 30 minutes. The beautiful marble floors, woodwork, stained glass, wildlife display and a historical photographic display are some of the features of the tour.

Parks for relaxation: Cheyenne's numerous parks are great for family picnics and relaxation. "Old Number 4004 Big Boy" is the world's largest locomotive and can be seen on display at the **Holiday Park**. Until 1956, this massive engine did the work of two conventional steam engines, carrying 28 tons of fuel and 25,000 gallons of water.

The **National First Day Cover Museum** in Cheyenne is the only museum of its kind in the world. This well-preserved collection is of first day covers of the rarest and most valuable stamps in the world. Its worth is nearly a million dollars. The museum stays open Monday through Friday 9 a.m. till 5 p.m. and may be visited free of charge.

There is a wide variety of motels, hotels, and restaurants for you to "hang your hat" in. If you expect to visit Cheyenne during Frontier Days, accommodation should be booked ahead of time. If you plan to explore the wilderness in Wyoming, stop at the Wyoming Travel Commission in Cheyenne on Interstate 25, and collect all the necessary information, maps and brochures.

A hard-working ranch hand drives the cattle out to pasture.

Not too far from Cheyenne, about 30 miles (50 km), are the **Vedauwoo Rocks**, a popular stop for rock climbers, photographers and picnickers. The name means "earthborn" in the Cheyenne language. This jumbled mass of unusual rock formations is located on Pole Mountain between Laramie and Cheyenne.

Trailblazing women: On your way out of Cheyenne west, about 50 miles (80 km) is the town of **Laramie** which is also one of Wyoming's oldest cities. The town was named after the legendary French-Canadian trapper, Jacques La Ramie, whose name was also given to a military post, a mountain range, a peak, a river, a county and a section of the Wyoming plains all in the Rockies area. La Ramie, a free trapper working the southeastern part of Wyoming, was said to have been killed by unfriendly Native Americans along the banks of the river that bears his name.

Laramie has a history and foundation very similar to that of Cheyenne. This city, called "The Gem City of the Plains", made history by having the first woman in the world serve on a court jury in 1870. Another "first" occurred when "grandma" Louiza Swain went to the polls and became the first woman in the world to vote in a general election.

Wyoming was the first state in the country to give women the right to vote. This happened in 1869 when the Wyoming Territorial Legislature passed resolutions that offered "married women in their separate property, and the enjoyments of fruits of their labor", and a school law providing equal pay for female school teachers. The women of Wyoming were trailblazers in the pursuit of women's rights. The leader of the suffragettes, Susan B. Anthony, rejoiced that Wyoming was "...the first place on God's green earth which could consistently claim to be the land of the free!"

The first chance for the vote came in 1870 when the majority of the one thousand women in Wyoming went to the polls. After the initial excitement, this event was soon forgotten. In 1889, when the State Constitution was being drawn, there was a threat to repeal suffrage. Mrs Theresa Jenkins, a women's rights activist, organized a demonstration for every woman in Cheyenne to come to the capitol and insist that they keep their voting rights. The demonstration was successful and that night Mrs Jenkins went home and delivered a baby girl.

Some of Laramie's other points of interest include the **Geological Museum**, the **Fine Arts Center** and the **Rocky Mountain Herbarium**. The Herbarium, located on the third floor of the Aven Nelson Building, contains more than 320,000 specimens of Rocky Mountain plants and is one of the best known herbaria in the country. **Fort Sanders**, 3 miles (5 km) from Laramie, **Laramie Plains Museum**, and the **Overland Trail Art Gallery** are also worth visiting.

Wyoming was, and continues to be, "the land of the cowboy". Folk here take pride in maintaining the traditions of the Old West, while keeping in step with the world's technological developments in agriculture and farming.

Wyoming cowboy prepares for the ride ahead.

BOZEMAN, MONTANA

Americans are fond of remembering the West's many mining camps as rambunctious and ramshackle towns thrown up overnight when gold or silver was discovered. Towns and cities of today's Rockies that had such beginnings proudly and nostalgically remind themselves and their visitors of their romantic heritage.

In doing so, they blithely overlook the certainly less romantic aspects of daily life. The myth would convince us that all the men in town spent every waking minute working their claims, and that the only women present were the gaudily dressed "soiled doves" of the saloons. When darkness fell over the diggings, the men repaired to saloons to consume rye whiskey – and nothing else – while playing poker until dawn.

Bozeman, Montana, did not start out that way. It came into existence because of the miners' needs. Men who devoted themselves to seeking elusive mineral riches during a short summer season had no time to plant crops.

Bozeman sits in a wide and fertile valley with mountains ringing the horizon. Even though we think of the concept as a 20th-century one, Bozeman was a planned community. On August 9, 1864, a group of settlers sat down and decided to establish a farming community. They would make their money by supplying food to the mining camps located in the mountains north and west of here. The group voted to name their town for the man who had conceived the idea and who had brought some of them here, John M. Bozeman.

Bozeman leads the way: It was the beginning of a stable community. Some of the great Rockies family fortunes were begun by those who were wise enough to venture West to serve as merchants, freighters, cattle ranchers and farmers. Untold thousands who came only for the precious metals went home penniless, while those who brought in and sold them the necessities of life usually profited and stayed.

John Bozeman seems to have learned that lesson the hard way. In 1862 he, too, came West to make his fortune as a miner, and failed. Wintering at Bannack, Montana Territory, he joined with John M. Jacobs in designing a shorter route north from Fort Laramie to Montana's new gold camps. Later to become known as the Bozeman Road, it was popular with gold-seekers for three years, although it was considerably more difficult and dangerous than the competing route laid out by former mountain man Jim Bridger.

Red Cloud's war: Hardship was not to stand in the way of those afflicted with gold fever. Bozeman's route offered less water, less forage for the horses, and passed through the prime hunting land of the Sioux Indians. Having been pushed westward long enough by white settlement, the Sioux were by now unwilling to give up this game-rich area. Led by Red Cloud, they fought. The new wagon route became known as the "bloody Bozeman", and the Sioux efforts are still remembered as Red Cloud's

Preceding pages: Bozeman Sweet Pea Festival. Left, morning light over Lone Mountain. Right, a special sight – the great horned owl.

War. Red Cloud and his people won, and the US Army officially closed the three-year-old route.

John Bozeman, having initiated the problem, retired from guiding wagon trains over this route after the first year. Upon the founding of Bozeman, he settled in Montana to farm and to serve as a probate judge. But in 1867, as John was traveling into eastern Montana to solicit a flour contract with the army, he was killed by Blackfeet Indians. They were not the Sioux, but perhaps it was poetic justice.

In death as in life, John Bozeman assisted his namesake town. Bozeman residents appealed to the federal government for military protection from Indian raids such as the one that killed their founder. They received Fort Ellis, a cavalry post which, naturally, became another market for the produce of Gallatin Valley farms surrounding the town. By 1880, when it was 16 years old, Bozeman had 3,800 residents, but its subsequent growth has been much slower: 50 years later, the population had not quite doubled. Today Bozeman has 22,000 people, half of them students at **Montana State University.**

Studying at "Moo U": This public institution opened as the Agricultural College of the State of Montana in 1893, with eight enrolled students and no campus. Although it is now a university, and the largest in the state's system, it is known as "Moo U" by those who remember its beginnings. Important research into improved crop and livestock production continues at the university: there is also an excellent film and television department, along with art, architecture, engineering, social services and nursing programs.

On the university campus is the **Museum of the Rockies**, a well-designed modern museum dedicated to telling the story of this region from prehistoric times to the 20th century. The museum sponsors summer season paleontological and archaeological digs, which have uncovered significant dinosaur remains as well as evidences of Native-American cultures. Finds from these digs as

The story of John Bozeman is depicted in this town mural.

well as farming relics are on exhibit.

Special changing exhibits feature art or historical objects from the museum's collections, as well as works by contemporary western artists and artisans. An annual western art show and sale occurs from late June to mid-July. The museum is open seven days a week, closed January 1 and December 25. There is an admission charge; group tours can be arranged on request.

Bright lights to red lights: Cultural events centered on the university are not the only ones Bozeman offers. Like many other small and isolated Rockies towns, Bozeman has cultivated a tradition of self-sufficiency in entertainment. In 1890, the ornate **Bozeman Opera Houe** opened, hosting various musical and theatrical performers – from Sarah Bernhardt to Al Jolson – and lecturers over the years. For a different clientele, a red-light district of at least six "sporting houses" (of prostitution) operated in a most businesslike way. From 1900 to 1912, each house paid a monthly fine to city hall for breaking the law. The opera house and the "sporting houses" are long since gone.

The 1970s saw a rebirth of interest in preserving historic Bozeman buildings. All along Main Street, the central downtown business district, brick "business blocks" dating from the late 19th century were restored to their original exterior appearances. Even though their interiors are modern stores and offices, a stroll down Main Street is a pleasant view of the West's past.

Bozeman supports 15 small art galleries and dealers, offering exhibits and sale of works in all media from weaving to photography, painting to jewelry, from artists around the western United States.

The Sweet Pea Festival: The annual Sweet Pea Arts & Crafts Festival (taking place in the second week in August) combines display and sales with a carnival-like offering of foods, fun runs, a semi-serious triathlon, outdoor musical performances and open-air Shakespeare theater, performed by a Montana repertory company that tours throughout the state each summer.

The Sweet Pea Festival began in 1906, celebrating a major industry in town: production and packing of seed peas for sale to farmers throughout the nation and canning of peas for food consumption. During World War I, the festival was discontinued and wasn't revived until 1978. By then, the seed pea and canning industries were gone from the town, but many backyard gardens still blossomed annually with sweet pea flowers, so the Sweet Pea Festival was resurrected.

Cattle ranching is also a part of Bozeman's heritage, and so, too, is the cowboy. "Cowboy art" is available in the galleries – realistic paintings of western landscapes and ranching scenes past and present. Cowboy cafés offer the hearty food that fuels ranch hands for long days, and western clothing stores supply their Stetson hats, Levi jeans, bandanna handkerchiefs and boots with heels designed for various kinds of work. Cowboy bars offer country-western music for listening or dancing.

Educated cowboys: In mid-June, Bozeman welcomes the National Intercollegiate Rodeo Association Finals, a rodeo for the best student competitors from more than 200 colleges in the United States, including 10 in Montana. These are young people attending college on rodeo scholarships, who have qualified for this event by virtue of their performances in rodeos between competing schools during the preceding academic year. They are competing both as individuals and as team members representing their schools.

A specially-groomed indoor arena at Montana State University houses the finals events, each night for a week. Related events include a "Miss College Rodeo" pageant, a cowboy golf tournament and an art show.

Because of its small size, Bozeman does not offer mass transportation. But visitors who rent cars to tour the surrounding area will find it worthwhile, summer or winter.

Bridger Bowl, 11 miles (18 km) north of town, offers downhill ski slopes noted for their dry powder snow. With five double chairs, 2,000 vertical feet (610 meters) and The Ridge (made famous by Warren Miller). There is plenty of cruising as well as steep terrain.

West of Bozeman on I-90, the **Madison Buffalo Jump** vividly explains how Plains Indians hunted the buffalo in the ages before they had horses. Working toward a cliff such as the one at this site, they herded the animals into a stampede over the side. At the kill site below, the buffalo were slaughtered and butchered in a process putting to use every part of the animal – hide, meat, bones, sinews, even bladders (which became inflated "footballs" for children's play). Interpretive signs at the Madison Buffalo Jump explain the use of the site as a camp during the buffalo preparation, and also give examples of archaeological finds from the area.

Neighboring scenic parks: The nearby **Headwaters State Park**, also along I-90 and well-marked, is where the Jefferson, Madison and Gallatin rivers converge to form the **Missouri River**. Within the park, visitors experience the landscape as Captain Meriwether Lewis did on July 27, 1805, when the Lewis and Clark expedition reached this point. The Captain noted in his journal: "we arrived at 9 a.m. at the junction of…the Missouri and the country opens suddenly to extensive and beautiful plains and meadows which appear to be surrounded in every direction with distant and lofty mountains…"

Interpretive signs tell the story of this area's use before whites came, and of the Lewis and Clark expedition. One of their purposes in exploring the vast "Louisiana Purchase" of lands obtained from France was to discover the fabled "Northwest Passage", a hoped-for water route to the Pacific Ocean. At the headwaters of the Missouri, they knew that no such water route existed, for here the Missouri stopped.

South of Bozeman, through the beautiful **Gallatin Canyon**, is one of the gateways to **Yellowstone National Park**. Throughout this area of clear trout-filled streams and lushly green-forested mountain peaks are guest ranches with year-round recreation facilities, including skiing, fishing, pack

Shoshone National Forest from Red Lodge Road.

trips, horseback riding, golfing, swimming and primitive or deluxe lodgings.

About one day's drive north from Bozeman is **Glacier National Park**, which crosses from Montana into Canada as Waterton Park. It is aptly named for the glaciers that remain upon its craggy, glacier-sculpted peaks, providing some of the most breathtaking scenery in the country.

Glaciers and eagles: Glacier Park is not nearly so developed with road networks and tourist facilities as is Yellowstone National Park. Only one road crosses from the east to the west entrance – **Going-to-the-Sun Highway**, which crosses the Continental Divide on Logan Pass. This narrow road, built for yesteryear's smaller cars, is cut shelf-like high up on the solid rock of the Garden Wall escarpment. It does truly seem to head for the sun.

These mountains show well the effect of glaciation on the hard rock faces when a mammoth ice sheet once covered the region. Cirques, or high mountain basins scoured out by glaciers, are in evidence, but the remaining glaciers are tiny compared to the ancient ones.

Alpine meadows of wild flowers bloom in late spring and early summer, and perpetual snowfields allow visitors to go cross-country skiing in the warm summer sun. While the park is open in some areas for winter cross-country skiing, Going-to-the-Sun Highway cannot be cleared of snowdrifts until June – and snows begin again in September or October. This is definitely a place to visit in summer.

At a lower elevation, however, is one of the grand sights of the Rockies. In October, bald eagles, an endangered species protected here, swarm to feed on spawning salmon.

Camping and bears: Hiking is the way to see Glacier Park, and trails exist thoughout. Backcountry camping is allowed, and campgrounds and lodges by lower elevation roadsides are provided. This is a habitat for grizzly and black bears, so rangers close camp grounds or trails where bears have been sighted and visitors are alerted on arrival.

ke in the
ster
ational
rest.

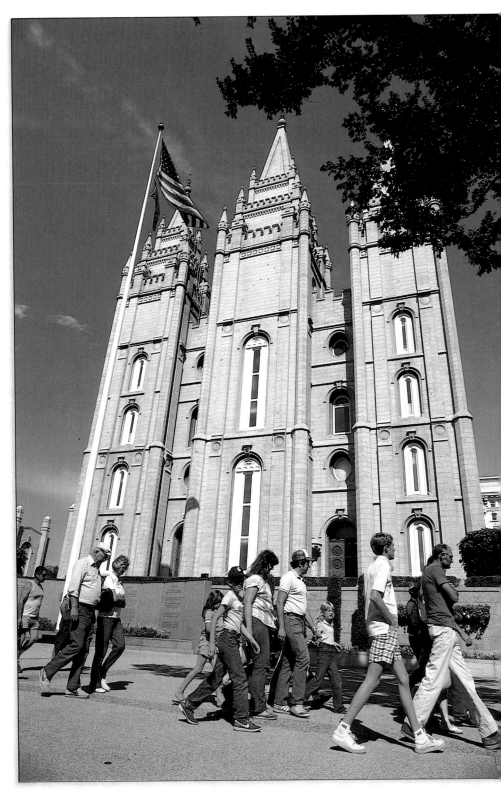

SALT LAKE CITY, UTAH

Years ago, Salt Lake City enjoyed the reputation of being a strait-laced provincial western town. In the eyes of the "well-traveled" visitor, only two distinctions redeemed the city from mediocrity. One, as the capital of the Great Basin kingdom of the Church of Jesus Christ of Latter-Day Saints (Mormons), Salt Lake City seemed like a foreign land to most Gentiles (non-Mormons) – an exotic encounter in his own homeland for the American visitor and a unique experience to those traveling from abroad. The distinct Latter-Day Saints' heritage left an indelible imprint on the city's history, architecture and lifestyle, which visitors readily discern. Two, the city's physical setting also placed Salt Lake City in the guidebooks as a memorable place to visit in the western Rocky Mountains. The city's matchless setting between the towering, jagged, snowclad Wasatch Mountains to the east, and the copper-pitted Oquirrh Mountains to the west, with the blue Great Salt Lake shimmering off to the northwest, brought tourists to this city of Zion in moderate droves

But after scanning the peaks and vistas, "bobbing" in the unsinkable salty waters, gawking at the Mormon citizenry and suspecting everyone of polygamy, boredom set in and soon the visitor asked, "Is there life in Salt Lake City after the local Woolworth's closes?" The answer was no.

But not today! For Salt Lake City is a premiere urban oasis in a rising new American West. The city now has not only vistas and virtue, but also vitality.

Due to a wave of outside influences during the last decade – the influx of energy-related and electronics industries, banking and corporate interests – coupled with the phenomenal growth of Wasatch ski resorts (only minutes away from downtown), Salt Lake City has leaped into modernity boasting a contemporary, cultured, uncrowded, vibrant lifestyle envied by all its Rocky Mountain urban rivals. Salt Lake City is still a "clean" city, but at no time is it ever dull.

This prosperity has created a benign tension between those "of the kingdom" and those outside the kingdom, placing the city squarely at a crossroads between the new "Gentile" growth and the saintly heritage of the region. So far, a beneficial balance has been struck between the the two, making the area a Rocky Mountain Zion for all.

Temple Square: By day, the heart and hub of Salt Lake City is the sandstone and adobe walled 10-acre (4-hectare) grounds of **Temple Square**, naturally the place to begin a visit. Shortly after his arrival at Salt Lake Valley in 1847, Brigham Young, with cane in hand, consecrated the site between two forks of City Creek for the construction of the church's temple. For over 40 years thereafter, oxen teams dragged and hauled granite blocks from nearby quarries in the Wasatch Mountains until the majestic, six-spired neo-Gothic Latter-Day Saints (LDS) Temple stood completed. Gold-leafed and conspicuously statued atop the Temple is the angel figure of Moroni, blowing his horn to announce the Second Coming of Christ. The Temple itself is used for the holy ordinances of the LDS church, such as baptisms, weddings and family "sealing" ceremonies, and is open only to Mormons with "recommends" from their ward bishops. But the general public can amble about within the manicured grounds of Temple Square (a delight at Christmas time, when it is aglitter with thousands of lights) where two visitors' centers provide exhibits of Mormon history and beliefs. While on the Temple grounds, of note is the **Sea Gull Monument** commemorating the "miracle of the gulls" who saved the Mormon pioneers' first crop from swarms of crickets, and **Assembly Hall**, a place of worship. And one should not miss a visit to the acoustically sensitive home of the Mormon Tabernacle Choir, the **Tabernacle**, and its magnificent organ with 11,000 pipes, considered to be one of the world's finest pipe organs.

From Temple Square it is only a short walk in several directions to other noteworthy LDS church sites in this district of

Salt Lake. Going out the west gate of Temple Square you cannot miss the mausoleum-housed **Museum of Church History and Art** where religious exhibits on church leaders, western art, the Mormon westward migration, and other subjects provide additional knowledge for travelers. Directly east of Temple Square is a full block clustered with Church-related buildings. Passing out the south gate of Temple Square and heading east, the route is marked by the **Brigham Young Monument** (depicting Brigham Young, the frontiersman Jim Bridger and the Shoshone Indian Chief Washakie) and the elegant, historic **Hotel Utah**. Directly north and east, the hotel is flanked by magnificent fountains, flowered gardens and leisurely lawns that comprise the grounds to a complex of other noteworthy LDS buildings.

A genealogical library: The Family History Library, next to the Museum of Church History and Art, houses the LDS genealogical library (largest in the world). Almost one million rolls of microfilmed records of births, baptisms and deaths from around the world are stored in its archive collection, and a staff of librarians, speaking 40 languages, will guide you to the roots of your family lineage.

Brigham's Beehive House: Directly south from the Church Office Building, across the plaza, are the former residences of Brigham Young and many of his 27 wives. The **Beehive House** (1853–54), on the southeast corner of the block, was the official residence of Brigham Young, where, as an LDS church president and Utah territorial governor, he received many prominent visitors. The charming three-storied Federal and Greek revival styled residence, which is now a National Historic Landmark, is named for the unique hand-hewed beehive sculpture resting on the roof's cupola; and its restored interior pine-paneled walls and period decorations quickly draw you to the Mormon past. Next door stands the **Lion House** (1855), a "supplementary" domestic residence for Brigham Young and his wives where

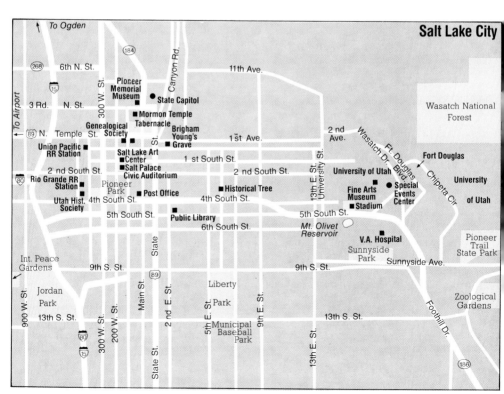

many of his 56 children grew to age. An impressive sculptured stone lion guards this communal residence's entrance. The main floor lodged Young's many wives in individual quarters, and the 20 gabled dormers on the second story marked the rooms of the older children. Though the Lion House is closed to the public (the LDS church now uses it for social purposes), more of the Mormon pioneer past can be discovered by walking westward back to the Brigham Young Monument and heading three blocks northward on Main Street, passing the elegant **McCune Mansion** (home of Alfred McCune, a mining pioneer and millionaire) on the right, to the **Daughters of Utah Pioneers'** or **Pioneer Memorial Museum**. The volunteer DUP Museum is crammed, nook and cranny, with pioneer memorabilia, from dolls to military collections – enough Mormon paraphernalia and belongings to overwhelm any visitor.

The State Capitol: Across the street from this monument to the Mormons', the secular world of the Gentile past and present begins with a tour of the **Capitol Hill** area. The Renaissance Revival copper-domed **State Capitol**, the temporal seat of power in Utah, overlooks Temple Square and the rest of the valley. On a clear day or night, from the steps beneath its Corinthian marble columns, the perfect photographic view of the Wasatch Mountains and the platted streets below is seen. Inside rises a 165-ft (50-meter) rotunda, arching over the building's attractions: the 23-karat gold-leaf state reception room, an exhibition hall displaying Utah's attractions and history, and marble staircases leading to the galleried chambers of state government. Outside there is a 40-acre (16-hectare) park with lawns and strolling gardens and other sites to visit such as the restored **Council Hall** (first meeting place for the territorial legislature), **White Memorial Chapel** (a Gothic steepled former LDS chapel), and **Memory Grove**, a secluded park in **City Creek Canyon** east of the Capitol where many downtown workers spread out picnic lunches on the banks of City Creek.

Surrounding Capitol Hill are two historic residential districts. West of the State Capitol is the **Marmalade Historic District** – its streets named after fruits – where many early English and Scandinavian immigrants resided. East of City Creek Canyon and accessible from Temple Square is the **Avenues Historic District**, where one can find a wide variety of residential architectures, including many restored Victorian houses. A number of mansions and buildings here are noteworthy and within short walking distance from Temple Square. They include the **Cathedral of the Madeleine** (a gray sandstone Catholic Romanesque style church with stained-glass sanctuary windows) and the mansions of two prominent Utah silver magnates who owned the Silver King Mine in Park City, the **Keith Brown Mansion** and the **Thomas Kearns Mansion**, which is now used as Utah's governor's mansion.

Tracing the way back to Temple Square, you can shrug off spiritual values in favor of the commercial and cultural ones which are to be found in the

ioneer
luseum, Salt
ake City.

downtown district of Salt Lake.

Gentile pursuits: The secular life begins with downtown's many shopping areas which are easily reached from all of Salt Lake's major hotels. Commercial Salt Lake City is compactly and conveniently arranged to meet all one's shopping dreams. South of Temple Square is four-story **Crossroads Plaza** (America's largest downtown shopping mall) where more than 100 shops and stores, three movie theaters, 22 restaurants or cafes, and a rooftop sports facility are all available. Across Main Street from the plaza, an additional 60 beautiful stores and 12 restaurants are located in the ZCMI **Center**, operated by the LDS church. In addition, three blocks west of Temple Square is a 30-acre (12-hectare) multi-purpose commercial complex, the **Devereaux Plaza** at **Triad Center**. It features fine shops, restaurants, private social clubs, an ice-skating rink, and the restored **Devereaux Mansion** at the center of the complex.

The vitality of Salt Lake's shopping district is only a small reflection of the growing prosperity and energy of the city. Almost daily, a new construction crane lifts its head toward the desert blue skies as the moribund pre-1970s lifestyle fades into the distant past. An energetic cultural and recreational life is evident everywhere in Salt Lake City. Ice-cream parlors and movie houses, popular local weekend diversions, still abound, but now there is a Gentile night life as well!

Capping Salt Lake City's new cultural life are a number of nationally acclaimed restaurants and dozens of hot nightspots and clubs. No "liquorbythedrink" (one word in Utah) except in private bottle clubs (where visitor memberships can be purchased) is still the norm, but the nightlife in Salt Lake is no longer just a night of bingo, as new "to-be-seen-at" social clubs proliferate and compete to meet the demands of Gentile immigrants and local "jack" (inactive) Mormons.

Cultural oasis: Summertime is Salt Lake's best downtown season. The city now features a variety of activities for

The Mormon Tabernacle Choir.

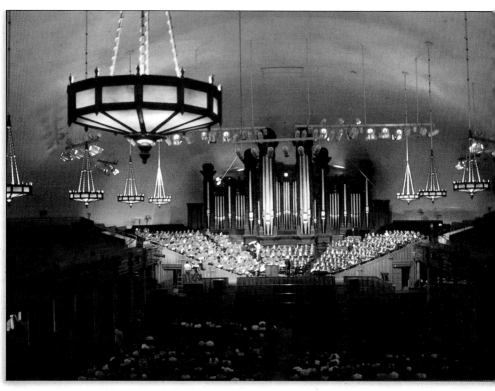

both Mormons and non-Mormons alike, such as arts and ethnic festivals where one can buy local crafts and art works with one hand while eating Greek *souvlaki* and Navajo *tacos* with the other. Or one can buy tickets to shows and entertainment at the nearby **Salt Palace Convention Center**, where activities range from concerts, circuses and rodeos to cheering Salt Lake City's very own professional basket-ball team, the Utah "Jazz".

If one has "higher" culture in mind, Salt Lake City has everything in the performing arts any cosmopolitan visitor could desire, for this western urban center is an oasis of culture in the Rocky Mountains, where nationally acclaimed music, theater and dance companies now reside. **Symphony Hall**, an architectural and acoustical gem, houses the world-renowned **Utah Symphony Orchestra**, while next door the **Salt Lake Art Center** offers the best work of Utah artistry along with visiting national exhibits. Several blocks away at the **Capitol Theater**, performing arts have no equal in the Rocky Mountain West when the **Utah Opera Company** and **Ballet West** take to fulfilling their busy calendar of engaging works.

Pioneers of the past: Downtown Salt Lake is not the only attraction for those seeking entertainment and fun. Within easy access from downtown Salt Lake are other areas that offer varied experiences. To the east is Salt Lake's **Emigration Visitors District**, a scenic triangle of entertaining, historic, educational and cultural attractions situated near the mouth of **Emigration Canyon**. At the **University of Utah**, whose medical school implanted the world's first artificial heart in Barney Clarke, one can stroll around the vast, gardened campus overlooking the panoramic valley below, visit the collections and exhibits at the **Museum of Fine Arts** and the **Museum of Natural History** or tour 9,000-acre **Fort Douglas**, a National Historic Landmark, which was established in 1862. The museum here displays exhibits on Utah's military history. From here, it is only a short hop to

The Mormon Assembly Hall, Salt Lake City.

Hogle Zoo on Sunnyside Avenue, where 1,000 exotic animals await your visit. Directly across from Hogle Zoo, Utah's pioneer past comes alive in a recreated typical Mormon settlement, **Pioneer Trail State Park**. The park's attractions include "**This is the Place**" **Monument**, commemorating the Mormons' entry into the valley, **Brigham Young's Forest Farm House,** an authentic social hall, a pioneer store, and pioneer craft demonstrations. It is an excellent picnic spot from which to observe what the pioneers may have felt as they entered the Salt Lake Valley from the Wasatch Mountains and saw the Great Salt Lake in the west.

Nostalgic fun: The **Trolley Square District** is six blocks southeast of downtown along Seventh East. It centers around a series of renovated 1908 trolley car barns turned into a bustling, brick-paved shopping, dining and theater area known as **Trolley Square,** an area reminiscent of Boston's Faneuil Hall and San Francisco's Ghirardelli Square. A few blocks south on Seventh East is **Liberty Park** where on landscaped lawns under shady pines, one can enjoy watching people swim, play tennis, and paddle on the ponds. After visiting the park's ivory, two-storied adobe **Isaac Chase Home and Mill** with its period furnishings, take a leisurely walk and listen to the trumpeter swans, the rare Andean condor and hundreds of other bird species at the **Tracy Aviary**.

The **Other Side of the Tracks District** literally designates an area with a rich ethnic heritage on the west side of the railroad tracks that pass through the city only a few blocks away from downtown. Railroad buffs may want to visit the nostalgic **Union Pacific Depot**, where western scenes are depicted on murals and stained glass, or the renovated **Rio Grande Depot**, two blocks to the south and now the Amtrak Depot and the **Utah State History Museum**, which offers many exhibits on Utah's rich and varied past. Continuing west from these sites, one can visit the unique **International Peace Gardens** representing 18 countries, or travel out to the **Utah State Fair Grounds** for such seasonal events as the western style state fair in the second week of September.

Beyond the city's immediate environs, several of Salt Lake's scenic satellite areas, such as **Great Salt Lake Desert/Oquirrh Mountain Tour** await discovery in a day's drive. The **Great Salt Lake Park** is a must for any visitor. A visitors' center, marina, beaches and a gift shop can be reached from exit 104 off Interstate 80. The lake, in one of its flooding cycles, has inundated the causeway to **Antelope Island**, and beautiful beaches, bird rookeries, and a small herd of buffalo (American bison) are temporarily inaccessible. Near the sailing marina on the lake's southeastern shores are breathtaking views of the Great Salt Lake, Antelope Island, mountainous **Stansbury Island** to the west, and spectacular sunsets.

Along the western shores: Traveling west along the lake's shores, one has many choices of what to do next. Far west of the **Oquirrh Mountains** are the **Bonneville Salt Flats**, famous site of numerous world land speed records.

Snowbird mountain.

270

Nearer to the western side of the Oquirrh Mountains unfolds the fascination of the American West, where Pony Express riders once carried the mail and where mining ghost towns named **Gold Hill, Ophir** and **Mercur** still capture the imagination. The culminating experience is a visit to the **Bingham Canyon Copper Mine** on the east side of the mountains, where the boast is that it is the "largest active, open-pit mine in the world, twice as deep as the Empire State Building is tall!"

Alpine Loop and Osmond Studios tours: After touring the Great Salt Lake sites west of Salt Lake City, the **Alpine Loop Tour**, 45 minutes south of the city, offers a variety of activities including some of Utah's most popular scenic excitements. Start the day with a tour of the **Osmond Studios** in North Orem, visit **Brigham Young University**, one of the nation's largest private universities, or even do some spelunking in famous **Timpanogos Cave National Monument**. Any one of these activities is only minutes away from the scenic beauty of Mount Timpanogos. Here one can wind past thawing springtime mountain streams on the 19th-century **Heber Creeper Stream Train** trip to **Bridal Veil Falls**, or in summer windsurf on **Deer Creek Reservoir** below the mountain's majesty, or cast eyes on an incredible alpine autumn by driving along the scenic loop from **Provo Canyon** to **American Fork Canyon**. Or finally, one can snow ski all winter at **Sundance**, movie star Robert Redford's ski resort on the flank of the high peak.

"Powder Perfect" Canyon country: Any season of the year, anywhere along the Wasatch Front, there are exuberant experiences, but the best Utah has to offer is surprisingly only minutes east from downtown Salt Lake in **Wasatch Canyon Country**. This is a relatively small area containing seven major ski resorts, four in **Big and Little Cottonwood Canyons** on the western side of the range and three near Park City on the eastern side of the mountains. All offer the "Greatest Snow on Earth" each and every winter.

"Powder perfect" is the only way to describe the skiing at **Alta** and **Snowbird**, both located in Little Cottonwood Canyon. With an annual snowfall of 500 inches (12.5 meters) of light, dry powder, and with lifts and trails unspoiled by crowds, you know immediately that from Thanksgiving to early summer you can anticipate the consummate skiing experience.

Skiing sensations: The "Alta Experience" is considered the ultimate mountain experience. Once you have tried Alta, you will go home and brag about it. Lifts named Sunnyside, Sugarload and Supreme take you to fluffy virgin powder almost every morning, and the resort's leisurely lodge life of superb dining, cozy fires, saunas, jacuzzis and a 100°F (38°C) outdoor swimming pool all contribute to a memorable experience. On the other hand, Snowbird has the reputation as the "Giantkiller" and is Utah's fast-paced, ultra-fashionable skiing resort. With 50 percent of its runs rated advanced/expert, this resort is a must for those seeking the ultimate

breathtaking descent. The Garaventa tram-ride to the top of 11,000-ft (3,550-meter) Hidden Peak is just spectacular in itself. In addition to alpine grandeur, Snowbird has excellent lodges, restaurants and bars to entertain you throughout the night.

If you are searching for skiing that is less commercial, slower-paced and more family oriented, **Solitude** and **Brighton** ski resorts in Big Cottonwood Canyon are the best destinations. It is here that "locals" learn to ski. If you're friendly, one may even adopt you and show you his favorite secret slopes and runs.

"Greatest snow on earth": From Big Cottonwood Canyon, it's over to **Park City** on the east side of the Wasatch Range, where one finds resorts ranging from ruggedly wild Parkwest to world-class Park City to Utah's newest ski area, the "unspoiled, uncrowded, uncommonly civilized" Deer Valley. All three are located only minutes from the heart of frontier flavored Park City. This historic mining town, nestled in the heart of Wasatch ski and hiking coun-

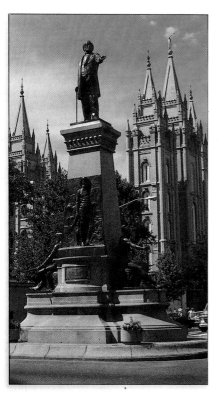

Left, Mormon leader, Brigham Young. Right, one of Young's many wives.

try, has a lifestyle and lively nightlife to match. Uncommon vacation condos, boutiques, gourmet restaurants, private bottle clubs and such annual events as the winter **United States Film Festival** and the summer **Park City Arts Festival** have transformed this once booming Utah mining town into a wealthy skiing mecca and summer vacation spot.

On the outskirts of Park City is another one of Utah's favorite local skiing areas, **Parkwest**. Its rugged powdered terrain, reflected in runs named Bad Hombre, Slaughterhouse, and Massacre, gives clues to the challenge ahead. After putting your skiing skills to the test there, a little more ambiance might seem enticing and the Park City ski resort is the obvious answer.

Park City is the largest ski area in Utah, presenting well-balanced runs from wide open beginner slopes to famous powdered bowls like Jupiter, Blue Slip, and Puma that challenge the advanced skiers. But if pampered poshness is your dream, then your skiing destination is luxurious **Deer Valley**.

Valets will unload your skis, attendants will watch over them in special ski corrals, and Stein Ericksen, Olympic gold medal winner and resort director, will see that you have a relaxing and sumptuous skiing vacation.

Wildlife, wild flowers and waterfalls: The Wasatch canyons hold not only the "Greatest Snow on Earth" but also the "Greatest Hiking on Earth". In the spring, summer or fall, in any of the main canyons, like Big and Little Cottonwood Canyons, and lovely **Millcreek Canyon**, or in any of the smaller canyons, such as **Neff's Ferguson** and **Lamb's Canyons**, the traveler will find a hiker's and rock climber's paradise. Numerous well-marked trails crisscross the canyons leading the hiker or picnicker to meadows of wild flowers full of wildlife, splendid pine and aspen forests; or to hidden, but easily accessible, mountain streams, foaming waterfalls and pristine lakes. Hiking, scenery, photography, fishing, picnicking, and camping are all only minutes away from Salt Lake City, in several different directions.

A strip mining operation near Salt Lake City.

Joseph Smith

(1805–1844)
"I teach the people
correct principles and
they govern themselves."

Mormonism, the most American of major religions, always had an ambivalent relationship with the rest of the nation. Mormon (officially, the Church of Jesus Christ of Latter-Day Saints) is the name of the largest branch of followers of founder Joseph Smith. Mormon experience in many ways repeats American experience, but for more than the first half century of their history Mormons confronted fellow citizens across a gulf of seemingly endless hostility. They were considered a peculiar people with odd, un-American attitudes, and for a while they toyed with the idea of building a separate nation. On the other hand, it is hard to imagine how Mormonism could have spread anywhere but on the intellectually and socially turbulent North American frontier.

That frontier was the prime source of America's symbolic identity and national character. Mormon culture, born and nurtured on the frontier, selected from the available components of that identity, choosing from the Puritan sense of mission and divine selection, freemasonry's cult of secrecy and brotherhood, pseudo-intellectual attempts to explain Native American origins, and the swirl of social, religious, and economic experimentation that gripped a young nation in the romantic era of the early 19th century. Mormons saw danger and excess in the wilderness, and they, like other Americans, tried to subdue it, pursuing an orderly, civilized ideal of neat farms and great cities – an ideal made possible by a steady, strengthening flow of immigrant converts to new orthodoxies like American ideology and Mormon theology. The parallels between the religion's and the nation's experiences became more apparent in the 20th century after the Latter-Day Saints, under duress, abandoned their most idiosyncratic ways – polygamy, theocracy, and communalism – and reembraced middle-class America. Further parallels could be observed in the 1980s as a Mormon vanguard led the national shift to the political right.

Through much of their history, the Mormons sought to organize their society along different lines. Today, their culture's uniqueness is composed of the residue of that distinct social order: their insulating sense that they are a different and special people, their rigid adherence to a set of values that they feel the modern world threatens, and an institutional framework that permeates their lives. Of course, they are no longer just an American people; they have achieved the international presence for which they worked

BRIGHAM YOUNG.—For sketch of life see Annex No. 91.

hard. They are emerging as a major religion, not major on the scale of the world's largest religions, certainly – their million members don't compare with 50 million American Catholics, for example – but their influence exceeds their numbers, and they are one of the world's fastest growing churches. Their 30,000 or so missionaries effectively spread a message first spoken by the son of an itinerant family in the primitive backcountry villages of upstate New York.

The "Burned-Over" district: Frontier New York in the first three decades of the 19th century underwent cycles of religious revivalism that historians call the Second Great

Left, Mormon founder, Joseph Smith, had a vision. **Right**, Brigham Young led his followers west across America.

Awakening. In hectic camp meetings, wandering evangelists competed for the souls of traditionally irreligious frontiersmen. The "burned-over district", as upstate New York was known because of the fervor that swept across it, had been peopled largely by descendants of New England's fervent Calvinist settlers, people like Joseph Smith's Vermont parents. In 1820, Joseph, a 14-year-old confused over religious choices, sought answers in prayer and had the first of a series of visions in which God and others told how true Christianity had been lost from the earth. Between 1823 and 1827 the Angel Moroni, the last survivor of a chosen people who had inhabited pre-Columbian America, revealed

and the leadership's retreat to Far West, Missouri. Devout Mormons expected to await the imminent second coming of Christ here, but instead they were violently attacked by Missouri mobs: 18 were massacred at the Mormon settlement at Haun's Mill, and Governor L. W. Boggs issued an order that the Mormons "must be exterminated or driven from the State".

After retreating to other parts of Missouri, they arrived in Illinois. Here Mormon culture truly blossomed, as the harassed people seemed to have found their "City on a Hill" on the swampy banks of the Mississippi, where they built the city of Nauvoo. Nauvoo was the largest city in Illinois of its time, and

the location of a buried set of gold plates that told the story of Moroni's people, the Nephites, and the ancestors of Native Americans, known as the Lamanites. Using a special instrument buried with the plates, Joseph translated them, completing the Book of Mormon and founding his church, with six members, in 1830.

From the moment his story leaked out, Joseph Smith and his followers were criticized, ostracized, and attacked by neighbors who considered him a charlatan. As membership slowly grew, the church moved, first to Kirtland, Ohio, where failure of a banking scheme in 1837 led to widespread apostasy

it benefited from a liberal state charter which gave its government – Smith and fellow church leaders – almost independent powers, including its own army, the Nauvoo Legion. But the problems that had repeatedly alienated neighbors arose again: the Saints asserted that as a divinely chosen people they would inherit the earth, and with their industrious accumulation of property, occasional boasting and military potential, they seemed poised to do it by force. They also tended to vote as a bloc, giving them the potential to control close elections. Always there were their unorthodox beliefs, which by the 1840s were rumored to include polygamy. A breaking point came when Smith ordered a Nauvoo newspaper run by critical ex-Mormons closed down and its presses smashed. Joseph and his brother Hyrum were arrested and taken to the Carthage jail, where, in June 1844, a mob murdered them.

Enter Brigham Young: Rather than disbanding, the bulk of the Mormons then rallied around Brigham Young, the head of their preeminent governing body, the Council of Twelve Apostles. In an unparalleled organizational feat (migrants were divided into companies of one hundred; support farms were established along the way; crews constructed trails and river ferries), Young led his people west in search of a new haven.

ies were at work. The Saints in Salt Lake City supported the poor's migration through donations to the Perpetual Emigrating Fund, which the migrants were expected to reimburse after establishing themselves. Some walked to Zion, pulling handcarts behind them, but in 1856 the Martin and Willie handcart companies started late and were trapped by snow in central Wyoming. In the worst tragedy of America's overland migration, between 200 and 225 people died before relief arrived.

Meanwhile, Brigham Young sought to build Joseph Smith's dream of the kingdom of God on earth. His visions of the new Mormon homeland were imperial: he pro-

VIEW OF SALT LAKE CITY, LOOKING WESTWARD ACROSS THE JORDAN VALLEY.

Twelve thousand moved across Iowa in 1846, to Winter Quarters near present Council Bluffs. This was the jumping-off point for the journey to the isolated and barren valley of the Great Salt Lake, the place Young, as the head of the first 148-person migration, chose as their refuge. Between 1847 and 1869, the year of the railroad's arrival, Mormon parties annually crossed the Plains from Winter Quarters, from other Mormon settlements and from overseas, where missionar-

Left, elegant interior of the Institute of Mormon Presidents. **Above**, a 19th-century view of Salt Lake City.

posed a new state of Deseret (the Book of Mormon name for beehive) encompassing all of present-day Utah, Nevada and Arizona and parts of Idaho, Wyoming, Colorado and southern California. Young sent out parties, carefully composed of men with useful occupations, to begin occupying this vast expanse. By 1855, a corridor of settlements stretched from Idaho down the west slope of the mountains to San Bernardino, California.

Mormons now had the chance for uninhibited open practice of their experimental social philosophy. After years of persecution, the Saints had found an isolated home away from the rest of the United States.

A theocracy in Utah: The organizational framework for Mormonism was the lay priesthood held by all adult males in the church. It was a patriarchal order that reached from priesthood-holding fathers in the family through bishops of neighborhood wards (similar to parishes) through other ascending levels to Brigham Young, the prophet, at the top. The overland migration had strengthened organizational ties; in the mountain West these were refined and institutionalized. Young's own charisma built up members' loyalty and willingness to obey but so did their sense of shared hardship and group destiny. Jedediah Grant, Mormon leader and first mayor of Salt Lake City, once said that Mormons' faith and testimony were different, much stronger, than that of other religions' adherents because the Saints were asked to believe so much more – especially God's appearance to men in modern times – in the face of great challenges. During the first years in the West, there was no clear line between ecclesiastical and secular government in Utah. Young was territorial governor, and church leaders held most government offices. Utah was, in effect, a theocracy where absolute obedience to a hierarchy was the norm.

That hierarchy pursued its goals of economic cooperation and self-sufficiency through careful planning. Living on the edge of the desert, the Saints first needed a different way of watering their crops than that used in the well-watered East. They hit upon the idea of extensive irrigation systems, the first widespread non-Indian use of irrigation in the United States. These systems were built by cooperative labor, and local church leaders allocated the water. They also distributed land for homes and farm fields according to members' perceived needs. The fields typically surrounded a small village, the focus of Mormon life, where the houses, farm buildings and stock corrals were situated in the middle of carefully laid out blocks. Each individual village strived toward its own self-sufficiency within the overall general economic and political independence of the kingdom of Zion.

Communal living: Manufacturing or raising specific products, especially those which otherwise would be imported, was encouraged and supported by the hierarchy. In the 1860s, the first of many local cooperative merchandising stores was opened (the mod-

ern ZCMI department store chain is a free enterprise descendant of these co-ops). Many of these operations included communally owned factories producing items such as clothing, furniture, textiles and dairy products. In the 1870s, Young encouraged the creation of United Orders in Mormon villages. In this most extreme Mormon communal experiment, members gave up private ownership of all property other than clothing and personal goods. Everything else was communally owned and managed. Most of these experiments, especially the United Orders, failed to achieve their ends, mainly because of Mormondom's growing connections to the outside world and economy. That

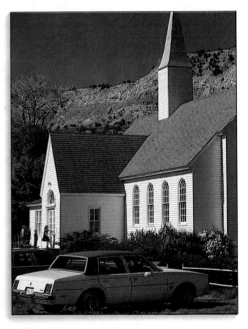

process began with the 1849 gold rush, which brought the desperate Saints a windfall in abandoned or traded goods as passing forty-niners lightened their loads to obtain badly needed Mormon farm products and livestock. Then it accelerated after the arrival of the transcontinental railroad in 1869.

The most infamous Mormon institution was polygamy. Joseph Smith first announced it to a small group of church leaders at Nauvoo. The extent of his own plural marriages is still debated. In the Rocky Mountains promised land, polygamy came out into the open, although only a small Mormon minority, those with enough wealth and influence, practiced it. But before long, it became the rallying point for national anti-Mormon forces. The early Republican party, for example, campaigned against what are known as the "twin relics of barbarism", slavery and polygamy.

There were other reasons why Mormons by the mid-1850s found themselves in a state of renewed conflict with other Americans. Foremost were the complaints of several federally appointed territorial officials who felt thwarted by Utah's theocracy. Probably seeking to divert national attention away from sectional conflicts over slavery, President Buchanan in 1857 sent Colonel Albert Sidney Johnston, 2,500 soldiers, and a new

Gentile governor, although Brigham Young continued to be the real authority in Utah.

Mormons and Indians unite: In a tragic sidelight to these tense events, Mormons and local Native Americans massacred 120 emigrants at Mount Meadows on the south California trail. Southern Utah Mormons, in the midst of a religious revival, were expecting the army's invasion. They knew that some haughty members of the emigrant train were from hated Missouri and had insulted other Mormon communities along the way. Many years later, John D. Lee, the only Mormon ever brought to justice for the crime, was executed at the massacre site.

During the Civil War, volunteer troops

territorial governor to enforce federal authority over the rebellious Mormons. In response, Brigham Young sent out guerrillas to harass the army, ordered his people to abandon Salt Lake City and retreat south, and prepared armed resistance. The bogged-down army, after spending a winter in camp at Fort Bridger, accepted a settlement negotiated by an intermediary and marched through Salt Lake City without incident to establish Camp Floyd far south of the city. The Mormons, in return, accepted their new

Left, a Mormon temple in Utah. **Above**, Brigham Young University is famous for its football team.

from California occupied Salt Lake City to insure Mormon loyalty to the Union. Their commander, Colonel Patrick Connor, was eventually known as the father of mining in Utah because he encouraged his soldiers to prospect in their spare time and helped develop some of Utah's earliest strikes. He was virulently anti-Mormon and hoped mining would encourage immigration of Gentiles to Utah. He was correct, and mining in places like Alta, Park City, and the Oquirrh Mountains eventually created a second, non-Mormon economy in the state.

After the Civil War, Congress stepped up its crusade against polygamy. In a series of acts culminating in the Edmunds-Tucker Act of 1887, stiff penalties were imposed for practicing polygamy. Polygamists were disenfranchised and prohibited from public office and jury duty, test oaths were introduced, the church was disincorporated and its property confiscated, the Perpetual Emigrating Fund was dissolved, and women's suffrage was abolished. Federal marshals hounded polygamists throughout the state while church leaders went underground. In 1890 Mormon president Wilford Woodruff (Brigham Young had died in 1877) publicly advised members "to refrain from conducting any marriage forbidden by the law of the land," thereby surrendering to overwhelm-

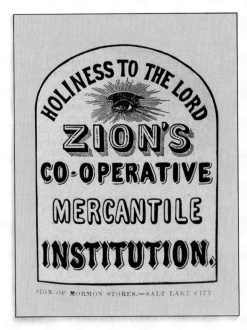

SIGN OF MORMON STORES.—SALT LAKE CITY.

ing federal powder. With the Woodruff Manifesto, as it was known, and the admission of Utah to statehood in 1896 after 50 years of waiting, church members took their first steps toward reconciliation with the rest of the nation.

Mormons in the 20th century moved further and further from their early attempts to build a perfect millennial community and embraced the more traditional social ideals of middle-class America. Members at first entered the Democratic and Republican parties in roughly equal numbers, ceasing to be a solid voting bloc, but in more recent years, more of them have adopted the predominant

Republican business ideology. The church's own economic strength rebounded gradually until after World War II, when the Latter-Day Saints grew into one of the country's wealthiest religions, with major investments in real estate, communications, insurance, and elsewhere. Mormon leaders keep in touch with members through an organized network so intricate that it could make most federal bureaucracies jealous. Members pay not only a tithe of 10 percent of their income, but also contribute to a building fund, a missionary fund, and a welfare fund.

Cultural differences: There are other distinctive cultural attributes of the Mormons – abstinence from alcohol and tobacco; the wearing of specially designed, sanctified undergarments; dedication to genealogical research, and the high value placed on education and the arts. But it was the increasingly conservative politics of many members, an attribute shared with many other Americans, which brought them much attention in the 1980s. Patriotism and traditional family values were suddenly popular. Ronald Reagan received his largest presidential vote margins in Utah. He considered the Mormon West one of his prime constituencies and brought a number of prominent Mormons (such as Education Secretary Ted Bell and pollster Richard Wirthlin) to Washington, DC to enter into national government.

Mormons, if anything, are fiercely partisan, and they take great pride in home-grown celebrities. They loyally follow the careers of well-known members like entertainers Donny and Marie Osmond and ex-football star and television personality Merlin Oslon. While there are many kinds of Mormons with widely different attitudes (political columnist Jack Anderson, for example, does not fit the Mormon stereotype and his religious persuasion is hence less well-known), there is still a striking uniformity among Mormons that lends credence to stereotypes. The Mormons, after all, remain a tightly unified people who largely conform to the wishes of their church leaders. As such, they are a people apart, one subculture in the endlessly fascinating hodgepodge of American society.

Left, a typical Mormon merchant's sign in the 19th-century. **Right**, representative Mormon leaders surround Brigham Young.

REPRESENTATIVE MORMONS.

1.—W. Woodruff.   2.—John Taylor.   3.—Mayor Daniel H. Wells.   4.—W. H. Hooper.   5.—President Brigham Young.
6.—Orson Pratt.   7.—John Sharp.   8.—George Q. Cannon.   9.—Orson Hyde.

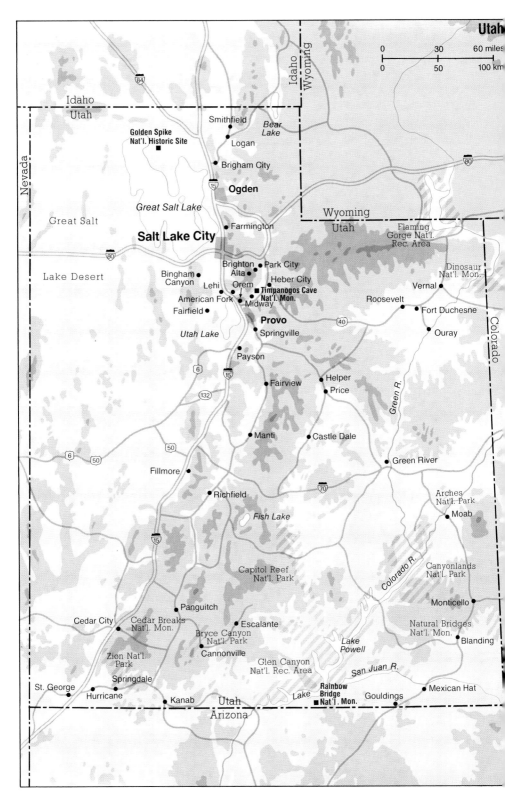

Utah

| 0 | 30 | 60 miles |
| 0 | 50 | 100 km |

Idaho
Utah

Nevada

Smithfield
Bear Lake

Golden Spike
Nat'l. Historic Site
Logan

Brigham City

Ogden

Idaho
Wyoming

Great Salt Lake

Wyoming
Utah

Farmington

Flaming
Gorge Nat'l.
Rec. Area

Salt Lake City

Great Salt

Dinosaur
Nat'l. Mon.

Lake Desert

Brighton
Park City

Bingham
Canyon
Alta
Heber City

Vernal

Lehi
Orem
Timpanogos Cave

Roosevelt

American Fork
Nat'l. Mon.
Midway

Fort Duchesne

Fairfield
Provo

Ouray

Utah Lake
Springville

Payson

Colorado

Fairview
Helper
Price

Manti
Castle Dale

Green R.

Green River

Fillmore

Arches
Nat'l. Park

Richfield

Moab

Fish Lake

Capitol Reef
Nat'l. Park

Colorado R.

Canyonlands
Nat'l. Park

Monticello

Panguitch

Cedar City
Cedar Breaks
Nat'l. Mon.
Escalante

Natural Bridges
Nat'l. Mon.

Bryce Canyon
Nat'l. Park

*Lake
Powell*

Blanding

Zion Nat'l.
Park
Cannonville

Glen Canyon
Nat'l. Rec. Area

San Juan R.

Springdale

St. George
Hurricane
Kanab
Utah
Arizona

Rainbow
Bridge
Nat'l. Mon.
Gouldings

Mexican Hat

Lake

NORTH UTAH

Its geography, its history, and its culture make northern Utah a land of transitions and contrast. Perhaps its most notable contrast is between the seclusion its people sought and the changes an intruding outside world kept bringing, but the contrast in its landscape, located astride a geological transition zone, is more readily seen. Two massive plates of the earth's crust clash together along the Utah, Idaho and Wyoming borders to form the energy-rich Overthrust Belt, one of America's more recent and productive oil fields. To the south and west is the Great Basin and its jewel, the Great Salt Lake, remnant of Lake Bonneville, whose prehistoric shore lines can be seen high on the mountain benches throughout northern and western Utah. To the north and east are towering mountains that arise abruptly from deep, expansive valleys formed by Bonneville and her children, the lakes and rivers of today. These valleys – Cache, Weber, Ogden's, Bear River, Bear Lake, and other smaller ones along the lake – were retreats: first for Shoshones, Bannocks, and Utes who ranged east to contest Plains Indians for buffalo; later for mountain men who cached their furs, held their rendezvous, and spent their winters; finally for Mormon farmers seeking a refuge where they could build their communities in peace. Always there was an outside world beyond the valleys of different and potentially hostile competitors.

Then the railroad came and finally effectively tied America's regional cultures together. Fittingly, the transcontinental railroad was linked, the symbolic transition and tie between East and West pinpointed in the **Promontory Range**, north of Great Salt Lake. Today, the sense of passage from one world to another can still be felt in northern Utah. There are few areas in America where one can get a better feeling of climbing from lowland to highland than along the front rising to the east of Great Salt Lake. Approaching the Utah border from Wyoming or Idaho, a traveler can detect the subtle but apparent differences in the farming villages that announce the Mormon core region. But also within and around those villages there is a strong sense of change as an older, rural way of life gives way to national security, energy and recreation industries – to name but a few of the modern equivalents of the mid-19th-century railroad.

Utah farmlands: Cache Valley, the heart of the remaining farm economy, is a good place to begin a visit to the region bounding Great Salt Lake's northern shores. Here where the winters are frigid, but the summers pleasant, are some of the most productive farms in Utah. Well-watered by Bear River and its tributaries, the beautiful green valley is almost completely surrounded by steep mountain ridges. Its name derived from the early trappers' practice of hiding their furs there. They called it Willow Valley, and many spent their winter layoffs here, taking advantage of the valley's abundant game.

Near the middle of the valley, on its

Swimming during ski season in a Snowbird heated pool.

eastern side where Logan River emerges from the mountains, is **Logan**. Upon approaching the city, a visitor may first see a castle high on one of Lake Bonneville's terraces. This is the **Logan Temple** of the Mormon church, an unornamented, gray limestone Gothic building with twin cupola-topped towers. Volunteer laborers constructed it with native materials between 1877 and 1884. The temple is not open to the public (although its grounds are), but a similar gray, cupola-crowned building is only two blocks west on Main Street, and visitors are welcome. This is the **Mormon Tabernacle**, begun in 1865, and completed in 1890. Another two blocks west and north brings one to the **Cache Country Relic Hall** on the lower level of the Chamber of Commerce building. Run by the Daughters of Utah Pioneers, the hall contains a fine collection of pioneer artifacts, including clothing, furniture, tools, and art.

There are numerous historic buildings in Logan. The old **Lyric Theatre**, home of a modern repertory company,

and the stately **David Eccles Home** are among the reasons **Center Street** is listed as a historic district on the National Register of Historic Places.

Utah State University, founded in 1888, sprawls across the benchland east of the city. Originally a land grant agricultural college, Utah State, like Logan, still has some of the flavor of its early years, both in its old buildings like **Old Main**, with its distinctive tower, and in its curriculum, which continues to emphasize programs in agriculture and natural resources. But it is now a complete university with distinctively modern facilities and a full range of course offerings. Each July and August, the campus hosts the Festival of the American West, including diverse activities ranging from a spectacular historical pageant to a fair, exhibits, reconstructed Old West streets, and conferences, all celebrating and highlighting the frontier experience.

The Wellsville area: South of Logan is Cache Valley's oldest settlement, **Wellsville**. Brigham Young first sent an

A view of Logan with the dominant Mormon Temple.

exploratory party into this valley in 1847. Their report was favorable, but settlers didn't return until 1856 when Peter Maughan and a party of friends and relatives drove several thousand cattle and horses to the site of Wellsville, called "Maughan's Fort" for many decades. Several houses and other buildings have survived from the village's early years. The town sits at the foot of the **Wellsville Mountains**, which climb 5,000 ft (1,500 meters) from the valley floor, a rise made more impressive by their narrow base. They have one of the steepest mountain faces in the United States. A few miles east of Wellsville is another colorful early Mormon settlement, **Hyrum**, and outside it is the **Hyrum Lake State Recreation Area** with complete boating and camping facilities.

Making cheese in a valley: Heading back north on the highway between Wellsville and Logan, stop off at the **Ronald V. Jensen Historical Farm** and **Man and His Bread Museum**, a 120-acre (50-hectare) living museum where a large collection of steam powered tractors, harvesters, threshers, wagons and other antique farm equipment is kept operating. The Jensen farm is only one sign of Cache Valley's agricultural tradition. One only has to cross the valley from south to north, passing through little villages such as **Mendon, Newton, Clarkston** and **Richmond** to see the hundreds of neat, modest farms among their dairy pasures and alfalfa fields. Although the area's farms produce varied crops, Cache Valley is best known for its cheese. A tour of the **Cache Valley Cheese Factory** in Amalga, north of Logan, and a taste of its product will demonstrate why. It's advertised as the world's largest maker of Swiss cheese; other equally tasty varieties are also produced. The factory is the other side of the coin to the modest-sized family farms, for agriculture in Cache Valley, like elsewhere, is big business.

Cache Valley extends several miles across the state border into Idaho, where there are two sites important to the re-

Abandoned ranch cottages in the dry Utah countryside.

gion's history. Five miles (8 km) north of Preston, Idaho, by the Bear River, is the **Bear River Massacre Site**, the place where a large band of Shoshone-Bannocks, accused of harassing overland migrants and settlers, camped in January 1863. Federal troops from Fort Douglas in Salt Lake City attacked them there. Led by Colonel Patrick E. Connor, the soldiers trapped the Native Americans in a ravine and, showing no mercy, killed at least 224. Their own casualties came to a total of 14 killed and 49 wounded. A few miles north of Preston, Cache Valley ends at **Red Rock Pass**, site of one of the world's great floods. After rising for thousands of years, ancient Lake Bonneville finally reached its maximum depth and broke through its rim here, draining into the Snake River.

Picturesque sites: For peaceful mountain beauty there are few areas that can beat the **Bear River Range** east of Cache Valley. Start with **Blacksmith Fork Canyon**, reached from Hyrum. A high walled canyon with good fishing and plenty of picnic sites, its main attraction is the winter feeding of hundreds of elk at **Hardware Ranch Elk Preserve**. With a primary mission to maintain herds through the winter and keep them away from local farms, the ranch now attracts visitors who are taken to view the feeding elk on sleighs drawn by Clydesdale horses.

Logan Canyon is a pleasant 30-mile (48-km) drive, from the narrow rocky banks of the **Logan River** at its lower end outside Logan city to the high parklands and sinks at its top. Along the way are superb fishing areas for German brown, rainbow and cut-throat trout; a steep 1½-mile (2-km) hike to the giant 3,500-year-old **Jardine Juniper**; a number of caves for the adventuresome to explore; a roadside drink of clean mountain water at **Rick's Spring**; and many scenic campgrounds like the one at pretty **Tony Grove Lake**. In winter, try some quiet, out-of-the-way skiing at **Beaver Mountain Ski Area.**

Summer activities at Bear Lake: From the summit above the Logan Canyon, look down on the breathtaking vista of

The Jupiter steam engine at Promontory Point.

286

the 21-mile (34-km) long, deep blue **Bear Lake** below. Summer boaters and water skiers flock to Utah's **Bear Lake State Park Marina** or other docks. Swimmers collect at **Idaho State Beach** on the northern shore or **Rendezvous Beach State Park** on the southern edge, and others find diverse pleasures at one of several resorts, like the largest at **Sweetwater**. The 200-ft (61-meter) deep lake also harbors the rare Bonneville cisco fish, which begins its run in January, attracting wading fishermen with dip nets to the ice-covered lake.

While small traditional Bear Lake towns like **Laketown** and **St Charles** still retain much of their character, Bear Lake is showing signs of overdevelopment. Its beaches and nearby hillsides are crowded with resorts and summer homes, and the quality of its once crystal clean water is deteriorating. It once drained one way, into Bear River; now Bear River's water is pumped back into the lake during the high runoff, a process gradually altering the temperature and ecology of the lake.

"Must-sees": To see truly rural Utah scenes, travel south from Bear Lake on State highways 30 and 16 to rustic, isolated **Randolph** and **Woodruff**. From the latter, head west, taking a seemingly endless climb past some of the most well-maintained and extensive snowmobile trails around to reach **Monte Cristo**, a spectacular picnic area among the clouds at 9,000 ft (2,740 meters). Then descend into **Ogden's Valley**, a rugged mountain valley with jagged edged **Pineview Reservoir** occupying much of its floor.

Near the reservoir is **Huntsville** and the home of the late David O. McKay, one of the Mormon church's most revered prophets. Not far from Huntsville is the **Abbey of Our Lady of the Holy Trinity**, a Trappist monastery that welcomes visitors and sells homemade bread and honey from its own hives. There is plenty of skiing to be had in the mountains surrounding Ogden's Valley – at **Snow Basin** to the south and at **Nordic Valley** and **Powder Mountain** to the north.

, copper
melting
ant near
Magnavox.

Ogden River drains west out of Pineview Reservoir down **Ogden Canyon** to the city of **Ogden**, all named after Peter Skene Ogden, the British fur brigade leader who passed this way in the 1820s. Ogden, Utah's second largest city, is where Miles Goodyear, commonly considered Utah's first non-Native American settler, built his home in 1846. He raised a garden and traded horses he bought in California to overland migrants. He eventually sold everything to early Mormon settlers, and now the **Miles Goodyear Fort Buenaventura State Historical Monument**, a reconstruction of his log stockade, commemorates him at a park off 24th Street in West Ogden. The actual **Goodyear Cabin** is located next to the **Daughters of Utah Pioneers Museum** on the same block as the Mormon Temple dedicated in 1972 and the older **Ogden Tabernacle**. A visitors' center is located at the latter.

Ogden grew with the railroad, becoming Utah's non-Mormon city after the tracks arrived in 1869. It was then Utah's commercial connection to the outside. The **Union Depot** at 25th Street and Wall Avenue wasn't built until 1924, but it is a classic reminder of the railroad's importance to the city. Designed in the Spanish Revival style, it houses the **Railroad Hall of Fame Museum** and the **John M. Browning Firearms Museum**.

A good way to sense the **Great Salt Lake's** beauty and size, as well as the varied topography and changing society around it, is to follow the old railroad's route north around the lake's northeastern shore. First take the highway through **Willard**, the **Golden Spike Fruitway** where countless fruit stands offer the many products of local orchards. Next is **Brigham City**, most successful home of Brigham Young's 19th-century experiments in cooperative living.

West of Brigham City you will come to the extensive marsh lands of the **Bear River Migratory Bird Refuge**, best visited in the fall or spring when hundreds of species of migrating birds pass the Great Salt Lake's shores. Turning west around the north end of the lake, one comes to **Corinne**, once the sin capital of Utah. Corinne, one of many western sin capitals spawned by the railroad, is now a quiet Mormon village on the Bear River. Just before turning south to the railroad's most historic site, look north where the huge **Thiokol Wasatch Division Plant**, the world's largest manufacturer of solid propellant rocket motors, can be seen. It is only one piece of evidence demonstrating Utah's heavy dependence on the national security industry and the federal government, known to be the state's largest employers.

In the Promontory Mountains, the **Golden Spike Historic Site** commemorates the joining of the Union Pacific and Southern Pacific in 1869. Drive south along the range to **Promontory Point** and look at the vast scene around you. You may then feel some degree of the threat, challenge and opportunity the first Mormon settlers faced when they chose to adopt this odd, diverse landscape as their home.

Below, ranch woman show the strains of time and toil. Right, springtime in the Rockies.

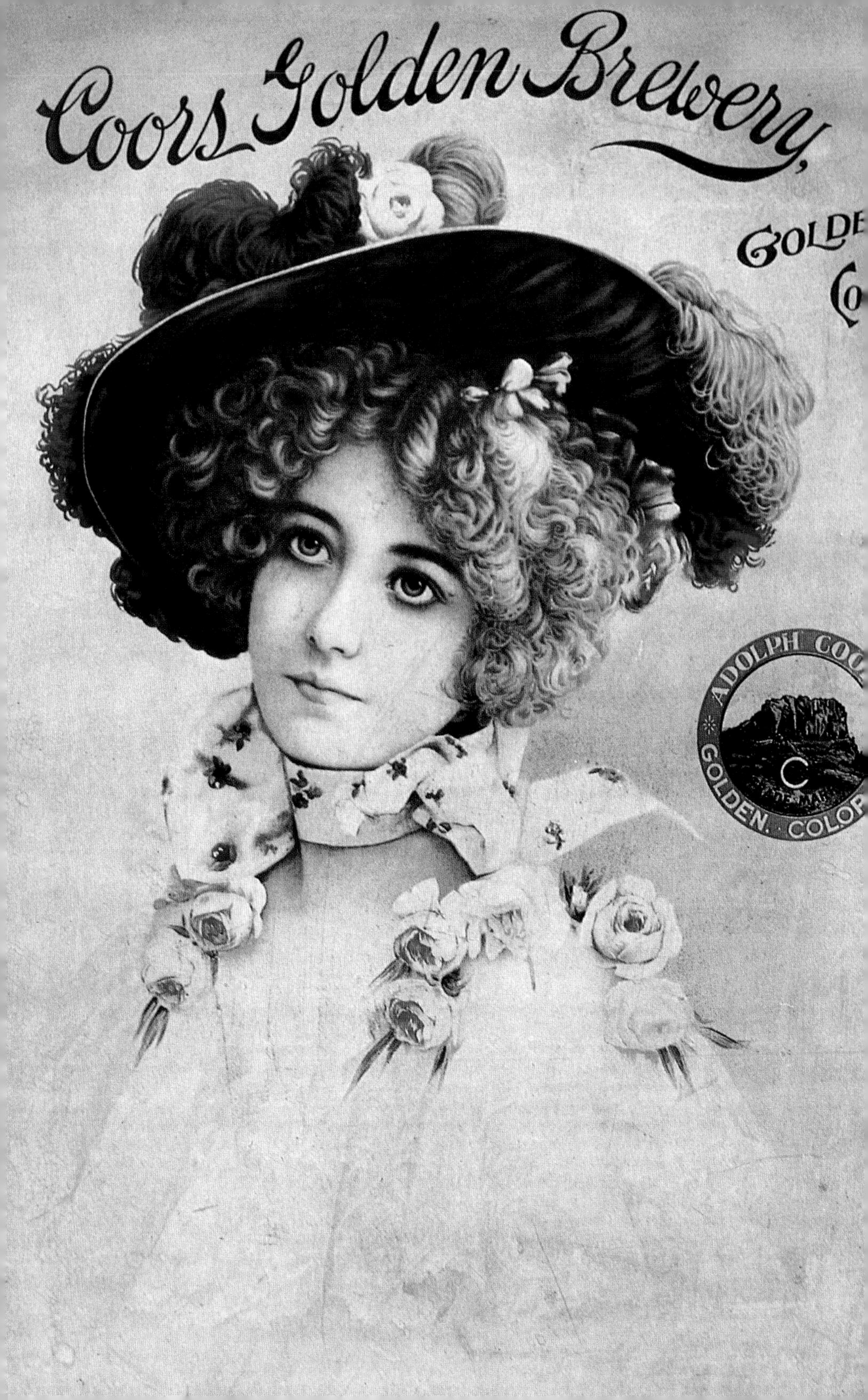
Coors Golden Brewery,
GOLDE
CO
ADOLPH COO
GOLDEN. COLO

THE NOBLE TIME

JUVENIA

— 1860 —

Golden Age ®

C O L L E C T I O N

STEEL - STEEL/GOLD - 18KT GOLD AND WITH PRECIOUS STONES

Worldwide list of JUVENIA Agents available on request

JUVENIA MONTRES SA - 2304 LA CHAUX-DE-FONDS - SWITZERLAND
Tel. 41/39 26 04 65 Fax 41/39 26 68 00

When it comes to planning an unforgettable vacation,

we wrote the book. *Amtrak's America.* A free, 82-page

IF YOU REALLY WANT TO SEE AMERICA, WE'LL SEND YOU A PERSONAL GUIDE.

travel planner that highlights the excitement of seeing

the country on Amtrak. With complete descriptions of

scenic routes. Our comfortable on-board accommoda-

tions. Even tour packages. And with over 500 destina-

tions, from cover to cover we'll take you coast to coast.

Amtrak's America. It's where great vacations begin.

For more information, or to order *Amtrak's America,*

call your travel agent or Amtrak at 1-800-USA-RAIL.

- ✂

Please send my free copy of *Amtrak's America:*

Name _____
                        Please Print

Address _____

City_____ State _____

Zip_____ Phone (   ) _____

Mail to: AMTRAK, Dept. 6000
P.O. Box 7717, Itasca, IL 60143

AMTRAK

THERE'S SOMETHING ABOUT A TRAIN THAT'S MAGIC.

TRAVEL TIPS

GETTING THERE

BY AIR

Most major and international carriers service the Western Rockies states of Colorado, Idaho, Montana, Utah and Wyoming. The major entry points to the Rockies are Denver in the east and Salt Lake City in the west. There are small airports covering the entire Rockies region. Some of the smaller airports are Colorado Springs, Pueblo and Grand Junction in Colorado; Boise, Twin Falls, Idaho Falls and Pocatello in Idaho; Bozeman, Helena and Great Falls in Montana; St George and Moab in Utah; Jackson, Casper, Cheyenne and Laramie in Wyoming. Some of the local and regional airlines travel to these airports.

The National Parks in the Rockies are easily accessible by air. The Jackson Airport is located in the Teton National Park. The other National Parks have airports within short distances of the Parks.

STAPLETON INTERNATIONAL AIRPORT

This airport is located 340 miles (550 km) west of the center of the Continental United States, just outside the city of Denver. Stapleton International Airport is the seventh busiest airport in the world and the sixth busiest airport in the United States, making Denver one of the major centers of air travel in the country. Over 25 million people land at this airport every year.

AIRLINES

Air travel in the Rocky Mountain region is limited to most large carriers and to a few regional airlines:
Mesa Airlines
Air Midwest

Continental Express
United Express

AIRLINES TO DENVER

American West, Tel: (1-800) 356-6611.
American, Stapleton Int'l Airport, CO 80207. Tel: 595-9304.
Continental, 9000 E. Smith Road, Suite 210, Denver, CO 80207. Tel: 398-3000.
Delta, 7555 E. Hampden #605, Denver, CO 80231. Tel: 695-8180.
Eastern, 443 Stapleton Int'l Airport, CO 80207. Tel: 623-4800.
Mexicana, Stapleton Int'l Airport, CO 80207. Tel: 832-5454.
Northwest, 707 17th St #120, Denver, CO 80207. Tel: 293-2376.
Piedmont, 2260 S. Xanadu Way #375, Aurora, CO 80014. Tel: 893-3567.
United, 7700 Smith Road, Denver, CO 80207. Tel: 398-4181.
US Air, Tel: (1-800) 428-4322.

AIRLINES TO IDAHO

Alaska Airlines
America West
Delta, Tel: (208) 383-3110.

AIRLINES TO MONTANA

Continental
Delta
Northwest
Northwest Airlink
United

AIRLINES TO WYOMING

Continental Express
Delta
United

AIRLINES TO UTAH

American
America West
Continental
Delta
Northwest
United

Most major commercial airlines arrive and depart from **Salt Lake City International Airport**, located on 4000 West, 900 North. For information write to AMF, Box 2204, Salt Lake City, UT 84122. Tel: (801) 539-2205. Commuter connections are available from Salt Lake City to cities in Utah and other Rocky Mountain States.

There are many smaller airports located in Utah which have flights to the resorts, national parks and some cities. For information write to: Utah **State Division of Aeronautical Operations**, Salt Lake City International Airport, 135 N. 2400 W., Salt Lake City, UT 84116. Tel: (801) 328-2066.

BY BUS

The **Greyhound Trailways** bus company provides services to the main cities and towns in the five Rocky Mountain states covered in this book. There are many other bus companies that serve specific areas. Denver serves as a hub for intercity bus services with Greyhound offering 24 daily arrivals and departures. Check the Yellow Pages for a listing of local bus companies.

• DENVER, COLORADO
Greyhound, 1055 19th St, Denver, CO 80203. Tel: (303) 292-6111.

• SALT LAKE CITY, UTAH
Greyhound, 160 West South Temple, Salt Lake City, UT. Tel: (801) 355-4684.

• CHEYENNE, WYOMING
Greyhound, 1503 Capitol Ave, Cheyenne, WY 82001. Tel: (307) 634-7744.

• BOISE, IDAHO
Greyhound, 1212 Bannock St, Boise, ID 83706. Tel: (208) 343-3681.

• BOZEMAN, MONTANA
Greyhound, 625 N. 7th St, Bozeman, MT 59715. Tel: (406) 587-3110.

BY TRAIN

Amtrak is a leisurely passenger line that provides an excellent service from coast to coast. In Denver there are six daily arrivals and departures serving Los Angeles, Seattle, San Francisco and Chicago. Westbound

trains pass through Glenwood Canyon, a spectacular route. Amtrack has rail passes for unlimited travel in the US which can be purchased only from a travel agent overseas. (Amtrack – Nationwide – Tel: (800) 872-7245.) In Denver, Amtrack operates from the Union Station (Tel: 893-3911). Amtrack office in Salt Lake City is located at 400 West South Temple (Tel: 364-8562).

HIGHWAY TRAVEL

Denver is served by interstate highways 25, 70, 76 and 225.

AAA **Auto Club**, 4100 E. Arkansas, Denver, CO 80222. Tel: 753-8800
Colorado Dept of Highways, 4201 E. Arkansas, Idaho Springs, CO 80452. Tel: (303) 567-9404. Ground transportation serves all major ski areas in Colorado. Hotel/condo reservation statewide.

TRAVEL ESSENTIALS

VISAS & PASSPORTS

Most visitors entering the United States, must have a valid passport, a visitor's visa and an international vaccination certificate depending on the country of origin. Canadian citizens entering the Western Hemisphere need not have a visa or a passport. Neither do Mexican citizens who possess a border pass.

Citizens of any country admitted to the United States on a single entry visa may visit Canada or Mexico for not more than 30 days and reenter the United States without a new visa, but only if the reentry falls within the original admission specifications.

MONEY MATTERS

The United States has no limit on the amount of money foreign visitors bring into the country. For your convenience, come with a supply of small bills, credit cards and traveler's checks (preferably in US dollars).

The basic US monetary unit is the dollar ($) which is equivalent to 100 cents. Coins are minted in 1¢ (penny), 5¢ (nickel), 10¢ (dime), 25¢ (quarter), 50¢ (half dollar) and $1. Silver dollar coins are very rare. Nickels, dimes and quarters are accepted by coin-operated vending machines, telephones and laundromats. Paper currency is printed in denominations of $1, $2, $5, $10, $20, $50, $100 and $1000 and are of the same color (greenbacks) with the value of each note clearly indicated on the bill.

Visitors who arrive by air can usually exchange their money at the gateway airport. Most shops and hotels in the Rockies area accept US traveler's checks, but be sure to have your passport on hand. Foreign currency will have to be changed at the bank. Most banks are open from 8 a.m. till 5 p.m. on weekdays. Some banks are open till 1 p.m. on Saturdays. In most states in the country there is a sales tax added to retail goods. This amount is different in each of the Rockies states.

HEALTH

Altitude: Give yourself time to get used to the new altitude. Some of the lower parts of the Rockies are a mile high and the ski areas can exceed 13,000 ft (4,000 meters). Avoid over-exhaustion and heed early warning signs of shortness of breath, fatigue or headache, by resting or returning to a lower altitude. If you have heart or lung problems check with your doctor before making the trip.

Sun: The Rockies sun can be very intense. Use highly rated sunscreens on all exposed areas of the skin and avoid the peak intensity sunshine. The direct sun rays reflecting off the snow can cause serious burns even on the coldest days. Wear sunglasses or ski goggles at all times specially when the ground is covered with snow.

Temperature: In the summer, to prevent heat exhaustion, avoid strenuous activities during the mid-day hours and drink plenty of fluids. In the winter, frostbite is a potential hazard. It generally occurs in the fingers, toes or other exposed areas of skin. Keep all skin covered from brisk wind and cold.

Equipment: It is important to take a variety of clothing, first-aid kit, sunscreens, insect repellents, drinking water (if traveling in wilderness areas), protective eye gear, and a map of the area.

WHAT TO BRING

As Rocky Mountain weather is so changeable, you should bring a variety of clothing to be comfortable. Most of the residents dress in layers so they can peel clothes off till they are comfortable. Most clothing worn in the Rockies area is very casual and often very sporty. Denver, the capital of the Rockies, is the city with the most sports shops in the world.

In the summer you will need shorts, T-shirts, lightweight dresses and slacks for the mornings and sometimes a light sweater or jacket in the evenings. A hooded sweatshirt, sweatpants, and tennis shoes or hiking boots are good summertime mountain attire. In the winter you will need a warm winter jacket, scarf, mittens, sweaters, hat, woollen pants, jeans, and warm footwear. For the slopes you will need one warm ski outfit, ski gloves, ski hat and sunglasses or goggles. You can find these things in the many ski shops at the resorts. Skis can be easily rented. A sunscreen is essential in the mountains so you can avoid being a victim of sunburns and windburns.

Remember to bring along your swimsuit so you can enjoy the different hot springs located in different parts of the Rockies. Most of the larger hotels have swimming pools and health spas.

QUARANTINE REGULATIONS

At the port of entry the State Department of Food and Agriculture may inspect all produce, plant materials and animals to see if they are admissable under the current quarantine regulations.

For the fastest weekend refunds anywhere in the world.

Ensure your holiday is worry free even if your travellers cheques are lost or stolen by buying American Express Travellers Cheques from;

Lloyds Bank

Royal Bank of Scotland

Abbey National[*]

Bank of Ireland

Halifax Building Society[*]

Leeds Permanent Building Society[*]

Woolwich Building Society[*]

National & Provincial Building Society

Britannia Building Society[*]

American Express Travel Offices.

As well as many regional building societies and travel agents.

[*]Investors only.

Not all travellers cheques are the same.

Travellers Cheques

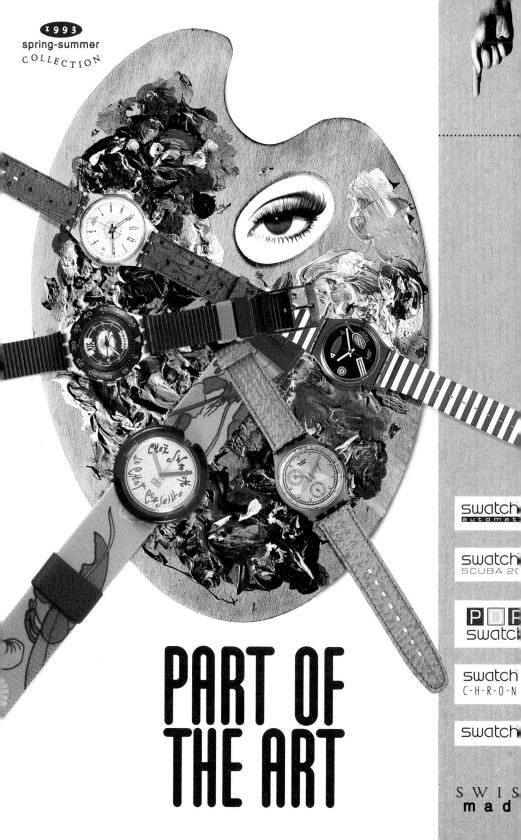

1993
spring-summer
COLLECTION

swatch
automat

swatch
SCUBA 2(

P O P
swatch

swatch
C-H-R-O-N

swatch

PART OF
THE ART

SWIS
mad

GETTING ACQUAINTED

The Rockies is the name given to a group of jagged, snow-capped peaks which run across the western part of North America. This chain of mountains stretches over 3,000 miles (4,800 km) and in some areas it is 350 miles (563 km) in width. The Rockies start in northern New Mexico and extend to the northern part of Alaska. They run from New Mexico through Colorado, Utah, Wyoming, Idaho, Montana and Washington. At the US border the Rockies stretch into the Canadian Rockies. This *Insight Guide* to the Rockies covers the states of Colorado, Wyoming, Utah, Southeast Montana and the eastern half of Idaho.

The Rockies are known for their scenic beauty and natural wonders. Many of the nation's national parks are in the Rockies including the oldest and the largest, Yellowstone National Park and the Rocky Mountain National Park. The Rockies are the starting place of mighty rivers like the Arkansas, the Colorado and the Rio Grande.

CLIMATE

The climate in the Rockies varies greatly depending on the season and location. Denver is almost a desert, receiving 15 inches (38 cm) of precipitation and 300 days of sunshine in a year. Denver's climate is ideal due to its low humidity and sunshine. Gold courses are active here even in January, as good weather prevails most of the year.

If you are a skier, the weather is perfect in the Rockies. Most ski areas have a dry climate, brisk temperatures, high elevations and unbeatable powder snow. In the summer most of the mountain areas are warm during the day and cool in the evenings. In most parts of the Rockies the spring and fall are cool and crisp.

The hallmark of the weather systems in the Rockies is the changeability. There can be a 50°F (10°C) difference from one day to another. Along with its wonderful weather are the brilliant golden aspens in the fall, the picturesque snow covered ranges in the winter and the meadows of wildflowers in the spring and summer.

TIME ZONES

The Rockies lie within the Rocky Mountain Time Zone. The time zone in all five Western Rockies states (Colorado, Idaho, Montana, Utah and Wyoming) is the same: one hour behind Chicago, two hours behind New York, and one hour ahead of Los Angeles. On the last Sunday in April, the clock is moved ahead one hour for Daylight Savings Time, and on the last Saturday in October the clock is moved back one hour returning to Standard Time.

Without taking Daylight Savings Time into consideration, when it is 12 noon in the Rockies, it is:

9 a.m. in Hawaii
2 p.m. in New York and Montreal
7 p.m. in London
8 p.m. in Bonn, Madrid, Paris and Rome
10 p.m. in Athens and Cairo
11 p.m. in Moscow
12.30 a.m. in Bombay, the next day
2 a.m. in Bangkok, the next day
3 a.m. in Singapore, Taiwan and Hong Kong the next day
4 a.m. in Tokyo, the next day
5 a.m. in Sydney, the next day

TIPPING

As in most parts of the United States, service personnel rely on tips for a large part of their income. Your gratitude in the form of a tip is most appreciated.

The accepted rate for porters at the airports is 50 cents per bag. Hotel bell boys and porters expect at least 50 cents depending on the location of your hotel or resort. A doorman should be tipped if he loads and unloads your car. It is not essential to tip chamber maids unless you have an extended stay in a small hotel or resort.

In most instances 15 to 20 percent is the going rate for other services like taxi drivers, barbers, hairdressers, waiters, waitresses and bartenders. Some restaurants include a service charge if the group is large. Tipping is not necessary in cafeterias and self-service fast-food restaurants.

WEIGHTS & MEASURES

Given below are the US equivalents of metric units.

1 inch (in) = 2.54 centimeters (cm)
1 foot (ft) = 0.305 meters (m)
1 mile = 1.609 kilometers (km)
1 square mile = 2.69 square kilometers
1 US gallon = 3.785 liters
1 ounce (oz) = 28.35 grams (g)
1 pound (lb) = 0.454 kilograms (kg)

ELECTRICITY

Most wall outlets have 110-volt, 60 cycle, alternating current. A transformer is necessary if you are using European or 220-volt equipment.

PUBLIC HOLIDAYS

State, local and federal agencies may be closed during the following holidays. Local businesses, banks and schools may also be closed.

New Year's Day: January 1
President's Day: February 18
Easter Sunday: First Sunday after spring equinox
Memorial Day: Last Monday in May
Independence Day: July 4
Labor Day: First Monday in September
Columbus Day: Second Monday in October
Election Day: First Tuesday after the first Monday in November, of even numbered years
Veterans' Day: November 11
Thanksgiving Day: Fourth Thursday in November
Christmas Day: December 25.

There may be additional holidays in the different Rocky Mountain states for local events.

EVENTS & FESTIVALS

IN COLORADO

JANUARY
National Western Stock Show and Rodeo, Denver.
Annual Cowboy Downhill/Torchlight Parade, Steamboat Springs.
Winterskoll, Snowmass.
Breckenridge World Freestyle Invitational/Ullr-Fest, Breckenridge.

FEBRUARY
US Alpine Championships, Copper Mountain.
Dog Sled Races, Granby.
American Ski Classic, Vail and Beaver Creek.

MARCH
World Cup, Aspen.
St Patrick's Day Parade, Denver.

APRIL
Spring Splash/Closing Day, Winter Park.

MAY
Annual Music and Blossom Festival, Canon City.
People's Fair, East Highschool, Denver.
Bolder Boulder Race, Boulder.

JUNE
Renaissance Festival, Larkspur.
Colorado Music Festival, Boulder.
Annual Aspen Music Festival, Aspen.
Madam Lou Bunch Day: "Original Bed Race", Central City.
Colorado Music Festival, Chautauqua Park, Boulder.
Donkey Derby Days, Cripple Creek.
Annual Blue Grass and Country Music Festival, Telluride.
"The Way it Wuz" Celebration, Steamboat Springs.
Independence Stampede (rodeo, parade, dance), Greely.
Twilight PRCA Rodeo, Alamosa.
Yacht Club Races, Grand Lake.

JULY
Colorado Shakespeare Festival, (weekends), Boulder.
The Ballet/Aspen Summer Dance Festival, Aspen.

Central City Opera Festival, Central City.
Pike's Peak Hill Climb, Cascade.
International Bike Classic, Boulder, Vail, Aspen Fruita, Grand Junction.
Invitational Snowmass Hot Air Balloon Races, Snowmass.
"World Famous Rooftop Rodeo", Estes Park.
Pow-wow Parade, Fairgrounds, Boulder.
Arts Festival, Durango.
Tennis Classic, Beaver Creek.
Cool Water Revival (windsurfing), Winterpark.

AUGUST
Boom Days Celebration, Burro Race, Leadville.
Pike's Peak or Bust Rodeo, Colorado Springs.
Jerry Ford International Gold Tournament/Concert, Vail.
Buena Vista Pack Burro Race (parade, crafts), Buena Vista.
Telluride Jazz Festival, Telluride.
Annual Telluride Film Festival, Telluride.
Festival of Mountain and Plain, Denver.
Colorado Springs Balloon Race, Memorial Park, Colorado Springs.

SEPTEMBER
Annual Scottish Highland Festival, Estes Park.
World Hang Gliding Championships, Telluride.
Annual German Harvest Festival; Oktoberfest, Larimer Square, Denver.
Snowmass Old Car Classic, Snowmass.
Crested Butte Marathon, Crested Butte.
Annual Triathlon, Aspen.
Annual Potato Day Festival, Carbondale.
Vailfest Weekend, Vail.

OCTOBER
Larimer Square Halloween Bash, Denver.
United Bank's Annual Denver Film Festival, Denver.

NOVEMBER
Veterans' Day Parade, Denver.
Larimer Square Christmas Walk, Denver.

DECEMBER
Georgetown Christmas Market, Georgetown.

Parade of Lights, Denver.
Snow Sculpture Contest, Beaver Creek.
All-Cal Ski Week, Vail.
Decemberfest, Denver.
Aspen Winter Concert Series, Aspen.

IN IDAHO

JANUARY
Winter Carnival, Schweitzer, Sandpoint.

FEBRUARY
Winter Carnival, McCall.

MARCH
Idaho State Champion Cutter and Chariot Races, Pocatello.

MAY
Salmon River Rodeo, Riggins.
Locust Blossom Festival, Kendrick.
Lake Coeur D'Alene Days Festival, Coeur D'Alene.
Kamloops and Kokannee Week (fishing derby), Sandpoint.
Priest Lake Spring Festival and Flotilla, Priest Lake.

JUNE
National Old Time Fiddlers Contest, Weiser.
State High School Rodeo Championship, Jerome.

JULY
Snake River Stampede and Festival, Nampa.
Kootenai River Days (parade, rodeo, lumberjack competition, pancake breakfast), Bonners Ferry.

AUGUST
Huckleberry Festival (parade, firemen's water fight, huckleberry judging contest), Priest River.
Pilgrimage to Old Mission (Indian Pageant including performance, encampment, traditional dinner), Cataldo.
Western Idaho State Fair, Boise.
Shoshone Bannock Indian Festival and Rodeo, Fort Hall.
Pierre's Hole Rendevous BBQ (parade and rodeo).

SEPTEMBER

Bunyan Days (lumberjack competition, antique auto show, parade, dances, games, carnival).

St Maries Lewiston Round up (cowboy breakfast rodeo and breakfast), Lewiston.

Wagon Days (pancake breakfast, vintage wagon parade, buggies, trappings), Ketchum.

Shoshone Bannock Indian Day, Fort Hall

OCTOBER

Four Nations Pow-wow, Lapwai.

Fiddlers Jamboree (jam sessions and Salmon River Art annual), Riggins.

DECEMBER

Traditional Basque Shepherder's Ball, Lamb Auction, Boise.

IN MONTANA

JANUARY

PRCA **Rodeo Finals**, Great Falls.

HCIA **Carnival**, Hardin.

Montana Winter Fair, Bozeman.

Winter Carnival, Big Sky.

Nashua Winterfest, Nashua.

Cabin Fever Days, Hungry Horse and environs.

EARLY JANUARY–LATE MARCH

Camera Safaris, Yellowstone National Park. Exciting guided tours through the northern section of the park, led by park naturalists. Car caravans are escorted, using CB radios. The 3–4 hour tours include information on wildlife, geology, and history.

FEBRUARY

Sno Fest, Anaconda.

Winter Carnival, Bozeman and Whitefish.

Boat Show, Kalispell.

MARCH

Annual Gun Show, Kalispell.

Charles Russell Art Auction, Great Falls.

Great American Ski Chase, West Yellowstone.

Red Lodge Winter Carnival, Red Lodge.

Oly Days, Big Sky.

St Patrick's Day Parade, Butte.

Doug Betters Winter Classic, The Big Mountain.

APRIL

MSU **Rodeo**, Bozeman.

Gem and Mineral Show, Billings.

Northern International Livestock Exposition and Spring Show, Billings.

Peak to Prairie Triathlon, Red Lodge.

Science Fair, Missoula.

Libby Arts Festival, Libby Memorial Gymnasium.

Northern American Skiing/Yachting Championship, The Big Mountain.

MAY

Stump Town Follies, Whitefish.

Bluebay Regatta, Polson.

Cherry Festival, Polson.

U. of M. Rodeo, Missoula.

Veterans' Memorial Pow-wow, Fort Belknap.

Roosevelt County Range Tour, Wolf Point.

Memorial Day Pow-wow, Lame Deer.

Horse Racing and Bucking Horse Sale, Miles City.

Western Heritage Art Classic, Billings.

Vigilante Parade, Helena.

JUNE

Governor's Cup Marathon, Helena.

US Open Fiddlers Contest, Dillon.

College National Finals Rodeo, Bozeman.

Midland Empire Horse Show, Billings.

Western Days Parade, Billings.

Red Lodge International Ski Race Camp/ Music Festival/Run to the Sun, Red Lodge.

VFW **Rodeo**, Hardin.

Demolition Derby, Hardin.

Wild West Days, Poplar.

Match Bronco, Wolf Point.

Jaycee Rodeo, Chinook.

Heritage Gun Show, Libby.

Viking Boat Regatta, Whitefish.

Big Sky Logging Championships, Kalispell.

Homestead Days, Hot Springs.

Jazz Festival, Helena.

JULY

Glacier International Horse Show/Quarter Horse Show, Kalispell.

Whitefish Cup Regatta/Lake to Lake Canoe Race, Whitefish.

Montana State Fiddlers Championship/ Wagon Burner Regatta/Independence Cup Regatta, Polson.

Great Western Montana River Race,

Missoula.
Arlee Pow-wow, Arlee.
State Fair Rodeo and Horse Races, Great Falls.
Central Horse Show, Fair and Rodeo, Lewiston.
Fort Belknap Indian Days, Fort Belknap.
Opeta-Ye-Teca Indian Days/Wild Horse Stampede, Wolf Point.
Annual Northern Cheyenne Pow-wow, Lame Deer.
4th and 5th East Fork Roping Club/Rodeo/Old Timers Rodeo, Broadus.
Youth Rodeo, Hardin.
Carbon County Fair/Rodeo/Beartooth Run, Red Lodge.
Billings Railroad Days, Billings.
Yellowstone Boat Float, Livingston.
Last Chance Stampede and Fair, Helena.
4th of July Parade, Butte.
Daly Days, Hamilton.
North American Indian Days, Browning.
Lewis & Clark Expedition Festival, Cut Bank.

AUGUST

Festival of Nations/Silver Bow County Fair, Butte.
Raft Race and River Remedy/Western Rendezvous of Art/Governor's Cup All Breeds Horse Show, Helena.
All Girl Rodeo, Dillon.
Bannack Days, Bannack.
Mile High Lake Catamaran Regatta, Georgetown Lake.
Sweet Pea Festival, Bozeman.
Eastern Montana Fair, Miles City.
Sun Dance, Lame Deer.
Crow Fair Celebration and Pow-wow, Chow Agency.
Miller's IGA Sanction Barrel Race/Madden's 4 State Roping/Espy Team Roping, Broadus.
White River Cheyenne Pow-wow, Busby.
Rocky Boys Pow-wow, Box Elder.
Western Montana Fair/Rodeo and Horse Races, Missoula.
Festival of Nations, Red Lodge.
Yellowstone Exhibition, Billings.
Western Rendezvous of Art, Helena Civic Center.

SEPTEMBER

Missoula Gun Show, Missoula.
Harve Festival Days, Harve.

All Indian Rodeo, Wolf Point.
Jaycees Demolition Derby, Wolf Point.
Harvest Festival, Glasgow.
Yellowstone Exhibition Fall Race Meet/Montana State Chili Cook Off, Billings.
McIntosh Apple Days/Ravalli County Fair, Rodeo and Horse Races, Hamilton.
Whitefish Summer Games, Whitefish.
Kalispell Art Show and Auction, Kalispell.
Montana State Draft Horse Show, Bozeman Fairgrounds.
Threshing Bee and Antique Show, Culbertson.

OCTOBER

Electrum, Helena.
Northern International Stock Show and Rodeo, Billings.
Octoberfest, Glendive.
Art-in-the-Park, Great Falls, C.M. Russell High School.

LATE OCTOBER–MID-NOVEMBER

Bald Eagle Gathering, Glacier Park, Apgar. An extraordinary event which occurs each fall as migrating eagles stop to feed on spawning Kokanee salmon in lower McDonald Creek. Park rangers are on hand each day to answer questions.

NOVEMBER

International Snafflebit Futurity, Malta.

DECEMBER

Good Neighbor Days, Anaconda.
Christmas Stroll, Bozeman Main Street.

IN UTAH

JANUARY

US Film and Video Festival, Park City.

FEBRUARY

Annual Winter Carnival, Park City.
Winterskoll Annual Winter Festival, Snowbird.
Park City Snow Sculpture Contest, Park City.

MARCH

Mormon Festival of the Arts, Provo.

APRIL

Park City Ski and Sail Race, Park City.

MAY

Utah Heritage Foundation Historic House Tour, Salt Lake City.

Spring State Square Dance Festival, Salt Lake City.

Annual Indian Arts and Crafts Exhibit and Sale, Salt Lake City.

Annual Sand Castle/Sculpture Contest, Salt Lake City.

JUNE

Utah Arts Festival, Salt Lake City.

Utah Scottish Association Highland Games, Salt Lake City.

Utah Pageant of the Arts, American Fork.

Annual Golden Spike, National Old Time Fiddle and Blue Grass Festival, Ogden.

JULY

"Days of '47", Salt Lake City.

Murray Fun Day, Murray.

Annual Festival of the American West, Logan.

AUGUST

Salt Lake County Fair, Murray.

Annual Park City Arts Festival, Park City.

Railroaders Folk Festival, Promontory.

SEPTEMBER

Annual Greek Festival, Salt Lake City.

Annual Oktoberfest, Snowbird.

Utah State Fair, Salt Lake City.

Ice Capades, Salt Lake City.

Fall State Square Dance Festival, Salt Lake City.

Swiss Days Celebration, Midway.

Bonneville National Speed Trials, Bonneville Salt Flats.

Ringling Bros Circus, Salt Lake City.

"Viva la Fiesta", Salt Lake City.

OCTOBER

Utah Symphony/Ballet West/Reportory Dance Theater & Utah Opera Co., Salt Lake City.

NOVEMBER

Performing arts season begins for Ririe-Woodbury Dance Company, Salt Lake City.

Utah Chorale, Salt Lake City.

DECEMBER

Tabernacle Choir Performances, Salt Lake City.

Ethnic Festival, Utah Museum of Fine Arts, Salt Lake City.

"Festival of Lights", Salt Palace, Salt Lake City.

Christmas Eve Torchlight Parades on Skis, Snowbird, Alta and Park City.

IN WYOMING

JANUARY

Wyoming State Winter Fair, Lander.

All American Cutters Races, Melody Ranch, Jackson.

FEBRUARY

Wyoming State Snowmobile Association Races, Riverton.

Snowsation, Saratoga.

Winter Carnival, Sheridan Creek Snow Oval, Dubois.

Five Shot Rabbit Hunt, Shoshoni.

Winter Carnival, Main Street, Pinedale.

MARCH

White Pine Ski Open, Pinedale.

Coors Rocky Mountain Speed Run Snowmobile Race Championship, Evanston.

Para Ski Championship, Jackson Hole Ski Area, Teton Village.

Boat, Sports and Travel Show, Events Center Casper.

Wyoming State Cross-country Ski Championships, Togwotee Mountain Lodge.

World Championship Snow King Hill Climb, Snow King Ski Area, Jackson.

APRIL

Pole, Paddle, Paddle Race, Jackson.

Togwotee Spring Fling 10 km Nordic Race, Togwotee Mountain Lodge.

MAY

Annual State Championship & Old Time Fiddle Contest, Shoshoni.

Old West Days, Jackson.

Rodeo Days, Thermopolis.

JUNE

Woodchoppers Jamboree, Encampment.

Indian Tribal Pow-wow, Sundance, Ft Washakie.

Laramie Jubilee Days Rodeo, Laramie.

Sheridan WYO Rodeo, Sheridan.

Boysen Pike Fishing Derby, Shoshoni.

Grand Teton Music Festival, Teton Village.

Green River Rendezvous, Pinedale.

Cheyenne Frontier Days, Cheyenne.

Cody Stampede (parade and rodeo), Cody.

Lander Pioneer Days (rodeo and parade), Lander.

AUGUST

Gift of the Waters Pageant, Thermopolis.

Wyoming State Fair, Douglas.

SEPTEMBER

Fort Bridger Mountain Man Rendezvous and Black Powder Shoot, Fort Bridger.

Cowboy Days, Evanston.

Oktoberfest, Worland.

One Shot Antelope Hunt, Lander.

LIQUOR LAWS

Laws regarding the purchase of alcohol in stores differ from state to state as to hours and days. However, throughout the entire US the minimum drinking age (purchase and consumption) is 21.

COMMUNICATIONS

NEWSPAPERS & MAGAZINES

The daily newspapers that are most widely read in Colorado are the *Rocky Mountain News* and the *Denver Post*. These and national newspapers are available at drug stores, grocery stores, bookstores and coin-operated newspaper stands. Weekly newspapers in Denver are *Denver Sentinel Newspapers, City Edition* and *Denver Downtowner*. The *Rocky Mountain Business Journal* is devoted to the business community, and *Up the*

Creek is for singles. Ethnic newspapers in Denver are *Intermountain Jewish News, Denver Catholic Register* and *Denver Rocky Mountain Jiho Times*, a Japanese English newspaper. A number of monthly magazines published in Denver are available in general stores. The *Denver Magazine* covers a variety of material about Colorado.

Most Rocky Mountain towns and cities have their own local newspapers. In Colorado, the *Boulder Daily Camera, Colorado Springs Gazette Telegraph, Colorado Springs Sun, Pueblo Chieftain-Pueblo Star Journal* and the *Grand Junction Daily Sentinel* have a wide circulation.

The major daily newspapers in Salt Lake City are the *Salt Lake Tribune* and the *Deseret News*. Most of the smaller towns in Utah have their own local newspapers. The *Standard Examiner* printed in Ogden has a wide circulation.

In Montana, some of the well circulated newspapers are the *Billings Gazette,* the *Bozeman Daily Chronicle*, Helena's *Independent Record*, Butte's *Montana Standard*, the *Great Falls Tribune* and the *Missoulian*.

The prominent daily newspapers in Wyoming are the *Casper Star Tribune, Cheyenne Wyoming Eagle* and the *Cheyenne Wyoming State Tribune*.

In Idaho the main newspapers are the *Idaho Statesman*; in Boise, the *Lewiston Morning Tribune*; the *Post Register* in Idaho Falls; the *Idaho State Journal* in Pocatello; and the Twin Falls' *Times News*.

TELEVISION

Most towns in the Rockies have their own local TV stations besides having the national networks and cable TV options. Complete listings appear in the daily newspapers. The *TV Guide* is a booklet, available at most grocery and drug stores, that lists the week's programs in the area. In the Rockies area, some of the major stations are:

COLORADO

Channel 14	KTVJ	Boulder
11	KKTV	Colorado Springs (CBS)
13	KRDO	Colorado Springs (ABC)
9	KBTV	Denver (ABC)
4	KCNC–TV	Denver (NBC)
31	KDVR	Denver
7	KMGH–TV	Denver (CBS)

6	KRMA–TV	Denver (PBS)
2	KWGN–TV	Denver
6	KREZ–TV	Durango

IDAHO

Channel			
4	KAID	Boise (PBS)
2	KBCI–TV	Boise (CBS)
6	KIVI	Boise (ABC)
6	KPVI	Pocatello and Idaho Falls (ABC)
10	KIBU–TV	Pocatello (PBS)
12	KUID–TV	Moscow (PBS)

MONTANA

Channel		
2	KTVO	Billings (CBS)
8	KULR–TV	Billings (ABC)
7	KCTZ	Bozeman
6	KTVM	Butte (NBC)
4	KXLF–TV	Butte (ABC)
12	KTVG	Helena (NBC)

UTAH

Channel		
30	KOOG–TV	Ogden
11	KBYU–TV	Provo (PBS)
5	KSL–TV	Salt Lake City (CBS)
20	KSTU	Salt Lake City
4	KTVX	Salt Lake City (ABC)
7	KUED	Salt Lake City (PBS)
2	KUTV	Salt Lake City (NBC)

WYOMING

Channel		
14	KCWY–TV	Casper (CBS, ABC)
2	KTWO–TV	Casper (ABC)
27	KLWY	Cheyenne
5	KYCU–TV	Cheyenne (CBS, ABC, NBC)
4	KCWC–TV	Lander (PBS)
5	KOWY	Lander (CBS, ABC)
13	KWWY	Rock Springs (CBS)

RADIO

Most American radios (in cars, hotel rooms and transistors) pick up two frequencies: the AM and FM. The FM frequency has fewer commercials and a greater range of programs. Most stations specialize in pop, classical, country, gospel or jazz music.

COLORADO

AM

1280	KBRQ	Denver (Country and Western)
1340	KHOW	Denver News (NBC)
950	KIMN	Denver (Top 40, Easy Listening)
1390	KJIZ	Denver (Easy Listening)
1090	KKBB	Denver (Easy Listening)
560	KLZ	Denver (Country and Western)
850	KOA	Denver (News and Talk)
910	KPOF	Denver (Classical)
930	KUIP	Durango (Easy Listening)
1470	KSIR	Estes Park (Easy Listening)
600	KIIX	Fort Collins (Country and Western)
1230	KEXO	Grand Junction (Contemporary)
1100	KREX	Grand Junction (Easy Listening)
620	KSTR	Grand Junction (Easy Listening)
1310	KFKA	Greeley (Farm News, Easy Listening)
1450	KYOU	Greeley (Country and Western)
1490	KQUC	Gunnison (Easy Listening)

FM

90.1	KCFR	Denver (Classical)
950	KYGO	Denver (Country and Western)
100.3	KLIR	Denver (Adult Contemporary)
103.5	KOAQ	Denver (Contemporary hits)
95.7	KPKE	Denver (Contemporary hits)
99.5	KVOD	Denver (Classical)
101.3	KIQX	Durango (Rock)
100.5	KRSJ	Durango (Country and Western)
93.3	KTCL	Fort Collins (Rock)
90.9	KCSU	Fort Collins (Educational)
99.9	KEKB	Grand Junction (Country)
90.3	KJOL	Grand Junction (Religious and Educational)
93.1	KQIX	Grand Junction (Easy Listening)
91.3	KUNC	Greeley (Easy Listening, News)
102.3	KVLE	Gunnison (Easy Listening)
97.7	KSPN	Aspen
90.5	KEPC	Colorado Springs

IDAHO

AM

670	KBOI	Boise
630	KIDO	Boise
103.1	KVNI	Coeur D'Alene
930	KSEI	Pocatello

FM

92.3 KBBK Boise
103.1 KCDA Coeur D'Alene
104.9 Pocatello

MONTANA

AM

730 KURL Billings (Religious, Specials)
970 KOOK Billings (Contemporary)
1230 KBMN Bozeman (Easy Listening)
1090 KBOZ Bozeman (Country)
550 KBOW Butte (Country and Western)
1370 KXLF Butte (Contemporary)
1400 KARR Great Falls (Top 40, Rock)
1310 KEIN Great Falls (Country and
Western)
1240 KBLL Helena

FM

88.9 KRER Billings (Educational)
93.3 KYYA Billings (Contemporary)
93.7 KBOZ Bozeman (Contemporary)
95.5 KQUY Butte (Adult Contemporary)
98.9 KAAK Great Falls (Adult
Contemporary)
92.9 KLFM Great Falls (Modern
Country)

UTAH

AM

1230 KOAL Price (Easy Listening)
960 KDOT Provo (Easy Listening)
1400 KFTN Provo (Modern Country)
910 KALL Salt Lake City (Adult
Contemporary)
1320 KBUG Salt Lake City (Adult
Contemporary)
1280 KDYL Salt Lake City (News)
570 KLUB Salt Lake City (Nostalgia)
630 KZJO Salt Lake City (Talk)
860 KWHO Salt Lake City (Classical)

FM

98.3 KARB Price (Country and Western)
88.9 KBYU Provo (Classical)
94.9 KLRZ Provo (Contemporary)
99.3 KRDC St George (Variety)
94.1 KLCY Salt Lake City
(Contemporary)
98.7 KCPX Salt Lake City
(Contemporary)
104.3 KSOP Salt Lake City (Country and
Western)

90.1 KUER Salt Lake City (Classical and
Jazz)

WYOMING

AM

1240 KFBC Cheyenne (Easy Listening)
1030 KTWO Casper (Easy Listening)
1230 KVOC Casper (Modern Country and
Western)
1340 KSGT Jackson (Easy Listening)
1330 KOVE Lander (Country and
Western)
1490 KOJO Laramie (Easy Listening)

FM

95.5 KTRS Casper (Top 40)
94.5 KAWY Casper (Rock and Jazz)
97.9 KFBQ Cheyenne
100.7 KKAZ Cheyenne (Adult
Contemporary)
97.9 KTAG Cody (Top 40)
96.9 KMTN Jackson (Adult
Contemporary)
97.5 KDLY Lander (Adult Contemporary)
102.9 KIOZ Laramie (Top 40)
96.5 KLWD Sheridan

POSTAL SERVICES

Post office hours vary in different areas of
the Rockies. Hotels and motels will be able
to advise you about the post office hours in
the area nearest to you. You can have letters
sent to you in care of General Delivery at the
main post office in the town you will be
spending time in. This mail has to be picked
up by you personally.

At press time the postage rates are as
follows: Letters within the United States are
29 cents for the first ounce and 23 cents for
each additional ounce. Postcards are 19 cents
within the United States.

Letters to Mexico are 35 cents and to
Canada, 40 cents.

Airmail letters to foreign countries are 50
cents for each half ounce.

Vending machines at airports, shops, bus
depots, train stations, hotel lobbies and drug
stores sell stamps.

A 24-hour express mail is available within
the United States.

Using the five-digit zip-code facilitates
quick delivery.

TELEGRAMS & TELEX

Western Union (Tel: 1-800 325-6000) will accept telex and telegram messages over the phone. Most major hotels have their own telex machines.

TELEPHONES

Public phones are located in hotel lobbies, restaurants, street corners, drug stores, garages, gas stations, bus depots and other general locations. In the national parks and forests, phones are available at the ranger stations. The cost of making local calls varies from 10 to 25 cents. Have plenty of change if you are making a long-distance call from a public phone. Long-distance rates decrease considerably after 5 p.m., and even more after 11 p.m. Overseas calls can be dialed direct from many areas in the Rockies. The operator will give you the code and dialing instructions.

Several hotels and state travel commissions have toll-free numbers. To find these out call (1-800) 555-1212. Each state in the Rockies has a different area code. These are: Idaho – 208, Montana – 406, Utah – 801 and Wyoming – 307; Colorado has two – 303 and 719.

EMERGENCIES

SECURITY & CRIME

Many areas of the Rockies are best enjoyed on foot and it is generally very safe to walk the streets. However, you should be careful when sightseeing, shopping and moving around.

Whenever possible travel with another person, especially after dark. Avoid deserted areas. Never leave your luggage unattended, at the airport, at your hotel or anywhere else. Clutch on to your purse and important documents.

If not driving, always lock your car and don't leave luggage, cameras and other valuables in view. Lock them in the trunk. At night, park in lighted areas.

Never leave money or jewelry in your hotel room, even if it is only for a short time. Always turn in your room key at the desk when going out. Free storage service is provided by most hotels.

Don't carry around extra cash. Use credit cards and traveler's checks whenever possible. When making purchases avoid making a display of large amounts of cash.

MEDICAL SERVICES

Being sick in America can be an expensive affair. Make sure you are covered by medical insurance while traveling in the Rockies. An ambulance can cost around $200, an emergency room treatment costs a minimum of $50, an average hospital room can cost approximately $300 per night.

It you need any medical assistance, turn to the Yellow Pages in the local directory for a doctor or pharmacy closest to you. In larger cities in the Rockies area there is usually a physician referral service whose number is listed in the directory.

Listed below are some of the facilities in Salt Lake City and Denver.

HOSPITALS

• SALT LAKE CITY
LSD **Hospital,** 8th Ave and C St.
Holy Cross Hospital, 1045 E. 100 S.
St Marks Hospital, 1200 E. 3900 S.
University of Utah Hospital, 50 N. Medical Drive.
Cottonwood Hospital, 5770 S. 300 E. (Murray)
Primary Children's Hospital, 320 12th Ave.
InstaCare Medical Center, 1344 Foothill Blvd.

• DENVER
Children's Hospital, E. 19th and Downing. Tel: 861-8888.
Presbyterian/St Luke's Medical Center, 719 E. 19th Ave and Williams. Tel: 839-6000.
Denver General Hospital, 777 Bannock St. Tel: 893-6000.
St Anthony's Hospital, 4231 W. 16th Ave. Tel: 629-3511.
(Flight for life-helicopter emergency service.)

PHARMACIES

Most modern drug stores stock a variety of medications and have a pharmacist on duty. Certain drugs can be prescribed only by a doctor. Chain drug stores like **Skaggs Drug Center** and **Walgreens** are located in many of the cities in the Rockies area. Most drugs and prescriptions are available in these drug stores. In Denver, King Soopers has over 25 stores all over town. This general supermarket has an excellent and moderately priced drug department. The Yellow Pages will have the specific locations of these stores. **Jolley Pharmacy** (900 E. 900 S.) in Salt Lake City is one of the primary pharmacies.

CLINICS & HEALTH CARE IN DENVER

Rose Medical Center at One Denver Place, 999 18th St (18th and Champa), Suite 250. Tel: 298-0891. Minor emergency care in downtown area. (8 a.m. to 4.30 p.m.)
Professional Respite Care, 1776 Jackson, Suite 410. Tel: 757-4808. (Nursing/attendant care for disabled or seniors, in home, hotel or while traveling.)
Bryner Clinic (and pharmacy), 745 E. 300 S.
Salt Lake Clinic (and pharmacy), 900 E. 333 S.
Intermountain Clinic, 700 E. 350 S.

EMERGENCIES & USEFUL NUMBERS

In case of an emergency dial **911** for police, fire, ambulance or any other emergency. If you dial the operator "0" and state the nature of the emergency you can receive some assistance. Another option, time permitting, is to check the inside cover of the local telephone directory for a list of emergency numbers.

The following numbers in Denver and Salt Lake City may come in handy.

• DENVER (Area Code: 303)

Tourist Information	892-1505
Travelers Aid	832-8194
Weather Conditions	639-1515
Road Conditions	639-1234
(north, south, east)	
Road Conditions	639-1111
(west, mountains)	
Dial-4-Health	443-2584

Dental Referral Service	798-7451
Bus Information	778-6000

• SALT LAKE CITY (Area Code: 801)

Weather	521-3650
FBI	355-7521
Time	933-9122
Utah Transit	263-3737
(highway information)	
Highway Patrol	533-5621

GETTING AROUND

FROM THE AIRPORT

Most of the major airports will have airport limousine services to take you to your hotel. Some hotels provide transportation back and forth from the hotel. Cabs are available outside the major airports. Yellow Cab has radio-controlled cabs and can be reached at (1-800) 525-3177.

Public bus service is available at some of the major airports.

DENVER AIRPORT TRANSPORTATION

Airport Limousine Service Inc., 3455 Ringsby Ct., Denver, CO 80216. Tel: (1-800) 525-3177. Leaves door 10 every 25 minutes.
Yellow Cabs, in Colorado, Tel: (1-800) 367-8294. In Denver, Tel: 292-1212. Elsewhere, Tel: (1-800) 525-3177. $10–$12 (approx.) from downtown to airport.
Zone Cabs, 2358 Washington, Denver, CO 80205. Tel: 861-2323. Radio-controlled cabs.

TRAVEL INFORMATION FOR INTERNATIONAL VISITORS

Private and public agencies offer the foreign traveler to the United States special fares and discounts for transportation and accommodation. Some of these are outlined below.

Visit USA is a discounted airline ticket

offered by many domestic airlines with discounts up to 40 percent off regular fares within the country. To qualify for this ticket, you must live at least 100 miles (160 km) outside the border of the United States and you must stop in at least two cities (not including the arrival and departure cities). Visit USA tickets are valid for one year and tickets must be confirmed 7 days prior to your arrival in the country and reservations must be made outside the United States.

Bus Services: **Greyhound** offers bargain rate passes for unlimited travel in the United States. The **Visit USA** bus tickets have to be purchased from your travel agent before you come to the United States. Discounted international rates are also available on point-to-point travel that could be purchased either overseas or in the United States.

BY TAXI

Taxis are available throughout the Rockies area, and are seen more often in the big cities. Rates vary depending on the company. Long-distance rides tend to be expensive.

BY JEEP

Colorado: The US Forest Service recreational maps are excellent guides for 4-wheelers. These can be purchased for 50 cents from the US Forest Service. Some resorts offer RV rentals for do-it-yourself jeepers or well-guided jeep tours. Popular jeeping areas are Ouray, Montrose, Telluride, Crested Butte, Alamosa, Creede, Steamboat Springs, Estes Park, Aspen, Vail, Leadville, Dillon, Lake City, Salida, Grand Junction and Gunnison. Good information sources are US Forest Service, Colorado Division of Parks and Recreation, Chambers of Commerce. Check the Yellow Pages under "Automobile", "Truck", "Camper" and "Recreational Vehicle".

CAR RENTAL

Visitors wishing to rent or lease an automobile after arriving in the Rockies area will find car rental offices in most tourist centers, airports and major hotels. Shop around for the best rates and terms. Most rental companies will rent their vehicles only to individuals at least 21 years old (sometimes 25),

having a valid driver's license (an international driver's license is acceptable) and a major credit card. some companies will require a high deposit (sometimes as high as $500) in case you don't have a credit card. Check with your travel agent for special package rates for car rentals.

American International Rent-A-Car	(1-800) 527-0202
Avis Rent-A-Car	(1-800) 331-1212
Budget Rent-A-Car	(1-800) 527-0700
Hertz Rent-A-Car	(1-800) 654-3131

MOTORING ADVISORIES

Winter Driving Tips: If you are stranded in a blizzard stay put in your car. Your car will be easier to locate than you. Run the car's heater sparingly and be careful of carbon monoxide poisoning. Make sure your exhaust pipe is not blocked by snow. Open a "crack" in your window for ventilation. Running the car for 20 minutes every hour should keep you fairly warm and conserve gas.

Emergency supplies for winter traveling by car are a warm sleeping-bag for each person traveling, extra winter clothes, high calorie non-perishable food, matches, candles, first-aid kit, flashlight, transistor radio with batteries, pocket knife, shovel with a long handle, tow chain, small sack of sand, water jug, basic tools for repairs, signal flares, axe, spare quart of gas and a distress flag.

In the Rocky Mountain area you can expect a blizzard even in the early fall. Driving on icy roads demands more skill than driving on dry roads. Check the weather forecast before venturing out into the mountains. Don't drive on icy roads if you can avoid it. Postpone your adventure; it's better than being stuck in the middle of nowhere in a snow storm.

Call for weather reports: Denver: (303) 398-3694; Statewide: (303) 639-1515.

WHERE TO STAY

The Rockies area and its surroundings harbor thousands of rooms in hundreds of diverse types of lodgings. The variety ranges from cozy family managed motels to large, luxury hotels, from alpine ski lodges to campgrounds and bed-and-breakfast accommodations. The Visitors' Bureaus and Chambers of Commerce in the Rockies States have made the selection easier by compiling information on accommodation, rates, amenities, services, schedule of events, etc. It is recommended that you write to these agencies before you start your journey. Most of the major hotels have toll-free numbers that can be obtained by calling (1-800) 555-1212. For information about the National Parks and Monuments please write to the **United States Dept of Interior**, National Park Service, Washington, DC 20240. (*See "Tourist Information" for the addresses of Visitors' Bureaus in the different states.*)

Many motels and hotels have reductions up to 35 percent for Visit USA participants. Hospitality packages offering prepurchased meals and accommodations are also available (*see also "Hospitality Program"*). Your travel agent can inform you about these benefits.

IN COLORADO

HOTELS & INNS

• ASPEN

Best Western Aspenalt Lodge, P.O. Box 428, Basalt, CO 81621. Tel: 927-3191. Located 16 miles (26 km) from Aspen/Snowmass on Frying Pan River in Basalt. Moderate rates. AAA.

Continental Inn, 515 S. Galena, Aspen, CO 81611. Tel: 925-1150. Aspen's largest lodge with indoor/outdoor pool, overlooking Aspen Mountain. (Write for rates.)

The Gant, P.O. Box K-3, Aspen, CO 81611. Tel: 925-5000. 140 units, 2 heated pools, hot tubs, saunas, tennis.

Bavarian Inn, 801 W. Bleeker, Aspen, CO 81611. Tel: 925-7391. West side of town, economical. (Write for rates.)

• BEAVER CREEK

Beaver Creek Resort, P.O. Box 7, Vail, CO 81658. Tel: 949-5750. Spectacular mountain setting, 195 units.

The Charter at Beaver Creek, P.O. Box 5310, BC, CO 81620. Tel: (1-800) 824-3064. Luxury, full service condominium hotel.

• BOULDER

American Youth Hostels Inc., P.O. Box 2370, Boulder, CO 80306. Tel: 442-1166. Hostels all over Colorado. (Write to them for details.)

Best Western Boulder Inn, 770 28th St., Boulder, CO 80303. Tel: 449-3800. Across from campus, 98 units, pool, sauna.

The Hilton Harvest House, 1345 28th St., Boulder, CO 80302. Tel: 443-3850. Resort hotel at the base of the Rocky Mountains.

Holiday Inn Boulder, 800 28th St., Boulder, CO 80303. Tel: 443-3322. Holidome recreation center, close to campus.

• BRECKENRIDGE

Blue River Condominiums, P.O. Box 1942, Breckenridge, CO 80424. Tel: 453-2260. Completely furnished, 36 units.

Beaver Run Resort, 620 Village Road, Breckenridge, CO 80424. Tel: 453-6000. Luxury resort with 329 rooms, and all facilities including its own ski lift.

The Village at Breckenridge Resort, P.O. Box 1979, Breckenridge, CO 80424. Tel: 453-2000. Luxury ski resort.

Summit Ridge Inc., 11072 Hwy 9, Breckenridge, CO 80424. Tel: (1-800) 525-3882. Homes and condominiums at varying rates.

• CENTRAL CITY

Golden Rose Hotel, 102 Main Central City, CO 80427. Tel: 825-1413. Restored Victorian Hotel, hot tub and sauna.

• COLORADO SPRINGS

The Broadmoor, P.O. Box 1439, Colorado Springs, CO 80901. Tel: (1-800) 634-7711. Pool, golf, tennis, alpine slide, 565 units.

Hilton Inn, 505 Popes Bluff Trail, Colorado Springs, CO 80909. Tel: 598-7656. Restaurant, pool, 222 units.

Palmer House Best Western, 3010 N. Chestnut, I-25 at Fillmore, Colorado Springs, CO 80907. Tel: (719) 636-5201.

• CRIPPLE CREEK

Imperial Hotel of Cripple Creek, 123 N. 3rd St., Cripple Creek, CO 80813. Tel: (719) 689-2922. Restored Victorian Hotel. Colorado's oldest melodrama, staged in the Gold Bar Room Theater.

• DENVER

The Aapartel, 1221 Clarkson, Denver, CO 80218. Tel: 867-9630. Tasteful one-bedroom apartments, near downtown. Seven days minimum stay.

The Brown Palace Hotel, 321 17th St., Denver, CO 80202. Tel: 297-3111. Historic downtown hotel 25 minutes from Stapleton Int'l Airport. Transportation provided, 460 rooms.

The Burnsley Hotel, 1000 Grant St., Denver, CO 80224. Tel: 830-1000. Small, super luxury hotel. Located near State Capitol. Suites and penthouse suites.

Executive Tower Inn, 1405 Curtis, Denver, CO 80202. Tel: 571-0300. Athletic club, shopping, 337 rooms.

Hyatt Regency, 1750 Welton St., Denver, CO 80202. Tel: 295-1200. Mobil 4 star, AAA, 540 rooms with tennis, swimming, award-winning restaurant, meeting facilities.

Holiday Chalet, E. Colfax at High St., 80218. Tel: 321-9975.

The Oxford, 1600 17th St., Denver, CO 80202. Tel: 628-5400. Elegant, restored 82-room hotel, near Union Station.

El Camino Motel, 1576 S. Colorado Blvd., Denver, CO 80222. Tel: 756-9487. Quiet, 14 family motel, 2 blocks north of I-25 on Colorado Blvd. (Weekly rates available.)

Holiday Inn Denver Downtown, 1540 Glenarm Place, Denver, CO 80202. Tel: 1-800-HOLIDAY. Prime downtown location, 396 rooms, all amenities.

Holiday Inn, 1474 S. Colorado Blvd., Denver, CO 80222. Six miles from the airport, free transportation, 253 rooms, revolving rooftop restaurant. (There are other Holiday Inns on I-70 and East Chambers, 1975 Bryant St and 9009 E. Arapahoe, Englewood. Call toll-free 1-800-HOLIDAY for information.)

Quality Inn South, 4760 E. Evans Ave., Denver, CO 80222. Tel: 757-7601. Exit 203 on I-25. Restaurant, lounge and 80 rooms.

Ramada Hotel Republic Park, 7007 S. Clinton, Englewood, CO 80112. Tel: 799-6200. 10-storied, 265-room hotel. Concierge Floor has glass ceilings. Teleconferencing, pool and lounge.

Denver Marriott Hotel (city center), 1701 California, Denver, CO 80202. Tel: 297-1300. Five restaurants, 612 luxury rooms with fitness center, convention facilities. (Other excellent Marriott Hotels are located on I-25 at Hampden Ave and 1717 Denver West Blvd Golden.)

The Denver Hilton, 1550 Court Place, Denver, CO 8202. Tel: 893-3333. Colorado's largest first-class hotel. Downtown on the 16th St Mall. 758 rooms.

Airport Hilton, 4411 Peoria, Denver, CO 80239. Tel: 373-5730. First class, 200 rooms. Full amenities, airport shuttle, children free.

The Westin Hotel Tabor Center, 1672 Lawrence St, Denver, CO 80202. Tel: 572-

9100. New luxury hotel, downtown, on 17th St Mall, 430 rooms.

Writers Manor Hotel, 1730 S. Colorado Blvd., Denver, CO 80222. Tel: 756-8877. Athletic club, nightly entertainment, 325 rooms.

Clarion Hotel Denver Airport, 3203 Quebec St., Denver, CO 80207. Tel: (303) 321-3333. First-class hotel, 10 minutes from downtown, all amenities, free limousine to airport, 588 rooms.

Sheraton Graystone Castle, 83 E. 120th Ave., Thornton, CO 80233. Tel: 451-1002. Unique castle architecture, large rooms, jacuzzi, mountain views, suites. (Other Sheraton Hotels are **Sheraton Denver Tech,** 4900 DTC Parkway, Denver, CO 80237; and **Sheraton Denver Airport**, 3535 Quebec St., Denver, CO 80207. Tel: 333-7711.)

Rodeway Inn, Denver Airport, 4590 Quebec St., Denver, CO 80216. Tel: 320-0260. Restaurant, lounge with weekend entertainment. Therma-sol rooms available.

Stapleton Plaza Hotel and Athletic Center, 3333 Quebec St., Denver, CO 80207. Tel: 321-3500. Two minutes from airport, 300 rooms, special week rate, athletic center.

Regency Hotel, 3900 Elati St., Denver, CO 80216. Tel: 458-0808. Metro hotel, 405 rooms, all amenities, free shuttle downtown.

Best Western Capri Hotel Plaza, 11 E. 84th Ave., Denver, CO 80221. Tel: 428-5041. Located on I-25 and 84th Ave. Close to Merchandise Mart, 107 rooms.

Brock Residence Inn (downtown), 2777 North Zuni, Denver, CO 80211. Aspen-like setting, free continental breakfast, evening cocktail party, 156 suites, downtown shuttle.

Chalet Motel, 6051 W. Alameda Ave., Lakewood, CO 80226. Tel: 237-7775. A small place with excellent service. French, Italian, German and English-speaking staff.

Bar X Motel, 5001 W. Colfax, Denver, CO 80204. Tel: (303) 534-7191. All suite hotel. Units have two rooms, kitchenette and all amenities. Free breakfast and evening cocktail party.

Condominium Short Term Rentals, 1190 S. Birch, Suite #101, Denver, CO 80220. Tel: 320-4823. (Write for brochure.)

Condo Inn Summit, 10651 E. Bethany, #140, Aurora, CO 80014. Tel: 671-7401. Luxury condos for short-term rentals. All facilities provided.

Denver East KOA, P.O. Box 579, Strastburg, CO 80316. Tel: 622-9274. Large, shady, pull-through sites, camping, cabins, playground, game room, cafe, easy access to I-70.

Youth Hostel, 630 E. 16th St., Denver. Tel: (303) 832-9996.

• **DILLON**

Dillon Super & Motel, P.O. Box B, Dillon, CO 80435. Tel: 468-8888. Economical lodging, 5 minutes from ski area.

Best Western Ptarmigan Lodge, 625 Colorow St., CO 80435. Tel: 468-2341. Located on the lake, central location for summer and winter activities.

Holiday Inn – Lake Dillon, P.O. Box 669, Dillon, CO 80435. Tel: 668-5000. Located on the lake, 15 minutes from Copper, Keystone, A-Basin and Breckenridge Ski Areas.

• **DURANGO**

Best Western Durango Inn, 21382 Hwy 160 W., P.O. Box 3099, Durango, CO 81301. Tel: (303) 247-3251. Beautiful location, close to Mesa Verde and Purgatory Ski Area.

Four Winds Motel, 20797 W. Hwy 160, Durango, CO 81301. Tel: 247-4512. Near Durango-Silverton train, on the way to Mesa Verde.

Quality Inn Summit, 1700 Country Road 203, Durango, CO 81301. Tel: (1-800) 228-5151. Pool, sauna, jacuzzis, 95 units.

Strater Hotel, 699 Main Ave., Durango, CO 81301. Tel: 247-4431. Restored Victorian hotel located downtown.

• ESTES PARK

Golden Eagle Lodge, P.O. Box 480, Estes Park, CO 80517. Tel: 586-6066. Historic hotel with magnificent view.

Holiday Inn Resort, P.O. Box 1468, Estes Park, CO 80517. Tel: 586-2332. Deluxe accommodations, pool, sauna, whirlpool.

The Stanley Hotel, P.O. Box 1767, Estes Park, CO 80517. Tel: 586-3371. Historic hotel, elegant, children under 17 free.

• GLENWOOD SPRINGS

Glenwood Hot Springs Lodge and Pool, Box 308, Glenwood Springs, CO 81601. Tel: 945-6571. World's largest mineral hot springs pool, athletic club, open all year.

Hotel Colorado, 526 Pine, Glenwood Springs, CO 81601. Tel: 945-6511. Restored historic hotel. Outdoor activities.

• IDAHO SPRINGS

Historic Indian Springs Resort, P.O. Box 1990, Idaho Springs, CO 80452. Tel: 825-6513. Hot mineral baths, deluxe lodgings.

• LEADVILLE

Mountain Mansion, 129 W. 8th St., Leadville, CO 80461. Tel: 486-0655, Historic hotel, 8 units, group rates.

• OURAY

Best Western Twin Peaks, P.O. Box 320, Ouray, CO 81427. Tel: 325-4427. Hot springs, whirlpool, luxury units.

• PUEBLO

Ramada Inn, 2001 N. Hudson, Pueblo, CO 81001. Tel: 542-3750. 180 units, pool, live entertainment, group rates.

• SNOWMASS RESORT

The Snowmass Club, P.O. Box Drawer G-2, Snowmass Village, CO 81615. Tel: 923-5600. Luxury resort, athletic club, tennis, golf, very exclusive.

Timberline Condominiums, P.O. Box 1-2, Snowmass Village, CO 81615. Tel: 923-4000. 96 condominiums, pool, sauna.

Woodrun Place, P.O. Box 6077, Snowmass Village, CO 81615. Tel: 923-5392. 55 units, steam shower, whirlpool, all facilities.

• STEAMBOAT SPRINGS

Sheraton at Steamboat, P.O. Box 774808, Steamboat Springs, CO 80477. Tel: 879-2220. 450 rooms, luxury hotel, pools, ski-in/ski out, sauna, live entertainment.

Storm Meadows Resort, P.O. Box AAA, Steamboat Springs, CO 80477. Tel: 879-1035. 260 units, pool, athletic club.

• TELLURIDE

New Sheridan Hotel, P.O. Box 980, Telluride, CO 81435. Tel: 728-4351. Victorian gem, 30 units, close to ski area.

• VAIL

Best Western Inn at Vail, 2211 N. Frontage Road, Vail, CO 81657. Tel: 476-3890. Resort hotel, shuttle bus to ski area.

Marriott's Mark Resort, 715 Lionhead Cir., Vail, CO 81657. Tel: 476-4444. 350 units, full service resort hotel.

Westin Hotel Vail, 1300 Westhaven Drive, Vail, CO 81657. Tel: 476-7111. 185 units, resort hotel next to forest.

Vail Home Rentals, 143 E. Meadow Drive, Vail, CO 81657. Tel: (800) 525-9803. Offers an extensive list of condominiums and private homes. Many homes have pools and saunas.

BED-&-BREAKFASTS & HOSTELS

American Youth Hostels, Box 2370, Boulder, CO 80303. Tel: 442-1166. Inexpensive accommodations in 21 Colorado cities and towns.

Bed-and-Breakfast Colorado, Box 12206, Boulder, CO 80303. Tel: 494-4994. Statewide reservations for private homes, ranches, farms and inns. All selected and include breakfast.

Bed and Breakfast Rocky Mountains, P.O. Box 804, Colorado Springs, CO 80901. Tel: (719) 630-3443 or (1-800) 825-0225. Nearly 100 homes and inns. In the city and the mountains, statewide reservations. Mansions, ski homes and ranches.

Colorado Campground Association (CCA), 5101 Pennsylvania Ave., Boulder, CO 80303. Tel: 449-9343. (Camping information, Colorado Directory free at Visitors' Centers.)

GUEST RANCHES

Aspen's T-Lazy Guest and Horse Ranch, P.O. Box 240, Aspen, CO 81612. Tel: 925-4614. 500-acre ranch in the heart of Marron Primitive Wilderness Area, 18 units, pool, lodges and cabins. (Write for details.)

Lost Valley Ranch, Rt. 2, Sedalia, CO 80135. Tel: 647-2311. Authentic horse-cattle ranch with cabins. 60 miles (96 km) north of Colorado Springs, children's discount.

Ah Wilderness Guest Ranch, P.O. Box 997, Durango, CO 81301. Tel: 247-4121. Modern cabins, horses, overnight pack trips.

The Aspen Lodge and Guest Ranch, Longs Peak Route, Estes Park, CO 80517. Tel: 586-4241. Rustic mountain lodges with a great view. Outdoor activities. (Write for details.)

Wilderness Trails Ranch, Box V, Bayfield, CO 81122. Tel: 247-0722. Open end-May to mid-September, and hunting season. Close to Durango, western lodge with log cabins.

Double JK Ranch, Box V, Estes Park, CO 80517. Tel: 586-3537. Family ranch, 9 miles (15 km) south of Estes Park. Home-cooked meals, hay rides. (Write for details.)

YMCA of the Rockies – Estes Park Center, P.O. Box 578, Association Camp, CO 80511. Tel: 586-3341. Adjoining Rocky Mountain National Park, activities for all ages.

YMCA of the Rockies – Snow Mountain Ranch, Box 558, Granby, CO 80446. Tel: 887-2152. Variety of summer and winter recreational activities for the family.

Arapaho Valley Ranch, P.O. Box 142DC, Granby, CO 80446. Tel: 887-3495. Open mid-May to end-September. Great fishing.

Sylvan Dale Ranch, 2939 N. County Road, 31 D, Loveland, CO 80537. Tel: 667-3915. Authentic working ranch resort.

S Bar S Ranch, Clark Rt., Steamboat Springs, CO 80487. Tel: 879-0788. Working cattle ranch, trout stream, ski, ride, open year-round. (Write for details.)

Skyline Guest Ranch, Box 67, Telluride, CO 81435. Tel: 728-3757. View of San Miguel Range, hiking and fishing.

For more information write to:
Colorado Dude/Guest Ranch Association, Box 300, Tabernash, CO 80478. Tel: (303) 320-8550.

IN IDAHO

HOTELS & INNS

• **BOISE**

Best Western Safari Motor Inn Inc., 1070 Grove St. Tel: 344-6556. 105 rooms, pool, free car to airport, downtown.

Boisean Motel, 1300 S. Capitol Blvd. Tel: (800) 645-3645. 135 rooms, pool, free car to airport, close to museum, parks and shops.

Holiday Inn Boise, 3300 Vista Ave. Tel: 344-8365. 265 rooms, pool, recreation center.

Red Lion Inn Downtowner, 1800 Fairview Ave. Tel: 344-7691. 182 rooms, suites, pool, entertainment.

Red Lion Motor Inn Riverside, 2900 Chinden Blvd. Tel: 343-1871. 308 rooms and suites, located on Boise River, restaurant, dancing, pool.

• **IDAHO FALLS**

Best Western Stardust, 700 Lindsay Blvd. Tel: 522-2910. 254 rooms, pool, also has live entertainment.

Quality Inn West Bank, 475 River Parkway. Tel: 523-8000. 198 rooms, reasonably priced, pool, overlooks falls.

Weston Lamplighter Motel, 850 Lindsay Blvd. Tel: 523-6260. 130 rooms, pool, electrical truck hook-up. (Weekly rates.)

• LEWISTON

Sacajawea Lodge, 1824 Main. Tel: 746-1393. 95 rooms, pool.

Churchill Motor Inn, 1021 Main. Tel: 743-4501. 62 rooms, pool, satellite TV, spa, senior citizens' rates.

Tapadera Motor Inn, 1325 E. Main. Tel: 746-3311. 81 rooms, pool, entertainment, cable TV.

• MOSCOW

Best Western University Inn, 1516 Pullman. Tel: 882-0550. 122 rooms, pool, sauna, putting green, entertainment.

Motel 6, 101 Baker St. Tel: 882-6639. 110 rooms, economical.

• POCATELLO

Best Western Cotton Tree Inn, 1415 Beach Road. Tel: 237-7650. 150 rooms, pool, racquet ball, tennis.

Holiday Inn, 1399 Bench Road. Tel: 237-1400. 206 rooms, pool.

Days Inn, 133 W. Burnside. Tel: 237-0020. 120 rooms, sauna, jacuzzi, breakfast.

Oxbow Motor Inn, 4333 Yellowstone. Tel: 237-3100. Reasonably priced, 184 rooms, pool, coffee shop.

Motel 6, 291 W. Burnside. Tel: 237-6667. Reasonably priced.

Quality Inn Pocatello, 1555 Pocatello Creek. Tel: 233-2200. 152 rooms, pool, whirlpool, sauna, entertainment.

• TWIN FALLS

Best Western Canyon Springs Inn, 1357 Blue Lakes Blvd N. Tel: 734-5000. 112 rooms, pool, senior citizens' discount.

Motel 6, 1472 Blue Lakes Blvd. N. Tel: 733-6663. 157 rooms, reasonably priced, pool.

Holiday Inn, 1350 Blue Lakes Blvd. Tel: 735-0650. Pool, 204 rooms, live entertainment, inroom movies, babysitting.

GUEST RANCHES & RESORTS

Grandview Lodge and Resort, Star Rt., Box 48, Nordman, ID 83848. Tel: 443-2433. Reeder Bay on Priest Lake. 28 units, restaurants, sea plane tours, snowmobile. (Write for details.)

Hill's Resort, Rt. 5, Box 162-A. Priest Lake, ID 83864. Tel: 443-2551. Located at Luby Bay on Priest Lake, fully equipped cabins, condos, beach location. (Write for details.)

Whitewater Ranch, Cascade, ID 83611. Tel: 382-4336. 90 miles (145 km) east of Grangeville, cabins, hunting, float boats, fishing, horseback riding. (Write for details.)

Cook Ranch, 5727 Hill Road, Boise, ID 83703. Tel: 344-0951. 50 miles south of Elk City. Lodge, family-style meals, snowmobile, hunting, horseback riding. (Write for details.)

Sawtooth Lodge, 1403 E. Bannock St., Boise, ID 83702. Tel: 344-6685. Located in Grandjean, cabins, RV facilities, hunt, fish, backpack, pack grips. (Write for details.)

Sulphur Creek Ranch, 7153 W. Emerald St., Boise, ID 83704. Tel: 377-1188. Middle fork of Salmon River. Lodge, cabins, 5-acre trout reservoir, ski, climb. (Write for details.)

Clark Miller Guest Ranch, Star Route, Ketchum, ID 83340. Tel: 774-3535. 12 miles (19 km) south of Redfish Lake. Six primitive fully equipped cabins, located on 300 acres of land, fishing streams. (Write for details.)

Sun Valley Resort, Sun Valley Lodge, Sun Valley, ID 83353. Tel: 622-4111. 550 units, pool, golf, tennis, ski.

Elk Creek Ranch, Island Park, ID 83429. Tel: 558-7404. Rustic luxury cabins 25 miles (40 km) north of Ashton. (Write for details.)

IN MONTANA

HOTELS & INNS

• BILLINGS

Best Western Northern Hotel, Broadway at First Ave. N., Tel: (1-800) 528-1234. Located downtown, lounge, live entertainment, children under 16 free.

Billings Plaza Holiday Inn, 5500 Midland Road. Tel: 1-800-HOLIDAY. Under 18 free. Pool, indoor recreation center, electronic games, restaurant.

Billings Sheraton Hotel, 27, N. 27th St., Tel: (1-800) 325-3535. Pool, Nautilus center, 300 luxury rooms, downtown.

• BOZEMAN

Best Western City Center Motor Inn, 507 W. Main. Tel: (1-800) 428-1234. Sauna, pool, Bridger Bowl Ski Area 15 miles (24 km).

Holiday Inn of Bozeman, 5 Baxter Lane. Tel: 1-800-HOLIDAY. Pool, airport limousine service, full service restaurant.

Thrifty Scot Motel, 1321 N. 7th Ave. Tel: (1-800) 228-3222. Economical, free continental breakfast, 8 miles (13 km) to airport.

• BUTTE

Best Western Copper King Inn, 4655, Harrison. Tel: 494-6666. 151 luxury rooms, pool, sauna, live music and dancing, coffee shop, dining.

Best Western War Bonnet Inn, 2100 Cornell Ave. Tel: 494-7800. Pool, jogging track, 134 rooms.

• GREAT FALLS

Best Western Heritage Inn, 1700 Fox Farm Road. Tel: 761-1900. Indoor recreation center, 2 pools, sauna, whirlpool, 250 rooms.

Fox Hollow Residence Inn, 1700 10th St. SW. Tel: 727-0702.

Sheraton Great Falls, 400 10th Ave. S., Tel: 727-7200. Luxury hotel, pool, full service.

• HELENA

Best Western Colonial Inn, 2301 Colonial Drive. Tel: 443-2100. Pool, sauna, truck parking.

Park Plaza Hotel, 22 N. Last Chance Gulch. Tel: (1-800) 322-2290. Downtown in historic mall.

• KALISPELL

Best Western Outlaw Inn, 1701 Hwy 93 S. Tel: 755-6100. 250 luxury rooms, 2 pools, sauna, spa, live music.

Cavanaugh's, 20 N. Main 752. Tel: 752-6660. Inn with restaurant and pool.

Red Lion Motor Inn, 1330 Hwy 2 W. Tel: 755-6700. Full service, hotel, pool.

• MISSOULA

Comfort Inn, 744 E. Broadway. Tel: (1-800) 228-5150. Pool, 89 luxury rooms, fishing, tennis, full service.

Red Lion Motel, 700 W. Broadway. Tel: (1-800) 547-8010.

Village Red Lion Motel Inn, 100 Madison. Tel: (1-800) 547-8010.

• WEST YELLOWSTONE

Best Western Executive Inn, corner of Gibbon and Dunraven. Tel: (1-800) 528-1234. Beautiful location, pool, fish, snowmobile.

Quality Inn Ambassador, 315 Yellowstone Ave. Tel: (1-800) 228-5151. Close to Yellowstone National Park. Pool, whirlpool, and restaurant.

Stagecoach Inn Travelodge, Madison and Dunraven. Tel: (1-800) 255-3050.

• WHITEFISH

Grouse Mountain Lodge, 1205 Hwy 93 W. Tel: (1-800) 321-8822. Luxury lodge, pool.

Bay Point Estates, 300 Bay Point Drive. Tel: 862-2331. Ski & gold packages, family retreat, pool.

Ptarmigan Village, Big Mountain Road. Tel: 862-3594. Pools, sauna, tennis.

RANCHES & RESORTS, HOSTELS & HOT SPRINGS

Birchwood Hostel, 600 S. Orange, Missoula, MT 59801. Tel: 728-9799. 22-bed dorm with bunk beds, fully equipped, bring food and sleeping-bags. (Reservations advised.)

Crystal Lakes Resort, Fortine, MT 59918. Tel: 882-4455. 40 condominiums, pools, cross-country skiing, hiking.

Dolezal Home Hostel, Rt. 2, Box 65, Ronan, MT 59864. Tel: 676-2154. Six-bedroom home, bring food. (Guests must have youth pass and reservations.)

Flathead Lake Lodge, Box 248, Bigfork, MT 59911. Tel: 837-4391. Dude ranch on Flathead Lake, riding, sailing, water-skiing, tennis, cottages.

Circle 8 Ranch, Box 729, Choteau, MT 59422. Tel: 466-5964. Modern cabins, riding, swimming, wilderness pack trips, hunting.

7 Lazy P Ranch, Box P, Choteau, MT 59422. Tel: 466-2044. Pack trips, hunting and fishing in Bob Marshell Wilderness. Cabins and home-style cooking.

Jackson Snyder Ranch, Box 1099, Lewistown, MT 59468. Tel: 538-3571. 2000-acre mountain ranch. Includes two meals.

Bar Y Seven Ranch, Brusett, MT 59318. Tel: 557-6150. 5000-acre working cattle ranch, fishing, hunting, snowmobile, cabins, family-style meals. (Write for rates.)

Sleeping Buffalo Resort, Star Rt. 3, Box 13, Saco, MT 59621. Tel: 527-3370. Hot springs resort, golf, fishing, hunting, pools.

Bill Sweet Hostel, Box 16, Darby, MT 59829. Tel: 821-3792. Pitch your tent or rent a tipi.

CB Cattle and Guest Ranch, Box 604, Cameron, MT 50720. Tel: 682-4954. Working ranch, riding. No children under 13.

Diamond J Ranch, Ennis, MT 59729. Tel: 682-4867. Cabins, riding, pool, fishing on Madison River.

Burnt Leather Ranch, McLeod, MT 59052. Tel: 222-6795. Working ranch bordering national forest. (Write for rates.)

Lazy K Bar Ranch, Melville Rt., Big Timber, MT 59011. Tel: 537-4404. 20,000-acre working cattle and horse ranch. One week minimum stay.

BYXBE Ranch, Pompey's Pillar, MT 59064. Tel: 987-2377. Hiking, rock hunting in 640-acre working cattle ranch.

Rooney Ranches, Tongue River Stage, Miles City, MT 59301. Tel: 784-2770. Two working ranches, hiking, skiing and riding. Camper hookups, family lodging in home.

IN UTAH

HOTELS & INNS

• ALTA

Rustler Lodge, Tel: 532-4061. 54 units, heated pool, saunas, skiing, suite available.

Alta Lodge, Tel: 742-3500. Ski lodge. (Call for details.)

• BEAVER

Best Western Piace Motel, 161 S. Main. Tel: 438-2438. AAA, 24 units, pool, golf, close to Holly Ski Resort.

Country Inn Restaurant and Fuel Stop, N. off-ramp interchange. Tel: 438-2484. 38 units, pool.

• CASTLE DALE

Best Western El Roy Inn, 80 S. Main. Tel: 586-6528. Pool, sauna, whirlpool, 75 units.

Meadeau View Lodge (Bed-and-Breakfast), 30 miles (48 km) east of Cedar City, on Nordic Ski Center, near Cedar Breaks.

• **DELTA**

Best Western Pendray Plaza, 527 E. Topaz Blvd. Tel: 864-3882. 83 units, restaurant, pool.

• **GREEN RIVER**

Best Western River Terrace, Tel: 564-3401. 51 units, pool.

Motel 6, east of Green River. Tel: 564-3266.

• **HEBER CITY**

Viking Lodge, 989 S. Main. Tel: 654-2202. 36 family units, playground.

Wasatch Motel, 875 S. Main. Tel: 654-2123. 20 units, pool.

• **KANAB**

Best Western Red Hills, 124 W. Center. Tel: 644-2675. 55 units.

Treasure Trail Motel, 140 W. Center. Tel: 644-2687. 28 units, pool, airport service.

• **MINERSVILLE**

Apache Motel Friendship Inn, 166 S. 400 E. Tel: 259-5755. AAA, 2-room units, pool.

Ramada Inn, 182 S. Main. Tel: (1-800) 228-2828. Pool, hot-tub/jacuzzi, AAA.

• **OGDEN**

Best Western Flying J Motel, 1206 W. 21st St. Tel: 393-8644. Pool, game room.

Holiday Inn, 3306 Washington Blvd. Tel: 399-5671. 109 units, pool, restaurant, airport service.

Ogden Hilton, 247 24th St. Tel: 627-1190. 288 units, indoor pool, 2 restaurants, game room.

• **PANGUICH**

Color Country Motel, 500 N. Main. Tel: 676-2386. 26 units, pool, AAA, close to 5 National Parks.

New Western Motel, 180 E. Main. Tel: 676-8876. Pool, 26 units.

• **PARK CITY** (Ski Country)

The Blue Church Lodge, 424 Park Ave. Tel: 649-8009. Units with kitchen, golf, tennis, skiing, horses.

Deer Valley Lodging, Deer Valley Road. Tel: 649-4040. Family units.

The Yarrow/a Holiday Inn Resort, 1800 Park Ave. Tel: 649-7000. 179 units, pool, restaurant.

Edelweiss Haus, P.O. Box 495. Tel: 649-9342.

Resort Property Management and Lodging, 592 Main. Tel: 649-6613. 25 units, condos, kitchen, playground.

Snowflower, 400 Silver King Drive. Tel: (1-800) 852-3101. 90 units, fully equipped, 2 pools, hot tubs, skiing.

• **PRICE**

Carriage House Inn, 590 E. Main. Tel: 637-5660. Pool and spa, restaurant.

• **PROVO**

Best Western Columbian, 79 E. 300 S. Tel: 373-8973. AAA, 28 family units, pool.

Best Western Cotton Tree Inn, 2230 No. University Pkwy. Tel: 373-7044. 80 units, peaceful setting, pool, spa.

Budget Host University Western Inn, 40 W. 300 S. Tel: (1-800) 368-4400. 29 family units, pool, playground.

The Provo Excelsior, 101 W. 100 N. Tel: 377-4700. Pool, 250 units, 2 restaurants, sauna, whirlpool.

• **Richfield**

Best Western High Country Inn, 145 S. Main. Tel: 896-5481. AAA, 65 units, airport service.

• **St George**

Best Western Thunderbird, 1000 E. 150 N. Tel: 673-6123. Family units, pool, sauna.

Hilton Inn, 1450 S. Hilton Drive. Tel: 628-0463. Pool, sauna, whirlpool, golf, tennis, 100 units.

Regency Inn, 770 E. St George Blvd. Tel: 673-6119. 49 units, pool, sauna, whirlpool.

• **Snowbird** (Ski Country)

Snowbird Ski and Summer Resort, Tel: (1-800) 453-3000. 571 units, kitchen, restaurant, pools, shopping.

• **Salt Lake City**

Hilton Hotel of Salt Lake, 150 W. 500 S. Tel: (801) 523-3344. 352 rooms, outdoor pool.

Holiday Inn & Holidome Downtown, 230 W. 600 S. Tel: (1-800) 238-800. 160 rooms, indoor pool, children's recreational facilities.

Hotel Utah, Main and S. Temple. Tel: (1-800) 453-3820. Children under 14 free, 500 rooms, restaurant.

Little America Hotel, 500 S. Main. Tel: (1-800) 453-9450. 850 rooms, 2 pools, all facilities.

Marriott Hotel, 75 South West Temple. Tel: (1-800) 228-9290. Pool, handicapped facilities, children's recreation.

Quality Inn City Center, 154 W. 600 S. Tel: (1-800) 228-5151. 250 rooms, outdoor pool, sauna.

Salt Lake Sheraton, 255 S. West Temple. Tel: (1-800) 325-3535. Pool, 502 rooms, children under 18 free when accompanied by adults.

Town House Motel, 245 W. North Temple. Tel: (1-800) 453-4511. AAA, 66 rooms reasonably priced, pool, children under 13 free.

Holiday Inn Airport, 1659 W. North Temple. Tel: (1-800) 238-8000. 91 rooms, no charge for children under 18 years, pool.

Salt Lake Airport Hilton, 5151 Wiley Post Way. Tel: (1-800) 528-0313. Tennis, paddle boats, pool, putting green, children free.

Motel 6, 1990 W. North Temple. Tel: 322-3061. Outdoor pool, reasonably priced. (No credit cards.)

Se Rancho Motel, 640 W. North Temple. Tel: 532-3300. 97 rooms, reasonably priced, outdoor pool, tennis.

BED-&-BREAKFAST

Bed N Breakfast Association of Utah, P.O. Box 16465, Salt Lake City, UT 84116. Tel: 532-7076. Reservations. (Write for listings.)

Brigham Street Inn, 1135 E. South Temple, Salt Lake City, UT 84102. Tel: 364-4461. National historic site, private baths, fireplace, Continental breakfast.

Eller Bed & Breakfast, 164 S. 900 E., Salt Lake City, UT 84012. Tel: 533-8184. State historical site, full breakfast, sauna. (No credit cards.)

• **Vernal**

Antlers Motel Best Western, 423 W. Main. Tel: 789-1202. Pool, playground, 53 units, AAA.

GUEST RANCHES, RESORTS & CABINS

Diamond Valley Guest Ranch, P.O. Box 712, St George, UT 84770. Tel: 574-2281.

Manning Meadow Ranch, 2052 E. 4500 South, Salt Lake City, UT 84117. Tel: 277-6928.

Rock Creek Ranch, P.O. Box 409, Duchesne, UT 84021. Tel: 353-4744.

Bryce Canyon National Park Lodge, TW Recreational Services, 451 N. Main, Cedar City, UT 84720. Tel: 586-7686.

Goulding's Lodge, Box 1, Monument Valley, UT 84536. Tel: 727-3231.

Zion National Park Lodge, TW Recreational Services, 451 N. Main, Cedar City, UT 84720. Tel: 586-7686.

Bullfrog Resort and Marina, Del E. Webb Recreational Properties Inc., Hanksville, UT 84734. Tel: (1-800) 528-6154.

Hilton Inn, 1450 S. Hilton Drive, St George, UT 84770. Tel: (1-800) 662-2525.

Prospector Square and Conference Center, P.O. Box 1698, Park City, UT 84060. Tel: (1-800) 453-3812.

Snowbird Ski and Summer Resort, Snowbird, UT 84092. Tel: (1-800) 453-3000.

Brian Head Ski and Summer Resort, P.O. Box 8, Brian Head, UT 84719. Tel: 677-2035.

Sundance, P.O. Box 178, Eden, UT 84310. Tel: 745-3511.

Nordic Valley Resort, P.O. Box 178, Eden, UT 84310. Tel: 745-3511.

Mt Majestic Lodge, Brighton, UT 84121. Tel: 364-3381.

IN WYOMING

HOTELS & INNS

• CASPER

Ramada Inn, I-25 & Center, 123 W.E. St. Tel: 235-5713. Full facilities, AAA.

Holiday Inn, 300 W. F St., Box 3500. Tel: 235-2531. 200 units, swimming pool, full facility hotel. AAA.

• CHEYENNE

Hitching Post Inn, 1700 W. Lincolnway. Tel: (1-800) 221-0125. Full service hotel, pool, 250 units, AAA.

Holiday Inn, 204 W. Fox Farm Road. Tel: 638-4466. Full service hotel, pool, 246 units.

Holding's Little America, P.O. Box 1529. Tel: 634-2771. Full services, 190 units, pool.

• CODY

Holiday Inn Convention Center, 1701 Sheridan Ave. Tel: 587-5555. Full service hotel, pool, 132 units.

Irma Hotel, 1192 Sheridan. Tel: 587-4221. Historic hotel built by Buffalo Bill, named after his daughter Irma.

• DOUGLAS

Plains Motel, 841 S. 6th St. Tel: 358-4484. Economical motel, 47 units, pool.

Holiday Inn, 1450 Riverband Drive. Tel: 358-9790. Full service hotel, pool, 117 units.

• EVANSTON

Best Western Dunmar Inn, Box 768. Tel: 789-3770. Full service hotel, 200 units, pool.

Western Budget Inn, 1936 Hwy 30 E. Tel: 789-2810. 115 units, pool.

• GILLETTE

Holiday Inn, 2009 S. Douglas Hwy. Tel: 686-3000. Full service hotel, pool, 161 units.

• JACKSON

American Snow King Resort, Box SKI. Tel: 733-5200. Full service resort, pool, 200 units.

Jackson Hole Racquet Club Resort, Star Rt. 362A. Tel: 733-3990. Full service resort, pool, 95 units.

Virginian Lodge, 750 W. Broadway. Tel: 733-8247. 149 units, full service lodge, pool.

Executive Inn-Best Western, 325 W. Pearl St. Tel: (1-800) 528-1234. Full service hotel, pool 59 units.

Wort Hotel, Broadway and Glenwood. Tel: 733-2190.

Holiday Inn, Box 1065. Tel: 742-6611. Full service hotel, 100 units, pool.

Ramada Inn, 1503 S. 3rd. Tel: 742-3721. Full service, pool.

• LITTLE AMERICA

Holding's Little America, Box 1. Tel: (1-800) 634-2401. 150 units, pool, full service.

• RAWLINGS

Quality Inn, 2222 E. Cedar. Tel: 324-6615. Full service, pool.

Holiday Inn, 1801 E. Cedar. Tel: 324-2783. Full service hotel, pool, 132 units.

• ROCK SPRINGS

Rock Spring Hilton Inn, 2518 Foothill Blvd. Tel: 362-9600. 150 units, pool, full facility hotel, AAA.

Outlaw Inn, 1630 Elk St. Tel: 362-6623. Full service hotel, one of the best western inns.

• SARATOGA

Saratoga Inn, Box 869. Tel: 326-5261. Full service hotel, 60 units.

• SHERIDAN

Sheridan Center Motor Inn, Box 4008, 612 N. Main. Tel: 674-7421. Full service hotel, pool, 142 units.

Trails End Motel, 2125 N. Main. Tel: 672-2477. Full service motel, pool, 83 units.

• TETON VILLAGE
(Adjoining Teton National Park)

Alpenhof, Box 228. Tel: (1-800) 733-3244. 40 units, pool.

Inn at Jackson Hole, Box 328. Tel: (1-800) 842-7666. 70 units, pool, full service.

The Sojourner Inn, Box 348. Tel: (1-800) 842-7600. 100 units, pool, AAA.

• THERMOPOLIS

Holiday Inn, Hot Springs State Park. Tel: 864-3131. Full service hotel, pool, 80 units.

DUDE RANCHES & RESORTS

Crossed Sabres Ranch, Box WTC, Wapiti, WY 82450. Tel: 587-3750. Located 9 miles (15 km) east of Yellowstone National Park. Weekly guest ranch, pack trips, park tours, rodeo, cookouts.

4-Bear Outfitters, 1297 Ln 10, Rt. 1, Powell, WY 82435. Fishing, hiking, hunting, wilderness horseback trips, special services for the handicapped. Historic trips to Cody.

Goff Creek Lodge, Box 155TC, Cody, WY 82414. Tel: 587-3753. Located 10 miles (16 km) from east entrance of Yellowstone National Park, deluxe cabins, trail rides, campfire get-togethers.

Bill Cody's Ranch Resort, P.O. Box 1390-T, Cody, WY 82414. Tel: (1-800) 621-2114. Modern mountain cottages, lounge, heated pool, whirlpool. Operated by Buffalo Bill Cody's grandson.

Flagg Ranch, P.O. Box 187, Moran, WY 83013. Tel: 543-2861. Located between Grand Teton and Yellowstone National Park, cabins, float trips, cookout rides.

Triangle X Ranch, Moose, WY 83012. Tel: 733-5500. Located 26 miles (40 km) northeast of Jackson, float trips, pack trips, hikes, ranch activities.

Jackson Hole Ski Area, P.O. Box 220, Teton Village, WY 83025. Tel: (800) 443-6931. Located 12 miles (19 km) northeast of Jackson Hotel, centrally situated.

Heart Six Guest Ranch, Moran, WY 83013. Tel: 543-2477. Located at the northeast end of Jackson Hole, modern cabins, pack trips, float trips on the Snake River.

HOSPITALITY PROGRAM

Many cities and communities in the United States have a "Meet Americans at Home" program when residents invite foreigners

THE WORLD IS FLAT

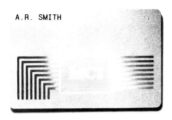

Our history could fill this book, but we prefer to fill glasses.

When you make a great beer, you don't have to make a great fus

into their houses. Different languages are on offer. Write to the **US Travel Service**, US Dept of Commerce, Washington, DC 20230, and request the "Americans at Home" folder.

CAMPING

Colorado: Colorado is teeming with camping sites. Colorado's National Forests, Parks and Monuments, Recreation Areas, State and private campgrounds give a wide choice of campsites. Most public campgrounds are equipped with water, tables, benches, fire gates, garbage containers, and simple toilet facilities (no showers). Private campgrounds offer electrical and plumbing hookups, showers, laundry facilities, and occasionally a swimming pool and clubhouse. Write to: US Forest Service, National Park Service, Bureau of Land Management, Colorado Division of Parks and Outdoor Recreation, Colorado Campgrounds Association. Also check "Campgrounds" in the Yellow Pages. Look for the "tree" symbol on the Colorado highway map.

Write for the "Roster of Rocky Mountain Summer Camps for Boys and Girls" which has a list of accredited camping facilities for young people. American Camping Association, Rocky Mountain Section, 400 S. Broadway, Denver, CO 80209. Tel: (303) 778-8774.

FOOD DIGEST

Whether a snack or a hearty dinner, eating in the Rockies can be fun. The large cities, small towns, mountain resorts, and alpine villages have a diversity of restaurants and cuisines. The steakhouses have become a standard institution, serving some of the best beef in the West. French, Italian, Asian and Latin American foods have proliferated and cuisine from different countries is surprisingly easy to come by.

The Rockies provides the best mountain trout, which is served in season in local restaurants. Fast-food places serving the traditional hamburgers, pizzas and tacos are plentiful. While more formal city restaurants require jackets and ties for men, the majority of eating places will welcome you in casual attire. Reservations are advisable for the popular restaurants. The Yellow Pages in each area gives a list of restaurants.

WHERE TO EAT

COLORADO

• **Colorado Springs** (Area Code: 719)

Dale Street Cafe, 115 E. Dale. Tel: 578-9898. (Wholesome eating.)

Edelweiss, 34 E. Romona Ave. Tel: 633-2220. (German and Continental cuisine, in a Bavarian setting.)

Pepe's, 2427 N. Academy Blvd. Tel: 574-5801. (Fine Mexican food.)

• **Durango**

L'Entrepoint Restaurant and Bar, 1769 Main Ave. (Gourmet French cuisine, Creole dishes, desserts, a variety of wines.)

The Ore House, 147 6th St. Tel: 247-5707. (One of Durango's oldest restaurants, seafood and steaks.)

Mr Rosewater, 522 Main St. Tel: 247-8788. (A deli serving a variety of soups, pastries, wines, juices, egg dishes.)

The Strater Hotel, 699 Main Ave. Tel: 247-4431. (Live ragtime music, all you can eat fish fry on Friday nights, luncheon buffet specials.)

Yesterday's, 800 Camino del Rio in Holiday Inn. Tel: 247-5393. (Rocky Mountain trout, prime rib.)

• **Aspen & Snowmass**

Andre's, 312 S. Galena. Tel: 925-6200. (International food.)

Country Road Ltd., 400 E. Main. Tel: 925-6556. (Bar and restaurant; fresh trout, sea food delicacies. Reservations advised.)

Crystal Palace, 300 E. Hyman Ave. Tel: 925-1455. (Large collection of stained glass. Gourmet food and music daily.)

Eastern Winds, 520 East Copper. Tel: 925-5160. (Szechuan and Mandarin specialities including Peking Duck.)

Guido's Swiss Inn, Hyman and Monarch. Tel: 925-1455.

Home Plate, 333 E. Durant. Tel: 925-1986. (Casual.)

Steak Pit, City Market Bldg. Tel: 925-3459. (Excellent steaks, prime rib, lobster, fresh fish, salad bar.)

• DENVER

Adirondacks, 901 Larimer. Tel: 573-8900. (Southwestern cuisine.)

Bay Wolf, 231 Milwaukee. Tel: 388-9221. (Specializes in veal and fish, live jazz music.)

Buckhorn Exchange, 1000 Osage.Tel: 534-9505. (This is a historic eating and drinking emporium.)

Cafe Kandahar, 2709 W. Main Littleton. Tel: 798-9075. (Continental cuisine with a ski museum.)

Campari's, Sheraton 4900 DTC Parkway. Tel: 779-8899. (Italian.)

Casa Bonita, 6715 W. Colfax. Tel: 232-5115. (Mexican.)

Churchill's Restaurant, 1730 S. Colorado Blvd. and I-25. Tel: 756-8877. (*Nouvelle cuisine*, nightly entertainment.)

Fins Oyster Bar and Restaurant, 1401 Larimer St. (Fresh seafood and other specialities. Downtown location.)

Fresh Fish Company, 7600 E. Hampden Ave. (Specializes in seafood.)

Gasho of Japan, downtown at 1627 Curtis. Tel: 892-5625; and 5701 S. Syracuse St. DTC. Tel: 773-3277. (Japanese steak house.)

H. Brinkers, 7209 S. Clinton, I-25 and Arapahoe Road. (Seafood, steaks, live entertainment.)

The Harvest, 430 S. Colorado Blvd. (Natural goodies.)

Hoffbran Steaks, 13th and Santa Fe. (Good steaks.)

Hudson's, 1800 Glenarm Place. (Red snapper, veal, lamb, prime rib, excellent desserts, entertainment.)

Imperial, W. Ninth at Speer. Tel: 698-2800. (Chinese.)

Le Central, 112 E. 8th Ave. Tel: 863-8094. (French.)

The Library Restaurant, 800 S. Colorado Blvd. (Fine food, cozy atmosphere.)

Magic Pan Creperie, 1465 Larimer St. (Fluffy crepes, souffles, delicacies.)

Manhattan Cafe, 1620 Market St. (New York-style atmosphere.)

Maxwells, 435 S. Cherry St. (Thick Sicilian pizza.)

Ming Dynasty, 4251 E. Mississippi, Glendale. (Mandarin, Szechuan, and Asian cuisine.)

North Woods Inn, 6115 S. Santa Fe Drive (in Littleton). Tel: 794-2112.

Old Spaghetti Factory, 1215 18th St. Tel: 295-1864. (Fun and inexpensive.)

Paradise Bar and Grill, 100 E. 9th Ave. (Excellent seafood.)

Pierre's Quorum Restaurant, East Colfax at Grant. (25 years of award-winning French cuisine.)

Red Apple Restaurant and Lounge, Rodeway Inn, 4590 Quebec St. (Steaks, seafood, salad bar.)

Rich's Cafe, 80 S. Madison St. (Specialities are salads, sandwiches, Mexican food. Opens till late.)

Sky Chef's, Stapleton International Airport. (Airline catering, restaurants, bar.)

Soren's, 315 Detroit. (Good eating, meat, fish and vegetarian food.)

Sushi Koi, 1626 Market St. (Japanese delicacies.)

Tante Louise, 4900 E. Colfax Ave. (Culinary treats, French country-style restaurant.)

Wellshire Inn, 3333 S. Colorado. (Lunch, dinner, Sunday brunch, full Continental service.)

Wilscam Restaurant, 1735 Arapahoe St. (Elegant restaurant, Continental cuisine.)

Zang Brewing Co., 2301 7th St. (Fun, casual with a Denver sports tradition before and after games.)

IDAHO

• BOISE

The Boarding House. (Moderately priced, Basque-style restaurant.)

The Gamekeeper, located in the Owyhee Plaza Hotel. (Top quality steaks, seafood, wines.)

Pengilly's. (Unusual lunches, served in an unique atmosphere.)

The Royal, located downtown. (Good food served, turn-of-the-century decor.)

• COEUR D'ALENE

The Cedars, Tel: 664-2922. (Excellent food, floating restaurant on Lake Coeur D'Alene.)

North Shore Plaza Restaurants, located in the Lakeshore complex with plush roof-top dining. (Shore Restaurant offers casual atmosphere, Templin's has excellent chicken-to-go.)

Osprey, 1000 W. Hubbard St. Tel: 664-2115.

• LEWISTON

Cedars III. (Moderately priced, hand-cut steaks, salad bar.)

Helm. (Excellent cooking, prime rib, shrimp, steaks. Children's menu.)

• TWIN FALLS

Morgan's Rogerson Restaurant. (Family dining, casual atmosphere, warm hospitality, moderate prices.)

• SANDPOINT

Garden Restaurant (Moderately priced, outdoor dining, Asian food, fresh seafood, roast duck.)

MONTANA

• BOZEMAN

Gene's Cartwheel Supper Club, located 7 miles (11 km) west on Hwy 191. (Full menu, steak, seafood.)

John's Pork Chop, 209 E. Main. Tel: 586-0029. (Original pork chop sandwich.)

Jordans Restaurant, 1104 E. Main. Tel: 586-9791. (Family meals, full menu.)

New Asia Kitchen, 1533 W. Babcock. Tel: 586-6362. (Chinese cuisine. Take-out orders accepted.)

UTAH

• CEDAR CITY

Sugar Loaf Cafe. (Excellent chicken and steak, moderate.)

• LOGAN

Country Kitchen. (Good family eating, moderately priced.)

Tijuana Tilly's, 6351 So State. (Mexican, American.)

Union Station, Union Square, 685 E. 9450 S. (American.)

Western Sizzling Steak House, 2222 W. 3500 S. (Steak, American.)

Zaccheo's Hansom House, 280 E. 800 S. (Italian, American.)

WYOMING

• CASPER

Benham's. (Steaks and businessmen's lunch.)

• CODY

Green Gables. (Smorgasbord, excellent food.)

Irma Grill. (Moderately priced steaks and ribs. Buffalo Bill's cherrywood bar)

• JACKSON

Alpenhof Garden Room, in Teton Village. (European gourmet restaurant. Veal, seafood and homemade pastries.)

Anthony's Italian Restaurant, 50 S. Glenwood, Jackson. (Authentic Italian cuisine.)

Lame Duck, in Jackson. (Featuring a variety of Asian dishes at reasonable prices.)

Soup Kitchen, in Jackson. (Fast-food, deli sandwiches, soups, salads, yoghurt, desserts.)

• LARAMIE

Diamond Horseshoe. (Moderately priced American and Chinese cuisine.)

• LANDER

Miner's Delight. (An exclusive restaurant in Atlantic ghost town serving Continental food.)

Calvary. (With excellent prime ribs.)

THINGS TO DO

NATIVE AMERICAN RESERVATIONS

Traveling through the Rockies allows you to discover vestiges of the colorful past of the Indian cultures…in sites, festivals, names, art, pageantry and descendants. The Native Americans have left a significant contribution in the Rockies for thousands of years.

If you plan to visit any of the reservations, you could write to the tribal headquarters ahead of time and get the schedule of events. During the summer months pow-wows and festivals go on in most of the reservations which are culturally enriching events.

COLORADO

Southern Ute Reservation, Tribal Headquarters, Ignation, CO 81137. (Mouche and Capote Ute tribes.)

Ute Mountain Reservation, Tribal Headquarters, Towaoc, CO 81334. (Wiminuche Ute tribe.)

IDAHO

Coeur D'Alene Reservation, Tribal Headquarters, Plummer, ID 83851. (Coeur D'Alene tribe.)

Fort Hall Reservation, Tribal Headquarters, Fort Hall, ID 83203. (Shoshone and Bannock tribes.)

Kootenai Reservation, Tribal Headquarters, Bonners Ferry, ID 83805. (Kootenai tribe.)

Nez Perce Reservation, Tribal Headquarters, Lapwai, ID 83540. (Nez Perce tribe.)

MONTANA

Blackfeet Reservation, Tribal Headquarters, Browning, MT 59417. (Blackfeet tribe.)

Crow Reservation, Tribal Headquarters, Crow Agency, MT 59002. (Crow tribe.)

Flathead Reservation, Tribal Headquarters, Dixon, MT 59831. (Salish and Kootenai tribes.)

Fort Belknap Reservation, Tribal Headquarters, Harlem, MT 59526. (Gros Ventre and Assiniboine tribes.)

Fork Peck Reservation, Tribal Headquarters, Poplar, MT 59225. (Assiniboine and Sioux tribes.)

Montana United Indian Association, Tel: 443-5350.

Northern Cheyenne Reservation, Tribal Headquarters, Lame Deer, MT 59043. (Northern Cheyenne tribe.)

Rocky Boy's Reservation, Tribal Headquarters, Box Elder, MT 59521. (Chippewa-Cree tribe.)

UTAH

Goshute Reservation, Tribal Headquarters, Ibapah, UT 84034. (Goshute tribe.)

Skull Valley Reservation, Tribal Headquarters, Grantsville, UT 84209. (Goshute tribe.)

Southern Paiute Reservation, Tribal Headquarters, Cedar City, UT 84270. (Southern Paiute tribe.)

Uintah and Ouray Reservation, Tribal Headquarters, Fort Duchesne, UT 84026. (Ute tribe.)

WYOMING

Wind River Reservation, Tribal Headquarters, Riverton, WY 82501. (Shoshone and Arapahoe tribes.)

RAILROADING

The Rio Grand Zephir, a scenic train trip between Denver and Salt Lake City, operates Monday, Thursday and Saturday with a return trip on Tuesday, Friday and Sunday. Advanced bookings advised. Write to: Colorado Scenic RR Association, 17155 W. 44th Ave, P.O. Box 641, Golden, CO 80427. Tel: (1-800) 866-3690.

Cripple Creek and Victor Narrow-Gauge Railroad: Trains depart every 45 minutes starting at 10 a.m. from Cripple Creek Museum from May 30 through the first weekend in October. Call 689-2640.

Cumbres and Toltec Scenic Railroad: Passengers have a choice of two all-day sightseeing excursions originating from the terminal at Antonio, Colorado, or terminal at Chama, New Mexico. Limited reservations are available for full-length trip between Antonio and Chama with return trip by van. Both trains leave their terminals at 10 a.m. and return at 5 p.m. This train operates Friday through Tuesday from mid-June to mid-October. For information and reservations write to: C&TS RR, P.O. Box 789, Chama, New Mexico 87520. Tel: (505) 756-2151; C&TS RR, Box 668, Antonio, CO 81120. Tel: 376-5483.

Durango to Silverton Narrow-Gauge: Passengers may ride the train round trip or ride the train one way (3 hours) and return on the Million Dollar Highway by motorcoach. Schedule is May 15–October 24, departure 8.30 a.m. daily, in the summer second departure 9.30 a.m. daily; October 25–November 29, 9 a.m. daily; November 30–May 14, 9.55 a.m. daily. Reservations advised at least one month in advance. Write to: Agent-Narrow-Gauge Depot, Durango, CO 81301. Tel: 247-2733. Weather permitting, this train operates through the year.

Georgetown Loop: 4-mile trip from Silver Plume to the end of the track and back. Operates daily except Mondays, June through Labor Day. Departures from Georgetown and Silver Plume depots. Tel: 670-1686.

FROM DENVER

Central City
Restored gold mining town, a National Historic District. Pan for gold, tour gold mines, Teller Opera House and Hotel, restaurants, antiques, shops and saloons. Located 34 miles (55 km) northwest of Denver.

Georgetown
Elegant, silver mining town with over 200 Victorian buildings. Shops, restaurants, Hotel de Paris, Hamil House, Georgetown Loop narrow-gauge railroad, silver mining tour. 34 miles (55 km) west of Denver.

Idaho Springs
Historic gold mining town. Shops, restaurants, attractions, 21 miles (33 km) west of Denver on I-70. National Forest information center in town for information on camping. Gateway to Mount Evans Highway, highest paved road in North America for automobiles. Free 14-mile (22 km) highway goes up to 14,260 ft (4,350 meters). Open June through Labor Day.

Boulder
Location of beautiful university town at foot of Rockies. University of Colorado, historic Boulder Mall downtown, shops, Victorian buildings, restaurants. 27 miles (43 km) northwest of Denver on highway 36.

Golden
Historic place just outside Denver. Coors tour, Colorado Railroad Museum, Heritage Square, Buffalo Bill Museum and gravesite, Colorado School of Mines. On the way to Golden, detour a few miles and visit the beautiful Red Rocks Amphitheater.

Sightseeing Tours

Best Mountain Tours by Mountain Men, 3003 S. Macon Circle, Aurora, CO 80014, Tel: 750-5200. One-day and half-day tours in four-wheel-drive vans to gold mines, mountains and ghost towns. Private charters also available.

Gray Line Bus Tours, Box 38667, Denver CO 80238. Tel: 289-2841. Two-hour to full-day tours to mountain parks, Colorado Springs, Gold mining towns, Rocky Mountain National Park.

Historic Denver Tours, 1330 17th St., Denver, CO 80202. Tel: 534-1858. Driving, walking, and van tours of the city's historic landmarks.

Pike's Peak Tours, 3704 W. Colorado Ave., Colorado Springs, 80904. Tel: (1-800) 345-8197.

Tours by Arrangement, Tel: 623-1492. The Arrangers Inc. offer half-day tours for groups in the city and surrounding areas.

FROM SALT LAKE CITY

City Creek Canyon
Enter the canyon off East Capitol Road. Paved road extends 5 miles (8 km) to Rotary Park. Great for picnicking and hiking. Canyon open from 8 a.m.–8 p.m.

Parley's Canyon
Most of this canyon is in Wasatch National Forest. Golfing, hunting in the fall and hiking are some of the activities available here. Many historical markers and cafes and service stations are located at the summit and near the golf course.

Mill Creek Canyon
This box canyon offers picnicking and hiking amidst oak, conifer and aspen. Picnic grounds and sports areas are available.

Emigration Canyon
Monument and Hogle Zoo are at the mouth of the canyon. Main entrance from Sunnyside Ave, Utah Hwy 85 connects with US 40 and I-80. Hiking and picnicking.

Big Cottonwood Canyon
In the Wasatch National Forest. At the top of the canyon is Brighton Ski and Summer resort. Picnicking, hiking and beautiful vistas.

Little Cottonwood Canyon
Effects of glaciation can be seen in this U-shaped canyon. At the end of the canyon are Alta and Snowbird Ski Resorts. Excellent rock climbing, hiking, picnicking and some fishing.

BACKPACKING

COLORADO: Over two thirds of Colorado is National Forest land with more than 400 public campgrounds. Excellent backpacking areas include Rocky Mountain National Park, Pike's Peak, West of Denver in the Mt Evans area, San Juan Mountain Range, north of Glenwood Springs, in the Flattops and the Rabbit Ears Pass area near Steamboat Springs, the Ten Mile Range south of Vail. For information write to: US Forest Service, National Park Service, Bureau of Land Management, US Geological Survey, Colorado Mountain Club. (*See below for a list of National Forests in each state.*) For renting and purchasing equipment check the Yellow Pages under "Mountain Climbing" and "Camping Equipment".

NATIONAL PARKS

There are 10 national parks in the five Rocky Mountain states covered in this book. Each Park has a variety of facilities, activities and regulations.

Entrance fees are charged at most of the Parks varying from 50 cents per person to $5 per vehicle. A Golden Eagle Passport can be purchased at all parks. Auto camping is allowed only in designated campgrounds mostly on a first-come, first-served basis. Most campgrounds have cold water restrooms and no hook-up for showers. In the summertime campgrounds get filled up early, and it's advisable that you reach your campground by early afternoon to ensure a site. The Ranger Station at the entrance of the Park will be able to advise you on what camp sites are available and also supply you with information on the Park. Winter operation of the Parks is often limited and some Parks have no water during the off-season.

Backcountry use in most of the Parks requires free permits for overnight stays. Many Parks require advanced reservations for overnight backcountry use as there are a limited quantity of permits available.

Most boats must meet state regulations on reservoirs, lakes and rivers in national parks. The use of motors is not allowed in some areas except in the case of emergencies.

Drinking water is available at most campgrounds. It is recommended that you check with the ranger responsible for the site re-garding the drinking water as some areas of the Rockies may have contaminated water.

All plants and animals are protected in the National Parks. It is against the law to molest them in any form. Most parks require that pets be kept on a leash or otherwise confined at all times. If you plan to bring your pet, please consult the ranger responsible for the Park ahead of time.

Off-road vehicle use is not allowed except on designated four-wheel-drive roads. Some Parks offer National Park Service (NPS) guided tours to organized groups that may require advanced reservations.

COLORADO

• **Mesa Verde National Park**, CO 81330. *Accommodations***:** Food, gasoline and lodging are available from mid-May to mid-October, no services are available rest of the year. Full interpretive services begin mid-June and continues through Labor Day. **Morefield Campground**, with single and group camp sites have six campsites for physically impaired persons. Commercial campgrounds are located close to the Park entrance.

Recreational facilities: NPS Guided Tours, self-guiding tour, guides for hire, picnic area. *Other facilities*: Museum, groceries, ice, Visitors' Center, handicapped access, restrooms.

• **Rocky Mountain National Park**, Estes Park, CO 80517. Tel: (303) 586-2371. *Accommodations*: Hotels, motels and lodges are available at Estes Park and Grand Lake, just outside the Park. The four campgrounds at Rocky Mountain National Park are all at an elevation above 8,200 ft (2,500 meters). **Moraine Park Campground**, located 3 miles (5 km) west of Head Quarters Visitors' Center, on Bear Lake Road has 250 campsites, including walk-in campsites, ranger station, sanitary dump station, public telephone and campfire amphitheater. Campsites can be reserved.

The **Glacier Basin Campground** located 9 miles (15 km) west of Estes Park on Bear Lake Road has 152 campsites plus 18 group campsites. Facilities include a ranger station, sanitary dump station, comfort station, telephones and an amphitheater. Campsites can be reserved.

Long Peak Campground is for tents only. It is 11 miles (18 km) south of Estes Park. There are 30 campsites, a ranger station and comfort stations. No reservations for this campground.

Timber Creek Campground, is on the west side of the Park and 10 miles (16 km) north of Grand Lake on Trail Ridge Road. Facilities include 100 campsites, a ranger station, comfort stations, sanitary dump station and an amphitheater. Timber Creek is on a first-come basis.

Recreational facilities: NPS Guided Tour, self-guiding tour, picnic area, backcountry use permits, hiking, mountain climbing, horseback riding, fishing, snowmobile route, cross-country ski trail.

Other facilities: Museum, restaurant, handicap access, restrooms and Visitors' Center.

MONTANA

• **Glacier National Park**, West Glacier, MT 59936. Tel: (406) 888-5441. Glacier National Park is open all year and comprises hundreds of miles of backcountry trails that lead to 50 living glaciers, many waterfalls and alpine gardens. Amtrack and regular bus travel are available to East and West Glacier. By car, use highways 2, 89 and 93. If you are traveling from Canada, use Alberta highways 2, 5 or 6.

Accommodations: Comfortable accommodations include two lodges, two hotels, two motor inns and cabins. The campgrounds have from 6 to 200 campsites. Write to the Park Superintendent for information.

Recreational facilities: NPS Guided Tour, self-guiding tour, backcountry use permits, mountain climbing, horseback riding, boating, fishing, picnic areas, cross-country ski trail, float trips, boating.

Other facilities: Groceries, ice, restaurant, restrooms, handicap access, Visitors' Center, boat rentals.

UTAH

• **Arches National Park**, 446 S. Main St., Moab, UT 84532. Depart from Moab and travel 5 miles (8 km) north via US 191 to the Park. Driving time through the Park is 2 hours but allow additional time for hiking.

Accommodations: Devil's Garden Camp-

ground is located in the Park, 18 miles (33 km) from the Visitors' Center. Motels and commercial campgrounds and other services are available in Moab.

Recreational facilities: NPS Guided Tour, self-guiding tour, picnic area, backcountry use permits, hiking.

Other facilities: Handicap access, restroom, Visitors' Center, museum and exhibit.

• **Bryce Canyon National Park**, Bryce Canyon, UT 84717. Allow 3 hours for the Park tour, with extra time for hiking.

Accommodations: Services and accommodations are available just outside the Park, in the surrounding communities. Camping is available year-round in the Park but water is only available in the summer.

Recreational facilities: NPS Guided Tour, self-guiding tour, hiking, backcountry use permits, picnic areas, cross country ski trail, horseback riding.

Other facilities: Museum, exhibit, groceries, ice, restaurant, handicap access, restrooms and Visitors' Center.

• **Canyonlands National Park**, 446 S. Main St., Moab, UT 84532. The Park can be reached from Moab traveling 60 miles (96 km) via US 191 and U-221. Allow around 3 hours to tour the Needles section of Canyonlands. Hiking, jeeping, river running or scenic flights are some of the best ways to explore this Park.

Accommodations: There are primitive camp sites located in four-wheel-drive areas of the Park. Piped water is available in the **Needles Campground** only. Anywhere else in the Park water must be carried in. Accommodations and services are available in Moab and Monticello.

Recreational facilities: Self-guiding tour, guides for hire, hiking, picnic areas, backcountry use permits, boating.

• **Capitol Reef National Park**, Torrey, UT 84775. This Park is accessible on U-24. Allow around 3 hours to drive through the Park.

Accommodations: There are no commercial facilities in the Park. There are two campgrounds located within the Park boundaries. The main campground 1 mile south of the Visitors' Center has 53 sites, comfort stations and fire places. Accommodations and services are available in Torrey, Bicknell and Loa.

Recreational facilities: Hiking, mountain climbing, horseback riding, picnic areas, NPS Guided Tour, self-guiding tour, boating.

Other facilities: Exhibit, Visitors' Center, handicap access.

• **Zion National Park**, Springdale, UT 84767-1099. Depart from St George and travel 46 miles (74 km) via 1-15 and U-90. Allow 3 hours to tour the Park and the Visitors' Center. TW Recreational Services operates accommodations and services to the Park from mid-May to mid-October.

Accommodations: Of the three campgrounds located within the Park, one is open year-round. Accommodations and services are available in communities just outside the Park and in St George.

Recreational facilities: NPS Guided Tour, self-guiding tour, picnic area, hiking, horseback riding, mountain climbing, backcountry use permit.

Other facilities: Museum, exhibit, restaurant, handicap access, Visitors' Center, restrooms.

WYOMING

• **Grand Teton National Park**, P.O. Drawer 170, Moose, WY 83012. Tel: (307) 733-2880.

Accommodations: Cabins, lodge facilities and rooms are available from 21 different concessionaires within the Park. Reservations are recommended for all facilities. A list of concessionaires and their addresses can be received by writing to the Park Superintendent. There are a number of campgrounds in the Park. **Colter Bay** (trailer village with hook-ups), **Lizard Creek, Jenny Lake** (no trailers), **Gros Ventre**, and **Signal Mountain**. The surrounding communities, specially Jackson Hole, are developed tourist areas with excellent accommodations and services. A maximum stay of 14 days is allowed in all the campgrounds except Jenny Lake which has a 10-day limit.

Food and lodging are offered at Colter bay, Jackons Lake, Jenny Lake and Signal Mountain Lodges in Moran. Signal Mountain has limited services in the winter.

Recreational facilities: Boating, boat rides, bus tours, fishing, hiking, horseback riding, interpretive program, mountain climbing,

skiing, snowmobiling, swimming, water skiing (allowed only on Jackson Lake), hiking, backcountry use permits, NPS Guided Tour, self-guiding tour, guides for hire.

Other facilities: Museums, exhibit, amphitheaters with naturalist talks, general stores, self-service laundry, restaurants, service stations, Visitors' Centers (Moose and Colter Bay), handicap access.

• **Yellowstone National Park**, P.O. Box 168, WY 82190. Tel: (307) 344-7381.

Accommodations: Within Yellowstone National Park are hotels, cabins, the Fishing Bridge Trailer Village and a number of campgrounds. These accommodations are open from mid-June through Labor Day. Limited accommodations are available off season with winter activities centering at Old Faithful. Reservations are advised specially during June and July. These can be made by writing to Yellowstone Park Co., Yellowstone National Park, 82190. Some of the lodges and hotels are **Roosevelt Lodge** (TW Recreational Services), **Canyon Village Lodge and Cabins** (588 units), **Lake Lodge and Cabins** (176 units), **Old Faithful Lodge/Cabins** (236 units), **Old Faithful Inn** (326 units) and **Old Faithful Snowlodge** (65 units). For information and reservations call (307) 344-7311.

Campgrounds are open from mid-June to mid-September, with limited camping during the rest of the year. The majority of campgrounds have been filled to capacity usually by noon during the summer. The ranger station at the entrance can inform you about which campgrounds have vacancies. When you arrive at a campground the ranger in charge will help you. Camping or overnight stopping is allowed only in designated areas. Your stay in the Park as a camper is limited to 14 days in the summer and 30 days during the rest of the year. Some campsites are restricted to hard-sided vehicles and some only for tents. Check with the ranger station for current information. Two campgrounds are available for organized groups and can be reserved ahead of time.

Recreational facilities: Boating, driving, horseback riding, stagecoach rides, boat and bus tours, hiking, NPS Guided Tours, self-guiding tour, back-country use permits, mountain climbing, fishing, bicycle trail, snowmobile route, cross-country ski trail.

Other facilities: Commercial airlines, railroad and bus lines provide service to Yellowstone National Park. Evening campfire programs, nature walks, museums, exhibits, handicap access, restaurants, general stores, laundry facilities (self-service), Visitors' Centers.

NATIONAL FORESTS

• **IDAHO**

Clearwater National Forest, Orofino, ID 83544.

Coeur d'Alene National Forest, Coeur d'Alene, ID 83814.

Kaniksu National Forest, Coeur d'Alene, ID 83814.

St Joe National Forest, Coeur d'Alene, ID 83814.

Nezperce National Forest, Grangeville, ID 83530.

Boise National Forest, Boise, ID 83702.

Caribou National Forest, Pocatello, ID 83201.

Challis National Forest, Challis, ID 83226.

Payette National Forest, McCall, ID 83638.

Salmon National Forest, Salmon, ID 83467.

Sawtooth National Forest, Twin Falls, ID 83301.

Targhee National Forest, St Anthony, ID 83445.

• **MONTANA**

Beaverhead National Forest, Dillon, MT 59725.

Bitterroot National Forest, Hamilton, MT 59840.

Custer National Forest, Billings, MT 59103.

Deerlodge National Forest, Butte, MT 59703.

Flathead National Forest, Kalispell, MT 59901.

Gallatin National Forest, Bozeman, MT 59715.

Helena National Forest, Helena, MT 59626.

Kootenai National Forest, Libby, MT 59923.

Lewis & Clark National Forest, Great Falls, MT 59403.

Lolo National Forest, Missoula, MT 59801.

• **COLORADO**

Arapahoe National Forest, Ft Collins, CO 80526.

Roosevelt National Forest, Ft Collins, CO 80526.

Grand Mesa National Forest, Delta, CO 81416.

Uncompahgre National Forest, Delta, CO 81416.

Gunnison National Forest, Delta, CO 81416.

Pike National Forest, Pueblo, CO 81008.

San Isabel National Forest, Pueblo, CO 81008.

Rio Grande National Forest, Monte Vista, CO 81144.

Routt National Forest, Steamboat Springs, CO 80477.

San Juan National Forest, Durango, CO 81301.

White River National Forest, Glenwood Springs, CO 81602.

• **WYOMING**

Bighorn National Forest, Sheridan, WY 82801.

Medicine Bow National Forest, Laramie, WY 82070.

Shoshone National Forest, Cody, WY 82414.

Bridger National Forest, Jackson, WY 83001.

Teton National Forest, Jackson, WY 83001.

• **UTAH**

Ashley National Forest, Vernal, UT 84078.

Dixie National Forest, Cedar City, UT 84720.

Fishlake National Forest, Richfield, UT 84701.

Manti National Forest, Price, UT 84501.

LaSal National Forest, Price, UT 84501.

Uinta National Forest, Provo, UT 84603.

Wasatch National Forest, Salt Lake City, UT 84138.

Cache National Forest, Salt Lake City, UT 84138.

COLORADO

Barbour Ponds State Recreation Area, 7 miles (11 km) east of Longmont. (Camping, sailboarding.)

Barr Lake State Park, 18 miles (29 km) northeast of Denver. (Picnic sites, sailboarding, hunting.)

Bonny State Recreation Area, 22 miles (35 km) north of Burlington. (Camping, water sports, hunting.)

Boyd Lake State Recreation Area, 1 mile (2 km) east of Loveland. (Camping, water sports, hunting.)

Castlewood Canyon State Park, 3 miles (5 km) south of Franktown. (Picnic sites, cross-country skiing.)

Chatfield State Recreation Area, 8 miles (13 km) southwest of Denver. (Camping, water sports, riding.)

Cherry Creek State Recreation Area, adjacent to southeast Denver. (Water sports, camping, snowmobiling.)

Crawford State Recreation Area, 1 mile (2 km) south of Crawford. (Camping, boating, cycling.)

Eldorado Canyon State Park, 8 miles (13 km) southwest of Boulder. (Picnic sites, rock climbing.)

Eleven Mile State Recreation Area, 8 miles (13 km) southwest of Lake George. (Camping, snowmobiling, hunting.)

Golden Gate Canyon State Park, 15 miles (24 km) west of Golden. (Camping, horseback riding, hunting.)

Highline State Recreation Area, 7 miles (11 km) northwest of Loma. (Camping, water sports, ice skating.)

Island Acres State Recreation Area, 15 miles (24 km) east of Grand Junction. (Camping, ice skating, sailboarding.)

Jackson Lake State Recreation Area, 22 miles (35 km) northwest of Fort Morgan. (Camping, watersports, hunting, cross-country skiing.)

Lanthrop State Park, 3 miles (5 km) west of Fort Collins.

Mueller State Park, 3 miles (5 km) south of Divide (closed).

Navajo State Recreation Area, 1 mile (2 km) south of Arboles. (Camping, hunting, water sports.)

Paonia State Recreation Area, 6 miles (10 km) west of Pueblo. (Picnic sites, water sports.)

Rifle Gap/Falls State Recreation Area, 7 miles (11 km) north of Rifle. (Camping, hunting.)

Roxborough State Park, (open by tour only) 15 miles (24 km) southwest of Denver.

State Forest, 21 miles (34 km) southeast of Walden. (Camping, cross-country skiing, snowmobiling.)

Steamboat Lake State Park, 26 miles (42 km) north of Steamboat Springs. (Camping, snowmobiling.)

Sweitzer Lake State Recreation Area, 3 miles (5 km) south of Denver. (Picnic sites, water sports.)

Trinidad State Recreation Area, 3 miles (5 km) west of Trinidad. (Camping, hunting, horseback riding.)

Vega State Recreation Area, 12 miles (19 km) east of Collbran. (Camping, hunting, snowmobiling, cross-country skiing, water sports.)

IDAHO

Priest Lake State Park, located 35 miles (53 km) north of Priest River on Priest Lake.

Round Lake State Park, 10 miles (16 km) south of Sand Point on US 95.

Farragut State Park, located 4 miles (6 km) east of US 95 at Athol.

Old Mission State Park, east of Cataldo, exit 39 off I-90.

Mowry State Park, accessible only by boat from Coeur D'Alene or Harrison to Grasser Point.

Heyburn State Park, located between Plummer and St Maries on Hwy 5.

Hell's Gates State Park, 4 miles (6 km) south of Lewiston on Snake River Ave.

Winchester Lake State Park, 1 mile (2 km) southwest of Winchester on US 95.

McCroskey State Park, 26 miles (42 km) north of Moscow on US 95.

Packer John State Park, 9 miles (15 km) northwest of McCall on Highway 55.

Ponderosa State Park, located just north of McCall on Payette Lake.

Eagle Island State Park, west of Eagle, off Hwy 44.

Veteran's Memorial State Park, located west of Boise at 36th and State St.

Lucky Peak State Park, (3 units) located 8 miles (13 km) east of Boise on Hwy 21.

Three Island State Park, 1 mile (2 km) west of Glenns Ferry.

Malad Gorge State Park, east of Bliss on I-84 exit 147.

Massacre Rocks State Park, 12 miles (19 km) west of American Falls.

Indian Rocks State Park, 25 miles (40 km) southeast from junction I-25 and 1-86 at Pocatello.

Bear Lake State Park, 18 miles (29 km) south of Montpelier on Hwy 89.

Harriman State Park, 18 miles (29 km) north of Ashton.

Henry's Lake State Park, 17 miles (27 km) southwest of West Yellowstone.

MONTANA

Bannack State Park, 5 miles (8 km) south of Dillon on I-15, then 21 miles (33 km) west on Secondary 278, and 4 miles (6 km) south on County Road.

Makoshika State Park, 2 miles (4 km) south of Glendive on Snyder Ave.

Medicine Rocks State Park, 25 miles (40 km) south of Baker on Montana 7, milepost 10, then 1 mile (2 km) west on County Road.

Missouri Headwaters State Park, 3 miles (5 km) east of Three Forks on US 10, then 3 miles (5 km) north on Secondary 286.

West Shore State Park, 20 miles (32 km) south of Kalespell, on US 93 milepost 93.

Wild Horse Island State Park, access from Big Arm State Recreational Area, via boat to Little Sheeko Bay (northwest side of island).

Giant Springs, edge of Great Falls on River Drive N. (A freshwater spring.)

Ulm Pishkun, off I-15, 12 miles (20 km) west of Great Falls. (A picturesque buffalo kill site.)

Lewis and Clark Caverns, just off I-90, 47 miles (75 km) east of Butte. (One of the largest known limestone caverns in the Northwest.)

UTAH

Lost Creek, 9 miles (15 km) north of Anaconda, on Montana 273.

Bear Lake Marina State Park, in Garden City, 1 mile (2 km) north on US 89.

Hyrum Lake State Park, in Hyrum, Utah.

Bear Lake Rendezvous Beach, Laketown, 3 miles (5 km) NW On Hwy 30.

Goosenecks of the San Juans, Mexican Hat, 4 miles (7 km) off Hwy 261.

Dead Horse Point State Park, Moab 34 miles (55 km) west on Hwy 313.

Millsite Lake State Park, Ferron, 4 miles (7 km) off Hwy 10.

Green River State Park, Green River, 2 miles (4 km) south of I-70.

Goblin Valley, Hanksville, 35 miles (57 km) northwest of Hwy 24.

Huntington Lake State Park, Huntington, 2 miles (4 km) northwest of Hwy 155.

Scofield Lake State Park, Soldier Summit, 17 miles (27 km) west of US 6.

Minersville Lake State Park, Beaver, 12 miles (19 km) west of Hwy 21.

Kodachrome Basin, Cannonville, 4 miles (7 km) south of Hwy 2.

Escalante Petrified Forest, Escalante, 5 miles (8 km) west off Hwy 12.

Coral Pink Sand Dunes State Park, Kanab, 35 miles (57 km) northwest of US 89.

Gunlock Lake State Park, St George, 16 miles (26 km) northwest of Hwy 56.

Snow Canyon State Park, St George, 5 miles (8 km) northwest of Hwy 18.

Starvation Lake State Park, Duchesne, 3 miles (5 km) west off US 40.

Steinaker Lake State Park, Vernal, 6 miles (10 km) north of Hwy 44.

Great Salt Lake, Saltair Beach, Salt Lake City, 15 miles (24 km) west off I-80.

Deer Creek Lake State Park, Heber City, 5 miles (8 km) southwest on US 189.

Wasatch Mountain State Park, Midway, off US 40, 189 or Hwy 113.

Utah Lake State Park, Provo, 4 miles (7 km) west off I-15.

Rockport Lake State Park, Wanship, 2 miles (4 km) south on US Alt. 189.

Otter Creek Lake State Park, Antimony, 4 miles (7 km) north on Hwy 22.

Plute Lake State Park, Junction, 5 miles (8 km) north on US 89.

Yuba Lake State Park, Nephi, 25 miles (40 km) south off US 91.

Paradise Lake State Park, Sterling, 3 miles (5 km) east off US 89.

WYOMING

Buffalo Bill State Park, located a few miles west of Cody. (Offers picnicking and minimum camping facilities. The adjacent reservoir features excellent trout fishing.)

Sinks Canyon State Park, 10 miles (16 km) southwest of Lander is in a spectacular mountain canyon. (Limited camping facilities, hiking trails, scenic overlooks, trout-filled pools are part of this park.)

Boysen State Park, in central Wyoming. (Surrounded by the Wind River Reservation. Good for overnight camping, fishing and water sports.)

Hot Springs State Park, at Thermopolis, is centered around the world's largest mineral hot springs. (Indoor and outdoor swimming pools, lodging accommodations and bath house are on the grounds.)

Seminoe State Park, located 34 miles (54 km) north of Sinclair, is surrounded by giant white sand dunes, antelope, sage grouse and sagebrush. (Fishing and camping.)

Edness Kimball Wilkins State Park, east of Casper, along the North Platte River, is currently under development.

Curt Gowdy State Park, is reached by taking the road (Wyo 210) west out of Cheyenne, and is midway between Cheyenne and Laramie. (Two reservoirs offer excellent fishing and water.)

Glendo State Park is at Glendo. (Overnight camping, commercial concession, cabin and trailer court facilities and marina operation. Good for fishing and boating.)

Guernsey State Park, is 3 miles (5 km) from the town of Guernsey. (This is Oregon Trail country, offering a museum and some camping.)

Keyhole State Park, is 4 miles (6 km) north of I-90, between Sundance and Moorcraft. Antelope, deer and wild turkey inhabit this western Black Hills area. The park is located along the shores of Keyhole reservoir and is a popular spot for fishing. The Devil's Tower National Monument can be seen from here.

TOUR PACKAGES

A prepackaged tour is often a lot cheaper than if you tried to assemble it yourself. There are also a variety of special interest tours that are offered in the areas of art, sports, skiing, horse riding, theater, etc., that your travel agent can help you with. The local Chambers of Commerce can give you a list of outfitters and guides that you can write to and make your own arrangements with (also see "Tour Operators" below). One of the most inexpensive ways for a family to explore the Rockies is to travel by car and stay in campgrounds. This is only possible in the summer.

TOUR OPERATORS

IN COLORADO

Contact your travel agent for special package tours for sightseeing and activities.

Grayline, Box 38667, Denver, CO 80238. Tel: (303) 289-2841.
Mesa Verde Company, P.O. Box 277, Mancos, CO 81328. Tel: 533-7731.
Maupintour and Tauck Tours offer Colorado package tours. Ask your travel agent.

IN IDAHO

Outfitters & Guides

Agalpah River Trips, P.O. Box 425, Salmon, ID 83467. Tel: 756-4167. (Backpacking, river running.)

Chamberlain Divide Outfitters, 205 E. 40th St., Boise, ID 83704. Tel: 343-8504. (Fishing, trail riding.)

Grizzly Mountain Outfitters, P.O. Box 809, North Fork, ID 83466. Tel: 865-2164. (Snowmobiling, guest ranch, big game hunting, bird hunting.)

Indian Creek Ranch, Rt. 2, Box 105, North Fork, ID 83466. Dial Operators, give #208-05-7121 ask Salmon operator for 24F211. (Trail riding, bird hunting, big game, snowmobiling.)

Lazy J Outfitters, Rt. 1, Kuna, ID 83634. Tel: 922-5648. (Snowmobile, river/lake fishing.)

Salmon River Experience, 812 Truman, Moscow, ID 83843. Tel: 882-2385. (River running, fishing, kayaking.)

Sun Valley Treking Company, P.O. Box 2200, Sun Valley, ID 83353. Tel: 726-9595. (Kayaking, X-C skiing, as well as technical mountaineering.)

Sun Valley Helicopter Ski Guides, P.O. Box 978, Sun Valley, ID 83353.

Teton Experience, P.O. Box 218, Rigby, ID 83442. Tel: 523-4951. (Trail riding, river running, fishing.)

Teton Mountain Touring, P.O. Box 514, Driggs, ID 83422. Tel: 354-2768. (X-C skiing.)

Whitewater Outfitters, Salmon River Air Rt., Cascade, ID 83611. Tel: 382-4336. (Jet boating, fishing, trail riding.)

Wilderness Learning, P.O. Box 431, Ammon, ID 83401. Tel: 524-1874. (Survival training.)

IN MONTANA

Outdoor Activities

Glacier Park Adventures, Tel: (406) 888-5333 (summer); (406) 862-4802 (winter).

Crazy Mountain Company, Chico Hot Springs, Pray, MT 59065. Tel: 333-4779.

Whitewater scenic float and fishing trips on the Yellowstone River. Guided hikes and ski trips. Group rates available.

Mountain Whitewater, P.O. Box 486, Bozemen, MT 59717. Tel: 995-4613. Whitewater scenic float and fishing trips on the Gallatin and Madison Rivers. Group rates available.

Venture Yellowstone, Box 846, Canyon Route, Gallatin Gateway, MT 59730. Tel: 995-4841. Scenic and whitewater trips down the Yellowstone and Gallatin Rivers. Group rates available.

Yellowstone Raft Company, Box 46, Gardiner, MT 59030. Tel: 848-7777. Rafting headquarters for southwest Montana and Yellowstone National Park. (Exclusive whitewater trip through the Bear Trap Canyon Wilderness Area on the Madison River.) Other half-day and full-day trips are available. Group rates.

Guided Outdoor Activities offered by TW **Recreational Services Inc. Stagecoach Rides**. The authentic Concord Stagecoach has exciting 45-minute rides through the rolling sagebrush country. Rides depart from Roosevelt Corrals. Between June 10 and September 9.

Old West Cookouts, cook a delicious meal outdoors at a site reached by a horse-drawn wagon near Roosevelt Corrals. Departs at 4.30 p.m. and 5.30 p.m., and returns by 7.30 p.m., June 10–September 9.

Sceniccruiser Rides, boats depart several times daily from the Bridge Bay Marina for a leisurely cruise on Yellowstone Lake. This is conducted by TW Recreational Services Inc., Yellowstone Park Division, Yellowstone National Park, WY 82190. Tel: 344-7901. June 15–September 23.

IN UTAH

Aerial Tours
Arrowhead Helicopters, P.O. Box 1343, Moab, UT 84532. Tel: 259-5956.

Park City Balloon Adventures, 2040 Sunnyside Ave., Salt Lake, UT 84108. Tel: 583-3120.

SkyWest Aviation, P.O. Box T, St George Municipal Airport, St George. UT 84770. Tel: (1-800) 453-9417.

Backpacking & Hiking
Ken Sleight Expeditions, P.O. Box 81185. Salt Lake City, UT 84108. Tel: 564-3656 (summer); 583-6255 (winter).

Excursion Train
Heber Creeper, Deer Creek Scenic Railroad, 600 W. 100 South, Salt Lake City, UT 84032. Tel: 654-3229.

Old Salty Railroad Inc., 549 W. 500 South, Salt Lake City, UT 84101. Tel: 359-8800.

Fly/Drive Tours
Mountain Tours, 1380 W. North Temple, Salt Lake City, UT 84116. Tel: 359-9996. Telex: 381-022.

Horse Packing
Calvin-Alpine Outfitters, 2567 E. Pringle Circle, Ogden, UT 84403. Tel: 479-6977.

High Country Adventure, Rt. #1 Box 118, Roosevelt, UT 84066. Tel: 722-3065.

Rell Enterprises, P.O. Box 14, St George, UT 84770. Tel: 574-2266.

Wild & Scenic Inc., P.O. Box 401, Moab, UT 84532. Tel: 259-8625.

Hunting & Fishing
Hatt's Ranch, Box 275, Green River, UT 84525. Tel: 564-3238.

Tavaputs Plateau Ranch, P.O. Box 786, Price, UT 84501. Tel: 564-3463.

United Sportsmen, P.O. Box 21141, Salt Lake City, UT 84121. Tel: 268-9557.

Jeep/Four-wheel-drive Tours
Adrift Adventures in Canyonlands Inc., 5620 S. Waterbury, Suite 203-A, Salt Lake City, UT 84121. Tel: 272-3442.

Tag-A-Long Tours, 452 N. Main St., Moab, UT 84532. Tel: (800) 453-3292.

National Park Tours

Allwest Leisure Tours, 451 E. Broadway, Salt Lake City, UT 84111. Tel: 532-2113.

Western River Expeditions, 7258 Racquet Club Drive, Salt Lake City, UT 84121. Tel: 942-6669.

Color Country Tours, 281 S. Main St., Cedar City, UT. 84720. Tel: 586-9916.

River Runners

Colorado River and Trail Expeditions Inc., P.O. Box 7575, Salt Lake City, UT 84107. Tel: 261-1789.

Moki Mac River Expeditions, P.O. Box 21242, Salt Lake City, UT 84121. Tel: 943-6707.

Mountain River Guides, 3325 Fowler, Ogden, UT 84403. Tel: 399-1297.

Tex's River Expeditions. P.O. Box 67, Moab, UT 84532. Tel: 259-5101.

Salt Lake City & Vicinity Tours

Allwest Leisure Tours, 451 E. Broadway, Salt Lake City, UT 84111. Tel: 532-2113.

Gray Line of Salt Lake City, 158 N. 400 West, Salt Lake City, UT 84103. Tel: 521-7060.

Mountain Tours, 1380 W. North Temple, Salt Lake City, UT 84116. Tel: 359-8677. Telex: 381-022.

IN WYOMING

Special Camps & Wilderness Schools

Wind River Wilderness Camp, Box WTC, 6878 S. Arapahoe Drive, Littleton, CO 80120. Tel: (303) 794-9518. Camp located in Bridger-Teton National Forest. (Wilderness and outdoor activities for teenagers. Backpacking, technical climbing, kayaking, glacier climbing, wilderness survival.)

Sodergreen Horsemanship School, Buford, WY 82052. Tel: (307) 632-7954. (10 day, live-in, intensive riding school.)

Western Wheels, Box WTC, 6878 S. Arapahoe Drive, Littleton, CO 80120. Tel: (303) 794-9518. (Offers bicycle tours to all ages through Teton and Yellowstone National Parks. Equipment furnished, bicycles can be rented.)

Jackson Hole Mountain Guides, Teton Village, WY 83025. Tel: (307) 733-4979. (Personal climbing instruction and guiding service.)

Rawhide Ranch Camps, 916 S. 11th St., Laramie, WY 82070. Tel: (307) 472-6115. (winter); Box 1810, Cody, WY 82414. Tel: (307) 587-2061 (summer). Camp for girls and boys ages 9–16 near Yellowstone National Park. (Horseback riding, fishing, archery, crafts, rodeos.)

Audubon Ecology Camp in the West, 4150 Darley, Boulder, CO 80303. Tel: (303) 499-5409. (Naturalists lead adults for two-week sessions of ecosystem studies in Wind River Mountains.) University credit available. June to mid-August.

Girl Scouts National Center West, Box 95, Ten Sleep, WY 82442. (The 14,134-acre center offers troop camping, special programs for girl scouts and their families.)

Siggins Triangle X Camp, Southfork Route, Cody, WY 82414. Tel: (307) 587-2031. Camp for 25 young people (ages 10–17). (Horse riding, fishing, tennis, dance, swimming, hiking, 8-day wilderness pack-trip.) June 25–July 24.

Teton Valley Ranch Camps, Box 8, Kelly, WY 83011. Tel: (307) 733-2958. Located in Jackson Hole. 5-week camps for boys and girls. (Activities include photography, pack trips, riflery, crafts, archery, fly tying and rodeos.)

Yellowstone-Grand Teton Photographic Expeditions, Box 3238, Jackson, WY 83001. Tel: (307) 733-5298. One and two-day guided tours for naturalists, photographers, filmmakers in Grand Teton and Yellowstone National Parks.

Skinner Brothers Guides and Outfitters, Box B, Pinedale, WY 82941. Tel: (307) 367-4675. (Family and adult, group pack trips and fishing trips.)

CULTURE PLUS

COLORADO

• ASPEN

The Aspen Art Museum, 590 N. Mill St. Exhibitions of art, photography, sculpture of local and international artists.

Aspen Historical Society Museum, 620 W. Bleeker St. History of silver mining, skiing, and ranching. (Walking tour of five or more can be arranged by reservation.) Open Tuesday–Sunday 1 p.m.–4 p.m. Closed holidays and 6 weeks in spring and fall.

Aspen Mountain Gallery, 555 E. Durant Ave. Graphics, painting, sculpture and jewelry.

Aspen Potters Guild, 107 S. Mill St. A unique shop selling porcelain, stoneware handcrafted by locals.

Bryne-Getz Gallery, 520 E. Durant Ave. Contemporary Southwest art, Native American jewelry, pottery.

Heather Gallery, 555 E. Durant Ave. Contemporary American art, crafts and woodworking.

Joanne Lyon Gallery, 525 E. Cooper Ave. Art Gallery.

The Thundercloud Corporation, Native American Indian Art.

• BOULDER

University of Colorado Museum, Henderson Bldg. Prehistoric life from the Plains and Southwest. Geological exhibits, art gallery, other displays. Open Monday–Friday 9 a.m.–5 p.m. Free.

Pioneer Museum, 1655 Broadway. Open daily in the summer 2 p.m.–5 p.m. and weekend rest of the year. Small admission charged.

Friske Planetarium, University of Colorado, Boulder Campus. Call 492-5001 for show times.

• CANON CITY

Canon City Municipal Museum, 612 Royal Gorge Blvd. Exhibits on the history of the area. Open Monday–Saturday 9 a.m.–5 p.m., Sunday 1 p.m.–5 p.m. Free.

Robinson Mansion, 12 Riverside Drive. Restored 1884 home with period furnishings. Open mid-April to mid-November, Tuesday–Sunday 9 a.m.–6 p.m; mid-November to mid-April, weekends only 1 p.m.–5 p.m.

• CENTRAL CITY

Central Gold Mine and Museum, 126 Spring St. Open daily May–September, 9 a.m.–5 p.m. Mine tour given. Admission charged.

Central City Opera House and **Teller House**, Eureka St. Both are restored historic buildings.

• COLORADO SPRINGS

Pioneers' Museum, 25 W. Kiowa St. Artifacts from Pike's Peak area, Native American displays. Open Tuesday–Saturday 10 a.m.–5 p.m., Sunday 2 p.m.–5 p.m. Free.

El Pomar Carriage House Museum, Lake Ave. Vehicles, saddles, riding accessories of 1890s. Open Tuesday–Sunday 10 a.m.–5 p.m. Free.

Colorado Springs Fine Arts Center, 30 W. Dale St. Prehistoric art of the Southwest, other collections. Open Tuesday–Saturday 9 a.m.–5 p.m., Sunday 1.30 p.m.–5 p.m. Admission free.

Manitou Cliff Dwellings Museum, US 24 Bypass. Open daily in the summer 9 a.m.–5 p.m. (except Friday); closed October to mid-May. Small admission charged.

Hall of Presidents, 1050 S. 21st St. 100. Wax figures of America's greatest and historical figures. Open 10 a.m.–5 p.m. daily.

National Carvers Museum, 14960 Woodcarver Road, 10 miles (16 km) north on I-25. Woodcarving exhibits and demonstrations. Open Monday–Saturday 9 a.m.–5 p.m., Sunday 10.30 a.m.–5 p.m. Admission charged.

Clock Museum, 21st St. at Bott Ave. Over 100 clocks. Open summers 9 a.m.–sunset. Admission charged.

Colorado Car Museum, 137 Manitou Ave. Cars of 1900 and custom-built cars belonging to celebrities. Open May–September, Monday–Saturday 9 a.m.–5 p.m., Sunday 10.30 a.m.–5 p.m; October–April, Saturday & Sunday 1 p.m.–5 p.m. Admission charged.

May Natural History Museum of the Tropics, 8 miles (13 km) southwest on SR 115. Tropical invertebrates from all over the world. Open May–September 8 a.m.–9 p.m. Admission charged.

US Airforce Academy, 10 miles (16 km) north on I-25. Visitors' Center has films, displays, self-guided auto tour. Open daily 8 a.m.–5 p.m. Free.

• CRIPPLE CREEK

Cripple Creek Museum, on SR 67. Relics from this old gold town. Open end-May to early October, daily 10 a.m.–5.30 p.m; weekdays only in the winter. Small admission charged.

The Imperial Hotel, restored historic hotel.

• DENVER

Celebrity Sports Center, 888 South Colorado Blvd. Tel: 755-3312. Family recreation: bowling, swimming, year-round waterslides, arcades, restaurants, bar, free childcare.

Colorado Renaissance Festival, 2660 S. Monaco, Denver, CO 80222. Tel: 756-1501. In Larkspur, a recreation of a 16th-century European marketplace. Weekends in June and July.

Civic Center Park. Fountains, monuments, outdoor Greek Theater, center of the city.

Colorado State Capitol, 30 Broadway and Colfax. Panoramic view of Denver and mountains. Free tours weekdays 9 a.m.–3 p.m.

Confluence Park, 15th St. and South Platte River. Man-made river, spot where Denver started in 1858.

Coors Brewery, 12th and East St., Golden, CO. 12 miles (19 km) west of Denver. Free tours and samples at one of the nation's largest breweries.

Denver Botanic Gardens, 1005 York St. Over 800 species of native and exotic plants. Open 9 a.m.–4.45 p.m. Admission free.

Denver's Zoo, at City Park off 23rd Ave. Modern Zoo with over 1500 specimens, beautiful setting. Open 10 a.m.–5 p.m. winter, 10 a.m.–6 p.m. summer. Admission free.

Elitch Gardens Amusement Park, W. 38th at Tennyson. Tel: 455-4771. Top-rate rollercoaster, flower gardens, log flume and amusement park rides and games. Open weekends in May, at noon June to Labor Day. Admission free.

Heritage Square, south of Golden on US Hwy 40. Reconstructed Colorado City from 1870s with crafts shops, restaurants, alpine slides and amusement rides. Open year-round. Admission free.

Hyland Hills Water World, 90th Ave. and Pecos St., Federal Heights, CO 80221. Tel: 427-SURF. One of America's largest water theme parks. Open Memorial Day through Labor Day. Features 5-ft (2-meter) waves and 14 water slides.

Lakeside Amusement Park, W. 44th Ave. and Sheridan Blvd. 40 major rides, games, speedway for stock cars. Open weekends in May, June to Labor Day. Admission free.

Larimer Square, 1400 block of Larimer St. Restored section of Denver's oldest street with courtyards, gas lamps, Victorian buildings, shops, outdoor cafes, nightclubs, restaurants, special events. Shops open in the evening. Free walking tour brochure available in shops.

Molly Brown House, 1340 Pennsylvania. Unusual Victorian House that belonged to the "Unsinkable Molly Brown" heroine of the *Titanic* disaster. Closed Monday in the winter. Admission free.

Red Rocks Amphitheater, north of Morrison on Hogback Road. 12 miles (19 km) west of Denver. An amphitheater that accommodates 8,000 set between 400-ft (122-meter) high red sandstone rocks. Panoramic views. Summer concerts. Free admission except when there is a performance.

Sakura Square, 19th St. and Lawrence. An entire block of oriental shops and restaurants surrounded by authentic Japanese gardens.

16th Street Mall, 16th St. from Broadway to Market St. Mile-long, tree-lined pedestrian path with stores, shops, restaurants and cafes. 12 fountains, special events, free shuttle bus rides.

United States Mint, W. Colfax and Cherokee St. Largest depository of gold outside Fort Knox. The Mint produces 5 billion coins annually. Free 20 minutes tours: 8 a.m.–5 p.m. weekdays, 9 a.m.–1 p.m. Sunday in summer, 9 a.m.–5 p.m. Saturday.

Denver Art Museum, 100 W. 14th St. Tel: 575-2793. 10-story, 28-sided structure covered with a million sparkling tiles, contains the world's greatest collection of Native American artworks, and 35,000 art objects in seven curatorial departments. Open Tuesday–Saturday 9 a.m.–5 p.m., Wednesday 9 a.m.–8 p.m., Sunday noon–5 p.m. Closed Monday. Admission free.

Museum of Western Art, 1727 Tremont Pl. Tel: 296-1880. Located in a one-time gambling den and brothel, this new museum has over 125 classical paintings and bronzes by artists like Remington, Russell, Moran, Bierstadt and Georgia O'Keeffe. Tuesday–

Friday 10 a.m.–6 p.m., Saturday 10 a.m.–5 p.m., Sunday–Monday 1 p.m.–5 p.m. Admission free.

Trianan Art Museum and Gallery, 335 14th St. Tel: 623-0739. European Masterpieces and Oriental art treasures. Fine selection in sales gallery. Monday–Saturday 10 a.m.–4 p.m. Admission free.

Buffalo Bill's Grave and Museum, top of Lookout Mountain exit 256 off I-70 West of Denver. Panoramic view from grave site. Summer 8 a.m.–5 p.m; winter 9 a.m.–5 p.m. Closed Monday. Admission free.

The Children's Museum, 2121, Crescent Drive. New and modern museum for kids of all ages. TV station, "hands-on" exhibits, supermarket, and 80,000 plastic balls. Call for hours on 571-5198. Admission free.

Colorado Historical Society, 1300 Broadway. A fabulous $22 million facility traces the colorful history of the Native Americans, gold miners and settlers of the Rockies. Exhibits, graphics, and dioramas. Tuesday–Saturday 10 a.m.–4.30 p.m., Sunday 12 p.m.–4.30 p.m. Closed Monday. Admission free.

Colorado Railroad Museum, 17155 W. 44th. Tel: 279-4591. Largest Railroad Museum in the Rockies. Open daily year round, 9 a.m.–5 p.m.

Denver Firefighters Museum and Restaurant, 1326 Tremont Pl. Tel: 892-1436. Collection of antique firefighting equipment. Open for tours, lunch and private parties. Monday–Friday 11 a.m.–2 p.m.

Denver Museum of Natural History, City Park. Seventh largest museum in USA and one of the great natural history museums of the world. Over 70 dioramas of international animals and hundreds of exhibits. Also includes the **Imas Theater** using the world's largest movie projection equipment on a 4.5x6.5 story screen: and **Charles C. Gates Planetarium** which offers a variety of changing shows. Open 9 a.m.–5 p.m. daily. Call 370-6300 for show times. Admission free for all three.

Forney Transportation Museum, 1416 Platte. Tel: 433-3643. Excellent collection of 300 cars, carriages, cycles, steam engines, rail coaches and "Big Boy" locomotive. Take I-25 to exit 211, 5 blocks east. Open Monday–Saturday 10 a.m.–5 p.m., Sunday 11 a.m.–5.30 p.m. Admission free.

Four Mile Historic Park, 715 S. Forest St. Tel: 399-1859. Restoration of this former stagecoach stop on the Cherokee Trail. Oldest home in Denver, working farm.

Grant Humphrey's Mansion, 770 Pennsylvania St. Tel: 866-3507. Turn-of-the-century mansion built by former Governor Grant. Monday–Friday 9 a.m.–3 p.m. Can be rented for private receptions. Admission free.

Pearce McAllister Cottage, 1880 Gaylord St. 1899 Dutch Colonial revival architecture and original interior furnishings, historical.

Arvada Center for the Arts and Humanities, 6901 Wadsworth Blvd. Tel: 422-8050. Nationally known artists perform in this beautiful arts center. Symphony, dance, theater, historical museum, art gallery and special events. Call for schedule.

Central City Opera Festival. Historic opera house in gold mining town of Central City offers great performances. Runs July and August. Call 571-4435 for schedule.

Colorado Shakespeare Festival, University of Colorado, Boulder. Outdoor theater. July and August. Call 492-8181 for schedule.

Denver Center for the Performing Arts, 14th and Curtis. A four-square block complex larger than the Lincoln Center in New York. Includes **Denver Center Theater Company**, the largest resident acting company in the West. Produces a season of eight plays on three stages. **Denver Center Cinema** screens 500 films a year, and hosts performances by **Opera Colorado and Colorado Ballet.**

Center Attractions, brings touring Broadway shows to the Auditorium Theater. Free tours of the complex on weekdays at 12.15 p.m. Box office: 893-4100.

Turner Museum, 773 Downing St. Tel: 832-0924. Prints by British artist J.M.W. Turner and American artist Thomas Moran. Open Sunday 1 p.m.–6 p.m., and by appointment.

• **DURANGO**

Joy Cabin, 23rd St. and Main. Tel: 247-0312. First home built in Durango furnished with antiques. Call for a guided tour.

Southwest Studies Center, Library Bldg, Fort Lewis College. Tel: 247-7928. Museum and study materials from the Southwestern United States. Monday–Friday 8 a.m.–5 p.m.

Top Atin Gallery, 145 W. 9th St. Large collection of tribal modern art, jewelry, pottery and Navajo rugs and weavings.

• **ESTES PARK**

Estes Park Museum, 200 4th St., Estes Park. Tel: 586-6256. Exhibits of local authors, artists and musicians. Call for tour or research.

• **EUREKA**

Clarke Memorial Museum, 240 E. St. Fossils, minerals, Native American artifacts, local historical materials. Open Tuesday–Saturday 10 a.m.–4 p.m; closed holidays. Free admission.

• **FORT COLLINS**

Pioneer Museum, 219 Peterson St. Prehistoric & contemporary Native American displays. Local historic items. Open Tuesday–Saturday 1 p.m.–5 p.m. Free.

• **GRAND JUNCTION**

Historical Museum and Institute of Western Colorado, 4th and Ute St. Geological, anthropological and historical displays. Open June–November, Tuesday–Saturday 10 a.m.–5 p.m., Sunday 2 p.m.–5 p.m. Free.

• **GREELEY**

Meeker Memorial Museum, 1324 9th Ave. Meeker's home containing personal and historical belongings. Open Monday–Friday 9 a.m.–noon, and 1 p.m.–5 p.m. Free.

Municipal Museum, new city complex. Local history. Open 9 a.m.–5 p.m. Monday–Friday (closed noon–1 p.m. for lunch).

• LEADVILLE

Tabor Home, 116 E. 5th St. Restored historical home. Open daily Memorial Day–Labor Day, 8.30 a.m.–8 p.m. Rest of the year 9.30 a.m.–5.30 p.m. Small admission.

Tabor Opera House, 308 Harrison Ave. Guided tours. Memorial Day–October, Sunday–Friday 9 a.m.–5.30 p.m. Small admission.

Healy House and Dexter Cabin, 912 Harrison Ave. Restored historical buildings. Open June to mid-October, daily 9 a.m.–4.30 p.m. Free admission

Heritage Museum and Gallery, 9th & Harrison. Period costumes, Leadville's history in dioramas, mining, geological and other displays. Contemporary western artists. Open Memorial Day through early September, daily 10 a.m.–9 p.m. Admission charged.

• LONGMONT

Pioneer Museum, 302 Kimbark. Open Monday–Saturday 9 a.m.–5 p.m., Sunday 1 p.m.–5 p.m. Free.

• MONTROSE

Ute Indian Museum, 2 miles (3.5 km) south on US 550. History of Ute Indians in dioramas, photos, prehistoric material and Indian artifacts. Open May to mid-October, daily 9 a.m.–5 p.m. Free.

• PUEBLO

El Pueblo State Historical Museum, 905 S. Praire Ave. Local history, iron and steel industry. Open Tuesday–Friday 9 a.m.–5 p.m; on Sunday and some holidays 10 a.m.–5 p.m.

Pueblo Metropolitan Museum, 419 W. 14th St. 37-roomed brick mansion of 1891. Open June–September 1, Tuesday–Saturday 9 a.m.–5 p.m., Sunday and holidays 2 p.m.–5 p.m; September–June 1, Tuesday–Sunday 1 p.m.–4 p.m. Admission charged.

• STERLING

Overland Trail Museum, 1.5 miles (2.4 km) east on US 6. Local pioneer exhibits. Open late-April to late-September, Monday–Saturday 9.30 a.m.–5 p.m., Sunday 10.30 a.m.-5 p.m. Free.

• SNOWMASS

Anderson Ranch Arts Museum, 5263 Owl Creek Road. Art, photography, ceramics. Open Monday–Sunday from 9 a.m.–5 p.m.

• VAIL

Colorado Ski Museum and Ski Hall of Fame Inc., 15 Vail Road, Vail. History of skiing from 1800 to today. Includes Ski Hall of Fame, ski exhibits and equipment.

IDAHO

• BOISE

Boise State Capitol, 8th and Jefferson St. Houses changing exhibits. Open 8 a.m.–6 p.m. daily. Admission free.

Boise Art Gallery, Julia Davis Park. Idaho artists, European, Oriental and American painting and sculpture. Open Tuesday–Sunday, 10 a.m.–5 p.m. Admission free.

Idaho State Historical Society, 610 N. Julia Davis Drive. Pioneer and Native American life, outdoor display. Open Monday–Friday 9 a.m.–5 p.m; Saturday, Sunday 1 p.m.–5 p.m. Admission free.

• FRANKLIN

Pioneer Relic Hall. Contains early artifacts, a steam engine Brigham Young shipped up the Missouri River. Open Monday–Friday 9 a.m.–5 p.m. Admission free.

- **IDAHO CITY**

Boise Basin Museum, Montgomery and Wall St. Small gold rush museum. Open Memorial Day–September. Admission free.

- **KELLOGG**

Catalado Mission, 11 miles (18 km) west off US 10 to Catalado Mission of the Sacred Heart 1848. Native American murals and handprints. Hand-carved altar. Open mid-April to September, 9 a.m.–dark. Small admission. Will open on request.

- **MONTPELIER**

Daughters of Utah Pioneers Historical Museum, 430 Clay St. Open June–August, Monday–Saturday 4 p.m.–9 p.m. Admission free.

- **MOSCOW**

Latah County Museum, 110 S. Adams. 1880 Victorian mansion, houses, dioramas, and artifacts illustrating local history. Open Wednesday and Sunday 2 p.m.–5 p.m., Saturday 10 a.m.–noon. Admission charged.

Appaloosa Horse Museum, Pullman Highway. Saddles and cowboy gear, Nez Perce artifacts. Open Monday–Friday 8 a.m.–5 p.m. Admission free.

- **POCATELLO**

Bannock County Historical Society, Center St and Garfield Ave. Early railroad, fur trade and Shoshone artifacts. Open Monday–Saturday 2 p.m.–5 p.m. Admission free.

Old Fort Hall Replica, Ross Park, 3 miles (5 km) south at 2nd Ave. Historic displays of houses, shops and buildings in the Fort. Open June to mid-September, daily 9 a.m.–8 p.m. April and May, Wednesday–Sunday 9 a.m.–1 p.m. Admission free.

Idaho State University houses a **Museum** and **Art Gallery**.

- **TWIN FALLS**

Twin Falls County Historical Museum, 3 miles (5 km) west on US 30. Pioneer life exhibits. Open Monday–Friday 10 a.m.–5 p.m., Sunday 2 p.m.–5 p.m. Small admission.

Herret Arts and Science, 1220 Kimberly Road. Museum, planetarium and observatory open on request. Open Monday–Saturday 9 a.m.–6 p.m.

- **WALLACE**

Coeur d'Alene District Mining Museum, 509 Bank St. Open Monday–Friday 10 a.m.–4 p.m; June–August, Monday–Saturday 9 a.m.–6 p.m. Mine tours and ghost town tours.

- **WEISER**

Historical Museum and National Fiddlers' Hall of Fame, 44 W. Commercial St. Contains local historic and folk music exhibits. Open June–Labor Day, Thursday–Saturday 10–noon and 1 p.m.–4 p.m. Admission free.

MONTANA

- **BILLINGS**

Yellowstone County Museum, On SR3 at Logan International Airport. Pioneer and Native American artifacts, old vehicles.

Western Heritage Center, 2822 Montana Ave, Billings. Collection of western history and Native American artifacts. Open Tuesday–Saturday 10.30 a.m.–noon, 1 p.m.–5 p.m; on Sunday 2 p.m.–5 p.m. Free admission.

- **BOZEMAN**

Museum of the Rockies, Montana State University, S. 7th and Kagy Blvd, Bozeman. Physical and social heritage of Northern Rockies. Open Monday–Friday 8 a.m.–5 p.m., Saturday–Sunday 1 p.m.–5 p.m. Admission free. Closed holidays and school vacation.

- **BROWNING**

Blackfeet Indian Reservation Museum of Plains Indian and Crafts Center (headquarters), half mile west at Jct US2 89.

Displays costumes, beadwork, carvings and other Blackfeet artifacts. Crafts for sale. Nearby is the **Museum of Montana Wildlife.** Dioramas, paintings and sculptures. Open early May–September, daily 7 a.m.–5 p.m. Admission charged.

• BUTTE

World Museum of Mining, W. Park Road, Butte. Mining displays, reconstructed mining camp, saloon, other buildings. Open June–September, daily 9 a.m.–9 p.m; October–May 10 a.m.–5 p.m. Admission free.

Copper King Mansion, 219 W. Granite St., Butte. Victorian home.

• DILLON

Beaverhead County Museum, 15 S. Montana St., Dillon. Tribal and pioneer artifacts, gold mining relics. Open mid June–August, daily 9 a.m.–5 p.m; September to mid-June, Monday–Friday 9 a.m.–5 p.m.

• GLASGOW

Pioneer Museum, half mile west on US2. Tribal artifacts and pioneer displays. Open June through Labor Day, Monday–Saturday 9 a.m.–9 p.m. Admission free.

• GREAT FALLS

Charles M. Russell Museum and Original Studio, 1201 4th Ave. N., Great Falls. Home of famous cowboy artist. Excellent collection of Russell paintings. Log studio, tribal and cowboy artifacts. Open mid-May through mid-September, Monday–Saturday 10 a.m.–5 p.m., Sunday 1 p.m.–5 p.m. Rest of the year open Tuesday–Saturday 10 a.m.–5 p.m., Sunday 1 p.m.–5 p.m. Small admission.

• HAVRE

H. Earl Clack Memorial Museum, on US 2 in Hill County Fairgrounds. Tribal exhibits, archaeological and geological displays, frontier life, buffalo era. Open Memorial Day–Labor Day, daily 9 a.m.–10 p.m. Free.

Glacier National Park Museum, W. Glacier. History of Glacier National Park.

• HELENA

Montana Historical Museum and C.M. Russell Gallery, 225 N. Roberts Road, Helena, across from the Capitol. Montana prehistory to now. Charlie Russell collection. Historical library. Open Monday–Friday 8 a.m.–5 p.m. (8 a.m.–8 p.m. summer); Saturday, Sunday and holidays, noon–5 p.m. Admission free.

Last Chance Train Tour. Runs daily from here in the summer to major points of interest.

Canyon Ferry Arms Museum, 10 miles (16 km) east on US 12, then 9 miles (15 km) north on SR 284 to Canyon Ferry Recreation Area. Native American and military artifacts. Open May to mid-October, daily 9 a.m.–9 p.m. admission free.

In Helena other interesting buildings are **Governor's Mansion, St Helena Cathedral, Northwestern Bank Pioneer Cabin** and **Kluge House.** Nearby ghost town Marysville.

• KALISPELL

Hockaday Art Center, 3rd St. and 2nd Ave. Open Monday–Saturday noon–5 p.m. Admission free. Traveling exhibits.
Conrad Mansion, Woodland Ave. Restored 1895 mansion.

• MILES CITY

Range Riders Museum, west on US 10, 12. Westward expansion and ranching memorabilia. Open June–August, daily 8 a.m.–8 p.m; April–May and September–October, 8 a.m.–6 p.m. Small Admission.

• MISSOULA

Gallery of Visual Arts, Turner Hall on University of Montana campus. Exhibits local work. Open Monday–Friday 10 a.m.–5 p.m; Saturday and Sunday 2 p.m.–5 p.m. Admission free.

Missoula Museum of the Arts, 335 N. Patte, Missoula.

Fort Missoula Historical Museum, Fort Missoula Bldg, 322 W. of S. Ave. Displays of Missoula timber industry, military commerce and agriculture.

• RED LODGE

Big Sky Historical Museum, south of town on US 212. Native American and pioneer artifacts, gun display. Open June to mid-September, daily 8 a.m.–9 p.m. Admission free.

• VIRGINIA CITY

Thompson Hickman Memorial Museum, Wallace St. Relics of gold days.

Virginia City-Madison County Historical Museum, Wallace St. Exhibits on the area's history. Open May–September, 8 a.m.–6 p.m.

• WOLF POINT

Wolf Point Historical Museum, 220 S. 2nd Ave. Native American and ranching exhibits. Open mid-May to September, Monday–Friday 10 a.m.–6 p.m. Admission free.

Poplar Museum, 21 miles (34 km) east on US2 in Poplar. A former jail. Displays Native American artifacts, arts and crafts. Open June–August daily. Small admission.

UTAH

• BRIGHAM CITY

Railroad Museum, located 7 miles (11 km) west on SR 83 in Corinne. Railroad cars, caboose, locomotives, photos and memorabilia, blacksmith shop. Open May–September, Tuesday–Saturday 9 a.m.–5 p.m., Sunday 2 p.m.–5 p.m. Admission free.

Golden Spike National Historic Site, 30 miles (48 km) west via SR 83 & unnumbered road to Promontory. Visitors' Center with exhibits, films, self-guided tour. Open daily June–August 8 a.m.–6 p.m; September–May, 8 a.m.–4.30 p.m.

• CEDAR CITY

Palmer Memorial Museum, 75 N. 300 W. Piute basketry, beadwork, other artifacts.

Open 8 a.m.–5 p.m. Monday–Friday (closed holidays). Free.

Museum of Southern Utah, west of Main St on Center St. (College Campus). Tribal and pioneer artifacts. Open Monday–Saturday 9 a.m.–5 p.m. Closed holidays.

• LOGAN

Daughters of Utah Pioneers Museum, 52 W. 2nd North St. Displays of Mormon pioneers. Open early June–late September, Monday–Friday 1 p.m.–5 p.m. or by appointment. Free.

Man and His Bread & Historical Farm, 5 miles (8 km) south on US 89, 91. Illustrates development of agriculture. Open daily in the summer.

• OGDEN

Daughters of Utah Pioneer Relic Hall, Tabernacle Square, 2150 Grant Ave. Pioneer furnishings and relics. Open June–September, Monday–Friday 1 p.m.–4.30 p.m. Free.

John M. Browning Gun Collection, 4 miles (7 km) south on US 89 at 450 E. 5100 S. Past and current models of Browning firearms. Open Monday–Saturday 8 a.m.–5 p.m., closed holidays. Admission free.

• PRICE

Prehistoric Museum, City Hall, Main & E. St. Open June–August, Monday–Saturday 8.30 a.m.–9 p.m; September–May, Monday–Friday 9 a.m.–5 p.m. Free.

• PROVO

Pioneer Museum, 500 N. 500 W. Pioneer artifacts of the region, pioneer village. Open June to mid-September, daily 9 a.m.–5 p.m. Free admission.

Fairview Museum of History and Art, 46 miles (74 km) south on US 89 in Fairview. Pioneer relics, old vehicles, Native American artifacts, paintings, sculptures, carvings. Open April–October, Tuesday–Saturday 10 a.m.–5 p.m., Sunday 2 p.m.–5 p.m. Free.

• ST GEORGE

Daughters of Utah Pioneers Museum, McQuarrie Memorial Bldg, 145 N. 100 E. Photos and relics of pioneers, who lived in primitive dwellings attempting to start a cotton industry. Free. Open June–August, Monday–Saturday 7 p.m.–9 p.m. Rest of the year by appointment.

• SALT LAKE CITY
All attractions are downtown within 1.5 mile (2 km) area.

Salt Lake Art Center, northeast entrance on West Temple. Changing art exhibits, sculpture court, art, photography, weekend films and lectures. Open Monday–Saturday 10 a.m.–5 p.m., Sunday 1 p.m.–5 p.m.

Symphony Hall, home of Utah symphony, interesting architecture. Free tours. Call 533-5626 for schedule. Box office: 533-6407.

Museum of Church History and Art, paintings, sculpture, historical memorabilia. Open April–December, 9 a.m.–9 p.m; January-March 10 a.m.–7 p.m. Tel: 531-3310. Admission free.

Temple Square, center of Salt Lake City. Free tours of the Tabernacle, North and South Visitors' Centers, daily every 15 minutes between 8 a.m.–8.30 p.m. (in summer) and 9 a.m.–7.30 p.m. (in winter). Mormon Tabernacle Choir rehearsals: Thursday 8 p.m., Sunday morning broadcasts are open to the public. (Be in your seat at 9.20 a.m.)

Beehive House, Brigham Young's official family residence, a National Historic Landmark, beautiful restored home with artifacts of the period. Open Monday–Saturday 9.30 a.m.–4.30 p.m., Sunday mid-day tours. Admission free.

LDS **Church Office Building**, extensive library for genealogical researchers. Open Monday 7.30 a.m.–6 p.m., Tuesday–Friday 7.30 a.m.–10 p.m., Saturday 7.30 a.m.–5 p.m. Tours of buildings, including 26th floor observation deck are available free. Call for details. Tel: 531-2190.

Hansen Planetarium, one of the finest plan-etariums in the world, largest of its kind between Denver and the West Coast. Facility has a space science library and museum. Open Monday–Saturday. Admission charged.

Promised Valley Playhouse, multi-million dollar restoration of a famous 19th-century theater. Playhouse has a full season of live music and dramatic productions from September to May. Summer offers a production of a family oriented musical Tuesday–Saturday at 7.30 p.m. free of charge. Tickets at Temple Square Visitors' Center. Box Office: 364-5678. Tours of the restored theater can be arranged, call 364-5697.

Liberty Park, from 900 to 1300 South, from 500 to 700 East, beautifully landscaped grounds, swimming, tennis and children's amusement park. Close to the Chase Mill, Brigham Young Home and **Tracy Aviary**. This 11 acre (4.5 ha) aviary has hundreds of birds including the rare Andean condor. Open at 9.30 a.m. daily. Closes at 8.30 p.m. in summer; 6 p.m. in fall and spring; 4.50 p.m. in winter. Admission free.

Hogle Zoological Gardens, this zoo is the home of over 100 animals from all over the world. Open daily at 9 a.m. Closes at 6 p.m. in summer; 4.30 p.m. in winter.

Utah Museum of Fine Arts, public general art gallery. Special collections include Navajo textiles, Southeast Asian sculptures, Japanese screens and prints, ceramics. Open Monday–Friday 10 a.m.–5 p.m., weekends 2 p.m.–5 p.m. Admission free. Tel: 581-7332.

Utah Museum of Natural History, on the University of Utah campus. Halls of minerals, biology, geology and earth science. Open Monday–Saturday 9.30 a.m.–5.30 p.m., Sunday noon–5 p.m. Tel: 581-6827.

Utah State Capitol, an attractive building, Corinthian style of marble and granite capped with a huge copper-covered dome. Open Monday–Friday 8.30 a.m.–5 p.m; and summer weekends 9.30 a.m.–6 p.m. Tour available. Admission free. Tel: 533-5900.

Pioneer Memorial Museum, 37 exhibit rooms. Dolls, handmade textiles, period furniture, artifacts. Open Monday–Saturday

9 a.m.–5 p.m; Sunday afternoons from May–
October. Admission free. Tel: 533-5759.

• VERNAL

Utah Field House of Natural History, 235
E. Main St. Outstanding museum with life-
size models of dinosaurs. Displays on bas-
ket-making, prehistoric cultures, fossils,
minerals, pioneer artifacts, regional wildlife.
Open daily 9 a.m.–6 p.m; summer hours 8
a.m.–9 p.m. Admission free.

Thorne's Photo Sudio, 18 W. Main St. Tools
and prehistoric artifacts of Utah. Open
Tuesday–Saturday 9 a.m.–6 p.m. Closed
holidays. Admission free.

WYOMING

Wyoming Pioneer Memorial Museum,
Wyoming State Fair Grounds, Douglas, WY
82633. Tribal artifacts, firearms, photos, antique cars. Open April–November, Monday–
Friday 9 a.m.–5 p.m., Saturday and Sunday 1
p.m.–5 p.m; December–March, Monday–
Friday 9 a.m.–5 p.m. Admission free.

• FORT BRIDGER

Fort Bridger State Historic site, Fort
Bridger, WY 82933. State Historic Site.
Military and Native American artifacts. Open
mid-May to mid-October, daily 9 a.m.–6
p.m. Weekends only mid-October to mid-
May. Admission free.

• FORT LARAMIE

Fort Laramie National Historic Site, Fort
Laramie, WY 82212. 15,000 item museum
of military and Native American artifacts
and a 3,000 book western library. Open Memorial Day–Labor Day 8 a.m.–8 p.m; Labor
Day–Memorial Day 8 a.m.–4.30 p.m. Free.

Grand Teton National Park, Moose Visi-
tors' Center, Jenny Lake Visitors' Center,
Colter Bay Visitors' Center, Indian Arts
Museum.

• JACKSON

Jackson Hole Historical Museum, 105 N.
Glenwood, P.O. Box 1005, Jackson, WY

83301. Artifacts of mountain men and Native Americans. Open daily 9 a.m.–9 p.m.
Children under 6 free.

• LANDER

Pioneer Museum, 630 Lincoln St, Lander,
WY 82520. Old West artifacts. Open June–
October; Monday–Saturday 9 a.m.–6 p.m.,
Sunday 3 p.m.–6 p.m; October–June, 1 p.m.–
4 p.m.(except Monday and holidays).

South Pass City State Historic Site, Route
62, Box 164, Lander, WY 82520. Historic
mining town. Open mid-May to mid-October,
daily 9 a.m.–6 p.m.. Admission free.

• LARAMIE

Laramie Plains Museum, 603 Ivinson Ave.,
Laramie, WY 82070. Historical and cultural
collection, photographs and manuscripts.
Open 9 a.m.–noon and 1 p.m.–4 p.m. (summer); 2 p.m.–4 p.m. February–December.

Rocky Mountain Herbarium, 3rd Floor,
Aven Nelson Bldg, University of Wyoming,
Laramie, WY 82070. 35,000 plant speci-
mens. Open 8 a.m.–5 p.m. (academic year)
Monday–Friday; 7.30 a.m.–4.30 p.m.
(summer) Monday–Friday. Admission free.
Guided tours on request.

• LUSK

Stage Coach Museum, 342 S. Main, Lusk,
WY 82225. Relics of pioneer days. Concord
Stage Coach from Cheyenne-Dreadwood run.
Tribal artifacts. Call (307) 334-3444 for hours.

• BUFFALO

**Johnson County Jim Gatchelle Memorial
Museum**, 110 Fort St., Buffalo, WY 82834.
Dioramas of Johnson County Cattle War of
1892, Tribal artifacts, pictures. Open 9 a.m.–
9 p.m., June–Labor Day. Admission free.

• CASPER

Old Fort Casper Museum, 14 Fort Casper
Road, Casper, WY 82601. Historic site,
Artifacts relating to Fort Casper, Central
Wyoming, reconstructed log structures. Open
all year, 10 a.m.–5 p.m. Admission free.

Nicolaysen Art Museum, 104 Rancho Road, Casper, WY 82601. Tuesday–Saturday 11.30 a.m.–4.30 p.m.

• **CHEYENNE**

Warren Military Museum, Bldg 210, F.E. Warren AFB, WY 82001. Memorial Day–Labor Day 1 p.m.–4 p.m., Monday, Wednesday, Friday and Sunday. Open all year on Sunday 1 p.m.–4 p.m. Admission free. Military uniforms, 19th-century artifacts.

Wyoming State Museum, Barret Bldg, 24th and Central. Cheyenne, WY 82002. Art, ethnographic material, historical material, gift shop. Open Monday–Friday 8 a.m.–5 p.m. Saturday 1 p.m.–5 p.m. Sunday (summer only). Admission free.

National First Day Cover Museum, 702 Randall Blvd, Cheyenne, WY 82001. Rare first day covers, stamps, flags of 50 States. Open Monday–Saturday 9 a.m.–5 p.m. Admission free.

Wyoming State Capitol, Cheyenne, WY 82001. Open Monday–Saturday 8 a.m.–5 p.m. Guided tours every 30 minutes in the summer. Admission free.

• **CODY**

Buffalo Bill Historical Center, P.O. Box 1000, Cody, WY 82414. Tel: (307) 587-4771. Fire arms, tribal art and artifacts, Buffalo Bill memorabilia. Western art and sculpture…one of the best museums in the world. Call for hours. Under 6 years free.

Old West Trail Town, 1 mile west of Cody. Frontier era buildings, cabins and horse-drawn vehicles.

• **DOUGLAS**

Fort Fetterman State Historic Site, Route 3, P.O. Box 6, Douglas, WY 82633. State Historic Site. Open mid-May to Labor Day 9 a.m.–6 p.m. Admission free.

• **RIVERTON**

Riverton Museum, 700 East Park, Riverton, WY 82501. Shoshone and Arapahoe relics.

Homestead cabin. Open daily June–September, 11 a.m.–6 p.m; October–May 10 a.m.–4 p.m. Admission free.

• **SHERIDAN**

The Sheridan Inn, Box 781, 5th and Broadway, Sheridan, WY 82801. Historic Site. Antiques and art gallery. Open daily 10 a.m.–10 p.m. year round. Admission free.

Medicine Wheel, on US 14A in Big Horn National Forest. Amazing construction in stone of almost perfect circle 70 ft (20 meters) across 28 stone spokes radiate like a wheel. Unknown origin.

Wyoming National Guard Museum, Buffalo Star Route, Box 57, Sheridan, WY 82801. National Guard artifacts, flags, uniforms, museum education. Open Monday–Friday 8 a.m.–5 p.m. Admission free.

• **SUNDANCE**

Crook County Museum, Sundance, WY 82442. General Wyoming history, art gallery: Open Monday–Friday 9 a.m.–5 p.m. Free.

• **THERMOPOLIS**

Hot Springs County Museum, 700 Broadway, Thermopolis, WY 82443. Tribal relics, fossils, minerals. Open June–Labor Day, Monday–Saturday 10 a.m.–8 p.m., Sunday 1 p.m.–5 p.m; Labor Day–May 31, daily 1 p.m.–5 p.m. Admission free.

Yellowstone National Park, Albright Visitors' Center, Canyon Visitors' Center, Fishing Bridger Museum, Madison Explorers' Museum, Norris Museum, Grant Village, Mammoth Hot Springs Visitors' Center. Free.

NATIONAL MONUMENTS & HISTORIC SITES

COLORADO

Bent's Old Fort National Historic Site, 35110 Hwy. 194 East, La Junita, CO 81050-0523.
Black Canyon of the Gunnison National Monument, P.O. Box 1648, Montrose, CO 81402.

Colorado National Monument, Fruita, CO 81521.

Curicanti National Recreation Area, P.O. Box 1040, Gunnison, CO 81230.

Dinosaur National Monument (Colorado and Utah), Box 210, Dinosaur, CO 81610.

Florissant Fossil Beds National Monument, P.O. Box 185, Florissant, CO 80816.

Great Sand Dunes National Monument, Mosca, CO 81146.

Hovenweep National Monument (Colorado and Utah), c/o Mesa Verde National Park, CO 81330.

IDAHO

Craters of the Moon National Monument, P.O. Box 29, Arco, ID 83213.

Nez Perce National Historical Park, P.O. Box 93, Spalding, ID 83551.

Atomic Energy National Historic Landmark, West of Idaho Falls. (The world's first Breeder Reactor #1.)

Hell's Canyon Recreation Area, Hellsgate State Park, Information Center, Lewiston. (Best viewed via jet or float boat.)

Sawtooth National Recreation Area, Stanley, ID. (Over half a million acres of recreational paradise.)

MONTANA

Big Hole National Battlefield, P.O. Box 237, Wisdom, MT 59761-0237.

Big Hole Canyon National Recreation Area (Montana and Wyoming), P.O. Box 458, Fort Smith, MT 59035.

Custer Battlefield National Monument, P.O. Box 39, Crow Agency, MT 59022.

Grant-Kohrs Ranch National Historic Site, P.O. Box 790, Deer Lodge, MT 59722. (216-acre historic ranch with demonstrations and tours.)

UTAH

Cedar Breaks National Monument, P.O. Box 794, Cedar City, UT 84720.

Glen Canyon National Recreation Area (Utah and Arizona), P.O. Box 1507, Page, AZ 86040.

Golden Spike National Historic Site, P.O. Box 394, Brigham City, UT 84302.

Natural Bridges National Monument, c/o Canyonlands National Park, 446 S. Main St,

Moab, UT 84532.

Rainbow Bridge National Monument, c/o Glen Canyon National Recreation Area, P.O. Box 1507, Page, AZ 86040.

Timpanogos Cave National Monument, R.R.3 Box 200, American Fork, UT 84003.

Flaming Gorge National Recreational Area, P.O. Box 278, Manila, UT 84046.

WYOMING

Devil's Tower National Monument, Devil's Tower, WY 82714.

Fossil Butte National Monument, P.O. Box 527, Kemmerer, WY 83101.

John D. Rockefeller Jr Memorial Parkway, c/o Grand Teton National Park, P.O. Box Drawer 170, Moose, WY 83012.

Fort Laramie National Historic Site, Fort Laramie, WY 82212.

LIBRARIES

Every city and town in the Rockies has a public library. The quality of each library can vary greatly depending on the location. Most of the larger cities have a library system consisting of the main library and several branch libraries in different parts of the city. The main library in Denver (1300 and Broadway) has the world's largest western library. Across the street from here is the State Historical Society which has a good research library and a collection of 75,000 photographs of William Henry Jackson.

Salt Lake City has the world's largest genealogical library, located in the LDS Church Office Building at Temple Square.

The different universities in the Rockies area have excellent libraries.

Non-residents cannot borrow library books, but are welcome to spend time in the libraries, reading material from newspapers, magazines to reference books. The use of all libraries is free.

BOOKSTORES

Bookstores are prevalent in most neighborhood shopping areas in the Rockies. Larger drug stores, grocery shops and general stores have a department for books, cards, magazines, postcards and other stationery. In the major cities the largest chain bookstores, **B. Dalton** and **Waldenbooks,** have stores in many locations. The Yellow Pages in the local directory give a list of the bookstores in the area. One of the best bookstores in the Rockies area is the **Tattered Cover Bookstore**, 2930 E. 2nd Ave, Denver, CO 80209. Tel: (303) 322-7727. This store is open daily, and has over 150,000 books, maps and services.

NIGHTLIFE

In the larger cities there is a variety of nighttime happenings. The problem isn't what to do but what to choose. A choice of music, theater, dance, cinema, disco, opera and more is yours. From famous performers to unknown talents, from Broadway performances to old-time melodramas, the bigger cities in the Rockies offer something to suit your taste. Outside the big cities abundant entertainment awaits you. Rodeos and festivals have their own nightly entertainment of dances, singers, square dancing, fairs and carnivals. In the smaller towns entertainment is usually confined to the weekends. In some places the nightly entertainment is limited to a motel lounge and bar or sometimes a roadhouse with a local band in the corner. The hotel receptionist or local residents, local newspapers and magazines are usually your best source of information. Listed below are some of the popular nightly entertainment in the cities of Denver and Salt Lake City.

DENVER

Boulder's Dinner Theater, 5501 Arapahoe, Boulder, CO 80303. Tel: 449-6000. Elegant atmosphere, gourmet dinner served by the performers along with an excellent Broadway musical.

Confetti, 350 S. Birch, Glendale, CO 80222. Tel: 320-0118. Denver's hottest night spot. Current music, video, lights and fashion.

Country Dinner Playhouse, 6875 S. Clinton, Englewood, CO 80110. Tel: 799-1410. Professional dinner theater from Tuesday through Sunday. Matinees during the weekends, 470 seats, buffet included.

Comedy Works, 1226 15th St., Denver, CO 80202. Tel: 595-3637. Denver's all comedy nightclub in Larimer Square. Open nightly, dinner/show package.

Heritage Square Opera House, Heritage Square, Box D-109, Golden, CO 80401. Tel: 279-7880. Great theater/restaurant specializing in unmatched comedy entertainment for 13 years. Reasonable prices, reservation required.

The Landmark Inn, 455 S. Colorado Blvd, Denver, CO. Folk music and 24-hour coffee shop.

"**Turn of the Century**", 8930 E. Hampden Ave., Denver CO. Nightclub with nationally known entertainers.

• DOWNTOWN DENVER
Live music of all varieties can be found all over the downtown area. **Ivory Piano Bar**, 1620 Market St is a quiet spot, and a popular jazz cantina **El Chapultepec,** at 20th and Market streets, provides good music. In the Larimer Square area are **Josephina's** for jazz, pop and wine, **Basin's Up** for local favorites and a 23-year-old piano bar, **Laffite**. An old jazz lounge is located in the Oxford Hotel on 1600 17th St called **Sage Restaurant** and the **Corner Room.**

• GLENDALE AND CHERRY CREEK
The **Bull and Bush**, 4700 Cherry Creek Drive S., offers a variety of musical talents. **Aspen City Limits**, 4501 E. Virginia Ave, specializes in local blues and jazz.

SALT LAKE CITY

Dead Goat, Arrow Press Square, a laidback beer bar decorated in Old Colorado style has a full service grill with dancing to live music during the weekends.

The Bay, 1130 E. 2100 S. A disco.

Broadway Disco, 34 South Main. A disco.

Matt Limburg's Dance Entertainment and Light Show, 2983 W. 3500 S. Disco and light show.

Thirteenth Floor, 161 W. 600 S. A disco.

Xenon, 909 E. 2100 S., 486-4261. A disco.

Cafe Viceuses Rumeurs, Salt Lake's new piano bar-cum-sushi bar. Decorated French bistro style, good food.

The Green Parrot, 155 W. 200 S. A casual cafe-style club with live music and dancing Thursday through Saturday.

SHOPPING

SHOPPING AREAS

Enormous shopping centers are a part of the suburban life in the United States. In the Rockies too, most of the towns and cities, resorts and mountain villages have their shopping malls. Shopping centers can be quite an adventure as there are a variety of shops, stores, fast-food restaurants, ample parking and sometimes beautiful landscaping, all under one roof. Specialty shops in America carry a wide range of products in a specific merchandise. Some shops specialize in books, jewelry, fabrics, cowboy clothing, crafts and other interesting items. You might have to venture off to find some of these specialty shops.

Some of the typical souvenirs of the Rockies are Rocky Mountain jade jewelry, buckskin jackets, cowboy shirts, hats, belts and boots, Native American jewelry, baskets, weavings and crafts, pottery and other crafts.

In the Rockies area there are a variety of stores and shops. Chain stores, discount stores, factory outlets, drug and grocery stores, department stores and small shops are some of the different kinds of stores accessible to you. The local newspapers usually advertise sales and discounts in the local shops.

DENVER

The leading department stores in downtown Denver are **The Denver, Fashion Bar, Joslins** and **May D & F**. Nationally known department stores and discount stores like **Sears, Walgreens, J.C. Penneys, Target, Wards, Woolworth's** and **Skaggs** are also here. The world's largest sports store **Gart Brothers** is located on 10th and Broadway. Shopping in Denver has always been an attraction. **17th St and 16th St Mall** with its free shuttle bus presents a mile of excellent shopping. **Larimer Square** offers interesting and quaint shopping in restored Victorian buildings. Antique shops are abundant on South Broadway, between 1300 and 1500 South. Every neighborhood has a shopping area and often a mall. **Cherry Creek North**, 2 miles (4 km) southeast of downtown, centered around 3rd and Detroit, has many intimate shops, restaurants and cafes. **Heritage Square** on Highway 40, near Golden, has wonderful arts and crafts for sale and a great amusement park for children.

An exciting shopping complex is **Tivoli**, which features shops through a restored brewery. This is located on 9th and Lawrence and specializes in high fashion shops, casual and elegant dining. A highlight of this area is a 12 screen cinema complex. **The Southwest Mall**, 8501 W. Bowles Ave (Littleton), is the largest mall in the West having over 200 shops and 5 major department stores.

There are factory outlets that sell name brand items at bargain prices. Check the newspapers and the Yellow Pages for these, especially before buying your ski attire.

SALT LAKE CITY

The ZCMI **Center**, in downtown Salt Lake City, is one of the largest malls in the United States. The stores are open from Monday through Friday from 10 a.m. to 9 p.m., and on Saturdays from 10 a.m. to 6 p.m. This center is closed on Sundays. One of the features of this shopping center besides the variety of shops is the several levels of parking for the customers.

Four floors of shops, stores, boutiques and restaurants are in one of the largest covered shopping malls in the country, the **Cross-roads Plaza**. The complex houses movie theaters, a sports complex, offices, and 8 levels of parking. The plaza is open Monday–Friday from 10 a.m.–9 p.m., Saturday from 10 a.m.–6 p.m. and on Sundays from 12 noon–5 p.m. The **Triad Center**, on South Temple and Third West, has many exclusive shops, boutiques and Utah's first millionaire's restored mansion. Other attractions include an outdoor summer theater, flowered terraces, fountains, ice skating and hot chestnuts in the winter. Triad Center and Theater is opened from 10 a.m.–6 p.m. daily. Old street lights, Victorian mansions, restored trolley cars along with specialty shops, theaters and restaurants are what you will find at **Trolley Square**. Shops are open from Monday–Friday from 10 a.m.–9 p.m., Saturday from 10 a.m.–6 p.m. with a few shops and restaurants opened on Sunday afternoons. Restaurants and theaters are open late during the week.

OTHER SHOPPING AREAS

Most of the ski resorts in the Rockies area have excellent shopping. **Vail** has a beautiful mall with specialty shops and restaurants. **Aspen** has a variety of shops and crafts stores. **Colorado Springs** is a large city and has many shopping centers in different parts of the city. In Cheyenne, Wyoming, the **Frontier Mall** along Del Range Ave. is the primary shopping complex. Downtown Cheyenne has a variety of shops and stores. **The Wrangler** has an excellent selection of western styled clothing. The **Eastridge Mall** is Casper, Wyoming, has over 90 shops and stores. In Boise, Idaho, the **Westgate Shopping Mall** and the **Overland Park Shopping Mall** are the main shopping areas.

The main malls in Montana are **Rimrock Mall** in Billings, **Main Mall** in Bozeman, **Southgate Mall** in Missoula and the **Holiday Village Shopping Mall** in Great Falls.

SPORTS

FISHING

COLORADO

Most of the 11,300 miles (18,185 km) of streams and 2,400 lakes of Colorado are open to public fishing. Best trout fishing spots are Grand Lake, Granby, Shadow Mountain, Green Mountain, Trappers Lake, Twin Lakes, Sweetwater Lake, Dillon Reservoir, Navajo Reservoir, Monument Lake, Vallecito Reservoir, Blue Mesa, and more than 200 other lakes on the Grand Mesa. A fishing license is required and is available at the numerous sporting goods stores as well as the Division of Wildlife. For more information write to: the Colorado Division of Wildlife, 6060 Broadway, Denver 80216. For recorded message about fishing conditions call (303) 291-7227.

Call for current fishing regulations. General fishing statutes and regulations apply to all State waters. The fishing season in Colorado is through the year.

IDAHO

A fishing license is essential for residents and non-residents in Idaho. Some waterways provide year round fishing. The licenses and copies of official fishing regulations can be obtained from vendors in most towns and the Idaho Dept of Fish and Game at 600 Walnut, Box 25, Boise 83707. Tel: (208) 334-3700.

MONTANA

For current information regarding fishing in Montana, write to: Montana Dept of Fish, Wildlife and Parks, 1420 East Sixth St., Helena, MT 59620. Tel: (406) 444-2535.

Montana, like most of the Rockies area, boasts thousands of miles of blue ribbon trout streams. Western Montana is famous for its rainbow, brown and cut-throat trout. In the Eatern part of Montana the waters are full of northern pike, channel catfish, large and small mouth bass, perch, walleye and sauger. The Yellowstone and Missouri Rivers offer a variety of fish including the rare paddlefish and shovelnose sturgeon. The Department of Fish, Wildlife and Parks will supply you with all the necessary information and a copy of the rules for fishing in Montana.

UTAH

The Flaming Gorge in the northeast and Lake Powell in south-central Utah are two man-made lakes that furnish splendid fishing. Utah, like most of the Rockies, has an abundance of lakes and streams well stocked with fish ranging from rainbow trout to cut-throat, kokanee salmon, Mackinaw, grayling, bass and walleye pike.

The regular fishing season is from end-May to end-November. Utah fishing regulations, limits, areas, and other information is available from Utah Division of Wildlife Resources, 1596 W. North Temple, Salt Lake City, 84116. Tel: (801) 533-9333.

WYOMING

Fishermen holding a valid Wyoming fishing license will have to purchase a fishing stamp if they want to fish in the Utah part of the Flaming Gorge National Recreational Area. A regular Montana fishing license is required to fish in the Montana part of the Bighorn Canyon National Recreational Area. A Wyoming license is not required to fish in the Yellowstone National Park but a free permit and package of regulations need to be collected from any park ranger station before you go fishing. Grand Teton National Park requires a Wyoming fishing license. The Wind River Reservation has special tribal regulations for fishing.

Fishing licenses can be purchased from selling agents, Game and Fish District Offices and national recreation areas. For more information write to: the Wyoming Game and Fish Dept., Cheyenne, WY 82002. Tel: (307) 777-7728.

HUNTING

Big game and small game hunting are very popular sports in the Rocky Mountains. All the states have their own regulations and require that you have a paid license to participate in this activity. Hunters unfamiliar with the rugged mountains might be advised to hire the services of a hunting guide. Some states insist that you complete a hunter safety training course before you can purchase a firearms hunting license. It is also required that you wear a certain amount of fluorescent blaze orange while hunting. This amount differs in each state. Many of the more rugged hunting areas can be reached by four-wheel drive vehicle but successful hunters do most of their hunting on foot. Check with the US Forest Service for local road closures and restricted areas before you go on your hunting expedition.

It is your responsibility as a sportsman to get permission from the landowner before you camp, hunt, fish or trap on his property. Some states have severe legal penalties for hunting, fishing or trapping on private land without written permission.

The unpredictable and varied climate of the Rockies requires that you bring a variety of clothing along with you. Some of the hunting grounds for deer and elk are in high altitude areas that require you to be in good physical condition.

A hunter needs to find out the specific dates, deadlines, application fees, hunter safety requirements, and other information before he takes off on a hunting trip. There are specific dates for receiving applications for certain animals. Most application fees are refundable. For some animals there are only a few permits available and to ensure fairness, random computer selections are made for the species where the applications exceed the available permits. Some states provide party applications. Write to the state wildlife agency for license applications, and a list of guides and outfitters.

COLORADO

Big game hunting for elk, deer, antelope, bears, mountain lions, bighorn sheep and mountain goats is available in Colorado. Some of the big game seasons require limited licenses through application and drawing, others have unlimited licenses that can be obtained at agencies or the Division of Wildlife offices in Colorado.

Deer and elk seasons are usually in October and November. Big horn sheep and mountain goat opens in late August, and antelope in September. Black bears are hunted in spring and also during the big game seasons. Mountain lions can be hunted during the big game season. Special archery, muzzle-loading and high country deer seasons are usually held prior to the regular deer and elk rifle season.

Most information and brochures can be obtained by writing to the Colorado Division of Wildlife (*see under "Fishing"*).

IDAHO

Idaho offers a great variety of animals and gamebirds with specific seasons. Like in the other Rockies States, the non-resident licenses are more expensive than the resident licenses. These are available from vendors all over the state and the Dept of Fish and Game. Along with this, request a copy of hunting rules and regulations for Idaho.

MONTANA

The minimum age for hunting is 12 years. Hunters between the ages of 12 and 17 years have to go through a hunter education course before they can legally hunt. The Dept of Fish, Wildlife and Parks will give you all the information about hunting requirements, licenses and seasons.

A combination big game hunting license can be purchased by non-residents which entitles a hunter to an elk, a deer, one black bear, an upland gamebird license and a fishing license; or there are special tags for only deer. Animals hunted in Montana include black bears, grizzly bears, mountain lions, antelopes, mountain goats, moose, and big horn sheep. Some of these animal have limited tags and licenses are obtained on a drawing basis.

UTAH

Utah has been known as one of the finest deer hunting areas in the country. Utah also has some excellent marshlands for waterfowl hunting. Other varities of game birds include pheasant, chukar, Hungarian partridge, forest and sage grouse, quail, mourning dove and cottontail.

Predator shooting and hunting for non-game animals like coyote, red and gray fox, bobcat and rabbit, are also permitted in Utah.

Minimum age for big game hunting is 16 and small game and waterfowl is 12 years. As hunting fees and regulations can change write for more complete information to Utah Division of Wildlife Resources.

WYOMING

Applications and fees must arrive at the Wyoming Game and Fish Department in Cheyenne by the last application date. Within 15 days they will inform the random number computer selection results. There is a non-refundable application fee for most of the animals in addition to the license fee. Write to the Wyoming Game and Fish Dept regarding individual licenses, party licenses, hunting rules and regulations and for a list of guides and outfitters. The cost of licenses vary, depending on the animal. If the person is unsuccessful in receiving a license the fee is non-refundable.

SKIING

COLORADO

For up-to-date guide to Colorado ski areas write to: Colorado Ski Country USA, 1560 Broadway, St 1440, Denver, 80202. Tel: (303) 837-0793. For updated snow reports call (303) 831-7669. For air travelers, check the Ski Information Booth at the Stapleton Airport in Denver. Many ski resorts are located within a few hours from Denver. Call your travel agent or write to the Chambers of Commerce for information.

Breckenridge, Breckenridge Resort Chamber, P.O. Box 1909, Breckenridge, CO 80424. Tel: (800) 221-1091. Open mid-November to mid-April.

Keystone, Keystone Ski Resort, Box 38, Keystone, CO 80435. Tel: (303) 468-4242. Open from October–April.

Steamboat Springs, Steamboat Springs, Box 774408, Steamboat Springs, CO 80477.

Tel: (303) 879-0740. Open late-November to mid-April.

Vail Resorts, Vail Resorts Association, 421 E. Meadow Drive, Vail, CO 81657. Tel: (1-800) 525-3875. (For Beaver Creek and Vail ski areas.) Open November–April.

Aspen Resorts, Aspen Resorts, 700 S. Aspen St., Aspen, CO 81611. Tel: (303) 925-9000. (For Aspen Mountain Ski Area, Snowmass Ski Area & Buttermilk Ski Area.) Open late-November to mid-April.

Copper Mountain Resort, Copper Mountain Resort, P.O. Box 3001, Copper Mountain, CO 80443. Tel: (303) 968-2882. Open November–April.

IDAHO

Bogus Basin, 16 miles (25 km) north of Boise via the Bogus Basin Road. For reservations and information: 2405 Bogus Basin Road, Boise, ID 83702. Tel: (1-800) 367-4397. Open December–April.

Schweitzer, 11 miles (17 km) NW of Sandpoint, 88 miles (140 km) northeast of Spokane. Schweitzer Reservations, P.O. Box 815, Sandpoint, ID 83864. Tel: (202) 263-9555. Open late-November to mid-April.

Sun Valley, 80 miles (128 km) north of Twin Falls, Sun Valley Co., Sun Valley, ID 83353. Tel: (1-800) 635-8261. Open end-November to mid-April.

Grand Targee, 78 miles (125 km) northeast of Idaho Falls. Grand Targee Reservations, Driggs, ID 83422. Tel: (1-800) 443-8146. Open mid-November to mid-April.

MONTANA

Bridger Bowl, Bridger Bowl, 15795 Bridger Canyon Road, Bozeman, MT 95715. Tel: (1-800) 223-9609. Open daily mid-December to mid-April.

Red Lodge, Red Lodge Ski Area, Post Office Drawer R, Red Lodge, MT 59068. Tel: (1-800) 468-8977. Open daily mid-November to mid-April.

Big Mountain, Big Mountain, Box 1215, Whitefish, MT 59937. Tel: (406) 862-3511. Open daily November to mid-April.

Big Sky, Big Sky Ski Area, Box 1, Big Sky, MT 59716. Tel: (1-800) 548-4486. Open daily mid-November to mid-April.

UTAH

Park City, 27 miles (43 km) east of Salt Lake City, via Interstate 80. Park City Ski Corp., P.O. Box 39-UP84, Park City, UT 84060. Tel: (1-800) 222-PARK. Open mid-November to end April.

Snowbird, 24 miles (38 km) southeast of Salt Lake City. Snowbird Ski and Summer Resort, Snowbird, UT 84092. Tel: (1-800) 453-3000. Open mid-November to early May.

Alta, 33 miles (55 km) southeast of Salt Lake City. Alta Reservations, Alta, UT 84092. Tel: (801) 742-2040. Open mid-November to May.

Deer Valley, 27 miles (43 km) east of Salt Lake City. Deer Valley Resort, P.O. Box 1525, Park City, UT 84060. Tel: (1-800) 543-3833. Open December 8 to April 7.

WYOMING

Teton Village, Jackson Hole Ski Corp., Box 290, Teton Village, WY 83025. Tel: (307) 733-2292. Ski area open mid-December to mid-April.

Jackson, Snow King Inc., Box 1137, 400 Snow King, Jackson, WY 83001. Tel: (307) 733-2042. Night skiing possible. Operates from mid-December to mid-April.

Pinedale, White Pine Lodge Ski Area, Box 833, Pinedale, WY 82941. Tel: (307) 367-4142. Open mid-December to mid-April. (Friday–Sunday). In January and February, open Thursdays too.

Casper, Hogadon Basin, Hogadon Basin, 1715 E. 4th St., Casper, WY 82601. Tel: (307) 266-1600. Open mid-December to mid-April, Wednesday–Sunday.

Cody, near Yellowstone National Park. Open mid-December to mid-April, Wednesday–Sunday.

Sleeping Giant, P.O. Box 790, Cody WY 82414. Tel: (307) 587-4044.

Centennial, Medicine Bow area. Open mid-December to mid-April, Wednesday–Sunday.

Medicine Bow/Snowy Range, Box 138, Centennial, WY 82055. Tel: (307) 745-5750.

SKI TOURING/ CROSS COUNTRY SKIING

COLORADO: Cross Country Ski Association, Snow Mountain Nordic Center, P.O. Box 169, Winter Park, 80482. Tel: (303) 887-2152.

SNOWMOBILING

COLORADO: The Colorado Division of Parks and Outdoor Recreation is responsible for registering and having regulations for this sport. All vehicles must be registered and proper display of the registration number is required. For information call Colorado Snowmobiling Association, Tel: (1-800) 235-4480. Write to: US Forest Service for a Forest Service map of the area you are interested in which will show trails and closure areas in the 11 National Forests in Colorado. For snowmobile sales and rentals, check Yellow Pages. Ask your travel agent for Ski/ Winter Recreation Package. Write to the local Chambers of Commerce. For club activity write to: Mile-Hi Snowmobile Club, Box 26368, Denver, CO 80226.

BALLOONING

COLORADO: The San Luis Valley in Southern Colorado is America's first ballooning resort. This Balloon Ranch is open May 15–February 15. Reservations are advised. Write to: Balloon Ranch, Box 41, Del Norte, CO 81132. Tel: 754-2533. Also check "Balloons" in the Yellow Pages.

BICYCLING

COLORADO: Free publication "Road rules, equipment requirements and safety tips for bicyclists" write to: Colorado Dept of High-

ways, 4201 E. Arkansas, Denver, CO 80222. Send SASE for free trail map: Colorado Plateau, Mountain Bike Trail Association, P.O. Box 4602, Grand Junction, CO 81502. For information about the International Classic write to: International Bicycle Classic, 1540 Lehigh, Boulder, CO 80303.

BOATING

COLORADO: World's highest registered anchorage at Grand Lake, skiing at Bonnie Reservoir, Granby, Shadow Mountain, Blue Mesa and Dillon are also major boating areas for large craft. Water skiing is a sport in more than 40 lakes in Colorado. All boats with motor or sails must be registered and display registration numbers. Write to: Colorado Division of Parks and Recreation, National Park Service, US Forest Service, Colorado Division of Wildlife, for more information and regulations.

RAFTING

COLORADO: More than 40 whitewater rafting companies are operating in Colorado. There are hundreds of miles of rivers in Colorado that can be rafted. Only the Yampa and Green Rivers in the Dinosaur National Monument require a permit. Permits must be obtained before January 15 of each year. For more information write to: Colorado River Outfitters Association, P.O. Box 1662 CR, Buena Vista, CO 81211. Consult your travel agent and Chambers of Commerce. Check "Float trips" and "Boat-rentals" in the Yellow Pages.

SPECTATOR

The Rocky Mountain area is packed with spectator sporting events. In the summer and the winter each state has its own sports events. Professional sporting events are prominent in Denver and Salt Lake City.

DENVER

Denver Zephyrs, minor league baseball. Mile High Stadium. Tel: 433-8645.
Denver Broncos, professional NFL football. Mile High Stadium. Tel: 433-7466.
Denver Nuggets, NBA basketball. McNichols Sports Arena, 1635 Clay. Tel: 893-6700.

University of Colorado Football, University of Colorado, Boulder. Tel: 492-5161.
Horse Racing, Arapahoe Park, 4100 S. Parker Road, Aurora, CO 80114, Tel: 699-2900. (Late May through early November.)
Dog Racing, Mile High Kennel Club, 6200 Dahlia. Tel: 288-1591. (Greyhound racing with parimutuel wagering.) June–August. Year-round off-track betting from other Colorado dog tracks.

SALT LAKE CITY

The Central Hockey League's **Golden Eagles** and the National Basketball Association's **Utah Jazz** play at the Salt Palace. The minor league baseball team, **The Gulls**, have their games at Derk's Field. University of Utah sports activities are played at the campus in Salt Lake City.

A full range of athletic events occurs at **Brigham Young University** at Provo. The BYU football team is usually one of the nation's top college teams. **Utah State University** in Logan and **Weber State University** in Ogden have many spectator sporting events during the year.

RODEOS

The Rockies is Rodeo Country and every week-end in the summer, you can find a rodeo somewhere in this area. In 1880 for the first time the sport developed as a professional entertainment. Today most modern rodeos have a parade that precedes the event. Listed below are some of the major events in a rodeo.

Saddle Bronc Riding: Saddle broncs are not trained to buck, but do so instinctively. The rider has to use a standard PRCA (Professional Rodeo Cowboys Association) saddle and buck rein which is a braided rope. The bronc rider is judged by the performance of his riding and the animal's bucking. Men are specially designated the job of helping the rider dismount from the horse when the riding time is up.

Bareback Riding: This event does not allow the use of stirrups or reins. The horse has a stiff leather strap that goes around the horse's belly and the cowboy has to hold on to this with one hand. The rider must spur the horse for 8 seconds and is disqualified if his free hand touches the horse of if he misses spurring the horse on the first jump.

Calf Roping: Within a given time limit the cowboy has to put the calf down and tie three of its legs together. The calf is given a 10-ft (3-meter) lead before the cowboy starts chasing it. The horse's job is to bring the cowboy close to the running calf and stop, so he can rope it.

Steer Wrestling: Here the cowboy grabs a 700-pound (320-kg) steer by its horns and wrestles it to the ground. The cowboy that performs this in the shortest time wins the event.

Bull Riding: A contest between small man and huge beast. Here a 150-pound (70-kg) man is pitted against a 1500-pound (700-kg) bull. The cowboy is required to ride one-handed with a loose rope, which is around the bull's belly. The other end of the rope is around the rider's hand. The ride is 8 minutes long and spurring is not required but will add to the score.

Barrel Racing: This event allows women to show their rodeo skills. Women run well-trained horses through a cloverleaf pattern at amazing speed. A fast horse and a good rider make this an exciting event.

The Wild Horse Race: Two men hold the wild horse long enough to saddle it and allow a third man to mount and ride it. This is an exciting event as there are many competitors.

Besides the professional rodeos, there are many special rodeos held in the Rockies area. These are all-girl rodeos, all-Indian rodeos, old times rodeos and college rodeos. If you write to the Chambers of Commerce, a list of rodeos and dates will be sent to you. For information about all the rodeos in Colorado, write to: Professional Rodeo Cowboys Association, 101 Pro Rodeo Drive, Colorado Springs, CO 80219. Tel: 593-8840.

Special Information

CHILDREN

In most of the cities in the Rockies, public parks, zoos, amusement parks, children's museums are great places to take your kids to. These places often have special attractions for kids. **Elitch Gardens** and **Lakeside Amusement Park** in Denver, the **Lagoon Amusement Park** in Farmington, Utah, offer a lot of fun for kids and adults. The **Renaissance Festival** at Larkspur is specially entertaining for children.

The national parks, forests and monuments offer educational and exciting times for the entire family. The outdoor life of the Rockies offers activities that children love to participate in. Conveniently located camping sites give children the space and freedom not found in hotels and motels. Many hotels and motels have baby-sitting services, playrooms, day-care centers, cribs, strollers, high chairs, etc., to make it more convenient for the family. Some of the ski resorts provide children's ski schools and day-care centers for the very young.

DISABLED

One of the newest groups that are exploring the travel scene are the handicapped travelers. Today extensive measures have been taken in many areas to offer safe and comfortable traveling for the physicially limited person. The wheelchair symbol is seen all over the Rockies area specifically demarking parking, toilets, ramps, camping, etc., for the handicapped. *A Travel Guide for the Handicapped* by Louise Weiss is an excellent book. The Chambers of Commerce, park services and other travel agencies will send special material for the handicapped traveler. The following will also supply you with material:

Rehabilitation International USA, 20 W. 40th St, New York, NY 10018.
Utah State Board for Vocational Education, 250 E. 500 S., Salt Lake City, UT 84111. (They have a handicapped guide to the city.)

A special book written for the handicapped is *Guide to National Parks and Monuments.* The book *Barrier Free* lists 300 roadside rest areas that have facilities for the handicapped and is available through the Commission at Washington DC. A list of tour operators who have tours for the handicapped could be obtained by writing to: **The Society for Advancement of Travel for the Handicapped**, 26 Court St, Brooklyn, NY 11242. TWA has published a special 12-page brochure named *Consumer information about Air Travel for the Handicapped.* This book explains all special travel arrangements that are available. Greyhound Bus System and Amtrack put out such publications too.

Further Reading

GENERAL

American Automobile Association. *Tour Book, AAA.* Va: Falls Church, 1984.
Bicidehaan. *Bike Rides of the Colorado Front Range.* Pruett Publishing Co., 1981.
Cahill, Rich. *The Colorado Hot Springs Guide.* Pruett Publishing Co., 1983.
Clifford, Peggy and John M. Smith. *Aspen/ Dreams and Dilemmas.* Chicago: The Swallow Press Inc., 1970.
Fodor's Rockies and Plains. New York: David McKay and Co. Inc., 1979.
Fosset, Frank. *Colorado, its Gold and Silver Mines, Farms and Stock Ranges and Health and Pleasure Resorts.* New York: Arno Press, reprint 1973.
Hansen, Harry. *Colorado, A Guide to the Highest State.* New York: Hastings House, 1970.

Hassick, Royal B. *Cowboys, The Real Story of Cowboys and Cattlemen.* London: Octopus Book Ltd, 1974.

Hopkins, Virginia. *The Colorado River: A Portrait.* London: Quatro Publications, 1985.

Hough, Robin. *The Friendly Native Guide Book to Utah.* Salt Lake City, n.p., 1979.

Lamar, Howard R. (editor) *The Readers' Encyclopedia of the American West.* Crowell, 1977.

Lord, Suzanne. *America's Travel Treasury.* Americans Discover America Series. New York: William Morrow, 1977.

Morgan, Dale. *The Great Salt Lake.* Albuquerque: University of New Mexico Press, 1973.

Peirce, Neal R. *The Mountain States of America: People, Politics and Power in the Eight Rocky Mountain States.* W.W. Norton and Co., 1972.

Roderunner Travel Guide to Big Wyoming. Jackson, Wyoming: Roderunner Travel Guide, 1983.

Rollins, Phillip Ashton. *The Cowboy.* University of New Mexico Press, 1979.

Stegner, Wallace. *The Gathering of Zion: The Story of the Mormon Trail.* Salt Lake City: Westwater Press, 1981.

Stone, Irving. *Men to Match My Mountains.* New York: Berkley Books, 1982.

Sudduth, Tom and Sanse. *Central Colorado Ski Tours.* Boulder: Pruett Publishing Co., 1977.

Wentworth, Frank L. *Aspen the Roaring Fork.* Denver: Sundance Publications, 1976.

Wiley, Peter and Robert Gottlieb. *Empires in the Sun: The Rise of the New American West.* G.P. Putnam's Sons, 1982.

Works Project Administration. *Utah Guide to the State.* (New revised edition.) Salt Lake City: Ward J. Loyance, Utah Arts Council, 1982.

Wyoming, A Guide to its History, Highways and People. Compiled by the workers of the Writers Program of the Work Projects Administration, University of Nebraska Press, 1981.

HISTORY

The American Heritage Book of Indians, American Heritage Publishing Co., 1961.

Atwood, Wallace. *The Rocky Mountains.* New York, 1945.

Buckholtz, C.W. *Rocky Mountain National Park: A History.* Boulder: Colorado Associated University Press, 1983.

Coues, Eliott. (editor) *The History of Lewis and Clark Expedition.* (3 volumes) New York: Dover Publication, 1965.

Hughes, J. Donald. *American Indians in Colorado.* Boulder: Pruett Publishing Co., 1984.

Lavender, David. *The Rockies.* University of Nebraska Press, 1968.

Mails, Thomas E. *The Mystic Warriors of the Plains.* Garden City: N.Y. Doubleday, 1972.

Miller, David E. *Great Salt Lake: Past and Present.* Salt Lake City: Publishers Press, 1977.

Swanton, J.R. *Indian Tribes of North America.* 1953.

GEOGRAPHY, WILDLIFE & NATURE

Bonney, Orrin H. and Lorraine G. Bonney. *Guide to the Wyoming Mountains and Wilderness Areas.* (Climbing Routes and Back Country). Chicago: Swallow Press Inc. *Montana Wildlife.* Helena: Montana Magazine.

Craighead, Frank. *Track of the Grizzly.* San Francisco: Sierra Club Books, 1979.

Mattheissen, Peter. *Wildlife in America.* 1959.

Nelson, Ruth Ashton. *Plants of Rocky Mountain National Park.* Colorado Associated University Press, 1982.

The Old West. (series) New York Time Life Books, 1974–77.

Ormes, Robert. *Guide to the Colorado Mountains.* Chicago: Swallow Press Inc., 1977.

Robbins, Michael. *Along the Continental Divide.* National Geography, 1981.

Schraff, Robert. *Exploring Yellowstone National Park.* New York: The World Publishing Co., 1969.

Sierra Club Guides to the National Parks, Rocky Mountains and the Great Plains. Stewart, Tabori and Co., 1984.

Wheat, Dough. *The Floater Guide to Colorado.* Billings and Helena, MT: Falcon Press Publishing Co., 1983.

Zwinger, Anne and Beatrice Willard. *Land Above the Trees.* New York: Harper and Row, 1972.

ART & PHOTOGRAPHY

Allard, William Albert. *Vanishing Breed.* Little, Brown and Co., 1983. Photographs of the Cowboy and the West.

Brownell, David and Nancy Tate (photography), John Sabella (text). *Aspen the 100 Year High.* New York: Books in Focus, 1981.

Hassick, Peter. *Frederic Remington.* Harry N. Abrams, Inc., 1973.

Hassick, Peter. *The Way West: Art of Frontier America.* New York: Abrams, 1977.

Nelson, Mary Carroll. *Masters of Western Art.* New York: Watson Guptill, 1982.

Westermeier, Clifford P. *Colorado's First Portrait.* University of New Mexico Press, 1970.

USEFUL ADDRESSES

TOURIST INFORMATION

Tourist information and useful literature can be obtained from tourist promotional agencies in each of the Rocky Mountain states. The following agencies will be very helpful.

• **COLORADO**
Denver and Colorado Convention and Visitors Bureau, 225 West Colfax Ave., Denver, CO 80202. Tel: (303) 892-1112.
Colorado Tourism Board, P.O. Box 38700 Dept TIA, Denver 80238. Tel: (1-800) 433-2656 or (303) 592-5410.

• **IDAHO**
Idaho Travel Council, 700 W. State St., Dept C, Boise 83720. Tel: (1-800) 635-7820 or (208) 334-2470.

• **MONTANA**
Travel Montana, Room 010, Deer Lodge, 59722. Tel: (1-800) 541-1447 or (406) 444-2654.

• **UTAH**
Utah Travel Council, Council Hall, Capitol Hill, Salt Lake City, UT 84114. Tel: (801) 538-1030.

• **WYOMING**
Wyoming Travel Commission, 1-25 College Drive, Dept WY, Cheyenne 82002. Tel: (1-800) 225-5996 or (307) 777-7777.

EMBASSIES & CONSULAR SERVICES

There are some consulates and other foreign government representatives located in Salt Lake City and Denver.

Belgium
In Los Angeles, Tel: (213) 857-1244.

Chile
In Colorado, Tel: (303) 424-4022.
In Los Angeles, Tel: (213) 624-6357.

Costa Rica
In Colorado, Tel: (303) 377-0050.
In Los Angeles, Tel: (213) 225-2464.

Denmark
Danish Consulate, 3100 S. Sheridan Blvd, Denver, CO. Tel: 980-9100

Dominican Republic
In San Francisco, Tel: (415) 982-5144.

Finland
In Los Angeles, Tel: (213) 203-9903.

France
French Honorary Consul, Western Federal Savings Bldg, Denver, CO. Tel: 831-8616.
French Trade Offices, 1840 Willow Ln., Denver, CO. Tel: 233-7484.
French Consul, University of Utah, Salt Lake City, UT. Tel: 581-6807. (Consulate General in San Francisco)

Germany
German Honorary Consul, 1801 Jackson Golden, Denver, CO. Tel: 279-1551.

Italy
Henry N. Aloia, (Cons) 2895 S. 800 E., Salt Lake City, UT. Tel: 466-7615. (Consulate Gen. in San Francisco)

Japan
In Los Angeles, Tel: (213) 624-8305.

Korea
Korean Consulate, Equitable Bldg, Denver, CO. Tel: 830-0500.

Mexico
Mexican Consulate, 1670 Broadway, Denver, CO. Tel: 830-0523.
Enrique Vazquez, (Cons), 182 S. 600 E., Suite 202, Salt Lake City, UT. Tel: 521-8503.

Netherlands
Netherlands Consulate, Suite 700, 910 16th, Denver, CO. Tel: 595-8833.

Norway
Norwegian Consulate, 1600 Sherman, Denver, CO. Tel: 733-7315.

Peru
In Los Angeles, Tel: (213) 651-0296.

Sweden
Swedish Consulate, Denver, CO. Tel: 758-0999.

Switzerland
Swiss Consulate, 430 S. Newland, Denver, CO. Tel: 499-5641.
Gottlieb L. Schneebeli, Consul, 617 8th Ave., Salt Lake City, UT. Tel: 532-1874.

United Kingdom
In Los Angeles, Tel: (213) 385-7381.

CHAMBERS OF COMMERCE

Cities and resorts throughout the Rockies have **Chambers of Commerce** to provide free information about the area. Lodgings, dining, shopping, medical, events, festivals, businesses, and other general information are areas in which they can be of assistance.

IN COLORADO (Area Code: 303)

Adams County Chamber of Commerce, 7100 Broadway, Bldg 1, Unit B, Denver, CO 80221. Tel: 426-1570.
Alamosa Chamber of Commerce, P.O. Box 120, Alamosa, CO 81101. Tel: 589-3681.
Arvada Chamber of Commerce, 7305 Grandview Ave., Arvada, CO 80015. Tel:

424-0313.
Aspen Chamber of Commerce, 303 E. Main St., Aspen, CO 81612. Tel: 925-1940.
Aurora Chamber of Commerce, 3131 S. Vaughn Way #622, Aurora, CO 80011. Tel: 755-5000.
Boulder Chamber of Commerce, 2440 Pearl St., P.O. Box 73, Boulder, CO 80302. Tel: 442-1044.
Breckenridge Resort Association, 555 S. Columbia Road, P.O. Box 1909, Breckenridge, CO 80424. Tel: 453-6018.
Brighton Chamber of Commerce, 1401 E. Bridge, Brighton, CO 80601. Tel: 659-0223.
Broomfield Chamber of Commerce, 740 Burbank St., P.O. Box 301, Broomfield, CO 80020. Tel: 466-1775.
Brush Chamber of Commerce, 301 Edison, Brush, CO 80723. Tel: 842-2666.
Buena Vista Chamber of Commerce, 343 US Highway 24 S., Buena Vista, CO 81211. Tel: 395-6612.
Burlington Chamber of Commerce, 410-14th, Burlington, CO 80807. Tel: 346-8070.
Canon Chamber of Commerce, P.O. Box 749, Canon City, CO 81212. Tel: 275-2331.
Central City Chamber of Commerce, City Hall, Central City, CO 80427. Tel: 573-0247.
Colorado Springs Chamber of Commerce, P.O. Drawer B, Colorado Springs, CO 80901. Tel: 635-1551.
Copper Mountain Resort Association, P.O. Box 1, Copper Mountain, CO 80443. Tel: 668-2882.
Cortez Chamber of Commerce, P.O. Box 968, Cortez, CO 81321. Tel: 565-3414.
Craig Chamber of Commerce, 1111 W. Victory Way, Craig, CO 81626. Tel: 824-5689.
Crested Butte Resort Association, Old Town Hall, P.O. Box 1288, Crested Butte, CO 81224. Tel: 349-6438.
Cripple Creek Two Mile High Club, P.O. Box 650, Cripple Creek, CO 80813. Tel: 689-2169.
Delta Chamber of Commerce, 301 Main St, Delta, CO 81416. Tel: 874-8616.
Denver Chamber of Commerce, 1600 Sherman St., Denver, CO 80203. Tel: 894-8500.
Denver Convention & Visitors' Bureau, 225 West Colfax Ave., Denver, CO 80202. Tel: 892-1112.
Dillon Chamber of Commerce, 50 Chief Colorow, Dillon, CO 80435. Tel: 468-6222.

Durango Chamber of Commerce, 111 S. Camino del Rio, P.O. Box 2587, Durango, CO 81301. Tel: 247-0312.

Englewood Chamber of Commerce, 180 W. Girard Ave., Englewood, CO. Tel: 781-7838.

Estes Park Chamber of Commerce, 500 Big Thompson Hwy, Estes Park, CO 80517. Tel: 800-44 ESTES.

Evergreen Chamber of Commerce, Evergreen, CO 80439. Tel: 674-3412.

Fort Collins Chamber of Commerce, P.O. Box D, Fort Collins CO 80521. Tel: 482-3746.

Fort Lupton Chamber of Commerce 330 Park Ave., Fort Lupton, CO 80621. Tel: 857-2714.

Fort Morgan Chamber of Commerce, 300 Main, Fort Morgan, CO 80701. Tel: 867-6702.

Georgetown Chamber of Commerce, 600 Rose, Georgetown, CO 80444. Tel: 567-4844.

Glenwood Springs Chamber of Commerce, 1102 Grand, Glenwood Springs, CO 81601. Tel: 945-6589.

Golden Chamber of Commerce, 611 14th St., Golden, CO 80402. Tel: 279-3113.

Granby Chamber of Commerce, P.O. Box 35, Granby, CO 80446. Tel: 887-2311.

Grand Junction Chamber of Commerce, P.O. Box 1330, Grand Junction, CO 81501. Tel: 242-3214.

Grand Lake Chamber of Commerce, P.O. Box 57, Grand Lake, CO 80447. Tel: 627-3402.

Greeley Chamber of Commerce, 1407-8th Ave., Greeley, CO 80631. Tel: 352-3556.

Gunnison Chamber of Commerce, 500 East Tomichi Ave., Gunnison, CO 81230. Tel: 641-1501.

Idaho Springs Chamber of Commerce, 2200 Miner St., CO 80452. Tel: 567-4844.

La Junta Chamber of Commerce, P.O. Box 408, La Junta, CO 81050. Tel: 384-7411.

Lake City Chamber of Commerce, Lake City, CO 81234. Tel: 944-2527.

Lakewood Chamber of Commerce, 12600 W. Colfax Ave., Lakewood, CO 80215. Tel: (303) 233-5555.

Las Animas Chamber of Commerce, 511 Ambrose Thompson Blvd., Las Animas, CO 81054. Tel: (719) 456-0453.

Leadville Chamber of Commerce, 809 Harrison Ave., P.O. Box 861, Leadville, CO 80461. Tel: (719) 486-3900.

Littleton Chamber of Commerce, 5600 S. Sante Fe Drive, Littleton, CO 80120. Tel: 795-0142.

Longmont Chamber of Commerce, 528 N. Main St., Longmont, CO 80501. Tel: 776-5295.

Loveland Chamber of Commerce, 114 Fifth St., Loveland, CO 80537. Tel: 667-6311.

Manitou Springs Chamber of Commerce, 354 Manitou Ave., Manitou Springs, CO 80829. Tel: (719) 685-5089, (1-800) 642-2567.

Meeker Chamber of Commerce, 710 Market St., P.O. Box 869, Meeker, CO 81641. Tel: 878-5510.

Monte Vista Chamber of Commerce, 1125 Park Ave., Monte Vista, CO 81144. Tel: 852-2731.

Montrose Chamber of Commerce, 555 N. Townsend, Montrose, CO 81401. Tel: (303) 249-6360.

Ouray Chamber of Commerce, 1222 Main St., P.O. Box 145A, Ouray, CO 81427. Tel: (1-800) 228-1867.

Pueblo, Chamber of Commerce, P.O. Box 697, Pueblo, CO 81002, Tel: 542-1704.

Rifle Chamber of Commerce, 101 Railroad, Rifle, CO 81680. Tel: 625-2085.

Rocky Ford Chamber of Commerce, 105 N. Main, Rocky Ford, CO 81067. Tel: (719) 254-7483.

Salida-Heart of Rockies Chamber of Commerce, 406 W. Rainbow Blvd., Salida, CO 81201. Tel: (719) 539-2068.

Silvertone Chamber of Commerce, 1360 Green St., P.O. Box 565, Silverton, CO 81433. Tel: 387-5654.

Steamboat Springs Chamber of Commerce, 625 S., Lincoln Ave., Steamboat Springs, CO 80477. Tel: 879-0880.

Sterling & Logan County Chamber of Commerce, 322 Poplar, P.O. Box 1683, Sterling, CO 80751. Tel: 522-5070.

Telluride Chamber of Commerce, 323 W. Colorado Ave., Telluride, CO 81435. Tel: 728-3614.

Trinidad-Las Animas County Chamber of Commerce, 309 Nevada Ave., Trinidad, CO 81082. Tel: 846-9285.

Vail Resort Association, 241 E. Meadow Drive, P.O. Box 308, Vail, CO 81658. Tel: 476-1000.

Westminster Chamber of Commerce, 3489 W. 72nd Ave., Westminster, CO 80030. Tel: 428-6597.

Wheatridge Chamber of Commerce, 6470 W. 44th Ave., Wheatridge, CO 80033. Tel: 423-3800.

Winter Park Resort Association, P.O. Box 3236, Winter Park, CO 80482. Tel: 726-4118.

Woodland Park Chamber of Commerce, 161 Walnut, P.O. Box W, Woodland Park, CO 80866. Tel: 687-9885.

IN IDAHO (Area Code: 208)

Aberdeen Chamber of Commerce, P.O. Box 276, Aberdeen, ID 83210. Tel: 397-4148.

American Falls Chamber of Commerce, 223 Idaho St., P.O. Box 637, American Falls, ID 83211. Tel: 226-2309.

Arco Chamber of Commerce, P.O. Box 837, Arco, ID 83213. Tel: 527-8559.

Ashton Chamber of Commerce, P.O. Box 624, Ashton, ID 83420.

Bayview Chamber of Commerce, P.O. Box 121, Bayview, ID 83803. Tel: 683-2243.

Bellevue Chamber of Commerce, P.O. Box 406, Bellevue, ID 83318.

Blackfoot Chamber of Commerce, P.O. Box 801, Blackfoot, ID 83221. Tel: 785-0510.

Bliss Chamber of Commerce, P.O. Box 65, Bliss, ID 83314. Tel: 352-9985.

Boise Chamber of Commerce, P.O. Box 2368, Boise, ID 83701. Tel: 344-5515.

Boise Convention Center, P.O. Box 2106, Boise, ID 83701. Tel: 344-7777.

Bonners Ferry Chamber of Commerce, P.O. Box 3, Bonners Ferry, ID 83805. Tel: 267-3156.

Buhl Chamber of Commerce, P.O. Box 28, Buhl, ID 83316. Tel: 543-6682.

Burley Chamber of Commerce, 1401 Overland, Burley, ID 83318. Tel: 678-7230.

Caldwell Chamber of Commerce, 300 Frontage Road, P.O. Box 819, Caldwell, ID 83606. Tel: 459-7493.

Cambridge Commercial Club, P.O. Box 56, Cambridge, ID 83610.

Cascade Chamber of Commerce, P.O. Box 26, Cascade, ID 83611. Tel: 382-4922.

Coeur d'Alene Chamber of Commerce, P.O. Box 850, Coeur d'Alene, ID 83814. Tel: 664-3194.

Cottonwood Chamber of Commerce, P.O. Box 15, Cottonwood, ID 83522. Tel: 962-3281.

Council Chamber of Commerce, P.O. Box 257, Council, ID 83612. Tel: (208) 253-4315.

Craigmont Chamber of Commerce, P.O. Box 257, Craigmont, ID 83612. Tel: 924-5975.

Driggs Chamber of Commerce, P.O. Box 92, Driggs, ID 83422. Tel: 354-2337.

Emmett Chamber of Commerce, 231 S. Washington, Emmett, ID 83617. Tel: 365-3485.

Fruitland Chamber of Commerce, P.O. Box 408, Fruitland, ID 83619. Tel: 452-4350.

Glenns Ferry Chamber of Commerce, P.O. Box 317, Glenns Ferry, ID 83623. Tel: 366-7486.

Gooding Chamber of Commerce, P.O. Box 177, Gooding, ID 83330. Tel: 934-4402.

Grangeville Chamber of Commerce, P.O. Box 212, Grangeville, ID 83830. Tel: 983-0460.

Hagerman Chamber of Commerce, Route 1, Hagerman, ID 83332. Tel: 837-4822.

Hailey Chamber of Commerce, P.O. Box 100, Hailey, ID 83333. Tel: 788-2810.

Harrison Chamber of Commerce, P.O. Box 24, Harrison, ID 83833.

Hayden Lake Chamber of Commerce, P.O. Box 122, Hayden Lake, ID 83835.

Homedale Chamber of Commerce, Homedale, ID 83628. Tel: 837-3271.

Hope-Clark Fork-Trestle Creek Chamber of Commerce, P.O. Box 515, Clark Fork, ID 83811. Tel: 266-1477.

Idaho Falls Chamber of Commerce, P.O. Box 498, Idaho Falls, ID 83402. Tel: 523-1010.

Jerome Chamber of Commerce, 112 S. Lincoln #3, Jerome, ID 83338. Tel: 324-2711.

Kamiah Chamber of Commerce, P.O. Box 1124, Kamiah, ID 83536. Tel: 935-2290.

Kellogg Chamber of Commerce, 712 W. Cameron, Kellogg, ID 83837. Tel: 784-0821.

Ketchum-Sun Valley Chamber of Commerce, P.O. Box 2420, Ketchum, ID 83340. Tel: 776-3423.

Kimberly Chamber of Commerce, Route 2, P.O. Box 629, Kimberly, ID 83341. Tel: 423-5360.

Kuna Chamber of Commerce, P.O. Box 123, Kuna, ID 83634. Tel: 922-5546.

Lava Hot Springs Chamber of Commerce, P.O. Box 668, Lava Hot Springs, ID 83246. Tel: 776-5221.

Lewiston Chamber of Commerce, 1030 F Street, Lewiston, ID 83501. Tel: 743-3531.

Lowman Chamber of Commerce, S. Fork Lodge, Lowman, ID 83637. Tel: 259-3322.

Mackay Chamber of Commerce, P.O. Box 207, Mackay, ID 83251. Tel: 766-2300.

McCall Chamber of Commerce, P.O. Box E, McCall, ID 83638. Tel: 634-7631.

Meridian Chamber of Commerce, P.O. Box 557, Meridian, ID 83642. Tel: 888-2817.

Montpelier Chamber of Commerce, P.O. Box 265, Montpelier, ID 83254. Tel: 847-1894.

Moscow Chamber of Commerce, P.O. Box 8936, Moscow, ID 83843. Tel: 882-3581.

Mountain Home Chamber of Commerce, Mountain Home, ID 83647. Tel: 587-4334.

Nampa Chamber of Commerce, P.O. Drawer A, Nampa, ID 83651. Tel: 466-4642.

New Plymouth Chamber of Commerce, Route 2, P.O. Box 26, New Plymouth, ID 83655. Tel: 278-3198.

Nez Perce Chamber of Commerce, P.O. Box 278, Nez Perce, ID 83543. Tel: 937-0347.

Orofino Chamber of Commerce, P.O. Box 2221, Orofino, ID 83544. Tel: 476-4335.

Parma Chamber of Commerce, P.O. Drawer B, Parma, ID 83660. Tel: 733-4644.

Paul Chamber of Commerce, P.O. Box 756, Paul, ID 83347. Tel: 438-5332.

Payette Chamber of Commerce, 700 Center Ave, Payette, ID 83661. Tel: 642-2362.

Pierce Chamber of Commerce, P.O. Drawer B, Pierce, ID 83546. Tel: 464-2323.

Pocatello Chamber of Commerce, P.O. Box 626, Pocatello, ID 83204. Tel: 233-1525.

Post Falls Chamber of Commerce, P.O. Box 32, Post Falls, ID 83854. Tel: 773-5016.

Preston Chamber of Commerce, P.O. Box 289, Preston, ID 83263. Tel: 852-2527.

Priest Lake Chamber of Commerce, Rt. 5, P.O. Box 206-E, Priest Lake, ID 83856. Tel: 443-2049.

Rexburg Chamber of Commerce, 134 E. Main St, ID 83440. Tel: 356-5700.

Rigby Chamber of Commerce, P.O. Box 217, Rigby, ID 83442. Tel: 745-6677.

Riggins Chamber of Commerce, P.O. Box 289, Riggins, ID 83549. Tel: 628-3456.

Rupert Chamber of Commerce, P.O. Box 452, Rupert, ID 83350. Tel: 436-4793.

Salmon Chamber of Commerce, 200 Main St, Salmon, ID 83867. Tel: 756-4935.

Sandpoint Chamber of Commerce, P.O. Box 928, Sandpoint, ID 83864. Tel: 263-2161.

Shelley Chamber of Commerce, P.O. Box 301, Shelley, ID 83274. Tel: 357-3231.

Shoshone Chamber of Commerce, P.O. Box 575, Shoshone, ID 83354. Tel: 886-2979.

Soda Springs Chamber of Commerce, P.O. Box 697, Soda Springs, ID 83276. Tel: 547-3331.

Spirit Lake Chamber of Commerce, P.O. Box 68, Spirit Lake, ID 83869. Tel: 623-4452.

St Anthony Chamber of Commerce, 110 W. Main St., St Anthony, ID 83445. Tel: 624-3296.

St Maries Chamber of Commerce, 825 Main St., St Maries, ID 83861. Tel: 245-2413.

Stanley-Sawtooth Chamber of Commerce, P.O. Box 59, Stanley, ID 83278. Tel: 744-3411.

Sun Valley-Ketchum Chamber of Commerce, P.O. Box 2420, Sun Valley, ID 83353. Tel: 726-4471.

Twin Falls Chamber of Commerce, 858 Blue Lakes Blvd. N., Twin Falls, ID 83301. Tel: 733-3974.

Victor Chamber of Commerce, P.O. Box 110, Victor, ID 83455. Tel: 522-1349.

Wallace Chamber of Commerce, P.O. Box 1167, Wallace, ID 83873. Tel: 753-7151.

Weiser Chamber of Commerce, 8 East Idaho, Weiser, ID 83672. Tel: 549-0452.

IN MONTANA (Area Code: 406)

Anaconda Chamber of Commerce, 306 E. Park, Anaconda, MT 59711. Tel: 563-2400.

Baker Chamber of Commerce, P.O. Box 849, Baker, MT 59313. Tel: 778-3317.

Belgrade Chamber of Commerce, P.O. Box 1126, Belgrade, MT 59714. Tel: 388-1616.

Big Fork Chamber of Commerce, P.O. Box 237, Big Fork, MT 59911. Tel: 837-5888.

Big Sandy Chamber of Commerce, P.O. Box 511, Big Sandy, MT 59520. Tel: 378-2247.

Big Timber Chamber of Commerce, P.O. Box 1012, Big Timber, MT 59011. Tel: 932-5131.

Billings Chamber of Commerce, P.O. Box 2519, Billings, MT 59103. Tel: 245-4111.

Bitterroot Valley Chamber of Commerce, 105 E. Main, Hamilton, MT 59840. Tel: 363-2400.

Bozeman Chamber of Commerce, P.O. Box B, Bozeman, MT 59715. Tel: 586-5421.

Broadus Chamber of Commerce, Powder River Commercial Club, Broadus, MT 59317. Tel: 436-2834.

Butte-Silver Bow Chamber of Commerce, 2950 Harrison Ave., Butte, MT 59701. Tel: 494-5188.

Chester Chamber of Commerce, P.O. Box 632, Chester, MT 59522.

Chinook Chamber of Commerce, P.O. Box 575, Chinook, MT 59523. Tel: 357-2264.

Choteau Chamber of Commerce, P.O. Box 256, Choteau, MT 59422. Tel: 466-5849.

Circle Chamber of Commerce, Circle, MT 59215. Tel: 485-2414.

Columbia Falls Chamber of Commerce, P.O. Box 312, Columbia Falls, MT 59912. Tel: 892-2072.

Columbus Chamber of Commerce, P.O. Box 783, Columbus, MT 59019. Tel: 322-4778.

Community Improvement Association, P.O. Box 313, Fort Benton, MT 59442. Tel: 622-5254.

Conrad Chamber of Commerce, 406½ South Main, Conrad, MT 59425. Tel: 278-7791.

Culbertson Chamber of Commerce, P.O. Box 633, Culbertson, MT 59218. Tel: 787-5821.

Cut Bank Chamber of Commerce, P.O. Box 1243, Cut Bank, MT 59427. Tel: 873-4041.

Deer Lodge Chamber of Commerce, 300 Main, Deer Lodge, MT 59722. Tel: 846-2094.

Dillon Chamber of Commerce, Beaverhead Chamber, P.O. Box 830, Dillon, MT 59725. Tel: 683-5511.

Ekalaka Chamber of Commerce, P.O. Box 297, Ekalaka, MT 59324. Tel: 775-6658.

Ennis Chamber of Commerce, P.O. Box 291, Ennis, MT 59729. Tel: 682-4287.

Fairfield Chamber of Commerce, Booster Club, P.O. Box 282, Fairfield, MT 59436. Tel: 467-2323.

Fairview Chamber of Commerce, P.O. Box 374, Fairview, MT 59221. Tel: 747-5226.

Forsyth Chamber of Commerce, P.O. Box 448, Forsyth, MT 59327. Tel: 356-2115.

Gardiner Chamber of Commerce, P.O. Box 81, Gardiner, MT 59030. Tel: 848-7681.

Glasgow Chamber of Commerce, P.O. Box 832, Glasgow, MT 59230. Tel: 228-2222.

Glendive Chamber of Commerce, P.O. Box 930, Glendive, MT 59330. Tel: 365-5601.

Great Falls Chamber of Commerce, P.O. Box 2127, Great Falls, MT 59403. Tel: 761-4434.

Hardin Chamber of Commerce, 200 N. Center Ave, Hardin, MT 59034. Tel: 665-1672.

Harlowton Chamber of Commerce, P.O. Box 694, Harlowton, MT 59036. Tel: 632-4223.

Havre Chamber of Commerce, P.O. Box 308, Havre, MT 59501. Tel: 265-4383.

Helena Chamber of Commerce, 201 E. Lyndale, Helena, MT 59601. Tel: 442-4120.

Hinsdale Chamber of Commerce, Hinsdale, MT 59241. Tel: 364-2221.

Hot Springs Chamber of Commerce, P.O. Box 580, Hot Springs, MT 59845. Tel: 741-2652.

Jordan Chamber of Commerce, Jordan, MT 59337. Tel: 557-2480.

Kalispell Chamber of Commerce, 15 Depot Loop, Kalispell, MT 59901. Tel: 752-6166.

Lakeside Chamber of Commerce, Westshore Chamber, P.O. Box 177, Lakeside, MT 59922. Tel: 844-3715.

Laurel Chamber of Commerce, P.O. Box 395, Laurel, MT 59044. Tel: 628-8105.

Lewistown Chamber of Commerce, P.O. Box 818, Lewistown, MT 59457. Tel: 538-5436.

Libby Chamber of Commerce, P.O. Box 704, Libby, MT 59923. Tel: 293-3222.

Lincoln Chamber of Commerce, P.O. Box 985, Lincoln, MT 59639. Tel: 362-4949.

Livingston Chamber of Commerce, P.O. Box 660, Livingston, MT 59047. Tel: 222-0850.

Malta Chamber of Commerce, 174 N. 1st St. E., Malta, MT 59538. Tel: 654-2234.

Miles City Chamber of Commerce, P.O. Box 730, Miles City, MT 59301. Tel: 232-2890.

Missoula Chamber of Commerce, P.O. Box 7577, Missoula, MT 59807. Tel: 543-6623.

Montana Chamber of Commerce, P.O. Box 1730, Helena, MT 59624. Tel: 442-2405.

Philipsburg Chamber of Commerce, P.O. Draw Q, Philipsburg, MT 59858. Tel: 859-3215.

Plains-Paradise Chamber of Commerce, P.O. Box 714, Plains, MT 59859. Tel: 826-5945.

Plentywood Chamber of Commerce, P.O. Box 4, Plentywood, MT 59254. Tel: 765-2810.

Polson Chamber of Commerce, P.O. Box 677, Polson, MT 59860. Tel: 883-5969.

Poplar Chamber of Commerce, P.O. Box 313, Poplar, MT 59255. Tel: 768-3323.

Red Lodge Chamber of Commerce, P.O. Box 998, Red Lodge, MT 59068. Tel: 446-1718.

Richey Chamber of Commerce, P.O. Box 279, Richey, MT 59259. Tel: 773-5887.

Ronan Chamber of Commerce, P.O. Box 254, Ronan, MT 59864. Tel: 676-4600.

Roundup Chamber of Commerce, P.O. Box 751, Roundup, MT 59072. Tel: 323-1966.

Saco Chamber of Commerce, Saco, MT 59261. Tel: 527-3361.

Scobey Chamber of Commerce, P.O. Box 91, Scobey, MT 59263. Tel: 487-5311.

Seeley Lake-Condon Chamber of Commerce, P.O. Box 516, Seeley Lake, MT 59868. Tel: 677-2880.

Shelby Chamber of Commerce, P.O. Box 488, Shelby, MT 59474. Tel: 434-2031.

Sidney Chamber of Commerce, 909 S. Central Ave, Sidney, MT 59270. Tel: 482-4375.

St Ignatius Chamber of Commerce, P.O. Box 216, St Ignatius, MT 59865. Tel: 745-2166.

Stanford Chamber of Commerce, Commercial Club, P.O. Box 386, Stanford, MT 59479. Tel: 566-2596.

Superior Chamber of Commerce, P.O. Box 252, Superior, MT 59872. Tel: 822-4643.

Swan Lake Chamber of Commerce, Hwy 83, Swan Lake, MT 59911. Tel: 886-2324.

Terry Chamber of Commerce, P.O. Box 677, Terry, MT 69349. Tel: 637-5782.

Thompson Falls-Trout Creek-Noxon Chamber of Commerce, P.O. Box 493, Thompson Falls, MT 59873. Tel: 827-4852.

Three Forks Chamber of Commerce, P.O. Box 1103, Three Forks, MT 59752. Tel: 285-6857.

Townsend Chamber of Commerce, P.O. Box 947, Townsend, MT 54644. Tel: 266-3161.

Troy Chamber of Commerce, P.O. Box 161, Troy, MT 59935. Tel: 295-4693.

Virginia City Chamber of Commerce, Vigilance Club, P.O. Box 295, Virginia City, MT 59755.

West Yellowstone Chamber of Commerce, P.O. Box 458, W. Yellowstone, MT 59758. Tel: 646-7701.

White Sulphur Springs Chamber of Commerce, P.O. Box 356, White Sulphur Springs, MT 59645. Tel: 547-3331.

Whitefish Chamber of Commerce, P.O. Box 1309, Whitefish, MT 59937. Tel: 862-3501.

Whitehall Chamber of Commerce, P.O. Box 667, Whitehall, MT 59759. Tel: 287-3343.

Wibaux Chamber of Commerce, P.O. Box 260, Wibaux, MT 59353. Tel: 795-2429.

Wolf Point Chamber of Commerce, P.O. Box 237, Wolf Point, MT 59201. Tel: 653-2012.

IN UTAH (Area Code: 801)

Brigham City Chamber of Commerce, 6 N. Main, Brigham City, UT 84302. Tel: 723-3931.

Bryce Canyon National Park, Visitors' Center, Bryce Canyon, UT 84717. Tel: 834-5322.

Cache Chamber of Commerce, 52 W. 2nd North, Logan, UT 84321. Tel: 752-2161.

Carbon County Chamber of Commerce, Municipal Building, 200 E. Main, Price, UT 84501. Tel: 637-2788.

Cedar City Chamber of Commerce, 286 N. Main, Cedar City, UT 84720. Tel: 586-4484.

Dinosaur National Monument, Visitors' Center and Quarry, P.O. Box 128, Jensen, UT 84035. Tel: 789-2115.

Duchesne Chamber of Commerce, P.O. Box 300, Duchesne, UT 84021. Tel: 738-2707.

Edge of the Cedars, P.O. Box 792, Blanding, UT 84511. Tel: 678-2241.

Golden Spike Empire, 2404 Washington Blvd. #100, Ogden, UT 84401. Tel: 621-8300.

Grand County Travel Council, 64 S. Main, Moab, UT 84532. Tel: 259-7531.

Green River Chamber of Commerce, 165 S. KOA River Blvd., Green River, UT 84525. Tel: 364-3651.

Information Center, P.O. Box 400, City Park, Panguitch, UT 84759. Tel: 676-2311.

Kanab Chamber of Commerce, P.O. Box 369, Kanab, UT 84741. Tel: 644-5868.

Monticello Visitor Center, 117 S. Main St., P.O. Box 217, Monticello, UT 84535. Tel: 587-2611.

Monument Valley Information Center, Monument Valley, UT 84536.

Orem City Chamber of Commerce, 777 S. State, Orem, UT 84601. Tel: 224-3636.

Park City Chamber/Bureau, 528 Main St., Park City, UT 84060. Tel: 649-6100.

Provo City Chamber of Commerce, 777 S. State, P.O. Box 738, Provo, UT 84603. Tel: 224-3636.

Richfield Chamber of Commerce, 220 N. 600 West, Richfield, UT 84701. Tel: 896-4241.

Roosevelt Chamber of Commerce, 332 South 200 E., Roosevelt, UT 84066. Tel: 722-4598.

Salt Lake Area Chamber of Commerce, 19 E. 220 S., Salt Lake City, UT 84111. Tel: 364-3631.

Springville Chamber of Commerce, 175 S. Main, Springville, UT 84663. Tel: 489-4681.

St George Chamber of Commerce and Information Center, 97 E. St George Blvd., St George, UT 84770. Tel: 628-1658.

Tooele County Chamber of Commerce, 90 N. Main, Tooele, UT 84074. Tel: 882-0690.

Vernal Chamber of Commerce, 50 E. Main, Vernal, UT 84078. Tel: 789-1353.

Wasatch County Chamber of Commerce, P.O. Box 427, Heber City, UT 84032. Tel: 654-3666.

IN WYOMING (Area Code: 307)

Afton Chamber of Commerce, P.O. Box 1107, Afton, WY 83110. Tel: 886-3810.

Buffalo Chamber of Commerce, P.O. Box 927, 55 N. Main, Buffalo, WY 82834. Tel: 684-5544.

Casper Chamber of Commerce, P.O. Box 399, 500 N. Center, Casper, WY 82601. Tel: 234-5311.

Cheyenne Chamber of Commerce, P.O. Box 1147, 301 W. 16th, Cheyenne, WY 82001. Tel: 638-3388.

Cody Chamber of Commerce, P.O. Box 2777, 836 Sheridan, Cody, WY 82414. Tel: 587-2298.

Douglas Chamber of Commerce, 318 – 1st St. W., Douglas, WY 82633. Tel: 358-2950.

Dubois Chamber of Commerce, P.O. Box 632, Dubois, WY 82513. Tel: 455-2556.

Evanston Chamber of Commerce, P.O. Box 365, 946 Front St., Evanston, WY 82930. Tel: 789-2757.

Gillette Chamber of Commerce, P.O. Box 1006, 314 S. Gillette, Gillette, WY 82716. Tel: 682-3673.

Glenrock Chamber of Commerce, P.O. Box 411, 506 W. Birch, Glenrock, WY 28637. Tel: 436-2754.

Green River Chamber of Commerce, 1450 Uinta Drive, Green River, WY 82935. Tel: 875-5711.

Greybull Chamber of Commerce, 613 Greybull Ave, Greybull, WY 82426. Tel: 765-2100.

Jackson Hole Chamber of Commerce, P.O. Box E, 532 N. Cache, Jackson Hole, WY 83001. Tel: 733-3316.

Kemmerer Chamber of Commerce, P.O. Box 1100, 800 Pine Ave., Kemmerer, WY 83101. Tel: 877-9761.

Lander Chamber of Commerce, 160 North 1st, Lander, WY 82520. Tel: 332-3892.

Laramie Chamber of Commerce, 401 Garfield, Laramie, WY 82070. Tel: 745-7339.

Lovell Chamber of Commerce, 336 Nevada, Lovell, WY 82431. Tel: 548-7552.

Lusk Chamber of Commerce, P.O. Box 690, 257 S. Main, Lusk, WY 82225. Tel: 334-2773.

Medicine Bow Chamber of Commerce, P.O. Box 456, Medicine Bow, WY 82329. Tel: 379-2311.

Meeteetse Chamber of Commerce, P.O. Box 38, Meeteetse, WY 82433. Tel: 868-2278.

Newcastle Chamber of Commerce, P.O. Box 68, 113 W. Main St., Newcastle, WY 82701. Tel: 746-2739.

Pinedale Chamber of Commerce, P.O. Box 176, 187 W. Pine, Pinedale, WY 82941. Tel: 367-2242.

Powell Chamber of Commerce, P.O. Box 814, 111 S. Day, Powell, WY 82435. Tel: 754-3494.

Rawlins Chamber of Commerce, P.O. Box 1331, 511 W. Spruce, Rawlins, WY 82301. Tel: 324-4111.

Riverton Chamber of Commerce, P.O. Box 469, 1st & Main, Riverton, WY 82501. Tel: 856-4801.

Rock Springs Chamber of Commerce, P.O. Box 398, 1897 Dewar Drive, Rock Springs, WY 82901. Tel: 362-3771.

Saratoga Chamber of Commerce, P.O. Box 1095, 102 W. Bridge, Saratoga, WY 82331. Tel: 326-8855.

Sheridan Chamber of Commerce, P.O. Box 707, 5th & I-90, Sheridan, WY 82801. Tel: 672-2485.

Shoshoni Chamber of Commerce, P.O. Box 324, Shoshoni, WY 82649. Tel: 876-2389.

Thermopolis Chamber of Commerce, 220 Park St, Thermopolis, WY 82443. Tel: 864-3192.

Torrington Chamber of Commerce, 350 W. 21st Ave., Torrington, WY 82240. Tel: 532-3879.

Wheatland Chamber of Commerce, P.O. Box 427, 600 - 9th, Wheatland, WY 82201. Tel: 322-2322.

Worland Chamber of Commerce, 120 N. 10th St., Worland, WY 82401. Tel: 347-3226.

TRAVEL INFORMATION SOURCES

COLORADO (Area Code: 303)

US Forest Service, Rocky Mountain Region Office, P.O. Box 25127, Lakewood CO 80225. Tel: 236-9431. (4-color map of any national forest, excellent guides showing trails, campgrounds, etc.)

Colorado Campground Association, 5101 Pennsylvania, Boulder, CO 80303. Tel: 499-9343. (Colorado maps, private campgrounds, fun things to do.)

The Colorado Trail, P.O. Box 260876, Lakewood. Tel: 526-0809.

Colorado Division of Highways, 4201 E. Arkansas Ave., Denver, CO 80222. Tel: 757-9982. (For information on highways.)

Colorado Division of Parks and Recreation, 1313 Sherman St. #618, Denver, CO 80203. Tel: 866-3437. (State parks, boating, RV and snowmobiling regulations, camping reservations: 1-800/328-6338.)

Colorado Division of Wildlife, 6060 Broadway, Denver, CO 80216. Tel: 297-1192. (For information on hunting and fishing.)

Colorado Guides and Outfitters Association, P.O. Box 31438, Aurora, CO 80041. Tel: 751-9274.

National Park Service, P.O. Box 25287, Lakewood, CO 80225. Tel: 969-2000.

US Bureau of Land Management, 2850 Youngfield St., Lakewood, 80215. Tel: 239-3600. (Quad maps – $1.50; statewide public lands – $2).

US Geological Survey, P.O. Box 25046, Denver Federal Center, Denver, CO 80225. Tel: 236-5829.

IDAHO (Area Code: 208)

Lewis and Clark Country, Box 8936, Moscow, ID 83843. Tel: 882-3581.

Treasureland, P.O. Box 2106, Boise, ID 83701. Tel: (1-800) 635-5240.

Magicland, Box 1844, Twin Falls, ID 83001.

Big Water Mountain Land Inc, P.O. Box 928, Sandpoint, ID 83864. Tel: 263-2161.

Pioneer Country, c/o Lava Hot Springs Foundation, Box 668, Lava Hot Springs, ID 83246. Tel: 776-5221.

Mountain River Country, Box 50498, Idaho Falls, ID 83402. Tel: 523-1010.

Idaho Department of Parks and Recreation, 2177 Warm Springs Ave, Boise, ID 83712. Tel: 327-7444

Idaho Department of Game and Fish, 600 S. Walnut, Boise, ID 83712. Tel: 334-3700.

Idaho Department of Transportation, 3311 W. State, Boise, ID 83707. Tel: 334-8000. (For highway information.)

Idaho State Historical Society, 610 N. Julia Davis Drive, Boise ID 83707. Tel: 334-3356. (For information on historic sites, museums.)

Idaho Bureau of Mines and Geology, Morril Hall, Rm 332, University of Idaho, Moscow, ID 83843. Tel: 885-7991. (For information on rockhounding and mining.)

Aeronautics and Public Transportation Division, 3843 Rickenbacker, Boise, ID 83705. Tel: 334-3183. (For information on fly-in recreation areas.)

MONTANA (Area Code: 406)

Visitor Services, National Park Service, P.O. Box 168, Yellowstone National Park, WY 82190. Tel: (307) 344-7381, ext 2283.

Montana Campground Owners Association, 3695 Tina Ave., Missoula 59802. Tel: 549-0881.

Montana Department of Fish, Wildlife and Parks, 1420 E. 6th Ave., Helena, MT 59620. Tel: 444-2535.

Bureau of Land Management, P.O. Box 36800, Billings, MT 59107. Tel: 255-2742.

National Park Service, Grant Kohrs Ranch National Historic Site, P.O. Box 790, Deer Lodge, MT 59722. Tel: 846-2070.

United States Forest Service, Northern Region, P.O. Box 7669, Missoula, MT 59807. Tel: 329-3511.

Montana Travel Planner, Tel: (1-800) 541-1447.

UTAH (Area Code: 801)

Utah State Division of Parks and Recreation, 1636 W. North Temple, Salt Lake City, UT 84116. Tel: 538-7221.

National Park Service, 125 South State, Salt Lake City, UT 84111. Tel: 524-4165.

Utah Travel Council, Council Hall Capitol Hill, Salt Lake City, UT 84114. Tel: 538-1030. (For information on travel, ski planning, campgrounds.)

Utah Division of Wildlife Resources, 1596 W. North Temple, Salt Lake City, UT 84116. Tel: 538-4200.

Ski Utah, Dept UTG, 307 W. 200 S., Salt Lake City UT 84101. Tel: 534-1779. (For information on snow conditions.)

Western River Guides Association Inc., Expeditions, Salt Lake City UT. Tel: 942-6669. (For information on river running.)

Antiquities Division, Utah Div. of State History, 300 Rio Grande, Salt Lake City, UT 84111. Tel: 533-5755. (For information on rockhounding and geology.)

Utah Arts Council, 617 E. South Temple, Salt Lake City, UT 84102. Tel: 533-5895.

Utah Department of Transportation, 4501 S. 2700 W., Salt Lake City, UT 84119. Tel: 965-4000.

WYOMING (Area Code: 307)

Wyoming Archives and Historical Department, State Office Bldg, East, Cheyenne, WY 82002. (For information on Wyoming museums.)

Wyoming Recreation Commission, Cheyenne, WY 82001. (For information on state parks and historic sites.)

Wyoming Geology Survey, P.O. Box 3008, University Station, University of Wyoming, Laramie, WY 82071. (For information on rockhunting and geology.)

Wyoming Highway Department, Cheyenne, WY 82002. (For information on highway.)

Wyoming Game and Fish Department, Cheyenne, WY 82002. (For information on hunting and fishing.)

Wyoming State Office, Bureau of Land Management, P.O. Box 1828, Cheyenne, WY 82001.

Wyoming Travel Commission, Tel: (1-800) 225-5996.

ART/PHOTO CREDITS

Photography by

202L	Boyles, Edgar
27, 29, 32, 33, 34L&R, 35R, 37, 43, 45, 46, 47, 68, 108, 275, 276, 277, 280, 281	Bruce Bernstein Collection, Courtesy of Princeton Library, NJ
184	Canova, Pat
30/31, 240	CM Russell Museum, Great Falls, Montana
103	Courtesy of the Aspen Chamber of Commerce
268, 279	Courtesy of the Salt Lake Valley Convention & Visitors' Bureau
17, 20, 21, 24/25, 26, 28, 35L, 39, 42, 44, 52/53, 57, 59, 61, 63, 64/65, 69, 70, 71, 74, 76, 77, 78, 79, 86/87, 128/129, 133, 135, 138, 140, 152/153, 156, 158, 159, 222, 236/237, 241, 242, 243, 244/245, 251, 252, 253, 271, 273, 274, 278, 285, 288	de Nanxe, Vautier
84/85	Faucher, Christine
173, 175, 177, 192	Ferro, Ricardo
54, 113, 141, 194, 225, 232, 235, 256, 258	Foster, Lee
22, 134, 142	Francis, Michael H.
155, 257	Hara Photographics
146	Heaton, Dallas & John
16, 23, 164, 228/229	McIntyre, Rick
100, 145, 195, 223, 226	Michael, Robert
3	Pinsler, Ronnie
4/5	Running, John
6/7, 8/9, 10, 12/13, 14/15, 19, 36, 41, 48/49, 50/51, 56, 58, 60, 62, 67, 80, 81, 92, 94, 95, 96, 99, 101, 122, 123, 124, 125, 126, 127, 136/137, 144, 147, 148, 149, 150, 160R, 161, 163, 165, 166/167, 168, 169, 171, 172, 176, 178, 179, 181, 182, 183, 185, 190, 191, 196, 204, 206/207, 208, 210, 211, 212, 213, 214/215, 216, 217, 219, 220/221, 227, 230, 233, 234, 238, 239, 246, 247, 248, 249, 250, 254/255, 260, 261, 262/263, 264, 267, 269, 272L&272R, 284, 286, 287, 289, 290	Tidball, Tom
55, 72/73	Tony Stone Worldwide
18, 66, 82/83, 90/91, 97, 98, 104/105, 106, 111, 115, 117L&117R, 118, 119, 120/121, 130/131, 132, 154, 157, 160L, 180, 186/187, 189, 193, 197, 198/199, 200, 201, 203, 205, 231, 270, 283	Viesti, Joseph F.

Illustrations   Klaus Geisler

Visual Consulting   V. Barl

INDEX

bison 21, 141, *251*
Bitterroot Mountains 40
Black Canyon of the Gunnison *216*, 217–218, 219
Blackfeet *see* Native Americans
Blackhawk 150
Black Hills 35, 248
Blacksmith Fork Canyon 286
Blossom and Music Festival, Canon City 218
blue grass 124
Blue Grass Festival, Telluride *see* Telluride Blue
   Grass Festival
Blue Mountains 38
boating 141, 234
Boettcher Concert Hall 123
Boggs, Governor L.W. 276
Boise 56
Bonneville, Capt. B.E. 38
Bonneville Lake 283, 284, 286
Bonneville Salt Flats 270
Bonny Reservoir 98
Book of Mormon, The 276
Botanic Gardens, Denver 177
Boulder *58*, 124, 125, 169, 182, 183, 184
Boulder Lake 225
Bozeman 257–261
Bozeman, John M. 257–258
Bozeman Opera House 259
Breakaway, The (dance festival) 123
Breckenridge 57, 107, 109–110, 191–193
Breckenridge Resort Association 110
Bridal Veil Falls 196, 271
bridge, suspension (over Arkansas River) 217–218
Bridger, James *34L*, 36
Bridger, Jim 34, 36, 41, 133, 134, 191, 257, 266
Bridger Bowl 117, 259
Bridger National Forest 223, 224
Bridger-Teton National Forest 224, 233, 234
Brigham City 288
Brighton Ski Resort 118, 272
Brown, D.R.C. 201, 203
Brown, J.J. 173
Brown, Molly *see* Tobin, Molly
Browning (John M.) Firearms Museum 288
Brown (Keith) Mansion 267
Brown (Molly) House *169*, 173
Brown Palace Hotel 174
Brush Creek Valley 203
Bryce Canyon National Park 26, *130–131*, 157–
   158, *157*
Buchanan, President 278
Buckskin Joe 218
buffalo 21, 70, 77, 140, 239, 259, 283
Buffalo Bill 240, 250
Buffalo Bill Cody's Grave and Museum 181
Buffalo Bill Historical Center *35L*, 36, 240–241,
   242, 243
Buffalo Bill Museum 241, 242
Buffalo Bill Wax Museum 181
Buffalo River 234
Buffet, Jimpson 205
Burbank, Luther 69
Burch, Leonard 75
Bureau of Indian Affairs (BIA) 76–77, 80
Butch Cassidy and the Sundance Kid (movie) 213
Buttermilk 114, 205

C

Cache Country Relic Hall 284
Cache Valley 283, 284, 285, 286
Cache Valley Cheese Factory 285
Campbell, Ben Nighthouse 212
Camp Floyd 279
Camp Hale 202
camping 98, 140, 225, 227, 234, 239, 261
canoes 146
Canon City 179, 180
Canyonlands National Park 158
Capitol, State (Wyoming) 251–252
Capitol Dome 156
Capitol Hill, Salt Lake City 266, 267
Capitol Reef National Park *19, 86–87*, 155–156,
   158
Carbondale 194, 205
Carson, Kit 35, 77
Cash, Roseanne 124
Cassidy, Butch 196, 225, 231
Castle Creek 202
Cataract Canyon 156
cattle 21, 43, 67, 68, 70, 93, 143
   branding 44
   ranching 20, 44, 57, 67, 70, 170, 240, 247–248,
     259
   roundups 44
   trade 44
Cave of the Winds 97, 181
caving, *see* spelunking
Cedar Point 219
celebrations *see* festivals
Celestial Seasonings Herb Tea Co. 124, 184
Celestial Seasonings Pavilion 125
Center for the Performing Arts, Denver 175
Central City 182
Central City Opera Festival *see* Opera Festival,
   Central City
   also see Opera House, Central City
Central Pacific Railway 43
Chaco 210
Chamber Music Festival, Telluride 123
Charbonneau, Toussaint 32, 40
Chatfield Recreation Area 99
Chautaqua Auditorium 126, 184
cheese 285
Cherokee *see* Native Americans
cherries 218
Cherry Creek Reservation Area 99, 169, 172
Cheyenne 57, *59*, 124, 247–253, *247, 248, 249, 250*
Cheyenne *see* Native Americans
Cheyenne Club 247–248
Cheyenne Frontier Days 101, 126, 249–251,
   249, 252
Cheyenne Frontier Days Rodeo 249–250
Cheyenne Mountain Zoo 179
Chivington, Colonel John 37, 78
Christians 28, 38
Christianity 28, 79
Church of Jesus Christ of Latter-Day Saints *see*
   Mormons
City Creek 265
City Creek Canyon 267
Civil War, The 37, 56, 133, 278
Claims Commission 80
Clark, William 32, 33, 40, 41, 76, 132, 133, 139,

INDEX

D

E

N

T

U

V

W